The Cairo Genizah and the
Age of Discovery in Egypt

The Cairo Genizah and the Age of Discovery in Egypt

The History and Provenance of a Jewish Archive

Rebecca J. W. Jefferson

I.B. TAURIS
LONDON • NEW YORK • OXFORD • NEW DELHI • SYDNEY

I.B. TAURIS
Bloomsbury Publishing Plc
50 Bedford Square, London, WC1B 3DP, UK
1385 Broadway, New York, NY 10018, USA
29 Earlsfort Terrace, Dublin 2, Ireland

BLOOMSBURY, I.B. TAURIS and the I.B. Tauris logo are trademarks of Bloomsbury
Publishing Plc

First published in Great Britain 2022

Cover design by Liron Gilenberg | www.ironicitalics.com
Cover image: Yemenite Liturgical Manuscript, c. 1830, with fragments hidden in the
binding. Isser and Rae Price Library of Judaica, photographed by Rebecca J. W. Jefferson.

A catalogue record for this book is available from the British Library.

A catalog record for this book is available from the Library of Congress.

ISBN: HB: 978-1-7883-1963-8
PB: 978-1-7883-1964-5
ePDF: 978-1-7883-1966-9
eBook: 978-1-7883-1965-2

Typeset by Deanta Global Publishing Services, Chennai, India
Printed and bound in Great Britain

To find out more about our authors and books visit www.bloomsbury.com and
sign up for our newsletters.

For Robert, Lily and Isaac

The honour of discovering the Genizah belongs to the 'nameless' dealers in antiquities in Cairo who for many years have continually offered its contents to the various libraries of Europe.

Solomon Schechter, 7 August 1897

Contents

Figures

Acknowledgements

Writing about the discovery of the Cairo Genizah is only possible thanks to the incredible work of hundreds of scholars, librarians and writers engaged with genizah fragments now and in the past. But I owe particular thanks to the following people whose key questions, insights, generous sharing of resources, guidance and all-round encouragement have been so immensely important to my research: Malachi Beit-Arié, Siam Bhayro, Piet van Boxel, Nina Caputo, Ezra Chwat, Mark Cohen, Peter Cole, Perry Collins, Giacomo Corazzol, Bess de Farber, Idan Dershowitz, Natalie Dohrmann, Mark Farber, Sarah Fargeon, Mark Geller, Noah Gerber, Nathan Gibson, Mark Glickman, Jessica Goldberg, Stacey Goldring, Haim Gottschalk, David Green, Wissem Gueddich, Mitchell Hart, Tapani Harviainen, Boruch Helman, Adina Hoffman, Lily Kahn, Jason Kalman, Sarah Kemp, Geoffrey Khan, Brian Keith, Arthur Kiron, Dragan Kujundzic, Eve Krakowski, Rachel Leket-Mor, Heidi Lerner, Shlomo and Daphne Leshem, Michael David Lukas, Jason Lustig, Arthur MacGregor, Ginessa Mahar, Michelle Margolis, Yoram Meital, César Merchán-Hamman, Emily Madden, Karen Miller, Bruce Nielsen, Ephraim Nissan, Judith Olszowy-Schlanger, Ben Outhwaite, Michael Press, Katalin Rac, Stefan Reif, Gary Rendsburg, Marina Rustow, Ediwn Safer, Gregor Schwarb, David Selis, Nadeen Shaker, Merrill and Robyn Shapiro, Robert Singerman, Renate Smithuis, David Starr, David Stern, Sara Sviri, Sarah Sykes, Laurie Taylor, Nadia Vidro, Ngaio Vince-Dewerse, Ronny Vollandt, Miriam Esther Wagner, Simone Weny, and Oded Zinger, as well as all the helpful librarians, archivists and staff in institutions with genizah fragments or pertinent archives, my former colleagues in the Genizah Research Unit, and everyone involved in the Friedberg Jewish Manuscript Society.

I am deeply grateful to Dean Judith Russell, the George A. Smathers Libraries administrators and the University of Florida for giving me opportunities to engage in research and for the award of a summer sabbatical. Likewise, to all the members of the wonderful Price family who have helped my research through their ongoing support for the Judaica Library. Thanks for support are also due to all my colleagues in the Center for Jewish Studies, the Department of Special and Area Studies collections, and across the libraries, most especially my chair, Elizabeth Haven Hawley.

I extend special thanks to Rory Gormley, commissioning editor at I. B. Tauris, and Yasmin Garcha, assistant editor, for their kind guidance and hard work steering the manuscript through to its final shape; to the copy editor, Mary Rapunga, and Joseph Gautham and Giles Herman and all the production team for bringing it through the many stages of publication. Similarly, for their role in the editorial process, I owe the anonymous reviewers a special thank you for giving their time so generously to offer crucial feedback and advice.

Finally, I must acknowledge my parents, Gloria and John Wilson, and everyone in my family, for their vital love, support and encouragement, now and in the past.

Distance may have divided us, but warm memories never fade. Likewise, I am thankful for the love and support of my parents-in-law, Susan and Melvin Jefferson, as well as Melvin's professional guidance on conservation. For maintaining my health with daily walks, I would be remiss if I didn't acknowledge my dogs, Annie and Julian. Last, but not least, I owe an enduring debt of gratitude to my truly wonderful husband, Robert, and children, Lily and Isaac, not only for their patience while I obsessed about all things genizah, but for always sustaining me with so much love and laughter. I dedicate this book to them.

Prologue

Among the many captivating stories my parents read or told me when I was a child, my mother's account of Howard Carter's discovery of 'wonderful things' in the Valley of the Kings rooted deeply in my mind. Although my career path would not be Egyptology, something about the discipline still called out to me, and it began to awaken more fully when I was an undergraduate studying Hebrew at University College London. It was here that I first heard the incredible story of 'the Cairo Genizah', a hidden chamber inside an ancient synagogue in Egypt, and the marvellous Indiana-Jones-like adventures of Solomon Schechter, its discoverer. The narrative went something like this:

see pp 84-86

In 1896, two intrepid women travellers brought back to Cambridge a sack of Hebrew manuscripts they purchased during a trip to Egypt. The twin sisters, Agnes Smith Lewis and Margaret Dunlop Gibson, could not decipher some of the manuscripts, so they invited their friend, Solomon Schechter, Reader in Rabbinics at Cambridge, over to their house to help them. Schechter identified one of the pieces as a medieval fragment from the Jerusalem Talmud; then he lighted upon one that was of even greater significance: a fragment of Ecclesiasticus. Schechter quickly realized that the fragment was from a medieval copy of the original Hebrew version of Ecclesiasticus, the lost Book of Ben Sira. He rushed to the library to check the piece against other old sources, and then he excitedly informed the sisters of his monumental discovery. Having noticed old fragments coming out of Egypt in recent years, Schechter realized that there could be other manuscripts of great importance to be found there, and he grew ever more anxious to go. He consulted with other professors at the university about how to get his travel funded, but his good friend, Charles Taylor of St. John's College, offered to defray his expenses to prevent any delays caused by bureaucratic university processes. When Schechter finally arrived in Cairo in December 1896, carrying with him letters of introduction from the university vice chancellor and the chief rabbi of England, he had to spend some time courting the good graces of the chief rabbi of Cairo. After drinking many cups of coffee and smoking cigarettes, the highly personable Solomon Schechter won over the rabbi to his cause, and it was not long before he was taken to see the ancient Ben Ezra Synagogue in Old Cairo. Inside the synagogue, he was directed to the far end of the women's gallery on the second floor. The beadle fetched him a ladder and he was allowed to climb up to look through a hole high up in the wall. Inside was a secret chamber, known as a genizah, where a massive pile of disused manuscripts had been hidden for over a thousand years. The rabbi invited him to take as much of it away as he liked, and so he did. Schechter spent the next weeks buried deep inside the dark and dusty chamber, wrestling with the battlefield of books inside, stuffing as many precious manuscripts as he could into sacks. By the end of his visit, he had gathered enough to fill seven large crates. After his hoard of over 140,000 manuscripts arrived in Cambridge, he and Charles Taylor donated them to the University Library.

Over time, the Taylor-Schechter Genizah Collection yielded many treasures: in addition to a wealth of important biblical, rabbinical and liturgical fragments, including autograph works, there were palimpsests, belles-lettres, legal documents, personal letters, medical and philosophical writings, children's scribbles, recipes and shopping lists. The parchment and paper fragments were mostly written in Hebrew and Arabic, but there were fragments in many other languages too. Many had been written in Cairo, but there were also writings from across the Near East and the Mediterranean, from France and Spain across to Yemen and India. Some of the papers represent the oldest records of Jewish life in existence; others shed light on the more recent past. Thanks to Schechter's great foresight, the Cairo Genizah revolutionized the study of Jewish religious, cultural and social life in the medieval Mediterranean, and it illuminated the world of the broader communities among whom they lived and with whom they interacted.

This was the basic thrust of the story as I heard it in my undergraduate years. Some mention was made of the other genizah collections around the world and the characters involved in acquiring them before and after Schechter but, for the most part, the other collections were treated as a 'walk-on' to the main event. While working as a bibliographer on the Taylor-Schechter Genizah Collection, I began to want to know more how they came into being and, in exploring their histories, I found that the traditional discovery narrative started to unravel. As I delved more deeply into the history of each collection through record books, archives, travelogues, memoirs, periodicals and catalogues, I realized that many elements were lacking from the Cairo Genizah legend. Little known or forgotten protagonists began to emerge and under-explored connections and networks in the trade of Hebrew fragments expanded the scope of the story exponentially. Even the idea of a single find spot for the hundreds of thousands of these fragments in collections around the world began to appear less credible.

Many scholars have enriched our knowledge about the Cairo Genizah through their investigations into aspects of its discovery.[1] Among them, Stefan C. Reif OBE who, in addition to his important work building the Cambridge Genizah Research Unit, was the first to provide an in-depth history of the Cambridge collections. Adina Hoffman and Peter Cole are the most recent scholars to have revealed many more significant details about the wider story, particularly in relation to Schechter's activities. And other scholars before me have also closely questioned the traditional discovery narrative, most notably Nehemiah Allony, Mark R. Cohen and Yedida Stillman and Eleazar Hurvitz. My own contribution to the field is to track down as much provenance history about the other collections as possible and then weave the stories together chronologically to discover the connections between them. This method not only reveals that the Cairo Genizah as it stands today was assembled rather than discovered, but it also shows that other sources from within Cairo and even outside of Cairo and Egypt are mixed up in this 'archive'.

The uncertainties surrounding the provenance of genizah collections closely mirror problems faced by papyrologists. In the case of Arabic papyri, as Marina Rustow points out in *The Lost Archive*, most of the extant pieces are still languishing undiscovered across various institutional collections.[2] This is because Arabic papyri, although keenly appreciated by a handful of scholars, mostly took a back seat to the more widely coveted and studied Greek papyri. Many pieces of Arabic papyri were recovered by chance rather than by design, and as a result their origins and current whereabouts situated among other papyri collections are not well documented. As Brent Nongbri demonstrates in *God's Library*, even the origins of the highly sought-after Greek papyri have been obscured thanks to the vagaries of the antiquities market. The papyri found at Oxyrhynchus is a good case in point and one that is particularly consonant with the discoveries of genizah fragments. As Nongbri points out, even though many of the pieces of papyri can be traced to a find spot, with regard to documenting all of their finds, the early discoverers were 'frustratingly vague'.[3] Pieces purchased from dealers were also interspersed among the fragments that were excavated, and they were not clearly differentiated in subsequent publications. Moreover, as revealed in this book, genizah fragments often became mixed up in sales of papyri by antiquities dealers, which further obscured the origins of both.

Still, the reader may ask why it should matter how a manuscript fragment reached its current destination when surely all that counts is the text it contains. It matters because the content cannot fully be appreciated or understood in isolation. The physical container that carries the content – the artefact – has undergone multi-temporal journeys in and out of different social settings that impregnate it with various meanings.[4] A handwritten copy of medieval Hebrew hymns may have been annotated, vocalized and recited one way by an owner in Jerusalem and another way by an owner living in Egypt. A manuscript buried in a tomb in Palestine was regarded and treated in a distinct manner from one that was hidden away in a synagogue in Iraq. A recovered fragment of the Bible meant more to some nineteenth-century scholars than a fragment of a medieval shopping list. Thus, the study of an artefact's life cycle, in which provenance plays a key role, furthers our understanding of the interplay between ideas, objects and people and the ways in which one transforms the other.

Provenance research, once the preserve of art historians, is gaining greater interest among scholars in many fields and, in this respect, it is now becoming a cross-disciplinary activity. As Nick Pearce and Jane C. Milosch observe in *Collecting and Provenance*, while the study of provenance takes the history of objects as its starting point, it usually ends up becoming the history of people.[5] Provenance research traces the arc that extends from the creator of an object through its users and owners across time.

In the case of genizah fragments, the legwork of deconstructing the 'archive' and reconstructing who found which fragments and where, and how they got to their current setting, involves painstaking and time-consuming research. The investigation, while fulfilling and rewarding, can also lead to errors, frustrating dead ends and gaps that seemingly cannot be bridged. Yet, looking into this history over the course of the past twelve years, connections that I once believed to be undiscoverable have suddenly come to light. Thus, this book, the result of my research to date, endeavours to fill in as many gaps as possible while recognizing there is still more to be done.

I've tried to write this book in a way that will appeal to uninitiated readers and genizah scholars alike. It is a story of general interest set in the age of discovery in Egypt and against the backdrop of the nineteenth-century trade in antiquities. It exposes how previously hidden old books and scrolls were disinterred, broken up for sales and fed into a growing market for fragments. It reveals how increased interest in and searches for fragments led to even greater fragmentation of the source materials, and how fragments from other sources became included in the mix. And it charts a vast international cast of players all acting with varying motivations and intentions in a race for the spoils.

The story begins with a discovery on the rooftop of the Ben Ezra Synagogue in 1864, and then discusses the nature of a genizah and the practice of using one. Each subsequent chapter covers a distinct period of Hebrew manuscript collecting. Chapters 2–4 cover three decades from the 1860s to the rebuilding of the Ben Ezra Synagogue at the end of the 1880s. The next nine chapters each concern a key period of one or two years within the 1890s, and the final chapter looks at some of the collections discovered in the twentieth century.

The material presented here is also intended to help scholars who work with genizah fragments understand more about the ownership and acquisition history of their objects of study. To this end, it includes an appendix with a list of the main institutional genizah collections, some brief provenance information for each one where possible, and a guide to finding the relevant chapters in the book. Overall, I hope that my work will demonstrate that tracing the provenance of disjointed collections is possible and that it will inspire others to scrutinize more closely the history of the collections they are studying, manage or own.

1

Hiding places for Hebrew manuscripts

IT COULD HAVE BEEN A HOWARD CARTER MOMENT. A concealed receptacle filled with wonderful manuscripts, accessed via the rooftop of Old Cairo's Ben Ezra Synagogue, was ripe for discovery by the time Jacob Saphir climbed up there in June 1864. But after toiling for two days to clear the debris from recent repairs blocking its entrance, Saphir finally gave up. The 42-year-old Jerusalemite envoy found little to inspire him among the fragmentary papers he managed to seize from under the dirt and dust. Nevertheless, he left the scene wondering what else lay beneath.[1]

In the year of Saphir's near-discovery, an era of momentous change was underway in Egypt with the appointment of the country's new leader, Ismāʿīl Pasha. Soon after he assumed leadership, Ismāʿīl began to capitalize on the ever-increasing demand for Egyptian cotton to realize his vision of Europeanizing his country. In 1862, severe shortages of cotton, resulting from the American Civil War, had prompted desperate Manchester industrialists to urge Egyptian leaders to expand their cotton production. Ismāʿīl heeded the cry, and by 1864 Egypt's imports of steam engines, machinery and coal had almost doubled, with around 40 per cent of the total cultivated land of Lower Egypt placed under cotton.[2] Europeans flooded in to take advantage of the new economic opportunities. Among them a sizeable number of Greek and Jewish immigrants who brought with them business and banking knowledge.[3] As the number of foreign inhabitants in the cities and towns of the Delta cotton-growing region expanded, houses needed building and public utilities had to be improved. Along with this sudden economic growth, Ismāʿīl initiated his grand plan to make the city of Cairo a showpiece of Egyptian progress by founding the Ministry of Public Works. Supplies of gas and municipal water were established in the following year and, by 1867, inspired by the displays of urban planning at the Universal Exposition in Paris, Ismāʿīl commissioned Pierre Grand, a Parisian civil engineer, to devise similar plans for Cairo. An Egyptian engineer, Ali Pasha Mubarak, was appointed as the first minister of Public Works and entrusted to carry out these plans. Under Mubarak's leadership, Cairo's suburbs, previously separate and distinct entities, were unified with Cairo and assigned to four administrative districts (*aqsam*): Bulaq, Shubra, Wayli and Old Cairo. Each district was assigned a head engineer to map the streets and alleys, a necessary first step in helping Pierre Grand realize his definitive map of Cairo in 1874.[4]

THE NAME 'OLD CAIRO' – based on the Arabic *Misr al-Qadima* or *Misr al-Atiqa* – was used by European travellers to refer to the fortress town of Babylon and the surrounding land, which was once the site of the first capital of Muslim Egypt (*Misr*). Babylon of Egypt was an ancient town situated on the east bank of the Nile. The Fortress of Babylon was built by the Roman emperor Diocletian on the site of a harbour and canal constructed by the emperor Trajan to connect the land to the Nile and Red Sea. During the Byzantine period, the area was inhabited by Coptic Christians and, possibly, a smaller population of Jews (although contemporaneous documentation regarding the latter is scant).[5] By the fifth century, Babylon expanded and encompassed a large area, with over forty churches, governed by a Coptic bishopric.

When the Arab general Amr ibn al-As captured Babylon in 641 CE, the fortress was renamed *Qasr al-Sham*. Babylon became part of the new town created at the site of the general's military encampment on the outskirts: *al-Fustat* from the Greek *fossaton* (camp). In time, al-Fustat became the new Islamic government's administrative capital, and as it expanded and achieved greater importance the whole territory was referred to as *Misr* (the Arabic name for Egypt). 'Amr extended protections to non-Muslims under an annual poll tax scheme, and land was granted back to the Copts enabling them to rebuild their churches.

After the Abbasid dynasty assumed the caliphate in the eighth century, a new capital, *al-Askar*, was established in the northeast, while the town within *Qasr al-Sham* remained mostly a Christian and Jewish enclave. A third capital city was founded by the Abbasids at *al-Qata'i* further north in the ninth century, and in the next century, the land was conquered by the Fatimid dynasty, which established its royal centre to the northeast at *al-Qahira* (meaning 'the victorious'). These first capital cities were girded by a vast ancient necropolis, the *Qarafa* (City of the Dead), located along the foot of the Muqattam hills; its expansion matched the eventual migration from al-Fustat in the south up to al-Qahira in the north. Saladin, founder of the Ayyubid dynasty, brought about a temporary regeneration in al-Fustat, building his own fortified city, the imposing Citadel, to its northeast on a high area of land in the Muqattam hills. Under the successive Mamluk dynasty, however, al-Qahira grew exponentially while large parts of al-Fustat fell into ruin and only the Christian and Jewish enclave within *Qasr al-Sham* (the Fortress of Babylon) remained mostly intact. By the nineteenth century, visitors to the suburb of what they dubbed 'Old Cairo' would find only traces of the once flourishing medieval life in al-Fustat among the architectural remains, pottery kilns and rubbish mounds, and in the buildings still standing and inhabited within the Fortress.[6] Little did they know that the written records of life under the medieval caliphate still existed and were hidden away in and around Cairo's medieval synagogues, and in the caves and tombs of the ancient cemetery.

As nineteenth-century Cairo was being reimagined, revitalized and redrawn once again, old things were replaced with new, and new things became seemingly old. During the next two decades, the city's medieval mosques, churches and synagogues, many of which had already undergone centuries of ongoing alteration and repair work, would be subject to more dramatic interventions. Under the leadership of the Ministry of Public Works, and later under the auspices of the Comité de Conservation des Monuments de l'Art Arabe, many of the city's old mosques were stripped of their later Ottoman additions, acquired thanks to centuries of layer upon layer of local preservation work, or they were rebuilt entirely anew in a neo-Mamluk style.[7] In the penultimate decade of the nineteenth century, several medieval buildings in Old Cairo, including the St. Barbara Church, the Hanging Church, the Church of St. George and the synagogue of Ezra the scribe, underwent major structural restoration projects. During this period, Cairo's other synagogues went through similar architectural loss and revival. By the 1880s, the 800-year-old Maimonides (or Rambam Synagogue) in the Jewish quarter was gone forever, replaced by a new structure which sat upon its ancient foundations. Synagogue rebuilding projects took place in Egypt's other expanding cities, like the medieval Eliyahu Hanavi, Zaradel and Azouz synagogues in Alexandria. And in the growing town of al-Mahallah al-Kubra, at the heart of the Delta cotton trade, the community replaced their 600-year-old al-Amshati Synagogue with an 1880s replica.[8]

Such dramatic changes also contributed to the dislocation of interior artefacts from their historical location either into new settings or out into the markets or the hands of private collectors. Items that were genuinely old were sold alongside pieces that were restorations or modern pieces fashioned to look old. By the middle of the century, increasing numbers of town criers traversed the passageways of the *souks* and bazaars announcing the latest 'interesting objects' for sale to the rising numbers of Western tourists keen to appropriate 'Oriental curiosities'.[9]

The ancient synagogue of Ezra the scribe (Ben Ezra) in Old Cairo was still in place when Jacob Saphir visited it six years earlier in 1858.[10] The building dated to the eleventh century and stood on the site of at least one and possibly two former synagogues. Yet, restoration work to strengthen and whitewash the walls, the building caretakers told him, was being planned. When he returned to Cairo in 1863, after a long and arduous emissarial journey to raise funds among wealthy merchant families in India, an undertaking which took him on an unplanned route through Egypt, Yemen, Indonesia, India, Australia, New Zealand and back, he encountered a different city. He recorded the changes in his travelogue:

> I found a new state of things here: the city as a whole had changed, with wide streets and fine new houses, especially in the Jewish areas. And the five large synagogues, which had been in the last stages of dilapidation . . ., were now demolished and new ones built in their place, large and tall, embellished with blocks of pure marble.[11]

Returning to Cairo again in 1864, he found evidence of the recent repairs on the roof of the Ben Ezra Synagogue: piles of roof rafters, boards, and other building debris obscuring a cache of manuscripts lying beneath and impeding his ability to discover anything of worth.

SAPHIR'S UNEXPECTED ADVENTURE IN 1858 began with a tour of the various Jewish communities of Egypt. As an envoy of a Jerusalem-based Lithuanian community known as the *perushim* (separate ones), Saphir's main purpose was to gather funds to restore the ancient Hurva Synagogue in Jerusalem. He was also a self-taught scholar, having made considerable efforts to advance on his early training in the rabbinic schools of the *perushim*. Influenced by their spiritual leader, the Vilna Gaon, who placed great emphasis on the philological study of Jewish religious texts, the *perushim* made notable efforts to integrate the secular sciences into their rabbinic studies. Saphir was therefore predisposed towards the ideas of a broader movement spreading across Central and Eastern Europe and into the Middle East through a Jewish 'Republic of Letters' known as the *Haskalah* (Jewish Enlightenment). The adherents of the *Haskalah*, the *maskilim*, regarded the Hebrew Bible as their main source and standard in reviving the Hebrew language. In the Bible, the *maskilim* saw the 'pure' Hebrew of their forebears, untainted by other languages. The *maskilim* promulgated their ideas through an active printing press, and particularly through the establishment of Hebrew-language periodicals. Intellectual enquiry into the history and nature of the Hebrew language was also increasing in the academies of higher learning; not only among the scholarly exponents of biblical criticism, but also within the nascent *Wissenshaft des Judenthums* (scientific study of Judaism) movement. Saphir, in spite of being a religiously observant rabbinic scholar with no formal academic training, was connected on the periphery to all these circles and ideas through his voracious reading and ongoing correspondence with other scholars.[12]

Saphir was particularly interested in the historical development of the Masorah: a Bible reading apparatus consisting of vowel signs, accents and extensive marginal notes. Since the Hebrew text is purely consonantal, which can lead to errors of pronunciation and interpretation, the Masorah was designed both to elucidate the Bible and to ensure its exact transmission. The authoritative version of the Hebrew Bible with its Masorah, called the Masoretic Text or the rabbinic Bible, was first printed in Venice in 1525 CE. The compiler of the Masoretic Text, Jacob ben Haim, had collated all the variant Masoretic notes he could find in the notable manuscript versions of the day, which themselves had been transmitted through the Middle Ages among the scholarly Jewish communities of Europe. Peering back further into the time before this period, the precise lines of transmission had become lost. Little was known of the work of those who invented the Masoretic system, apart from a few notable names, such as Moses Ben Naphtali and Aaron ben Asher, both of whom were credited with producing model Bible codices upon which other subsequent editions were based.[13]

Today, thanks to manuscript discoveries made in the nineteenth century, it is known that the Masoretic Text first emerged out of several Masoretic schools situated in the Near East in the sixth century CE. Three distinct traditions of vowelizing and pronouncing the Hebrew consonantal text were invented during the early Masoretic period, which were named according to their place of origin: Babylonia, Palestine and Tiberias. Since Bible scrolls copied for ritual purposes were prohibited from having extraneous marks on them, any vowel signs, accents and notes added to guide the reading were only permitted on non-liturgical copies of the Bible. Thus, hand in hand with the development of these reading traditions arose the development of the Hebrew Bible in book form (codex).

By the ninth century CE, the Tiberias tradition had become authoritative, and its system of vocalization prevailed. Evidence that a Palestinian school of vocalization had once existed was still unknown in the nineteenth century; evidence of the old Babylonian system (which unbeknown to many was still being used by some remote Jewish communities) had only recently come to light. The Tiberian tradition (the only one known at that time) was represented by a dynasty of scholars from the Ben Asher family. Its scion, Aaron ben Asher, was considered the most authoritative Masorete of all time: the creator of the model codex upon which the great medieval Jewish philosopher, Moses Maimonides, based his celebrated code of Jewish religious law, the *Mishneh Torah*. Even so, some of the model codices exhibited variants that were produced by the rival Tiberian school of Ben Naphtali, although no codex representing the entire Ben Naphtali system has been found.[14]

That so much mystery surrounded the development of the Masoretic Text, let alone the history of the Bible text preceding it, is not surprising given the overall paucity of manuscript evidence available to Hebrew scholars in the early to mid-nineteenth century. At the time of Saphir's emissarial trip, over ninety years before the momentous discoveries of the Dead Sea Scrolls in the caves of Qumran, ancient copies of the Hebrew Bible were unknown. A few years after the founding of the Palestine Exploration Fund in 1865, a correspondent in *The Jewish Chronicle* expressed hope that through their future explorations, ancient scrolls would one day come to light:

> The most precious relic that could be discovered by the Exploration Society would be some truly ancient scroll of the law or prophets, such as, undoubtedly, existed in every synagogue. And if manuscripts from Pompeii and Herculaneum are in our days being brought to light, why should we despair of meeting with a similar treasure in one of these synagogues, which have so long been hidden in the bowels of the earth?[15]

In Saphir's day, the oldest Bible scroll in existence was the Ezra Scroll in Bologna, Italy. According to the legends surrounding it, the scroll was gifted by some of the Jews of Provence to a Dominican Friar, Aimerico Giliani, in 1302. Aimerico took it to Bologna where it was stored in the Library of the Dominican convent of San Salvatore. The scroll's attribution to the biblical prophet, Ezra the scribe, rendered it so precious that it was kept locked up in a shrine whose duplicate keys were carefully guarded by the Dominicans and the Municipality, and its fame drew leading European Hebraists and biblical scholars to visit it. In 1802, the scroll was confiscated by Napoleon during the suppression of the monasteries, and in 1815 it was returned to the Dominican Library in Bologna only to be confiscated again and deposited in the University Library in 1866. From that time until 2013, it disappeared from notice having been mistakenly relabelled as a seventeenth-century scroll of unknown provenance.[16] When it was rediscovered in 2013, scholars were able to use radiocarbon dating and other tools of scroll analysis to date it more precisely to the twelfth or thirteenth century CE.

Aside from this legendary scroll, with its fabled origins, the oldest known complete copy of the Hebrew Bible was in codex form, and it was hidden out of sight in the Great Synagogue of Aleppo, Syria. It had been written by the scribe Solomon ben Buya'a and later corrected, punctuated and furnished with its Masoretic apparatus by Aaron ben Asher in about 930 CE. Today, the Aleppo Codex is regarded as the only known true representative of Aaron ben Asher's text and probably the famous model codex cited by Maimonides. But in the mid-nineteenth century, its provenance was still the subject of debate.[17] In order to date a Bible manuscript today, scholars can combine an analysis of its script type, with their knowledge of the historical development of the vocalization signs, accent marks and other marginalia, together with any complementary or conflicting information provided by the scribe in a colophon or epigram. Back then, Hebrew palaeographical analysis was still in its infancy; the precise development of the Masoretic Text, for which there were only later manuscript informants containing many variants, was still being traced; and the information in the available colophons might not be wholly reliable given that some contained corrections and additions, some were copied directly from an earlier codex and some were even forged. Most importantly, having rarely been seen, the Aleppo Codex had not yet been subjected to rigorous scrutiny. As to scrolls, since uniformity was assumed to be their underlying characteristic feature, their scholarly study was mostly neglected.

Certainly, much more material evidence from an earlier period was needed if scholars were to have reliable points of comparison from which to trace historical lines of development. Into this vast, but promising, black hole of knowledge stepped Saphir who, as he embarked on his Asia-bound fundraising mission, realized that the trip presented him with an opportunity to view Hebrew manuscripts and Bible scrolls held in other distant Jewish communities, to examine them for evidence of the Bible's historical transmission and to correct printed works against their earlier manuscript editions. In this latter enterprise, he followed in the footsteps of generations of Torah scholars living in Palestine and Egypt who, as Hebrew printing became established, set about correcting error-ridden texts.[18] With his in-depth knowledge of the Jewish sources and considerable linguistic talent – he knew at least five languages, including Arabic – he was well equipped to undertake the task.[19]

SAPHIR VISITED JEWS IN THE LOWER EGYPTIAN TOWNS OF Benha, al-Mahallah al-Kubra, Minyat al Qamr, Zifta, Tanta, Samannud and Mansoura in addition to communities in the major Egyptian cities of Alexandria, Suez and Cairo. Jews had lived in Egypt from at least as early as the fifth century BCE, as later attested by the discovery of a Jewish military colony in Elephantine. Large-scale Jewish settlement in the country first occurred, however, following the Greek conquest in 332 BCE. Synagogues were established in the major port city of Alexandria and other northern areas and over time communities settled further south, including most notably, the ancient cities of Dammuh in Memphis, Arsinoe in the Fayum, Oxyrhynchus and up the Nile as far as Syene (Aswan). By the medieval period (as subsequent manuscript discoveries would attest), there were at least ninety Jewish villages, towns and cities in the country.[20] Dammuh, in particular, was once a major Jewish town before it declined in the Byzantine period causing its inhabitants to shift north to the area of the Roman Fortress of Babylon. According to the fifteenth-century Egyptian historian, al-Maqrizi, the Kanīsat Mūsā (Synagogue of Moses) in Dammuh continued to be a major site of pilgrimage for Egyptian Jews through to his own day.[21] Ancient sites like Dammuh were in ruins by Saphir's time, and other medieval towns had dwindled down to just a handful of inhabitants; although for some, such as al-Mahallah al-Kubra, numbers were set to grow in the wake of Egypt's modern industrial development. Saphir noted the demographics of all these communities and described some of their living conditions, livelihoods and food-ways. He visited their synagogues – in Cairo he noted ten, and in the smaller towns he observed that many were situated within private homes – and he took a great interest in their varying religious customs. In spite of his own misgivings about offering a mere 'chattering of words' as opposed to producing a work of serious rabbinic study, the keen observations Saphir compiled in his travelogue help reconstruct the condition of Egyptian Jewry in that period.[22]

As to his descriptions of the Hebrew manuscripts he encountered along the way, they were sometimes the first account of such material to reach Western scholars. Indeed, he was the first person to publish information about an old Hebrew Bible codex that, although incomplete, was believed to be older than the Aleppo Codex. The codex was housed, along with numerous other incomplete Bible codices, in the *Dār Simḥa* Synagogue in the *Harat al-Yahud al-Qara'in* (the Karaite Jewish quarter), situated in the al-Gamāliyya neighbourhood in the eastern section of Cairo's *Harat al-Yahud* (the Jewish quarter) near to the city's thriving commercial area and soon-to-be antiquities hotspot, the Sharia al-Muski.

The Karaites were Jewish religious dissidents who rejected rabbinic law and adhered only to the law of the Bible. After the founding of their movement in eighth-century Baghdad, sections of the community moved westwards and settled in Jerusalem. The growth of the movement may be connected to the intense focus on creating an authoritative version of the Hebrew Bible among the Masoretic scholars of the eighth and ninth centuries.[23] From Jerusalem, Karaite communities migrated to other parts of Palestine and to Damascus and, with the rise of the Fatimids at the end of the tenth century, over to Egypt. During the Fatimid period, Karaite communities flourished and established themselves in Alexandria, al-Fustat and the cities of the Nile Delta.[24] Al-Maqrizi, and another contemporary Egyptian historian, Ibn Dumqaq, both referred to the existence of a Karaite synagogue in al-Fustat, but by the time the Egyptian Jewish historian Joseph Sambari visited the site in 1672, the building was in ruins.[25] The community may have left the area after a plague spread through the city in the thirteenth century, or after a sweeping fire burnt down many of its buildings in 1473. According to historical Karaite documents, their *Dār Simḥa* Synagogue in Cairo was in continuous use from the beginning of the sixteenth century.

The manuscript examined by Saphir, the Cairo Codex of the Prophets (now known as Codex Cairensis), was a medieval copy of the biblical books of the Former Prophets (Joshua, Judges, Samuel, Kings) and the Latter Prophets (Isaiah, Jeremiah, Ezekiel and the twelve minor prophets). It was a sumptuous codex produced on 600 pages of gazelle-hide with 14 decorated carpet pages in coloured ink and gold leaf. Its colophon, which he transcribed, stated that it had been copied in Tiberias in 895 CE, and Saphir reported that it contained further evidence to suggest that it was a product of the Ben Asher Masoretic school.[26] The colophon was later suspected as a forgery, and modern radiocarbon dating has placed it in the late tenth century rather than in the ninth.[27]

According to the traditions surrounding it, the codex had been given as a gift to the Karaite community in Jerusalem. The Crusaders seized it sometime later, and then, after being ransomed, it came into the possession of the Karaite community of Cairo. Despite the criticisms of a later twentieth-century observer, who lamented the way the Karaites treated their codices like talismans, the Karaites had always kept it safe within their custody, together with over twenty other Hebrew Bible codices, from the medieval period. They had also kept thousands of pages from their worn-out and defective manuscripts hidden away elsewhere within the building. Saphir did not see them, but others soon would.[28]

In the Ben Ezra Synagogue, Saphir was given the opportunity to see and report on things normally hidden from most visitors. On his first journey there in 1858, he recalled approaching the synagogue through dark, narrow streets until, coming out into a courtyard, he spied dilapidated buildings alongside other buildings that had been newly repaired. Some years earlier, the shabby state of the synagogue had been noted by a foreign gentile visitor who had peered inside through 'broken doors and windows' and inferred from the walls that the present building stood upon 'the substructions of older ones'.[29] Entering through a 'high hall' and descending several steps, Saphir found himself inside the main hall. Once inside, he was immediately struck by its neglected-looking state, and by the pieces of engraved wooden panelling scattered around, some of which had been removed to a 'special room' upstairs and some of which remained on the walls around the sanctuaries. He noted that they bore biblical verses and other ancient inscriptions, but many were so worn that only some verses from the Psalms were identifiable on them. He felt sure that details about the date of the building and its consecration must have once been present on the boards, but negligence and damage had left them inscrutable.

In a recess in the wall in the east corner five cubits (between 7 and 10 feet) high, he saw an ark containing three scrolls of the law set aside for use when there was a prayer quorum. On the right side, in another recess dubbed the Cave of Elijah (in whose name the medieval building had been formerly known) was the synagogue's most famous scroll which, like the Bologna scroll, was purported to have been handwritten by the biblical prophet, Ezra the scribe.[30] After he managed to persuade the nervous custodian that he would not die from opening the scroll, Saphir was allowed to climb up on a five-rung ladder to take a look. The scroll, about two feet in length, was enclosed in a wooden case overlaid with copper. Opening the case, as he balanced on his ladder, Saphir found the scroll to be so old and decayed that he warned the custodian it would fall to pieces if touched and that it was good to keep it hidden away.

Still alive, but apparently cursed, Saphir was duped by a confidence trickster during his travels through Lower Egypt and robbed of his luggage and travel funds. His planned journey from Egypt to India had to stop short at Yemen, where he disembarked at the busy port city of al-Hudaydah in search of further funding for his passage to Aden. Six days later, stuck with the possibility of having to reach Aden by land, he began a long trek across Yemen's interior, encountering perilous mountain tracks, mob attacks, starvation and plague along the way. Nevertheless, the experience proved transformative. The rich descriptions in his travelogue of Yemen's remote and isolated Jewish population, whose origins can be reliably dated to at least as early as the second century CE, were the first to reach Western Jewish readers. Moreover, the ancient religious customs Saphir encountered there, as well as the variant readings transmitted in their manuscripts, were of great interest to scholars in the growing field of biblical criticism. Saphir also brought home news about previously unknown Yemenite works of importance to rabbinic studies, such as the *Midrash Ha-Gadol*, a thirteenth-century commentary on the Pentateuch that preserved within it portions of ancient rabbinic texts considered lost. In addition to drawing scholarly attention to Yemenite traditions, the cache of manuscripts Saphir brought back with him, combined with reports of treasures still held in Yemen, drew immediate notice among an increasing number of European manuscript hunters.[31]

ABRAHAM FIRKOVICH WAS A VORACIOUS MANUSCRIPT HUNTER who later procured some of Saphir's Yemenite manuscripts before going on to pursue greater spoils in Nablus and Cairo. Born in 1787 in the city of Łuck, then part of the Polish-Lithuanian Commonwealth, Firkovich was raised by Karaite Jews. The Karaites of Łuck were a tiny minority group, and Firkovich grew up acutely aware of the paucity of historical materials pertaining to their history. As a young man, he was heavily influenced by his tutor, the self-taught Karaite scholar Mordechai Sultanski, who took a deep interest in Bible criticism and historical studies, as well as apologetic works that attempted to align Christian and Karaite beliefs.[32]

For Firkovich to gain greater knowledge of Karaite literature, he would need to seek out works in manuscript form as printed works were not commercially viable for such a small group of people. While still living in Łuck, he managed to obtain a handful of Karaite manuscripts from other nearby communities, and he started to earn a living as a tutor. But after becoming embroiled in a dispute with Sultanski in the 1820s, he left Łuck to serve as a tutor for the children of Crimea's Karaite spiritual leader, Simha Babovich. In addition to pursuing his own scholarship, Firkovich also tried to set up a printing press to publish classic Karaite texts and prayerbooks while, at other times, he continued to trade in books. After many vicissitudes in his life in the Crimea, he was finally appointed as Babovich's secretary.[33]

In 1830, Firkovich accompanied Babovich on a momentous trip to the Near East. As they travelled around from community to community, he uncovered a sizeable number of older Karaite manuscripts. He gained important Hebrew codices for his personal collection in Constantinople, and in Jerusalem he got hold of an unknown number of manuscripts from the eleventh- or twelfth-century Karaite synagogue that had been stored away in their genizah.

THE GENERIC NOUN 'GENIZAH', by its simplest definition, refers to any place in which worn-out or defective sacred writings can be hidden away or buried. The fundamental purpose of consigning sacred materials to a genizah was to shield the name of God from physical destruction. This rule not only covered all the various written forms of God's name, but it also extended to any building materials or utensils that were inscribed with such forms. Given the Persian origin of the word 'genizah', and its first appearance in the biblical book of Esther to denote a 'treasury', the concept of placing sacred materials away in some sort of safe place can probably be traced back at least as far as the post-exilic biblical period.[34] The earliest evidence of this practice may be the scrolls discovered stored or hidden in clay pots inside the caves at Qumran, and possibly the scrolls discovered buried during excavations in the synagogue ruins on Masada.[35]

References to the practice of genizah (i.e. verbal forms of the word connoting the act of consigning something to a genizah) appear in rabbinic literature, particularly in a section of the Talmud, known as tractate *Megillah*, which deals with the laws of the Jewish festival of Purim, as well as the laws surrounding the public reading of the Torah and other synagogue practices. In the uncertain world of the late Roman and early Byzantine era, the rabbinic sages probably realized, as they deliberated carefully over what things should be rescued from a fire, that they could not continuously guarantee the safeguard of their older sacred writings from pillage and destruction. In fact, the only way to guarantee the preservation of their ancient texts was to ensure the exact transmission of their contents (not their container) from generation to generation. And thus, they discussed at length which ceremonial items were considered sanctified and therefore worthy of putting away in a genizah and which items were merely accessories to ritual and could be thrown away. They also determined a hierarchy of sanctity whereby the synagogue and Torah scrolls were at the highest level of intrinsic holiness, and objects, such as the prayer shawl fringes (*tzitzit*), that only carried a quality of holiness due to their association with certain rituals or commandments, were at the lowest level. The objects of highest sanctity, once damaged, could not be renewed or recycled from out of the older materials. In other words, reusing old sacred materials was tantamount to defiling them. Elsewhere in the Talmud, the rabbis also used a verbal form of genizah to refer to the act of 'suppression' for works considered uncanonical, such as the Book of Ecclesiasticus. At any rate, the rabbinic deliberations on all these issues appear to have led to a wide interpretation of what should be kept from harm, and sometimes from harming, and consigned to a genizah. By the medieval period, the great Jewish philosopher and codifier Moses Maimonides ruled in his *Mishneh Torah* that anything written with 'sacred intent' by a Jew, or even a gentile (but not a heretic), such as a commentary on the law, should be put away in this manner.[36]

Indeed, the practice of genizah, in terms of what, how and where materials were put away and for how long, varied widely from community to community and over time. Genizahs, or more accurately *genizot* in the plural, as later discovered, were located in multiple places within and without synagogues: they could be found under floors or under stairs; in cupboards, niches or alcoves; in attic spaces or basements, and even, as Firkovich would discover, within synagogue walls. Some communities designated a single place of temporary storage in either a hidden or out-of-reach place; when the storage place was full the material was taken out and buried. Other communities created multiple storage places which were periodically emptied and taken for burial, or else the materials were simply moved from one storage place to another as each one filled up, or they were left permanently in place as though buried in situ. According to the Jewish explorer Israel Joseph Benjamin, genizot were meant to be inaccessible. Benjamin, a Jewish lumberjack who adopted the moniker Benjamin II (after the medieval explorer, Benjamin of Tudela), turned into a hunter of 'lost tribes'. On a tour of the East in the 1840s, he recorded information about the diverse Jewish communities he encountered along the way. Despite failing to notice the existence of any genizot in the Ben Ezra Synagogue, he did make a general note about the practice of genizah (Guenisa) during his visit to the town of Kabur-Kefil near the Euphrates:

In the interior of the Synagogue is a certain room, which is always kept shut; it is never even entered by the Jews, and is certainly therefore not accessible to any one else. It is a so-called Guenisa (place for the safe custody of ancient writings) in which old manuscripts are kept, which are said to date from ancient times, and to have come from different places. This place for the preservation of old relics is held in great veneration by the followers of every creed.[37]

Benjamin II's definition of a genizah room suggests to the reader that ancient materials of varied provenance could be discovered there and that the inaccessible room was a place of permanent preservation. Yet, he also added, in a contradictory footnote, that the Jews in the East and in Africa 'have still the custom of . . . burying them every two or three years in the cemetery'.

Even the practice of final interment differed: some communities buried their materials in locations around the synagogue grounds, while others buried them in the grave of a distinguished person, or else in their own dedicated plot; some communities encased them in clay pots before interment in a tomb, cave or hole in the ground; others conducted elaborate burial rituals involving processions and accompanying festivities. The London-based Jewish author and literary collector Philip Abraham described the traditions of such a ceremony in Jerusalem:

A great ceremony, called the 'Burying of the Law', lately took place in the Spanish Synagogue of Jerusalem. It happens once in every eight or ten years, and is accompanied with the following ceremonies: – There is in the 'Talmud Torah' synagogue a subterranean cave, wherein any old leaf torn out of any holy book . . . is deposited by all the Jewish inhabitants in Jerusalem of every Minhag [custom]. After eight or ten years, when the cave is full, these old papers and books are brought out and made into bales. This done, the Jews begin to assemble at a given time in the afternoon. A kosher, or faultless Sepher Torah . . . is brought by the Cacham Bashi, and carried by him and the other rabbis in turn at the head of the procession. He is followed by the other rabbis; next come the bales, about seventy or eighty in number, each carried by a Jew, and then the rest of the people. The procession winds its way slowly out of the Zion gate for some distance along the city wall, and then descends into the valley of Jehoshaphat, where the burial-ground is situated. Here is a very deep well, where the bales are finally thrown, amidst the singing of the joyous crowd.[38]

What was put away was also highly variable: some communities only buried their sacred writings (scrolls, Bible codices, prayer books, *mezuzot*, etc.) *known* to contain the name of God; while other communities placed in their genizot all manner of sacred and secular writings that *might* contain the name of God, as well as objects relating to ritual practice, such as the boxes for the *tefillin* (phylacteries).[39]

A number of nineteenth-century Christian scholars criticized the practice of genizah for being deliberately responsible for the disappearance of old, pre-Masoretic copies of the Hebrew Bible. In an article heralding the publication of the new English

Old Testament in 1885 (the revised edition of the King James Bible from 1611), the anonymous author, stated:

> When once the religious authorities of the nation had determined this text, it and it alone would be copied by the scribes. Manuscripts disagreeing from it would gradually disappear even if they were not deliberately destroyed as corrupt and misleading. The Jewish practice of 'concealing' worn-out or inaccurate copies is sufficient to account for the fact that there is no manuscript or even fragment of a manuscript containing anything but the 'Masoretic' text now in existence.[40]

A later scholar went even further to suggest that non-Masoretic texts were deliberately removed from circulation: 'Indeed, it may be that a wholesale destruction of early copies of the Old Testament took place upon the final establishment of an authoritative text, all copies not agreeing with it being put out of existence.'[41]

THE EARLIEST KNOWN ENCOUNTERS WITH GENIZOT include the experience of Simon Von Geldern who searched in one during a visit to Egypt in 1752 or 1753. A colourful member of a family of German 'court Jews', Von Geldern styled himself as a Holy Land emissary and journeyed in the Near East where he collected and sold books and manuscripts, mostly works of kabbalah. In his diary, he listed the places he visited and the purchases he made, including numerous visits to Alexandria and to the *Kahal Eliyahu Ha-Navi* (congregation of the Elijah synagogue). On folio 23 of his diary, he wrote the enigmatic note: 'I was in the synagogue of Elijah, of blessed memory. I searched in the genizah. I gave -:5.'[42] Unlike the other items in his list, this is one of the smaller payments, and his use of the Hebrew word for 'give' rather than the Hebrew word he uses elsewhere for 'paid' or 'bought' suggests that this small sum might have been offered as *bakshish*. Whatever, he saw inside this genizah, his notice of it was remarkably brief and decidedly underwhelming.[43] Nevertheless, this vague statement about a genizah in the Elijah synagogue, which may have been in Alexandria or Cairo, later assumed greater significance.

A more exciting encounter with a genizah was experienced fifty years later by the Scottish theologian and missionary Reverend Claudius Buchanan. In 1806, Buchanan travelled to Malabar to study the history of the Syrian Christians. While he was there, he also enquired after the Jewish communities of India and took an especial interest in their books. In Cochin, he was allowed to see a synagogue genizah, which he described as a 'Record Chest':

> Almost in every house I find Hebrew books, printed or manuscript; particularly among the White Jews. Most of the printed Hebrew of Europe has found its way to Cochin. . . . When I questioned the Jews concerning old copies of the Scriptures, which had been read in the Synagogues from age to age; some told me that it was usual to *bury* them, when decayed by time and use. Others said this was not always the case. . . . I was informed that the Black Jews possessed formerly copies written on *Goat Skins;* and that in the Synagogue of the Black Jews there was an old Record Chest, into which the decayed copies of their Scriptures had been thrown.[44]

After examining the contents of the 'Record Chest' with some of the synagogue elders, he tried to negotiate their purchase. But members of the community protested and entreated the local magistrate, Thomas Flower, for help. Flower confiscated the manuscripts and told Buchanan to leave while things calmed down. Upon his return, Flower decreed that the manuscripts would be delivered to Buchanan's house so that he could 'select what was *old*, and of little use to the Jews' and return to them 'what was *new*'. Buchanan eventually presented thirty-nine Hebrew manuscripts from the Cochin community to Cambridge University Library, including Bible and commentaries, liturgy, kabbalah, miscellanea and histories. Most of the pieces were only several centuries old; probably because the 'Record Chest' had been periodically emptied. Among the more notable pieces was an unusual eighteenth-century copy of an apocryphal work 'The Words of Gad the Seer', and a seventeenth-century history of the Jews of Malabar. Among the 'new' items that had been consigned to their genizah, the Jews of Cochin allowed Buchanan to take away their copies of the New Testament in Hebrew.

The oldest item was a Torah scroll believed to have been brought to India centuries earlier by Jewish merchants who hailed from Yemen. The scroll was constructed from the typical, red-dyed goat-skin leather used by the Yemenite Jews. In addition to emptying their small genizah, Buchanan also obtained copper facsimiles of the historic plates presented in the eleventh century by the king of Kerala to the Yemeni merchant, Joseph Rabban, granting land privileges to him and his successors. Buchanan's success notwithstanding, the news that some synagogues could contain ancient historical materials hidden or buried within them was slow to seep into the consciousness of nineteenth-century scholars who determined that everything consigned to a genizah was otherwise forever lost.

2

Seeking out the hiding places (1860s)

ABRAHAM FIRKOVICH REALI₂ THE POTENTIAL IN GENIZOT after finding manuscripts of great worth in the basement f the Jerusalem Karaite synagogue. After he returned from his travels in the Near East, he was appointed head of the Karaite publishing house in 1834. In addition to printing many Karaite works, he published several vehemently anti-Rabbanite tracts to prove Karaite antiquity and shield the Karaite community against accusations of deicide and of persecuting the early Christians. When an official government inquiry into the origins of the Karaites was sent to the Karaite leader, Simha Babovich, five years later, Firkovich was chosen to undertake the research. Armed with letters of credence from M. M. Muromtsev, the governor of Tavria, and Count Vorontsov, the governor-general of the Novorossiysk region, Firkovich was authorized to collect materials crucial to reconstructing Karaite history.[1]

During his expeditions into the Caucasus and Crimea, Firkovich acquired by various means, some more questionable than others, a collection of some of the world's greatest Hebrew manuscripts. Thanks to his memoir *Sefer Avne Zikaron* (Stones of Remembrance), as well as his extensive personal archive, the details of how and where he acquired many of them are known. One of his early finds was a copy of the book of the Latter Prophets from 916 CE, which he claimed he had discovered under the wooden floor of a Karaite synagogue in the Crimean city of Chufut-Kale. With great astonishment, he noted how the manuscript preserved evidence of the little-known Babylonian system of Hebrew vocalization with vowel signs written above the letters. During his stay in the city of Karasubazar (Belogorsk), he was able to obtain numerous old codices from the local Rabbanites by means of an exchange; a practice that was employed by many manuscript hunters who exploited the locals' desire for modern printed works:

> The local (Rabbanite) Krimchaks were rich in old [hand-] written books but lacking copies of the Bible for teaching their students, and I was rich in new copies of the Bible. So with them I made exchange with my new ones for the old ones among which they – and not I – made a choice. They gave me all the old ones, which were on parchment, because they were damaged from head to foot . . . holy books and also rabbinical works written on old and ancient parchment and paper, defective ones too, and I gave them thirty-two copies of the Bible printed in London.[2]

In the Karasubazar synagogue, Firkovich noticed that the students sitting in the *Beit Midrash* (study hall) were squeezed into a small space owing to an additional and unnecessary wall between their room and the room of the synagogue. When he asked the teacher why the community caused the students to suffer and not remove the wall, the teacher revealed that the space between the two walls stored all the community's worn-out, defunct and torn books. Firkovich noted that his soul leapt at these words as he contemplated the many ancient books that might be hidden there. His request to the elders of the community to open the wall, however, was met with resistance: the genizah he was told was protected from disturbance by an ancient ban; violating the ban would evoke a terrible curse upon the community. He told them not to be afraid, for it was he who, with the permission of the Governor, was requiring the wall to be opened. After reading his official letter aloud, the community members trembled and looked fearful, which he interpreted as a fear that he might uncover the secret that they originally hailed from the Karaites and would be forced to return to Karaism. As Firkovich stood vividly imagining their inner secrets, the community informed him that the ban originated in ancient times and that anyone overriding it would subject the town to a plague. Firkovich warned them that they were forcing him to go to the police and, upon seeing that they were intractable, he left to gain the help of the local mayor. The mayor, based on Firkovich's letters of credence, tasked several men to return with him to help break through the wall. At the synagogue, they met with a crowd gathered, he claimed, as though prepared for war. The mayor read the official letters to the crowd and, after assuring them that his actions provided them with immunity from any plague, the men took up their tools and broke down half the wall:

> And behold, the entire *geniza* was full of fragments and bundles of various books as much as the load of some carts. . . . I was inside the genizah searching and examining and I saw that I would not succeed in finding anything there because of the masses of bundles and the large amount of dust which filled my mouth and nose. . . . They took [the material] from my hands and carried [it] . . . to the *bet midrash*. . . . In great haste from noon until the evening . . . I searched among the fragments and bundles as far as possible and I chose from the useful objects those which in my eyes seemed to be the most valuable ones, those with a connection to the requested purpose.[3]

Following his foray into the Karasubazar genizah, Firkovich visited the fourteenth-century synagogue in the Crimean city of Kaffa (Feodosia). The Jewish community of Kaffa was founded by Jewish immigrants from the Black Sea region who arrived there at the same time as the Genoese were establishing the city as a major port of trade. In addition to the books and scrolls that the Kaffa community generated over the long course of its history, the first immigrants to the city had brought materials with them, many of which were the possessions of their ancestors in the Near East.[4] The synagogue was therefore rich in potential holdings; however, according to Firkovich's memoir, the synagogue wardens at Kaffa refused to even let him inside. They feared he would hand over their synagogue and treasures to the Karaites, and they warned him to keep his focus firmly on the Karaites to whose community he belonged. Firkovich explained that his official papers sanctioned him to search both Rabbanite and Karaite synagogues for ancient books. Still, the wardens would not grant him entrance until the legitimacy of his papers was confirmed by the local authorities. When Firkovich returned to the synagogue with the police, the courtyard had filled with members of the community who could not understand why they were being forced to take part in a Karaite project. The authorities explained that Firkovich would not be removing any of their complete books or scrolls, or anything still in use. He wanted only to see the place where they stored discarded books; those missing their beginning and end sections and Torah scrolls put away as unfit for use. The synagogue wardens finally disclosed that their old genizah was in the attic, but they warned that it was too dangerous to climb up there as the roof boards were all aged and rotten. With their old genizah inaccessible, they now used a vault hidden behind the Torah ark as a genizah. Firkovich reassured them that he was not afraid of the danger posed by the rotten attic boards. He suggested that new boards could be placed on top of the old boards to facilitate an entrance. Firkovich's accomplice, the local Karaite Rabbi, called upon several of his students to help. Two ladders were tied together to make one single ladder long enough to reach up to the attic window. The students climbed up the makeshift long ladder and by placing new boards on top of the old ones they could reach in to get the manuscripts. But they soon discovered that there were far too many pieces inside for the students to bring each manuscript down by hand, and so they resorted to tossing piles of papers out of the window, enough to fill several cartloads, until the place became so full of dust, they could no longer see each other. Firkovich searched through the piles and, according to his description of them, selected twelve of the best looking and most valuable pieces he could find. He did not explore the materials in the second genizah: the Rabbanites insisted that his raid should be over by the afternoon prayers. Besides, the job had become too overwhelming. In obeyance with the wardens' wishes, the students placed the remaining piles of papers in sacks and emptied the sacks into the second genizah through an external window behind the south wall.[5]

The vault, which now held manuscripts from the old genizah as well as its own, was penetrated four years later in 1843 when the German economist and agricultural scientist, Baron August von Haxthausen, visited the city as part of a Tsarist-sponsored, Empire-wide rural study. Curiously, given their earlier resistance to a stranger viewing and raiding their manuscripts, the Rabbanite Jews in the city purportedly went out of their way to invite Haxthausen to visit their synagogue and view their treasures. Haxthausen attributed this unexpected invitation to a feeling of jealousy on the part of the Rabbanites that the Karaites had received a visit from him. The jealousy he sensed was most likely based on the community's shrewd realization that any visitor having the ability to influence Russian rural policies should be cultivated as a potential advocate whose positive impression of the community and its synagogue could be beneficial.

Haxthausen's initial reluctance to accept the invitation was overcome by an offer too tempting to resist: the opportunity to see a large collection of ancient manuscripts inside the synagogue vaults. His description of the visit is extremely brief: he simply described the synagogue as large and interesting. His tantalizing account of the genizah, however, provides the only known description of that space and its contents:

> Behind the chair of the Rabbi was a vault entered through a low opening, into which a person could only creep on his hands and his knees. It was quite dark;

lights were therefore brought, and we crawled in. There was doubtless a large collection of manuscripts, but lying torn and in great confusion, in a heap above ten feet high: it would have taken a week to inspect them even superficially.[6]

Towards the end of the nineteenth century, a rebuilding project on the Kaffa synagogue brought to light some clay pots containing old parchment scrolls. Some of these pieces were sold off to various interested buyers; the rest appear to have been lost. The vault had also been searched at some point during this period by the synagogue's rabbi, Aron Hershkovich Begam. In a private letter to the English lawyer and manuscript hunter, Elkan Nathan Adler, probably in response to Adler's own queries about the subject, Begam reported that he had ordered the vault emptied. Yet, after 'two days of hard work in the dust', he noted that 'we did not find any [complete] manuscript or ancient printed book'. Begam blamed Firkovich for taking everything of worth, and he reported to Adler that nothing valuable was left.[7] Since, according to Haxthausen, there had once existed a 10-foot pile in the vault, it can only be assumed that either the bulk of the manuscripts had been removed and buried during the renovations, or that the potential scholarly value of the contents of scrappy old manuscript fragments was still underappreciated when Rabbi Begam cast his eye over the dusty remnants. But the potential historical information within these fragments would never be unlocked: the synagogue was closed by the Soviets in 1923, and the building (and whatever was left inside or buried near it) was finally destroyed by Nazi air raids in 1941.

THE FIRST FIRKOVICH COLLECTION WAS PURCHASED IN 1863 by the Russian government for the price of 100,000 silver roubles. The collection of 1,500 books and documents, which had been stored with the Odessa Society of History and Antiquities, was first known as the Odessa Collection and later, after he acquired and sold a second large manuscript collection to the Imperial Library, as the First Firkovich Collection. The purchase even gained international attention and, as recounted in the 'Weekly Gossip' of the *Athenaeum* literary magazine, Firkovich's collecting mission was cast in a romantic light:

> He sacrificed his fortune for rare and old manuscripts; bore without murmuring long separations from his family; subjected himself to all sorts of privations, and often endangered his own life. . . he has lived for months in churchyards and burial-places. . .; he has penetrated synagogues and other likely places, where the Jews used to hide books. . . . Thus he succeeded in collecting 124 Hebrew original copies of the Old Testament, which are older than all other Hebrew codices in any of the libraries of Europe. Twenty-five of the manuscripts in Mr. Firkowitch's collection were written before the ninth, and twenty before the tenth century. Five of the manuscripts on leather are maintained to be the oldest of all documents on the Scriptures hitherto discovered.[8]

Some of Firkovich's acquisitions have a firm provenance since he listed and described the outstanding pieces in his memoir, *Avne Zikaron*. Other pieces deemed less significant were left undescribed. Thus, for many of the manuscripts in the First Firkovich Collection, it is not known whether they were found in a genizah in Kaffa,

Karasubazar or some other Crimean synagogue or cemetery or whether they were Karaite or Rabbanite in origin or use.[9]

One of the greatest mysteries is the find spot for the collection's most famous piece: the Leningrad Codex B19a, the oldest complete codex of the Hebrew Bible from 1010 CE. Today it is known that the Bible's original scribe, Samuel ben Jacob, practised his profession in al-Fustat, and its original commissioner, Mevorakh ben Joseph, was a Persian Karaite living in Egypt. The codex was later sold to another Persian Karaite, one Ibn Kujik, and then afterwards to a leading Rabbanite, Masliah ben Solomon ha-Kohen, head of the Jerusalem Yeshivah (rabbinic academy). In 1489, the codex was donated to the Karaite synagogue of Damascus. Firkovich did not explain how he managed to obtain the codex some 400 years later, let alone how or when it might have left the Near East. The only clue appears in his memoir where he notes that he took all the ancient books and 'bundles' he had found 'and also the very precious twenty-four [volume] book that was written in 1010 in Egypt and brought from Damascus' to Odessa. One plausible theory is that the Bible codex was brought over by Karaite immigrants from Damascus in the nineteenth century and donated to the leader of the Russian Karaites, Simha Babovich, in gratitude for his help.[10] At the very least, the incomplete object biography of this monumental manuscript is symbolic of the inscrutable provenance surrounding so many of the manuscripts owned (and sometimes shared) by both Rabbanites and Karaites.

In addition to the information that can be gleaned about the collections he gained from his travels, the letters in Firkovich's archive reveal that he hoped to gain manuscript collections through his correspondence with disparate Karaite groups in remote areas of the world. In 1851, he sent a letter to a community in Hamadan, Iran, enquiring after their numbers, history and books. Presenting himself as someone who had been 'decorated with a medal' for his discoveries of antiquities, he asked that all ancient books (or copies) be sent to him. He also asked the addressee for any information about groups in Africa, Ethiopia and China. As far as the available evidence suggests, Firkovich did not receive a response from Iran.[11]

FIRKOVICH TOOK A SECOND TOUR OF THE NEAR EAST IN 1863 as part of another book-scouting mission. The tour, which covered the cities of Jerusalem, Nablus, Jaffa, Aleppo, Damascus, Alexandria and Cairo, would culminate in the addition of a second collection comprising several thousand manuscripts acquired from multiple sites and suppliers. One of his suppliers, Jacob Saphir, was already back home in Jerusalem by the time that Firkovich arrived there in October 1863. It is not clear how the two first met, but Saphir's travelogue recalls that they discussed the Aleppo Codex. Saphir asked Firkovich if, during his planned visit to the city of Aleppo, he could try to check a copy of the codex's dedication page against the original manuscript. Few people were granted access to the precious manuscript; the copy that Saphir handed to Firkovich had been made for him by Rabbi Yaakov Ze'ev, an emissary who had spent a year living in Aleppo back in 1855.

While residing in Jerusalem, Firkovich was also heavily engaged in funding and directing plans for the renovation of the medieval Karaite synagogue in Jerusalem. The project was undertaken after consulting historic documents relating to all the Karaite buildings in Jerusalem and with a view to producing a faithful restoration, but it also incorporated many new elements, including extensions to the size of the building, a new cupola with glass windows over the entrance, the addition of a coffee room, and the creation of a new ark for the Torah scrolls and a genizah under the ark.[12]

No ancient manuscripts appeared to surface in the building at this time: it's possible that Firkovich had already removed most of them in 1830, or that anything left had either been buried or taken away by others. While this extensive five-month project got underway, Firkovich visited Aleppo. His letters to Babovich indicate that he had been secretly shown the Aleppo Codex, but that he was barred soon after from seeing it again. According to Firkovich, the injunction arose due to his discovery that the manuscript showed signs of prior Karaite ownership and the current owners' fears that he would take it away from them 'by the force of the authorities'. They did, however, copy out for him parts of the text he had most wanted to examine.[13]

Paradoxically, in this case, it may have been better for its long-term preservation as a complete manuscript had Firkovich managed to take the Aleppo Codex away with him. The codex went missing during the Syrian anti-Jewish riots of 1947, only to resurface in Israel in 1958 with significant parts lost (around eighty-six folios), including its dedication page.[14] At some point after he returned to Jerusalem, at the end of 1863, or early in the winter of 1864, Firkovich returned the copy of the dedication page to Saphir with his notes added to the margins, including an emendation to the name of the scribe, which posited him as the Karaite, Shelomo ben Yeroham.[15] A version of this copy was published by Saphir in his travelogue, together with his own commentaries. Firkovich's surprising, and later contested, observations and emendations to the dedication page were placed in the footnotes. In addition to this informational exchange, Firkovich purchased books and manuscripts from Saphir, adding to his growing second collection of materials from the cache of manuscripts that Saphir had acquired in Yemen.

In March 1864, two emissaries from the Karaite community in Hīt, Iraq, visited Firkovich in Jerusalem. Their small, walled town, lying west of Baghdad on the Euphrates River, had once served as the centre of Karaism in Iraq, but by the time of Firkovich's engagement with the community, their numbers had dwindled to less than 100. Henry Aaron Stern, a Hebrew-Christian missionary, visited them in 1854 and described their synagogue as 'a sable, dusky room, consisting of just four smoked mud walls. The floor was covered with a tattered piece of carpet, and a small stool stood in one corner.' Stern sold them four Bibles and five New Testaments, but he did not mention being shown any of their scrolls in return. Only in the Rabbanite synagogue of Mosul did he report seeing 'a pile of more than a hundred and twenty scrolls of the law'.[16] Based on his letters to his son-in-law, Gabriel, Firkovich's interactions with this community were more involved than Stern's. The emissaries revealed to him that the community members back in Hīt were contemplating immigrating to Jerusalem. They also let it be known, probably in response to Firkovich's queries, that there were many manuscripts hidden in their genizah and in their homes.[17]

Firkovich provided them with 5,000 piastres to fund their travel back home and he requested they return with 'all the manuscripts, the complete and defective ones and even the torn and decomposed pages'. The emissaries promised to return before the Feast of Weeks holiday, which fell in June that year. They took with them a letter from Firkovich addressed to the community of Hīt which promised financial support to help them all relocate to Jerusalem. He sent books with the emissaries and promised to supply more after the move. In return, he asked the congregation to bring with them every single manuscript in their possession: manuscripts both on parchment and paper, old and ancient, complete and defective, and even anything torn, fragmentary and decomposed. This, he informed them, would be the way to recompense him for his help.[18] This detailed directive not only reveals the extent to which Firkovich would go to satisfy his bibliomania, and his method of leaving no stone unturned in his search for items of historical importance, it also shows his realization that others did not attach the same importance to fragmentary or defective manuscripts and that he would need to specify exactly what he wanted or else run the risk that scrappy (but significant) 'sheets' or fragments would be overlooked or discarded.

Subsequent scholarly analyses of his collection reveal that Firkovich did indeed acquire materials from Hīt; however, the pieces are interspersed among at least 500 other unprovenanced pieces in the collection that were brought over from Damascus, Aleppo and Jerusalem. Where colophons or other historical data are not present, scholars have had to rely on other clues such as the type of vocalization present to try to determine their origin.[19]

Testimony preserved in a nineteenth-century travelogue shows that the Karaite community of Hīt eventually moved to Jerusalem, but not long after they arrived there at some point in the 1880s – and certainly before 1884 – they returned to their native town in Iraq.[20] Even though it must be supposed that the emissaries had travelled back to Jerusalem to exchange their manuscripts for funding, Firkovich apparently did not gain everything they owned. In 1881, a collection comprising Karaite manuscripts from Hīt, mixed in with Karaite manuscripts from Cairo, were sold to the British Museum through the Jerusalemite dealer, Moses Wilhelm Shapira.[21]

A FUTURE CURATOR OF A WORLD-CLASS HEBRAICA COLLECTION was visiting St. Petersburg in March 1864. Adolf Neubauer, a 32-year-old Jewish scholar based in Paris was getting his first taste of collection building as part of an official commission to visit and report on Firkovich's Odessa Collection. Born in Hungary in 1831, Neubauer's natural aptitude enabled him to progress easily from a traditional childhood Jewish education with his father to studying at the feet of Solomon Judah Leib Rapoport, the chief rabbi of Prague, a leading proponent of the *Wissenschaft des Judenthums* (scientific study of Judaism) movement. Neubauer was deeply influenced by Rapoport's critical approach to the study of history and languages and wide-ranging knowledge of Jewish literature, and this training enabled him to pursue more advanced studies at the University of Prague and the University of Munich.

In the late 1850s, Neubauer was employed in the Jerusalem consulate of the Austro-Hungarian Empire, and he took the opportunity while in Palestine to tour around and inspect the condition of his brethren. His various observations, some scathing, filled the pages of *The Jewish Chronicle* newspaper for thirteen weeks.[22] Most significantly for this story, he was allowed to visit the Karaite synagogue in Jerusalem and gain access to its genizah, out of which (prior to Firkovich's renovation project) he purchased several

Karaite grammatical texts, including manuscripts of the tenth-century Karaite, David ben Abraham al Fasi, compiler of the first biblical Hebrew dictionary. His subsequent work on al Fasi's grammar reveals that, like other scholars of the *Wissenschaft des Judenthums*, Neubauer took a strong interest in the Karaites and Karaism,[23] and that he had come to realize that medieval Hebrew manuscripts (Karaite and Rabbanite) were key components to the critical study of Jewish history. During the next few years, Neubauer published numerous scholarly articles based on manuscript discoveries in the leading relevant journals of France, Germany and Hungary, and in recognition of his skills in appraising manuscripts, he was appointed to survey Hebrew collections around central Europe, eventually leading to his commission to examine the Odessa Collection in 1864.

The collection made a great impression on him, and Neubauer quickly published his first discoveries – ancient Jewish gravestone inscriptions in the Crimea (later revealed as forgeries) – in a notice in a Russian journal on 16 March 1864.[24] In a fuller report, two years later, Neubauer provided descriptions of the Karaite manuscripts in the collection, including excerpts from a travel book which recounted the pilgrimage of the Crimean Karaite, Samuel ben David, to Jerusalem in 1641. As he travelled through various countries on his way to the Holy Land, Samuel ben David recorded his impressions of the Jewish communities and synagogues he visited along the way. In his description of the Karaite Synagogue in Cairo, he revealed that the community owned fourteen Torah scrolls as well as books in Judeo-Arabic. He also chronicled the existence of thirty-one Rabbanite synagogues in the entire province of Cairo. In the Rabbanite synagogue of Old Cairo, he noted four scrolls, and his failed attempt to view the famous scroll of Ezra. This synagogue, he believed, had been owned formerly by the Karaites and snatched away from them by the Rabbanites.[25]

While the young Neubauer spent his winter pouring over the treasures in Firkovich's first collection, the elderly Firkovich was busier than ever, gathering information about important manuscripts hidden in other cities in Palestine. An official decree (*Firman*) signed by the Sultan's deputy enabled him to establish and use contacts within the Turkish administration and diplomatic corps in Jerusalem, including the English consul, Albert Cohn, to ensure the success of his mission. In addition, his standing within the Karaite community as a major benefactor furnished him with willing helpers and scouts from among the community members. In fact, in the month prior, one of his local agents, Shabbetai Levi, brought him news that important old copies of the Pentateuch were to be found in the Samaritan synagogue in Shechem (Nablus) and his close friend David ha-Levi, the Karaite community leader, served as his spokesperson and Arabic interpreter.[26]

THE SAMARITANS CLAIM DESCENT FROM THE NORTHERN TRIBES of Israel, according to their own traditions, and they regard themselves as the bearers of the true Israelite faith. Some of their traditions trace their development as a distinct ethnic and religious group back to the pre-exilic period; others assert that the split occurred after the Assyrian conquest of the Kingdom of Israel (Samaria) in the eighth century BCE. However, historical sources relating to Samaritan origins are far removed from the period, and the earliest direct references to the group emerge in the Bible from the

Second Temple period and in the writings of the Roman Jewish historian, Josephus. As far as historical sources can confirm, the split with mainstream Judaism occurred during the start of the Hellenistic period towards the end of the fourth century BCE. Their main sacred text, the Samaritan Pentateuch, comprising the first five books of the Hebrew Bible written in the Samaritan alphabet, has around 6,000 differences between it and the Masoretic Text. One major disagreement between the two versions of the Bible concerns the location of the Temple. The Samaritans disavowed Jerusalem as the Holy City and claimed that God chose to place the Temple on Mount Gerizim near Nablus.[27]

By April, Firkovich was in Nablus visiting the community and attempting to forge a special relationship with them. As part of this effort, he put forward the idea that the people the Assyrians had expelled from Samaria in the eighth century BCE were proto-Karaites. It is not known whether he himself fully believed this ahistorical theory (Karaism was founded in the eighth to ninth century CE), but it certainly aligned with his efforts to promote his community's legal standing by investigating possible common ancestry with other early pre-Talmudic groups of Jewish origin.[28] It is also not entirely clear how well this argument of shared heritage was received by the Samaritan community; but following numerous daily meetings with the Samaritan priests, elders and other leaders of the community, Firkovich finally received permission to view their precious sacred books. But before he could even get his hands on them, he was warned from the outset that they were banned from selling them. Thus, to acquire important manuscripts for his collection, Firkovich was impelled to think of a suitable inducement. Having seen the dilapidated state of their synagogue, he realized that by promising to fund the restoration of the building – whose present state of preservation, he argued convincingly, displayed a certain amount of profanity – he could help restore their religious standing. If they were to give him the gift of their books in exchange, it would thereby offset any betrayal of their sworn oath never to sell their books. The argument struck a chord; still, the Samaritan priests confined Firkovich to bargaining with the discarded manuscripts in their genizah. When he balked at the idea of paying large amounts of money for discarded books, the Samaritans explained that the manuscripts in their genizah represented a form of income for them as they were often used to satisfy the requests of explorers and antiquarians: 'though they are not precious articles' they told him, 'if the geniza leaves our possession, we shall never enjoy any more profit [from it].'[29]

Firkovich's recollection of this event, if wholly true, reveals that prior to his visit, other collectors had been content to take a few hand-picked leaves from the Samaritan synagogue without having their interest piqued to acquire more. It also shows that the Samaritan genizah was more of a permanent storage room than a site of burial like the genizah in the walls of the Karusabazar synagogue or the inaccessible attic space and vault of the synagogue of Kaffa. Firkovich paid the Samaritans 2,000 silver roubles, but rather than paying directly for the repairs, he signed a letter which gave the money to four Samaritan businessmen who promised to extract a tithe each year to give to the Samaritan High Priest.[30] In all, Firkovich acquired 1,350 items from the Samaritan genizah; he later sold them to the Imperial Public Library in St. Petersburg for over four times the amount he had paid for them.

FIRKOVICH AND SAPHIR RETURNED SEPARATELY TO CAIRO in May 1864. Over the course of several days, Saphir repaid numerous visits to the Ben Ezra Synagogue with a type of dogged persistence that encouraged the synagogue custodians to share information about a rooftop genizah holding ancient books. This genizah, he related, was enclosed in a square house (enclosure) on the roof of the synagogue. And the synagogue itself, he explained, was two and a half storeys high.[31] This detail is key because it has been the cause of much subsequent confusion regarding the location and size of the genizah. Prior readings of Saphir's account have assumed that this phrase, in which he uses the feminine pronoun *hi'* (she or it), referred to the genizah (a feminine noun). Thus, in standard Hebrew his description, *ve-hi'mele'a gova šte qomot va-ḥeṣi* should be translated as 'and it [the genizah] was full to the height of two and a half storeys'. This idea was puzzling, mostly because it presented a physical impossibility. However, recent research has shown that nineteenth-century Eastern European writers of Hebrew often used the feminine pronoun in combination with the masculine noun when using collated noun phrases such as *bet ha-knesset ha-zot* 'this house of assembly' (synagogue).[32] This distinctive usage certainly occurs elsewhere in Saphir's travelogue. Thus, what he meant to convey was that synagogue itself was 'the full height of two and a half storeys', which, of course, makes more sense. And so, on 8 May 1864, Saphir made his first appeal to climb up there to the rooftop genizah, but he was rebuffed by the custodians' tale of a snake curled up over its entrance.

Around the same time, Firkovich, together with his grandson, Samuel, was busy exploring a large genizah belonging to the Karaites, the location of which, although he didn't say so explicitly, was probably within the *Dār Simḥa* Synagogue.[33] The old scrolls and manuscripts preserved in its arks, cupboards and other storage spaces had most likely been transferred out of the community's former synagogue building in Old Cairo. According to their inscriptions, some of the manuscripts retained in the *Dār Simḥa* originally hailed from the Karaite synagogue in pre-Crusader Jerusalem (including the most famous one, the Codex Cairensis).[34] Others had been transferred to Cairo over time from Jerusalem, and by the Karaite community of Damascus in the nineteenth century. Thus, the treasure trove of scrolls, manuscript books and documents stored there – many of which were in Judeo-Arabic, providing a rich resource for the history of Judeo-Arabic literature – would prove irresistible to Firkovich. Based on his prior success, he employed his tactic of promising to fund building renovations to the tune of 1,000 silver rubles in exchange for hauling away the contents of the community's genizah.

While Firkovich and his grandson got to work on emptying the Karaite genizah, Saphir, undeterred from his own quest, set about gaining official permission to see the Ben Ezra Synagogue genizah. On 5 June 1864, just one day before Firkovich departed from the city to meet with Albert Cohn, the consul in Jerusalem, Saphir re-visited the Ben Ezra Synagogue armed with the rabbinic authorization needed to persuade the custodians to grant him access. Once again, they tried to discourage him from climbing up to the roof: issuing dire warnings and laughing at him for being willing to court the danger of snakes. Resolute, and with the help of some *bakshish*, and the promised protection of an amulet, Saphir convinced them to bring him a ladder and he climbed up to where he found the rooftop opening, the point from which, he noted, worn-out old books could be thrown into the genizah. The fears expressed by the custodians suggests that they did not go up there often, at least not since the building repairs of 1858, which had made the site, according to Saphir, mostly impenetrable. His main observation on the genizah was that it was a 'square house on the roof of the synagogue' – a structure that was closed on four sides, but from an open top (either the top of the roofbox or the newly opened roof) materials could be thrown inside:

> The custodian showed me the way to go up and also brought me a ladder to climb because the genizah is in a square house on the roof of the synagogue and closed on its four sides without an opening at its side and the roof is open from above that there they will place or throw worn and torn books.

He then described the height of the synagogue and the recent repairs to the roof that had made the rooftop a difficult place to navigate:

> And I went up on the ladder, and it [the synagogue] is the full height of two and a half storeys but at the time they repaired the synagogue they placed there from above also all the boards and broken rafters and also the heaps of dust and stones and piles of dirt that spilt there from the roof when it was opened.

Finally, he confirmed that the work of two days did not yield any results, nor any dangerous encounters with snakes. Moreover, he left future scholars with a tantalizing (and possibly misleading) statement about what else might lie beneath waiting to be uncovered:

> And after I toiled two days and was tired of the dust and dirt I found and brought up several leaves of different old books and manuscripts but I didn't find in them any information or benefit but who knows what else lies beneath because I became sick of looking but also a snake or scorpion I did not find and disaster did not befall me thank God.

Saphir's narrative of his visit to the Ben Ezra Synagogue in the summer of 1864 provides the only extant description of a genizah in its environs before the synagogue was rebuilt. Thirty-two years later, in 1896, the discovery of a genizah hidden within the walls of the newly built synagogue, when combined with Saphir's seeming prophetic statement about what lay beneath, would lead scholars to try to align the two discoveries and try to make them one and the same.[35]

When Firkovich returned to Cairo in October, he visited the Ben Ezra Synagogue and spent three days there, mostly chronicling its many inscriptions (some of which he believed were Karaite). In describing the visit to his son-in-law, Gabriel, he related how he had opened *the* genizah; however, unlike Saphir's account, his description of its location was frustratingly vague:

> Of the work of the genizah it will need to continue about one month, and after it I have in my mind to extract the genizah from under the dust that is in the

synagogue connected to Ezra the scribe according to the wishes of the Hakham-Basi [chief rabbi]. And I have already opened it and I have seen that there is a hope to find also in it writings of value . . . when the Hakham-Basi heard tell of the wonderful things that are within the genizah of our brethren the Karaites here with me, a fire of desire burned within him to open also their *genizot*. Although, I still have not been with him and I have not spoken with him on this matter, and the Hakham-Basi Rabbi Nathan of Alexandria . . . also he agreed to open the *genizot* that are there. And if you will come, my friend, you will be able to take part in their opening and I am certain that you could find even more precious things than in other places . . . for Egypt is the place of the sages of antiquity.[36]

While he provided little information about the Ben Ezra Synagogue genizah, Firkovich's reference to genizot in the plural is key, revealing that, according to the Cairene and Alexandrian Jewish authorities, there were many places in their synagogues and around their cities for the storage of worn-out, ancient books and manuscripts. Even so, Firkovich's grand ideas never materialized: his funds ran out, and he was impelled to return to Russia.[37] The precious books and manuscripts that had evaded Firkovich's grasp remained tucked away in a Karaite synagogue; a genizah on the roof of the Ben Ezra Synagogue was left unexplored; and ideas about opening the city's other *genizot* were soon forgotten. Dust blew back in from the Muqattam hills, and the wonderful things buried in and around Cairo would lay hidden for a while longer.

3

Discovering the manuscript treasures of Egypt (1870s)

GREVILLE JOHN CHESTER WAS ARRIVING IN EGYPT on his first extensive visit there just as Abraham Firkovich was leaving Cairo with his Karaite genizah spoils. By 1863, ill health, no doubt exacerbated by an unsanitary local environment and constant uphill struggles against inexorable social injustices, caused Chester to relinquish his incumbency as vicar in the parish of Sheffield. Following the death of his mother, and with only one brother and three sisters still living, an income in trust allowed him to dedicate the rest of his life to travel and writing. After a brief stint travelling in the Americas, he began to take annual five- or six-month trips to the Mediterranean and Near East.

Chester's excursions typically began in November and took him from London to Malta or Italy, through the Levant and into Egypt. Once in Egypt, he would disembark at Alexandria, spend several days in the European enclave of Ramleh, and then get the train to Cairo where, after stopping at various historic sites along the way, he would take up a room in the 'excellent' Hotel du Nil. From this base he usually spent the month of December scouting out the local markets in and around Cairo, Old Cairo, Giza, Memphis and Sakkara.[1] In January, he got on board a *dahabiyeh* (houseboat) and sailed up the Nile, stopping at old and new archaeological sites along the way. Before and after his Nile trips, Chester would also visit Palestine, Lebanon, Syria, Turkey and Greece.

Over time, Chester transformed into a collector extraordinaire and, according to the pioneering archaeologist, William Matthew Flinders Petrie, he became a 'notable figure in Egyptian matters'.[2] When the Irish-born author W. J. Loftie came to write his book on Egypt in 1879, he could describe Chester as often being 'the exclusive repository' of information on the subject,[3] and as one of Chester's obituarists noted, 'His long experience in Egypt, combined with an instinctive perception, had given him an authoritative knowledge of the true and the false. Relying on this, dealers used to bring to him at Cairo antiquities not only from Egypt but from all parts of the Levant.'[4] Chester's connections enabled him to buy and then sell or donate hundreds of artefacts to British museums every year.

By the time he was in his forties, the man who had once been laid low by the unsavoury conditions of the Sheffield slums, had also become, in the words of Sir Walter Besant, secretary of the Palestine Exploration Fund, 'an explorer of no mean order'.[5] Chester's explorations included a visit to the ancient port city on the Isle of Arwad (Syria), at which point he was probably the only living European to have landed on its shores, and an audacious journey across the biblical sites of Lower Egypt and along the proposed northern route of the Exodus down to the treacherous swamps of Lake Bardawil (Serbonis). His first explorations around Egypt, however, were less dramatic; but for this story they were no less important. Between 1872 and 1873, he began scouting out the country's ancient churches and monasteries. Chester was aware of the manuscript treasures that had come to light in earlier decades from the Egyptian monasteries in the Wadi el-Natrun (*aka* the Nitrean desert), particularly the sixth-century monastery known as the Deir al-Surian (the Syrian Monastery), and he was keen to see if any remained. Little could he imagine that the discoveries he was about to make of fragmentary manuscripts in genizah-like storage rooms, and his arbitrary removal of some of them, would be replicated years later in a synagogue in Old Cairo, or that his actions would form part of a long chain of random, unchecked and often undocumented, removals and dispersals from such repositories.[6]

In documenting his own visit to the Wadi el-Natrun, Chester mentioned some of the more notable manuscript hunters who preceded him, including Robert Curzon (later Lord Zouche) and the Archdeacon Tattam, whose famous searches had sparked 'considerable interest' in the area.[7] Their exploits had only just come fully to light with the publication of the British Museum's third volume of the *Catalogue of the Syriac Manuscripts*. In his preface to the volume, William Wright, professor of Arabic at Cambridge, described at length the various means by which over 500 volumes from the 'once magnificent' library of the Deir al-Surian, as well as manuscripts from other monasteries, had been transferred to the British Museum.[8]

While these particular manuscript hunters of the mid-nineteenth century were not looking for Hebrew manuscripts, their encounters with hidden manuscript repositories and the methods they employed to empty them are analogous to the later exploits of the genizah hunters. Given that Chester was connected to both worlds, it becomes clear that the experiences of the earlier hunters inspired and informed the later ones. Their combined activities, together with the activities of earlier and contemporaneous collectors of thousands of Arabic manuscripts, all share the same dubious distinction of having contributed towards a massive 'book drain to Europe', from Islamic countries that was largely facilitated by European and American consuls, as well as aided and abetted by other individuals wielding administrative power.[9]

COPTIC MANUSCRIPTS WERE HIGHLY SOUGHT-AFTER objects by nineteenth-century biblical scholars, given the early roots of the language. Among those interested in obtaining these covetous items, the most fervent was the Reverend Henry Tattam, the Archdeacon of Bedford, and an independent Coptic scholar. In 1828, Lord Prudhoe (Algernon Percy) visited the Coptic Bishop in Cairo and asked for help to find materials to assist Tattam's research. Upon visiting the Deir al-Surian monastery and bribing the monks with 'presents of some comforts and luxuries of which their situation in the desert deprived them', Lord Prudhoe was allowed to enter the library and select some manuscripts for purchase. Prudhoe shared the information with Tattam that the monastery held a small room with a trap door in which 'books and parts of books, and scattered leaves, in Coptic, Ethiopic, Syriac, and Arabic, were lying in a mass'.[10]

Before he could travel there himself, Tattam was almost pipped to the post. In 1833, the English traveller and author, Robert Curzon visited the Deir al-Surian monastery and was taken to the *Kas'r*, a type of tower room. Offering a dubious accusation of neglect, repeated in other nineteenth-century accounts of manuscript discoveries, Curzon observed that some manuscripts were 'lying on the floor, while others were placed in niches in the stone wall'. Through a 'French gentleman in Cairo', probably the Coptic scholar, Jean Dujardin, he was informed that the truly ancient manuscript treasures in the monastery were hidden inside the oil cellar. After allegedly plying his hapless guides with drink, Curzon encountered in the cellar a genizah-like closet where he spied a 'mass of loose vellum pages' and extracted four books from 'out of their literary grave'.[11]

After Tattam finally received funding for his mission, the consul-general, Colonel Patrick Campbell, provided him with an introduction to the Coptic Patriarch in Cairo, and accompanied him on a visit to the Patriarch's library. This connection enabled Tattam to gain letters of introduction to the heads of the other churches and convents: letters which also directed them to show him all their manuscripts.[12]

In the Deir al-Surian monastery, Tattam observed that they owned 'a great quantity of MSS' not only in Coptic and Arabic but also in Syriac. Among the earliest inhabitants of the monastery were Syrian Orthodox monks who moved from Tagrit in Iraq in the ninth century CE to settle among the existing Coptic monks. They brought books with them, produced their own works, and received books as contributions from the nearby Christian Tagriti community living in al-Fustat. This joint Syrian and Coptic occupancy of the monastery, documented in its building inscriptions and wall paintings, and through the products of its scriptorium, ceased in the seventeenth century after the Syrian Orthodox monks had become gradually absorbed into mainstream Coptic life.[13]

Even though the present-day monks were reluctant to part with their centuries-old books, they graciously allowed Tattam to visit the tower and vault where he noted some 'very old and valuable Syriac MSS'. In a deviation from his own Coptic-centric plan, he requested and was allowed to select 'six quarto or small folio volumes' from among them. Inside the tower, he was shown another room which held Coptic and Arabic manuscripts, and after pressing them even further, the monks allowed him to see yet another concealed apartment that held additional books. In the Abbot's room, they permitted him to look at the special Coptic and Arabic Lexicon, but this one they declined to sell due to a written prohibition that forbade them to part with it.[14]

During a visit to Deir Amba Bishoi (the Red Monastery), Tattam encountered 'a vaulted apartment . . . so strewn with loose leaves of old liturgies that scarcely a portion of the floor was visible. . . . In some parts the manuscripts lay a quarter of a yard deep.'[15] From the Deir Abu Magar (the Monastery of Saint Macurius) he acquired 'a great number of fragments and loose leaves, from which he selected about a hundred'. He purchased another four Syriac manuscripts from the Deir al-Surian and, after returning there for a third or fourth time, he obtained 'a large sack-full of splendid Syriac manuscripts on vellum', and several volumes including a copy of the Pentateuch in Coptic and Arabic and the Four Gospels in Coptic.[16]

Even though he had acquired a hoard of valuable manuscripts for the British Museum, it was clear that many treasures remained hidden in the monasteries. In 1842, Tattam received a fund from the Museum Trustees with which to negotiate the purchase of the remainder of the Deir al-Surian library. Tattam also received a letter from the archbishop of Canterbury to convey to the Patriarch of Cairo. The letter described Tattam's mission on behalf of the British Museum, as well as a specimen of a new translation of the New Testament in Arabic and Coptic that he would be bringing with him as a special offering to the Coptic community.[17]

The success of Tattam's second mission depended on the help of a local *sheikh* who had some sort of 'influence' with the monastery's superior. An agreement was negotiated between the various parties, and a local agent was appointed to fetch the manuscripts from the superior and bring them to the *sheikh*'s house. After three days, Tattam would be allowed to visit the *sheikh* and bargain for the manuscripts. Following a clandestine night-time meeting, Tattam left with an unspecified number of boxes, which were parcelled up and sent off to Alexandria. According to the classification numbers in the British Museum catalogue, Tattam acquired 314 volumes. Even though he assumed that his agreement had been for their entire collection, many manuscripts, according to William Wright, remained 'concealed and withheld' in the monastery library.[18]

Three years later, William Cureton, sub-librarian in the Bodleian Library and assistant keeper of manuscripts at the British Museum, enlisted the help of an Alexandrian merchant, Auguste Pacho, to find the remaining manuscripts in the Deir al-Surian. Pacho, a fellow Copt, lived with the monks for six weeks, gaining their confidence to such an extent that they showed him the remainder of their library and even, purportedly, 'began to treat with him for the purchase of it'. According to Cureton, Pacho 'swept up . . . every fragment from the floor' and oversaw the packing of the books so that the (alleged) 'greed or superstition of the monks' would not prevent him from securing every piece. Yet, Pacho himself could not resist the lure of profit, and he ended up withholding some of the volumes and selling them to the Russian Imperial Public Library for a greater sum.[19]

The Deir al-Surian manuscripts proved extremely important for biblical scholarship. They included one of just two extant manuscripts comprising the earliest Syriac translation of the Gospels, possibly from the third century CE, as well as a fourth-century commentary bearing witness to an even earlier lost translation of the Gospels, known as the Diatessaron.[20] At the end of his lengthy preface to his catalogue of the world's largest collection of Syriac manuscripts, with all its breathtaking tales of subterfuge and derring-do, Wright tantalizingly stipulated that 'Nor have we yet reached the end of the matter. Within the last two years a rumour has gone abroad of their being for sale, somewhere in Cairo or Alexandria, no less than thirty or forty vellum manuscripts.' The source he was certain was the Deir al-Surian.[21]

GREVILLE CHESTER'S EARS WERE RINGING WITH THESE STORIES as he set off around the Wadi Natrun. But his first attempt to see the *Kas'r* of the Deir Abu Magar monastery was not successful: following a recent robbery from their library the monks resolutely refused him access. In the Deir al-Surian, he reported that the library still contained a 'small collection of old, but not ancient, books and MSS'. And it must have been with some measure of disappointment that he noted: 'All the treasures have long since disappeared.' In reporting his visit to the Deir Amba Bishoi, Chester divulged his fervent hope to find ancient manuscripts or at least manuscripts on vellum. Inside a *Kas'r* within the monastery's Church of El Adra, he found a floor scattered with leaves of Coptic and Arabic manuscripts. Not only did he italicize the word 'leaves', but he also emphasized the fact that they were made of 'Charta Bombycina' (paper from cotton rags) and that among them were only 'a few atoms of vellum'. Again, perhaps with some measure of bitterness, he noted: 'The Ancient MSS. have all been sold.' In the *Kas'r* library of the Deir al-Baramus, he likewise encountered 'a considerable collection of MSS. on cotton paper in excellent preservation, but of no great antiquity'. In an adjoining room, he found fragments and loose leaves. On these, he made no further comment. In fact, one would not guess from his short and unexcited descriptions that he most likely came away with some of the pieces he dismissed since he later donated nine fragments to the British Museum, which have been identified as coming from the monastery of Amba Bishoi.[22]

Chester's relative lack of success in penetrating further into the monasteries was due in part to his lack of connections. Tattam went armed with letters of introduction and an endorsement from the archbishop of Canterbury, the British Museum Trustees, and the Coptic Patriarch, and he received help on the ground from the Christian Missionary Society, the consul-general, and a local *sheikh*. Chester, by comparison, was self-funded and self-motivated. It was still early days in his manuscript hunting career, but he had already begun to build local networks, and in his article on the *Dayrs* he acknowledged the editorial help of 'Mr. Girgis Melad, an accomplished Coptic friend at Cairo'.[23]

That same year, in 1873, the introduction to Murray's *Handbook for Travellers in Egypt* offered thanks to Chester, to whom 'readers of the Handbook are indebted for a most interesting paper on the Coptic Churches of Old Cairo – a subject which has never before received the attention it merited'. While exploring the churches of Old Cairo during the year prior, and carefully noting aspects of their exterior and interior elements, Chester had encountered and described the 'Jewish Synagogue' only twelve years past its most recent restoration and still looking in reasonable condition (at least enough not to warrant one of his more acerbic comments). Repeating the popular notion that the building, known locally as *al-Shamiyin* (or, per Chester, *Ish Shammain*), was 'anciently the Christian church of S. Michael', he decried with devout indignation its 'present state of profanation'.[24] Notwithstanding this partisan view, he found the synagogue to be a curious and interesting old building of great architectural interest, and he made careful notes of its Basilica-like shape; the dimensions of its nave, apse and aisles; the number of pillars; the elegant wooden leaf work and the Hebrew inscriptions around the walls. Chester's detailed description included the additional observation that the eastern extremity of the edifice had been reconstructed, and on the building's exterior he espied a bricked-up doorway. He also made a note of the 'fine view' of the limestone Roman walls and semi-circular flanking towers of the Fortress of Babylon afforded from behind the synagogue. Unlike other visitors, most notably the prelate and early Egyptologist, Richard Pococke in his *Description of the East* (1743), Chester made no mention of the synagogue's eponymous Ezra Scroll. Only in his follow-up article about the *Dayrs* did he append the point that, according to al-Maqrizi, the ancient synagogue kept 'a copy of the Holy Scriptures alleged to be in the hand-writing of Ezra the Scribe!'[25]

THE LEGEND OF THE SO-CALLED SCROLL OF EZRA was, as Chester pointed out, captured in the work of the celebrated Egyptian historian, al-Maqrizi. The reference is found in his *al-Khitat*, a fifteenth-century encyclopaedic history of Egypt and the topography of its major cities. In his second volume, al-Maqrizi focused on his hometown of Cairo, and he included descriptions of the eleven synagogues known to him at the time. Of the synagogue in *Kaṣr al-Sham*, he recorded local legends about its antiquity:

> It is old: over its door there is in Hebrew script and engraven upon wood [an inscription to the effect] that it was built in the year 336, Seleucid Era; before the second destruction of Jerusalem by Titus about 45 years, and before the Hijrah about 600 years. In this synagogue there is a copy of the Torah, about which all are agreed that it is in the handwriting of Ezra the prophet who is called in Arabic al-'Azīr.[26]

In 1473, about five or six decades after al-Maqrizi documented the site, a fire in Old Cairo caused massive damage to the interior and roof of the synagogue. By 1481, a visiting Italian merchant, Meshullam of Voltera, observed that the ancient city was 'completely in ruins'. Yet, when another Italian visitor, Rabbi Obadiah of Bertinoro, arrived there in 1488, the synagogue had been restored, and the great rabbinic scholar was able to testify to its beauty and grandeur. The scroll, however, was noted as stolen and lost forever as the ship on which it was being transported had sunk.[27]

At some point over the course of the next century, the scroll (or a scroll) reappeared. In 1610, an Italian Rabbi, Menachem de Lonzano, claimed to have seen the Ezra Scroll while living for a short time in Egypt. In comparing old manuscript versions of the Pentateuch for his work on the Masorah, *Or Torah* (Light of the Torah), he noted that he had personally inspected the copy. De Lonzano's visit was recorded by the Egyptian Jewish historian, Joseph Sambari, who in his chronicle *Divrei Yosef* (Joseph's Sayings) of 1673, related that the famous scroll had been moved to Syria.[28] Notwithstanding its alleged wanderings and disappearances, the legend of the scroll was kept alive so that almost a century later, Richard Pococke could report hearsay about its existence from his recent visit to the synagogue and that 'they say the book is in a niche about ten feet high, before which a curtain is drawn, and lamps are kept always burning before it'.[29] Pococke's description of the synagogue – indexed in his published account as '*Synagogue*, at Cairo, pretended to be of great antiquity' – and its scroll was repeated in numerous gazetteers, theological dictionaries, travelogues and geographies printed in the early nineteenth century.

By mid-century, both synagogue and scroll became better known to Jewish readers thanks to the rise in scholarly transcriptions and translations of Hebrew manuscripts. Rabbi Obadiah Bertinoro's account of his visit in 1488 was first published in 1863 by the Russian-born Hebrew scholar Senior Sachs in a recently established German-language periodical for Jewish studies *Jahrbuch für die Geschichte der Juden und des Judenthums*.

It was translated into German by scholar and future Bodleian librarian Adolf Neubauer for the same volume. A version in French was produced in 1866 by scholar and future Bibliothèque Nationale librarian Moïse Schwab just as Jacob Saphir's more contemporary description of the hidden, decaying scroll was being made accessible to Hebrew readers through the publication of his travelogue.

In 1872, the same year that Chester made his first foray into the Ben Ezra Synagogue, an English-language version of Bertinoro's letters was produced by Sachs and Neubauer for one of the first publications issued by the newly formed Society of Hebrew Literature in London. The editors added a note to Bertinoro's description of 'where the scroll of Ezra used to be placed' that the place is 'still shown, and a perpetual light is kept burning there'. On Bertinoro's observation that a wall inscription testified to the synagogue building having been 'built thirty-eight years before the destruction of the second temple' (i.e. in 32 CE), Sachs and Neubauer commented that the inscription 'no longer exists' and that a psalm was now 'inscribed on this spot'. But to add to the many puzzles and legends surrounding this building, they credited the Jews 'who are living there' with saying that the inscription had been 'destroyed by the flames when the synagogue was burnt down some years ago'. Since no record of a fire destroying the synagogue in the modern era exists, the locals may have been referring to the 1473 fire. This is even more perplexing, as this fire occurred before Bertinoro's visit. To confound the issue even further, Sachs and Neubauer cited two Arab historians, Abdallatif (aka 'Abd al-Laṭīf Baghdādī, Muwaffaq al-Dīn) and al-Maqrizi, who both testified that the inscription on the building marked its founding *forty-five years* before the destruction of the temple (i.e. in 25 CE).

DR JAMES ANDREW SANDILANDS GRANT was another treasure hunter and visitor to the Ben Ezra Synagogue who, in 1872, provided the first and only mention of a genizah-like hiding place within the walls of the medieval building. Dr Grant was a Scottish physician whose service to the Egyptian government earned him the title of 'Bey'.[30] He lived in Cairo from 1868 to his death in 1896, working primarily as a surgeon to the British Consulate at Cairo. In his spare time, Grant Bey became a familiar figure on the archaeological scene thanks to his great personal interest in ancient Egypt. His own collection of Egyptian antiquities in his house in Cairo – described by himself, as well as by those who attended his regular Wednesday-evening archaeological soirees, as a museum – was given after his death to the Museum of Aberdeen University.[31] According to Grant's brief testimony, he secured a ladder to climb up to a niche ten feet above the ground where he espied 'a Hebrew MS. of portions of the Bible' deposited inside. No further details were supplied, but the notice concluded: 'Portions, at least, of this MS., which still awaits proper examination, are supposed to be very old'.[32]

Grant Bey's enigmatic description evokes images of manuscript fragments or a partial codex rather than a whole scroll. In addition, the height of the niche, while the same height as the one in the description supplied by Pococke in the eighteenth century and possibly the same height as the one reached by Saphir's five-rung ladder, does not fit with later sightings in the 1880s which put the niche at 15 or 16 feet, not 10 feet. Either the scroll and its location changed over the course of a decade or he saw one of several niches (or genizot) that existed within and without the Ben Ezra Synagogue.[33]

Chester, a good friend of the Grants, was blissfully unaware of the many mysteries surrounding the evolution of the synagogue structure, and its hiding places, and he was one of the few visitors not to have been exposed to any manuscripts or told the legend of the scroll while on the site.[34] Nevertheless, thanks to his report, a concise (if questionable) description of the building was added to Murray's *Handbook*. Would-be British travellers were now informed of its history as 'the desecrated Christian Church of St. Michael' fallen victim to Jewish moneylending, as well as select highlights: its resemblance to a Basilica in miniature, its numerous wood inscriptions and its fine view of the Roman fortress.

Large numbers of travellers and treasure hunters were about to descend on Cairo thanks to the recent expansion of Thomas Cook Tours, and the recent opening of Cook & Son's first Middle East office on the grounds of the popular Shepheard's Hotel. The hundreds of thousands of British pounds that Cook's passengers had added to the country's economy since the first Cook tour of Egypt in 1869 were welcome to its quixotic leader, the Khedive Ismāʿīl Pasha. Having taken out massive, unfettered loans from foreign entities to fund his ambitious building projects, including a stake in the Suez Canal, he had already created an untenable national debt of almost £100 million. Pleased with Cook's success, the Khedive also granted the company the right to take tours up to the Second Cataract.

With Lower Egypt much more easily traversed thanks to a rapidly expanding rail network, and Upper Egypt now opened up thanks to Cook's steamships, the Nile was transformed into a grand tourist resort.[35] For Egyptians, it was a mixed blessing: the tourists brought cash and stimulated the growth of new industries catering to them, including the rise in the antiquities market, but some home-grown tourist ventures, like the institution of the dragoman, which had previously met all the logistical needs of independent travellers, suffered; and the development of native-born archaeological expertise was deliberately held back.[36]

The ancient monuments were at greater risk too. Despite the existence of cultural heritage laws in Egypt, irreversible damage would be wrought to the millennia-old landmarks through increased foot traffic, the illicit removal of relics as souvenirs, and even by the traveller graffiti left scribbled on the walls.[37] As the number of foreign visitors and semi-permanent residents increased so too did foreign involvement in Egypt's domestic affairs.

One visitor, who would have an impact on travel to Egypt and on the future safety of its monuments, first toured the country in the same year that the fourth edition of John Murray's *Handbook* was released. Yet, the London-born novelist and journalist, Amelia Blanford Edwards, did not go to Egypt as one thirsty, in Murray's words, 'for "doing" all possible countries', but rather by accident, having been driven out of Europe by unexpectedly high rainfall for the time of year. Arriving in Cairo on 29 November 1873, Edwards and her companion, Lucy Renshaw, spent several days exploring the city before embarking on a long voyage up the Nile to Wadi Halfa on the border with Sudan. This experience altered her life's course: Edwards's infatuation with the land and its ancient history, and her concern for the ongoing damage being wrought to its monuments, eventually led her to establish Britain's first professional archaeological society, the Egypt Exploration Fund, in 1882.[38]

On the journey back down the Nile, she noted that their arrival at Luxor brought out all the city's dealers and she disparaged the forgers, diggers and dealers all working hand in hand to drive a 'roaring trade'. Yet Amelia Edwards was no less immune to the thrill of the hunt for antiquities, noting unabashedly that 'we enjoyed it none the less because it was illegal. Perhaps we enjoyed it the more'.[39] She would not buy anything, however, 'without first taking the opinion of the English Consul'.

Aside from printed handbooks, which were still limited in number and scope, nineteenth-century visitors to Egypt could gain guidance and assistance from their consulates. Consular agents were appointed from among the local population by the European and American embassies to serve as their respective country's representatives in the cities most likely to be visited by their citizens. The agents were usually businessmen of good repute, and such a position of trust offered them a certain standing in the international community as well as diplomatic protection. As a result of their unique status, many of the consular agents became involved in the antiquities trade, often supplying the consuls general under whom they served.

The consuls general were responsible for overseeing and regulating trade in respect of the mercantile interests of their nations, but as these appointees themselves were usually selected from among their nation's leading traders and businessmen there was often a clash of interests.[40] In addition, many of the European consuls were trained Orientalists whose knowledge of Semitic languages and position of power gave them the inside edge when it came to acquiring and making a profit from large-scale manuscript sales. The steady expansion of Europe's national museums in the mid-nineteenth century was due in no small part to the role played by these strategically placed middlemen.[41]

In addition to using their consular agents, tourists could gain help, both in terms of travel advice and advice on buying antiquities, from the British and Anglo-American missionaries living in Egypt. The American Mission of the United Presbyterian Church established a permanent presence in Egypt in the 1850s to focus greater efforts on converting the native Orthodox Christians, the Copts, to Protestantism.[42] The clergymen and their families who were sent to run the Mission's medical facilities and schools, and to distribute Bibles and other Christian literature, took a keen interest in Egyptian archaeology, particularly where it served to underpin their beliefs and teaching about the Bible. One of the key missionary contacts for visitors to Cairo, someone who was later connected to the treasures of the Ben Ezra Synagogue, was the Reverend Gulian Lansing.[43] A native of New York, Lansing was first appointed to the church's foreign mission in Syria in 1850 and then to Alexandria in 1856. His main method of outreach to the Coptic communities was through the sale of Bibles, and his lively journal abounds with tales of his donkey rides loaded up with books.[44]

But not even Lansing could entirely resist taking possession of certain antiquities. In 1862, he had visited the Deir al-Surian monastery and from there obtained a mystical book which was 'five hundred and seventy years old'.[45] Among the treasures he later acquired in the 1880s was a 42-foot-long Egyptian papyrus roll, Book of the Dead, found during excavations at Sakkara, which he donated to the Theological Seminary at New Brunswick. To the British Museum he sold the eponymous 'Papyrus Lansing' – seven papyrus fragments containing a New Egyptian 'Miscellany' or anthology of texts – and donated twenty-six Coptic papyri that had been excavated near Asyut.[46]

FOR SOUVENIR-HUNGRY TOURISTS LOOKING FOR PAPYRUS, Murray's *Handbook* warned against the enticement of fake antiquities. The number of forged papyrus manuscripts was increasing in line with demand, particularly after 1877, when large discoveries of Greek papyri fragments were made by farmers digging for fertilizer in the Fayum region in Upper Egypt. The rich soil deposit, known as *sebakh*, which was composed of the remains of ancient mudbrick buildings mixed with centuries of decomposed plant and animal debris, was in high demand for use in the burgeoning cotton-growing industry. The high concentration of nitrates in *sebakh* was also needed to produce saltpetre in the manufacture of gunpowder.[47]

The first papyrus fragments to come to light surfaced among the ruins of the ancient city of Arsinoe. No other circumstance surrounding their discovery (such as exact location or condition upon disinterment) was recorded. And the details of how they were passed on and distributed to European institutions were mentioned almost in passing in the academic journals of the day. Thus, according to the *Zeitschrift für Ägyptische Sprache und Altertumskunde*, the oldest journal for Egyptology, the Greek papyrus rolls were somehow acquired by Gustav Travers, the German Consul in Cairo, who succeeded in obtaining them by designating them for the Berlin Museum.[48] Another crop was acquired by Otto Theodor Graf, a Viennese merchant, and forwarded to the Austrian Orientalist, Josef von Karabacek, who realizing their importance commissioned Graf to find more. The English Consul in Cairo, E. T. Rogers, sent to London 'some fragments of papyri with Cufic inscriptions, a kind of passport and some letters'.[49] And over a thousand pieces came into the hands of Greville Chester who sold them on to the Bodleian Library, Oxford, in 1878 for £20.[50]

Increased demand for papyrus from overseas institutions likewise impelled the *sebakh* farmers, dealers and middlemen to find, sell and distribute whatever fragments could be located among the rubbish heaps, cemeteries and ruins of the Fayum and in other Egyptian towns of the Delta region, such as al-Fustat and Abusir.[51] In addition to the Greek papyri, fragments in Arabic, Persian, Coptic, Syriac and Latin came to light, and twelve fragments in Hebrew, mostly from the seventh century, were found in the Berlin consignment and later published by the German-Jewish scholar and bibliographer, Moritz Steinschneider, in 1879.

In advancing the scientific study of Judaism and Jewish history, collectors and scholars were increasingly on the lookout for important manuscript witnesses, lost great works or little-known editions, but ideally in complete codex form. Yet, concurrent with the birth of papyrology, even mere fragments of Hebrew manuscripts started to gain notice and appreciation. In 1876, the year before the Fayum papyri came to light, Adolf Neubauer, now in the position of sub-librarian at the Bodleian Library, was commissioned to travel to St Petersburg to report on the Imperial Library's Second Firkovich Collection. The collection consisted of over 1,000 separate volumes of fragments that Firkovich had gathered during his visits to the Karaite synagogues in the Near East.

In comparing it to Firkovich's 'First Collection' – the one he reviewed in 1864 – Neubauer observed that the new collection had few complete works but was of 'much more value' for it contained hundreds of fragments of books that had been considered lost. He concluded his report by offering up an enticing inducement to the university authorities to go treasure hunting in the numerous 'Genizoth' of the eastern Rabbanite synagogues, which, if the treasure hunter was 'competent', could also yield 'a rich harvest of Mohametan and Syriac manuscripts'.[52]

The idea that treasures could be uncovered in the genizot of the East still did not gain broad notice. Added to the fact that most people were simply unaware of their existence was the prevailing belief that consignment to a genizah signified the death knell of a manuscript. In 1877, one year after Neubauer's report, an anonymous article in *The Times* under the headline 'Massorah' referred to the downside of genizot while praising the research being carried out in the field of biblical studies by a scholar named Christian David Ginsburg.

Ginsburg was born in 1831 to a Jewish family in Warsaw and educated in a rabbinical seminary. He converted to Christianity at the age of fifteen and found his way to England where he worked for the Liverpool branch of the Society for Promoting Christianity among the Jews. By the age of twenty-six, he had turned his full attention to scholarship and, for the rest of his life, working as an independent scholar; he built up a reputation as a formidable Hebraist, earning him an honorary doctorate from the University of Glasgow. His opus magnum *The Massorah*, published in four volumes between 1880 and 1905, was an in-depth study of the critical reading apparatus of the Hebrew Bible collated from all the manuscript editions of the Hebrew Bible he was able to hunt down and consult.

The Times article of 1877 explained to readers that Ginsburg had turned his attention to the Masorah because as a type of 'marginal directory' it provided an invaluable key to the Old Testament. It also explained the challenge Ginsburg faced due to the paucity of complete manuscript copies of the Hebrew Bible available to consult. This dearth, the writer informed, was due in part to Christian barbarism towards Jews and their property in the Middle Ages, and the 'wholesale destruction of MSS. by Christians' during that time. The destruction caused to ancient Bible manuscripts could also be attributed, he claimed, to the Jewish practice of committing them to rot in a genizah. By treating their manuscripts in this way, the writer concluded that all their potential treasures were lost for 'No Hebrew MS. was therefore preserved by the Jews merely on the ground of antiquity'.[53]

4

Increasing demand for Hebrew
manuscripts (early 1880s)

MOSES SHAPIRA WAS AMONG THE MANUSCRIPT HUNTERS who realized that not all was lost, and that ancient copies of Bible manuscripts and scrolls could still be retrieved from their hiding places. Little is known of Shapira's early life beyond the fact that he was born in 1830 to a Jewish family in Kaments-Podolsk in the Russian Empire, probably received a Yeshivah education, and at the age of twenty-five embarked on a fateful journey with his grandfather to Palestine. When his grandfather died on route, he was helped by a group of missionaries in Bucharest, and he underwent conversion to Christianity.

Styling himself as Moses *Wilhelm* Shapira, he finally reached Jerusalem, where the Anglican Christian mission trained him in carpentry and hired him as a part-time librarian and missionary. At some point in the early 1870s, he established a shop in the Christian Quarter of the Old City of Jerusalem, out of which he sold books and curios to ever-increasing numbers of visitors to the Holy Land.[1]

Some of his first manuscript sales may have been acquired from local hiding places such as the caves and ancient tombs in the Kidron Valley. One of the tombs that attracted the most attention was Absalom's Tomb, as it provided an entrance to a more extensive burial cave system known as the Cave of Jehoshaphat.

THE LEGENDS SURROUNDING THESE ANCIENT MONUMENTS, and their visible lure drew multiple visitors, and some even attempted to gain entrance to them whenever possible. In 1842, the writer of a Jerusalem handbook described how a pilgrim priest, seeing the tomb of Jehosaphat open for an internment, encountered 'a considerable quantity of Hebrew manuscript on parchment, reduced by time to a state of soft-red leather'. Some of the manuscripts were given over to the Latin Convent Patriarch and some to the British consul.[2]

This may have been one of the incidences that led the Jerusalemite rabbinic authorities to print a document that, in part, accused members of the Anglican church of raiding their ancient genizot. In 1845, the accused members sent a translation of the document to the vice-consul, purporting that it had been created by the Jews for the sole purpose of raising alms in Europe. Among several complaints levelled at the Anglican community was the following claim:

They cannot turn their hands from destruction, but go in secret to the caves of Geniza (גניזה) which are without the city, where are buried all the sacred writings, the Books of the Law, and the Holy Vessels, Tiphilim (Phylacteries), Mezuzoth & Instruments of Commandments (תשמישי מצות) and they kindle a flame of fire, and burn all the divine appointments which were hid in the earth.³

The Anglicans for their part expressed outrage at the idea that they would be 'wantonly and sacrilegiously burning Copies of the Sacred Book of the Law of God'. Nevertheless, the person to whom they sent their grievance, vice-consul William Tanner Young, was the same person who had apparently received the manuscripts from the tomb of Jehoshaphat in 1842. A second incident that may have inspired the creation of the rabbinical document was recorded by the Swiss Oriental scholar, Titus Tobler, who published a work on the topography of Jerusalem and its environment in the 1850s. In a letter sent to the Palestine Exploration Fund in 1875, he noted that the ancient tombs could not be fully investigated since the Jews continued to bury their dead near the monuments and 'will not allow them to be disturbed'. He related his own experience in the matter: 'In 1845 I made a plan of the so-called grave of Jehoshaphat, and carried off a prayer girdle, which I showed to a Jew. Soon afterwards the entrance was stopped up.'⁴ In 1857, the American journalist, William Cowper Prime, visited Palestine and in his travelogue, *Tent Life in the Holy Land*, he recorded his adventures, including crawling through the Akeldama tombs in the Kidron Valley where he encountered and disturbed piles of human bones and skulls. But in gaining entrance to the more celebrated tombs of Absalom and Jehoshaphat, he was, like Tober, similarly unsuccessful:

> Behind the tomb of Absalom is a subterranean tomb, called that of Jehoshaphat, which is kept closed, and in which the Jews of the city are allowed to claim a certain proprietorship. Of its contents I was unable to learn any thing; and I regretted much arriving one day a few minutes after it was closed by a Jew who had entered it. The common story is, that they keep here concealed a book of the law, and sundry valuable relics; but in a situation so exposed to night robbers I scarcely think this probable. The tomb, however, is closed, and the front heaped over with earth.⁵

Ten years later, however, the British engineer, Charles Warren, reported a breach of the tomb by someone 'in search of old copies of the law'. The chief rabbi of Jerusalem believed that Warren had opened up the tomb as part of his excavations for the Palestine Exploration Fund, and he wrote to the local village *sheikh* to ask that it was closed back up. Warren sent back word that the opening of the tomb had been carried out by someone else, and the *sheikh* confirmed that if it had been an engineer like Warren the tomb would have been closed back up and no one would have been any the wiser; ergo, it must have been a tomb raider too careless to cover up his tracks.⁶ The next year, in 1868, a British tourist visiting Palestine for health reasons reported seeing scrolls recovered from 'the tomb or monument of Absalom' in the Valley of Jehoshaphat on sale in a Jerusalem bookstore owned by 'a converted Jew'.⁷

Shapira's earliest sales to Europe included two Torah scrolls that he sent to a bookseller in Frankfurt in 1869. The bookseller Johannes Alt in collaboration with the

Masoretic scholar, Seligman Isaac Baer, compiled a sixteen-page catalogue describing the scrolls, one of which Shapira had told him came from Sana'a in South Arabia and the other from Hebron in Palestine. The catalogue contained a signed authentication of the scrolls' antiquity from Constantin von Tischendorf. The physical characteristics of Shapira's scroll from Sana'a were what are now known as typically Yemenite: the leather was sheepskin, it was a reddish-brown colour, and the text was written on fifty-one lines per column, as opposed to the usual forty-two lines.[8] This scroll was unusual in that it was made up of sections, some of which were older and some more recent, and some of the letters were described as overwritten. Baer noted that a detached fragment of the scroll containing verses of Leviticus had an inscription on the back revealing that it had once been owned by an Abu' ali Said in 1058 CE.[9]

In 1872, an English traveller by the name of Amy Fullerton-Fullerton recorded a visit to Shapira's shop in her travel diary and, in addition to being shown various old Jewish manuscripts, she also noted that the proprietor was 'the agent for inquiry in Samaria, as to some, supposed, very ancient Books of the Law kept in the synagogue at Nablous'.[10] Another visitor to Shapira's shop in 1873 similarly remarked on Shapira's sources. In March of that year, a Mormon of Utah, George A. Smith, was touring Palestine. In a letter home to the Mormon leader, Brigham Young, he observed seeing Shapira's parchments 'some of them very old, dug from beneath the ruins of synagogues both in Palestine and Arabia'.[11]

After being implicated in the famous scandal surrounding the forgery and sale of a large cache of so-called Moabite pottery in the mid-1870s, Shapira re-emerged at the end of the decade as someone determined to rebuild his reputation and livelihood as a purveyor of antique books and manuscripts. It didn't take him long to realize that the demand for ancient manuscripts was high and that there were eager buyers in Europe and America. It is not clear how he acquired his early Yemenite materials, but after making some initial sales of Yemenite scrolls and manuscripts in Berlin, Shapira realized that the writings of this remote Jewish community were sought after and profitable, particularly early copies of the Yemenite *Midrash Ha-Gadol*.[12]

A LOCAL YEMENITE AGENT WAS THE BEST, and perhaps the only way to acquire these antiquities. Such a connection may well have been Hayyim Habshush, a Yemenite coppersmith and later historiographer of Yemenite Jewry, and the connection appears to have been made after 1869. In that year, Habshush, with his extensive self-taught topographical knowledge, was first noticed by the Adrianople-born French-Jewish orientalist, Joseph Halévy, who was on a mission to find ancient Sabaean inscriptions. Halévy was sent on behalf of the French Académie des Inscriptions et Belles-Lettres at the request of the Semitics scholar, Ernest Renan. Renan had read Halévy's accounts of his travels to Abyssinia in 1867 on behalf of the French organization, the Alliance Israélite Universelle (AIU) and, in his zeal to collect every possible Semitic inscription, he realized that it would have to take a Jewish traveller like Halévy to be able to cross the tribal borders of Yemen and blend in. The AIU joined the Académie in sponsoring Halévy's Yemen mission to gain a report on the condition of Yemen's Jews, despite having undermined his previous findings about the Abyssinian Jews by questioning their lineage and rejecting his calls for aid to them.[13]

The founding principal of the AIU, established in Paris in May 1860, was to assist Jews around the world who were suffering from religious discrimination, and to defend their civil rights and protect their religious freedoms. The idea arose after the Damascus Affair of 1840, a notorious blood libel case which prompted many leading Jewish intellectuals and philanthropists to realize that an organization to support world-wide Jewish cooperation and solidarity was needed. In addition to providing relief and diplomatic assistance, members of the AIU were convinced of the need to advance the social and economic situation of Jews in Near Eastern countries through the provision of schools that would inculcate French education and culture and provide them with fluency in the language of commerce and diplomacy.

Concurrent with these developments, the AIU sought to establish its own Jewish library. The idea, first conceived by the society's secretary, the historian Isidore Loeb, was announced in the first issue of the AIU's *Bulletin* as one of its statutes. Membership of the society required a six-franc donation that could be given in either money or books. Article nine of the statute declared that: *la société réunira dans le local de ses séances les livres, journaux et documents interessant les Israélites* (the society would begin to assemble in the local premises of its meetings the books, newspapers and documents of interest to Jews),[14] and subsequent reports began to list the many book donations from its members, together with a list of the growing number of members from around the world. The AIU also funded scientific explorations and publications, including, for example, supporting Jacob Saphir's intended publication of his journey to Yemen through the purchase of fifty subscriptions.[15]

From Halévy's perspective, his mission on behalf of the Académie to gather ancient linguistic evidence was a crucial step towards proving the lineage of Semitic languages and a key component in defending Semitic cultures in the face of growing academic debates surrounding race and language. Once in Yemen, Halévy was determined to explore the Al-Jawf region for the ancient inscriptions: an area that no other European had visited since the Roman period. Yemenite Jews, though isolated, were used to receiving random travellers, occasionally Christian missionaries like Joseph Wolff in the early 1800s or, most often, Holy Land emissaries like Jacob Saphir collecting alms for the Jerusalem poor.[16] In spite of their own equally poor circumstances, the payment of such alms was regarded as a mutually beneficial act since it helped distant communities maintain their connection to the spiritual centre of Jewish life, as well as form associations that could be important in providing vital assistance during an hour of need. As civil unrest in the country made travel between the towns perilous and strangers an object of suspicion, Halévy chose to gain the trust and help of the Yemenite Jews by adopting the guise of a Jerusalemite rabbi. Impressed by Habshush's ability to track down and decipher inscriptions, he hired him as his local guide. Leading Halévy through Yemen's interior into remote towns, Habshush increased his own expert knowledge of the many different Jewish communities existing in his homeland and, through his enquiries, he learnt a great deal about their customs and their books.[17]

Many years later, when Eduard Glaser, an Austrian Jewish Orientalist, arrived in Yemen, similarly on the hunt for Sabaean inscriptions, he impressed upon Habshush the importance of committing to writing his experiences journeying with Halévy. Habshush decided that his travelogue should go beyond merely documenting the famous European explorer's encounter with Yemen, it should provide the world with a more accurate portrayal of the land and its people from within. In addition, Habshush's travelogue offered occasional insights into some of the books he encountered on route. For example, in the synagogue of Banu Qamis in the town of Milh, district of Nihm, he found a Yemeni Bible codex from the fifteenth century, which contained within it a sheet of writing from the tenth century; an introduction to another codex described as a 'Persian version'; two books of the Psalms written between the twelfth and fourteenth centuries, and a third book being a copy of the second part of Maimonides *Guide for the Perplexed*.[18]

It is in Habshush's writing that a brief hint of his relationship with Shapira arises. In describing his first visit to a Jewish graveyard in the ruins of Baraqish, which left him wondering how the tombstone inscriptions related to his own ancestry, Habshush made a note of a subsequent visit that he took there 'Years later, while buying old books for Moshe ben Natanel Shapira (who deluded us into selling them)'.[19] Habshush's book buying period probably refers to the late 1870s when Shapira acquired the bulk of his Yemenite manuscripts, many of which were sold to the British Museum and some to Berlin. Habshush's remark is also telling because it suggests that in his efforts to acquire old books for Shapira, he realized that many ancient manuscripts were buried in Jewish graveyards.

Shapira, according to a note in his handwritten catalogue, visited Yemen at least twice. At the time of writing the note, which was either late in 1880 or in 1881, he had visited Yemen for three months during the summer of 1879 and again during the winter of 1880.[20] However, in 1877, Shapira had already sold forty Yemenite manuscripts to the British Museum. The sale included several near-complete codices of the *Midrash Ha-Gadol*. Whether he acquired these during an earlier excursion there is unclear, but he most likely received Habshush's help during his 1879 trip, given that it involved trekking across more remote parts of the country. At some point, Shapira realized that he would have to hide his Christian persona and go by his Hebrew name, Moses ben Netanel, if he were to succeed in living with the community and securing their trust. It was no doubt this disguise that helped him 'delude' Habshush and others into selling their possessions. In his description of one of the Bible commentaries he obtained there, he noted that it was 'the only one known to my knowledge in Yemen, with very great dificulties [*sic*] I was able to get it'. In the introduction to one of his catalogues, he referred obliquely to 'The amount of difficulties to get theses [*sic*] books!' No specific names or types of exchanges were noted in the catalogue; only a hint of the struggle to 'destroy the curses and bans, lying since centuries upon them' and to 'overcome the supperstishness [*sic*] of this people' was mentioned.[21]

After completing his three-month visit in 1879, he published an account for *The Athenaeum* of the flora and fauna he encountered in some of the lesser traversed regions of Yemen.[22] He also gathered information about Yemenite towns, synagogues, religious customs and writings and noted these down when pertinent to describing the manuscript at hand. In his introduction, he observed that the coastal towns did not possess manuscripts and only a few were to be found in the smaller towns. Like Jacob Saphir before him, he discovered that the pedigree scrolls once owned by private individuals had been ransacked centuries before. In Sana'a, he recorded the existence of twenty-one synagogues but, as far as he was aware, only four of them held manuscripts.

Inside these synagogues he observed that some of the 'Old books or M. S. S. are here as well as in Egypt kept in a special shrine in the wall not far from the Toras, more as a relique or Talisman, than for studying them'. This description recalls the niche (or niches) in the synagogue in Old Cairo where the scroll of the Law attributed to Ezra the scribe was kept and revered, as well as the special cupboards of the Rabbanite synagogues, and the side-cupboards in the Karaite synagogue that the British-born, American scholar of Semitics, Richard Gottheil, would later find in Cairo, stuffed with ancient manuscript codices.[23] Shapira paid close attention to the names of scribes that were mentioned to him or to those that were written in the colophons of the manuscripts in order to build up his knowledge of what to look out for. For example, he noted when the locals told him that books written by Benayah ('Bunai') were the most trusted in terms of correctness, and that the Benayah family of scribes had produced over 400 biblical books.

Shapira's handwritten introduction to his catalogue reveals the lengths to which the Yemenites went to protect or redeem their scrolls and books from would-be plunderers and pillagers, including hiding them in cisterns or ransoming them 'for the highest sum'. Sulayman b. Yosef Qare, the chief rabbi of Sana'a, told Shapira about a Bedouin raid during Passover in the early part of the nineteenth century that had resulted in the vandalization of their property and the plunder of their possessions. The same tale had been related twenty years earlier to Jacob Saphir to whom the Yemenites had confided: 'There's nothing that can't be replaced. . . . But our Torah scrolls, and our ancient manuscripts can never be replaced.'[24]

While there is no firm evidence that he stole them, Shapira got his hundreds of Yemenite manuscripts for a steal. In 1914, Rabbi Yihye Qafih, then chief rabbi of Sana'a, in his work on the kabbalah entitled *Wars of the Lord*, recalled how the community lost their books through cheap, unauthorized sales:

> Many of our multitudes sold old books that they had inherited from their ancestors to uncircumcised people who came to Yemen, such as Moshe ben Netanel [Shapira], who dwelt in the house of our master and teacher, Avraham Salah. He himself sold him a Taj [biblical codex] of Prophets and Writings. . . . And we were powerless to take it away from him. . . . Many ancient manuscripts were sold to him and to others cheaply.[25]

THE REVEREND ARCHIBALD HENRY SAYCE WAS EXCITED BY SHAPIRA'S YEMENITE MSS, and he quickly shared the news of their acquisition with the Royal Asiatic Society in May 1881. At the time he viewed the MSS, Sayce was an Oxford scholar who specialized in the Assyrian language, but over the course of his lifetime he developed his linguistic talents to the extent that he was eventually able to write in about twenty ancient and modern languages. When Shapira showed him the manuscripts he'd brought back from Yemen, Sayce was surprised to see that one of the manuscripts had a colophon stating that it was written in 945 CE. Sayce followed up on his letter with an announcement in *The Academy*:

> I can guarantee the great value of some of them from my own inspection of them; one, for instance, which is written according to a hitherto unknown system of

punctuation, would be the earliest Hebrew text of the Old Testament in existence if any confidence can be placed in one of its colophons. . . . It would be a pity if the collection were allowed to go to Berlin like its predecessor.[26]

Responding to Sayce's notice, Christian David Ginsburg informed the public that the British Museum had selected 'no less than forty MSS' from the collection Shapira had brought to England in 1877, including fifteen 'Rolls of the Pentateuch', as well as fourteen of the manuscripts from his 1879 Yemenite hoard. But in a rebuke to Sayce and Shapira, Ginsburg went on to explain that while the British Museum never rejected any manuscript of importance it would not be led astray by ignorance and sensationalism:

> The foreign dealers who bring over these MSS., as a rule do not know much about their value, and often ask most extravagant prices. This renders it very difficult to deal with them; and the difficulty arising from their ignorance and their determination to bargain is greatly increased by notices in the public press of their collection which they entirely misunderstand.[27]

Yet Shapira, for all his 'foreign' ignorance and questionable methods of buying and selling manuscripts, did in fact pay close attention to the items in his possession. In describing the codex that Sayce had examined, he noted that the 'epigram' could read either AD 1145 or 945, and he noted how unsafe it was to trust epigrams that were not in the handwriting of the original scribe.[28]

THE GREATEST LOSS OF YEMENITE MANUSCRIPTS occurred through migrations to Palestine and other parts of the Ottoman Empire in the late nineteenth century, and as a result of relocations to Israel in the mid-twentieth century. It is not known exactly what first compelled groups of Yemenite Jews to immigrate to Palestine beginning in 1881, but it seems most likely that economic hardships in Yemen combined with increasing awareness of economic opportunities in Palestine through recent Jewish philanthropic efforts were factors. Three groups comprising twenty families arrived in Jerusalem at some point in the summer or fall of 1881. A larger group of around 300 people left Sana'a in 1882, but a cholera epidemic at the port forced them to turn back: some of them were able to take alternative routes out of Yemen to Alexandria or to Jerusalem and Jaffa; some got stuck without sustenance in other Yemenite towns and either converted, starved or tried to make their way back to Sana'a; and others eventually ended up in Jerusalem or in Bombay and Cairo. When they reached their final destinations, they struggled to integrate into the economic life of their new homeland and often faced extreme poverty and a lack of housing.[29] One means of generating an income was through the sale of the manuscripts and scrolls they had brought with them.

An early purchaser of Yemenite manuscripts in Jerusalem was someone who would be connected to one of the major collectors of genizah manuscripts, the Austrian Jewish scholar and bibliophile, David Kaufmann. The buyer was Mordechai Adelmann (previously known as Moritz Adelmann or Edelmann) and Adelmann began to supply Kaufmann with Oriental manuscripts soon after he moved to Jerusalem in 1881.

Adelmann had been born in Heydekrug to a Jewish Orthodox family, and he took an early interest in the Haskalah movement, which led him to Vienna in the 1870s in search of a broader education. Unlike many of the learned friends he made there (including David Kaufmann and Solomon Schechter) Adelmann's later scholarly activities took place in the public realm rather than within the confines of an academic institution. He devoted much of his time to writing and editing articles for the burgeoning Jewish press and, in seeking material for these pieces, he scoured the European libraries looking for little-known Jewish manuscripts to study and expound.

In Vienna, he grew close to the Hebrew writer and editor, Peretz Smolenskin, and he contributed articles to Smolenskin's early Jewish nationalist journal, *Ha-Shachar* under his own name as well as under various pseudonyms (such as Meyuhas and Ben Zvi). His nationalist tendencies led him to establish the Lemaan Zion Society of Frankfurt: an organization intended to support Jewish charitable institutions in Palestine. While living in Paris for a few years, Adelmann established a friendship with Eliezer Ben-Yehuda (later known as the father of modern Hebrew) and, together with the scholar Baer Goldberg, he conceived of a Hebrew journal *Haye 'Olam* dedicated to publishing unknown Jewish works in ancient manuscripts. The journal was short lived with only one issue published in 1878; perhaps because, as Adelmann had once told his friend Rabbi Benjamin (aka Yehoshua Radler-Feldman), his work on studying manuscripts in the Vatican Library had earned him a commission from the Vatican to seek out ancient materials in Persia and Iraq. The commission may have been a failure since Adelmann also divulged that among numerous hair-raising adventures, he was attacked and robbed while travelling on a boat going down the Tigris to Basra.[30]

Adelmann settled in Jerusalem in 1881 and first earned a living as a teacher in the German-Jewish Orphanage School and as a storekeeper near the Jaffa Gate. Within a short time, he had founded the weekly newspaper, *Ha-Tzvi* (the Gazelle), which was afterwards taken over and made famous by Eliezer Ben-Yehuda. He also continued to work tirelessly on behalf of the Lemaan Zion Society by helping to maintain and extend the *Yishuv* (Jewish settlement in Palestine) through garnering moral support and raising funds from his Jewish contacts in Europe.

He was instrumental in setting up new Jewish settlements in towns such as Ramleh (in the plain of Sharon) and Kerak (in Transjordan east of the Dead Sea region) and ensured that, in addition to their economic needs, their religious needs were met through the supply of ritual objects and Torah scrolls. Adelmann promoted the settlers' self-sufficiency through the supply of equipment for small businesses, and he gave them support by helping establish hospitals and dispensaries. He also gave critical assistance to poor immigrants arriving at the port of Jaffa and to Jerusalem.[31] It may have been thanks to this work with various communities across Palestine that at least one Yemenite liturgical manuscript found its way from Jerusalem to David Kaufmann in 1881.[32] This was followed by a Kabbalistic Yemenite manuscript comprising several hundred folios in 1882.

THE BODLEIAN PURCHASED SOME SHAPIRA MSS after Sayce had publicized them in July 1881. The British Museum purchased around eleven of them but decided against buying them all.[33] The sale included four copies of the *Midrash Ha-Gadol*, as well as some commentaries and a prayer book, but as to the rest it's likely they felt too uncertain of the dates given in the colophons. Shapira himself had made a note of some of the difficulties concerning the dates in his catalogue. In the description of one biblical codex he noted:

> The Jews mostly try to spoil the date before they let it pass to other hands. Sometimes because they wish to say that the M.S. is from the time of עזרא [Ezra] & any latter dates do not satisfy them, & mostly for supersticious [*sic*] purposes – it seems to me judging by the old forms of the letters which are alike the form of letters of one my M.S. now in Berlin in the Imperial Library dated 1222 & also to one I possess of the date 1295 to be of about AD 1250 – the possessors of it made a present of it to the well known synagogue in Sanaa called now כניסת בית פנחס אלעראקי [Kenisat bet Pinhas al-Iraqi].[34]

Even if they had read Shapira's catalogue, they were clearly unconvinced by his attempts to date some of the manuscripts. Yemenite manuscripts were still too little known, and they may have distrusted his knowledge and, based on his past involvement with forged artefacts, his character.

At this point, Shapira seems to have turned his full attention to collecting Karaite manuscripts, which to all intents and purposes was safer ground. As part of this effort, he seems to have made good connections with some key members of the Karaite community in Cairo. In addition to acquiring substantial Karaite codices and fragments of Karaite manuscripts, he also obtained nine incomplete Torah scrolls which he listed as 'From Geniza of Kairo' and which probably referred to the Karaite genizah given that there is a distinction between the nine items on this list and the tenth. The tenth item is a scroll at the very end of the list which is described as '[ditto] fragments of the so called roll of Ezra ha-Sofer [the Scribe] from the synagogue at Old Cairo see appendix very old'. The words from 'so-called' to 'very old' at the end of the sentence are crossed through, suggesting that Shapira had erred somehow in the description or identification of this piece.[35] Notwithstanding the error, it is certain that he (or an agent) had paid a visit to the Ben Ezra Synagogue where, like Grant Bey in 1872, these fragments were discovered.

A GROUP OF CLANDESTINE VISITORS TO THE BEN EZRA SYNAGOGUE also found fragments from the so-called Ezra Scroll (or some other scroll) in 1881. The group was led by Rev. Gulian Lansing who, by this time, had been running the successful American Mission based in Cairo for two decades. Lansing was fluent in Arabic and deeply knowledgeable about ancient Egypt, he also took a deep scholarly interest in the Hebrew Bible. In his history of the American Mission, Lansing's close partner in Cairo, the Reverend Andrew Watson, recalled that Lansing was a 'fine Hebrew scholar' who kept his Hebrew Bible and Oriental dictionaries close by, reading and studying every day often into the night.[36] Lansing had established the Mission's central premises in Cairo's main tourist area, near the Shepheard's Hotel overlooking the el-Azbakeya Gardens, on deserted ground where the dragomans used to pitch their tents. In addition to this three-story building, which included a church, schools and apartments for the

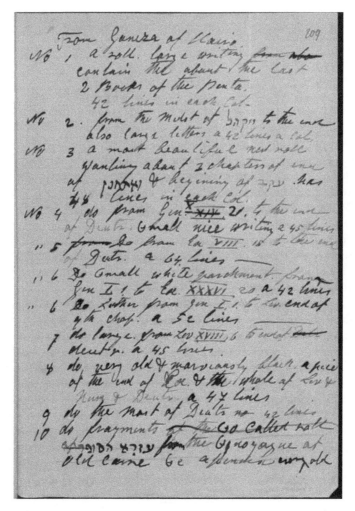

Figure 4.1 MS. Or. Fol. 1342, a page from Moses W. Shapira's handwritten catalogues.

missionaries, an American cemetery was established in Old Cairo. The schools were regarded as key to converting the local population (in this case the Coptic Christians) and they were considered as 'a wedge to enter the local community'. By 1900, the Mission could boast that it had converted 12,500 Copts to Protestantism.[37] With his linguistic skills and broad network of contacts, both native and foreign, Lansing was regarded as an expert on local matters. Greeted by all who passed him on the streets of Cairo, he often served as a key intermediary for European and American visitors to the city, many of whom stayed at the Shepheard's.[38]

A vivid report of Lansing's guided tour to see the famous Ezra Scroll was sent to the *Christian Union* journal in March 1881 by the Reverend James Meeker Ludlow, a nineteenth-century writer of Bible-themed novels. In fact, Ludlow resisted sharing with readers a lengthy description of their visit to the Great Sphinx in favour of relating the tale of an expedition 'which not many tourists, I fancy, have taken; while fewer still, if any, have met with the success which we attained'. And as if to drive home the point and ramp up the excitement, he added that the scroll was 'so jealously guarded that even our best scholars, who have made distant journeys, have departed without the sight'. Ludlow described how they approached the ancient synagogue through the debris-ridden streets of the Coptic quarter, and how they had to descend 'as if entering a cellar' to its entrance. Having reached their target, they were disappointed to find that the building was all locked up with the custodian gone from Cairo with the keys. Undeterred, and using a method 'sufficiently familiar to travellers in the East, the visitors found an 'open sesame'. Alone inside the gloomy old building, they expressed great joy at the opportunity to visit without the 'watchful eyes of the priest' upon them, especially someone who was known for resisting the 'lure of bakshish' in his refusal to allow visitors to see the 'oracle'. After describing the synagogue's dark interior, marble pillars and a stone marking the spot where Jeremiah once stood, Ludlow proceeded to relate their close encounter with the scroll:

> In a dark corner, some fifteen feet from the floor, hung a little curtain against the wall. Near by was a moveable ladder. It was the work of a moment to explore the closet behind the curtain with the aid of a candle. There were the venerable 'two rolls'. A detached piece of the manuscript, containing five or six columns or pages, was brought down. It was yellow and rotten with age, though originally of the toughest vellum.[39]

The group had brought two Hebrew Bibles with them: one containing the Samaritan text and the other a traditional Hebrew text upon which their own 'Old Testament' was based. The Samaritan text was taken along in response to the debates raging about biblical criticism in the scholarly journals of the day, including in the recently founded *Presbyterian Review*. The Samaritan Pentateuch was regarded by scholars in the field of biblical criticism as having the potential to bear witness to an earlier version of the Hebrew Bible given certain key differences in its text and the fact that the Samaritans had eschewed rabbinic law. The interlopers were thus keen to see if this scroll purported to be from the biblical period was likely to agree with the Samaritan text and after comparing the two, they reported that it did not.

Ludlow ended his tale of their furtive visit and partial mutilation of a Torah scroll with the hope that Lansing would one day succeed in convincing the synagogue authorities 'to bring the whole of this heirloom of the church out into the full daylight'. At any rate, Ludlow's account, along with various others in the 1870s and early 1880s, all recalled a dilapidated building which was regarded as notable for its age, marble pillars, Jeremiah stone and Ezra Scroll at best, or for being a dark and dirty disgraced former church at worst.[40] None of the visitors, including the one most familiar with the building, mentioned any other manuscripts within or without the environs of the building.

An American journalist who later wrote about the event for the American theological journal, the *Universalist Quarterly and General Review*, stated that he had held off from immediately publishing Ludlow's report of 'so valuable a manuscript', in the hopes that something 'additional would come of it'. In an editorial that is revealing both for its attitudes towards Egyptian patrimony and the growing interest in recovering 'the true text' of the Bible, the writer proposed:

> Now that the English are supreme in Egypt, having everything in their own way, would it not be a favorable time to secure this rich 'find' and test the question of its age and value? It might be of great service in helping to determine the true text from which the new revision of the Old Testament is being made. At any rate, we trust that something will be done to rescue it from the dangers of Egyptian guardianship.[41]

And much later still, Edith Louisa Butcher, the wife of Dean Charles Butcher, the Anglican chaplain in Cairo, recalled the event in her detailed history of the Coptic Church.[42] Butcher's portrayal of this incident is significant, not only for its insights into the state of the scroll and its subsequent disappearance (it was removed after the incident and replaced with a relatively modern scroll) but also for its silence on the existence of anything known as a genizah. This silence is particularly curious as, by the time she came to write the introduction in June 1897, a large genizah had just been found in the synagogue by someone who was known to her. Two protagonists appear in Butcher's account, described in a footnote as a Scotsman and an American. Since Lansing and Ludlow were both Americans, and since the anonymous figures in Butcher's sorry tale are said to have returned to the scene on two further occasions, it is possible that the people to whom she referred were Lansing, and his close friend, the Scottish-born physician and archaeologist, Grant Bey.[43] Bey had existing knowledge about a hidden manuscript in the Ben Ezra Synagogue, as he had reported to *The Athenaeum* back in 1872, and the current whereabouts of the scroll she claimed had been revealed to them by a 'treacherous Jew' (Moses Shapira?).

Shapira catalogued the Karaite MSS he'd acquired from Cairo and also from Hīt in Iraq between 1881 and 1882. How he acquired the Hīt manuscripts is unknown. Even though the British Museum records suggest that he had travelled there, he may have just as easily obtained them when the Karaite Jews of Hīt temporarily relocated to Jerusalem in 1881. As to the Cairo manuscripts, it seems likely that many were acquired with the help of someone called Mosheh al-Qudsi the second. In between serving as the community's chief rabbi, between 1856 and 1872, al-Qudsi was a scholar, scribe and seller of Karaite manuscripts like his father before him. Both father and son had devoted their talents to copying important old texts in preference to writing their own original works, as they both believed it helped keep the texts' traditions alive.[44] Included in Shapira's Karaite sales were several medieval works copied by a Moshe Ha-Levi, which must have been al-Qudsi's father since Shapira noted that he was deceased by this time. Ha-Levi himself explained in one of his colophons that he had copied his work from an older manuscript found in the genizah. In defending his selling of modern copies of ancient works, Shapira wrote in his catalogue that he knew Ha-Levi to be 'a most honest upright man' and someone who despised Firkovich's methods of forging manuscripts to make them appear older than they were.[45] The testimonial is intriguing, especially given the fact that Shapira himself would later be declared a major forger of ancient manuscripts.

In July 1882, Charles Pierre Henri Rieu, keeper of Oriental manuscripts at the British Museum, informed the Trustees that he was honoured to report 'that a collection of 138 Jewish MSS. has been offered by Mr Shapira of Jerusalem for £700'. The manuscripts, he told them, were 'collected by Mr. Shapira in the town of Hit on the Euphrates, the sect of an ancient community of Cairaite Jews'. Despite this slight misreporting, which left Cairo out of the picture, Rieu continued to point out that

> The 48 MSS. written in the Arabic character . . . form the newest and most valuable part of the collection. They represent a school of Biblical reading and exegesis little or unknown in Europe, and the transliteration they give of the Hebrew text in the Arabic character is likely to prove of some importance for a critical study of the Old Testament.

As to the price requested, Rieu explained that it amounted to about £5 a piece and that with 'The contents being in great part new, and a large proportion of the MSS. of so early a date, it would have been worth much more, but for the fragmentary character and more or less dilapidated condition of the MSS'.[46] Rieu's characterization of the state of the manuscripts as 'fragmentary' is worth noting as many of the pieces in Shapira's collection were in far less a fragmentary state and were overall better preserved than fragments later classified as having been derived 'from the Cairo Genizah'.[47]

In July 1882, an article in *The Times* highlighted the treasures recently brought from Yemen through the travels of Jacob Saphir, Joseph Halévy and Moses Wilhelm Shapira. It singled out the Bible scrolls with their Babylonian vowel-points and the little-known literary products of the Jews of Persia written in 'Hebreo-Persian', some of which had also been acquired by Adolf Neubauer in Paris. The article emphasized the potential of such manuscripts to shed new light on significant works of Jewish literature. Most importantly, it concluded that travellers and consuls in the East needed to be aware of these things so that they could 'keep a watchful eye on manuscripts of this kind for the benefit of our great libraries'.[48]

DAVID KAUFMANN WAS KEEPING A WATCHFUL EYE from afar. During 1883, Kaufmann bought at least fourteen substantial manuscripts, mostly liturgical, including five Yemenite items, from the same quarter. For most of the pieces, Kaufmann simply recorded that they were *gekauft in Jerusalem* (bought in Jerusalem) but on some of them he supplied a bit more detail. On the flyleaf of a collection of *selichot* (penitential hymns), he noted in purple ink that it had come from his friend 'M. Adelmann in the Holy city of Jerusalem', and in the same pen on the flyleaf of a *Machzor* (festival prayer book) according to the North African rite, he wrote that it had come from his friend, M. Adelmann.[49] In an article published that year, he also acknowledged his friend's 'indefatigability' for finding him a manuscript copy of an Algerian lament (*qinah*) that retained important lost information regarding the epitaph of the famous medieval Spanish Rabbi, Isaac ben Sheshet.[50] Adelmann may have purchased some of these manuscripts from yeshivah collections, or from collections in the private hands of affluent Jerusalemites or from individuals selling off their inheritances. Such manuscript collections had been amassed by rabbinic scholars who, in previous centuries, transported their libraries with them to Jerusalem from their former homes across the Ottoman Empire.[51]

In July 1883, Shapira arrived in London bringing with him fifteen strips of leather which were inscribed in a Paleo-Hebrew script. The text appeared to represent an ancient copy of parts of the biblical book of Deuteronomy, which Shapira claimed had been found in caves on the eastern shore of the Dead Sea. The potential discovery drew in publicity from around the world and Christian David Ginsburg was appointed by the British Museum to evaluate the manuscripts. After several weeks of transcribing and analysing them, Ginsburg publicly declared them to be a forgery.

The affair was noted by David Kaufmann, who was now curious to find out if there were indeed ancient treasures to be discovered in Palestine. In January 1884, Adelmann sent him a short, enigmatic letter telling his 'Lieber Freund' that his activities in this field would have to end, at least as far as Jerusalem was concerned. He had made every effort to acquire an unspecified something for Kaufmann but had not met with success. Moreover, he informed him, he had not managed up to this point to visit any other cities in Palestine as part of his searches, but that he would be willing to do so at his special request. However, a set of liturgical fragments in Kaufman's collection was later

Figure 4.2 MS. A410, from the David Kaufmann Collection. Kaufmann's handwritten note verifies that he acquired it from Jerusalem from his friend M. Adelmann.

recorded as having been 'aus einer Genisah in Jerusalem gekauft 1883 u. 1884' (bought from a Genizah in Jerusalem in either 1883 or 1884).[52]

In between this letter and Adelmann's next, Shapira had relocated to Rotterdam. In March 1884, he shot himself in his hotel room. In all, 167 Yemenite manuscripts and scrolls remained unsold in his home in Jerusalem. When Adelmann wrote to Kaufmann again it was August, and he was in Jaffa. He informed his Austrian friend that he was sending him some manuscripts that he had bought in Hebron and some from Yemen, and he stated that he was intending to seek out other areas in the region known to have been inhabited since ancient times. He also shared news about what was left of the Shapira collection in Jerusalem, letting him know that an American Jew had already bought it all for 6,000 francs. The American was Adolph Sutro, a California-based engineer and philanthropist of German-Jewish extraction, and later Mayor of San Francisco. By way of good news, however, Adelmann assured Kaufmann that plenty of Yemenite codices, the type known as a 'Crown' (*Taj*), were still available from other sources. The *Taj* was a copy of the Hebrew Bible with extensive Masoretic notes, sometimes accompanied by an Arabic commentary known as the *Tafsir*. Several of them, he explained, had been in Shapira's collection, and while they were once considered hard to find, they were now more common, fetching between 80 and 120 francs. Adelmann closed his letter with the tantalizing statement that a substantial amount must still be in the possession of the Yemenite Jews who had recently arrived in Jerusalem.[53] While he did not receive a *Taj* that year, Kaufmann gained another six manuscripts from Jerusalem, including one Yemenite liturgy, and another three between 1885 and 1886.

5

Collectors and dealers on the rise (late 1880s)

Abraham Harkavy at the Imperial Library in Russia kept his eyes open for Hebrew scrolls and manuscripts of note. This is perhaps an understatement, for as the author of well over 300 books and articles on subjects ranging across the broad spectrum of Jewish history and literature, from the biblical period to the Middle Ages through to modern Jewish Russian history, and as the primary bibliographer of the Imperial Library's Hebraica collections, this distinguished Russian Jewish scholar was a prolific consumer of primary source materials. At the same time, he was also a cautious researcher. In his work to catalogue the Firkovich collections, his encounter with materials he suspected had been altered and forged by Firkovich, no doubt taught him great circumspection when evaluating purportedly ancient materials. Perhaps it was due to these instructive experiences, or perhaps it was just his pedantic nature with its focus on pure scholarship, that his published account of his trip to the East in 1886 is frustratingly void of human content.

The trip, sponsored by the Russian Imperial Library, was undertaken with the express intent of surveying (and purchasing where possible) biblical manuscripts. Of his visits to several genizot, he simply listed and described the manuscripts he viewed, introducing them with the words 'among the various papers that I found in the genizot of Jerusalem, Egypt, and Damascus.'[1] Beyond this simple statement, he provided no detail of exactly which genizot he penetrated and where they were located in those cities, let alone how he gained entrance, how long he stayed or his overall impression of what he encountered there. Most of the manuscripts he reported seeing were predominantly Karaite. His transcription of the colophon of the Codex Cairensis reveals that he spent time in the Karaite Synagogue in Cairo's Karaite Jewish quarter.[2] His mention of the synagogue belonging to the community of native-Arabic-speaking Jews (*mustarabim*), and to a twelfth-century Sephardi Torah scroll he viewed there, may have been a reference to the Maimonides Synagogue in the rabbanite Jewish quarter.[3] In Jerusalem, in addition to visiting an unspecified genizah, Harkavy paid a visit to the Russian Archimandrite Antonin (Kapustin), a noted archaeologist and collector, who was adding Hebrew manuscripts to his collection. Harkavy described their contents, including an outstanding Torah scroll in Yemenite script.[4] The fact that Antonin's notable collection of genizah manuscripts, including fragments that matched items found later in the Ben Ezra Synagogue, was not mentioned by Harkavy implies that Antonin had not yet acquired them. At some point in time, Harkavy amassed his own small collection of fragments that he later donated to the society for the

Promotion of Culture among the Jews of Russia. When the society became integrated into the Library of the Institute for Jewish Proletarian Culture in 1929, the fragments integrated too. And when the library was closed in 1936 and its contents transferred to the Vernadsky Library in Kiev, so the fragments moved again. But the circumstances surrounding Harkavy's original acquisition of them are still unknown.[5]

AMERICAN INSTITUTIONS WERE ALSO KEEN TO ENRICH their collections by sending well-connected scholars abroad to scout out treasures. One of these was John Gulian Lansing, the son of Reverend Gulian Lansing of the American Mission in Cairo. John was born in Damascus and grew up in Egypt, and he later went on to become a scholar of Oriental languages, the author of America's first published Arabic grammar, and the Gardner A. Sage Professor of Old Testament Language and Exegesis in the Brunswick Theological Seminary in New Jersey. Having already benefitted from his Cairo connections, through his father's donation of a Book of the Dead and his own donation of an Egyptian mummy, the New Brunswick Theological Seminary resolved in June 1887 to procure a fund from $200 to $500 for John Gulian Lansing to spend on purchasing 'curiosities' in Egypt. Lansing was travelling back to Cairo that summer to look after his ailing father.[6] Private buyers of antiquities did not often publicly record the prices they paid, but such information can sometimes be gleaned from their papers and journals, institutional record books and sales catalogues.[7] That same year Bernard Quaritch, the German-British bookseller, published the last general catalogue of his complete stock, which included some of the late Shapira's manuscript collection. In addition to presenting his notorious Deuteronomy strips for sale at £25, Quaritch also listed some of Shapira's Yemenite scrolls. Two complete Pentateuch scrolls out of the nine on offer were available for a mere £5. Given that the bookseller's profit margin was greater than that of the original vendor, Lansing could certainly afford to purchase many 'curiosities' on his trip.

After returning to New Jersey in November, Lansing published an account in *The Independent* magazine of his visit to the Karaite Synagogue in Cairo to see their manuscript treasures. Following a general description of the Karaite Jews, including their present number in Egypt, the location of their synagogue and the 'excellent appearance' of their 'chief priest', Lansing described several of the outstanding manuscripts he was permitted to view among the twenty or so kept in the synagogue. One of these was the Codex Cairensis, which he noted was 'almost entire' with portions missing only from the Pentateuch and the Writings. Unlike Richard Gottheil, who viewed the manuscript in 1905 and expressed horror at the way it had been stuffed into an ill-fitting box, Lansing reported that the manuscript was in fine condition. After several days spent examining the piece, he concluded that 'it was found to contain no variations from the *Textus Receptus*'.[8]

Lansing continued to describe three other special manuscripts in the collection: 'The Largest Manuscript', later than the first but well preserved and complete and written by a 'Nasa ben-Fudlan' (Nissi ibn Fadlan) who 'presented it to the City of Jerusalem';[9] 'The Finest Manuscript', illuminated with Levitical symbols in raised gold with a complete Masorah; and another 'fine' manuscript, with the entire text and 'very full' Masorah, which was one of the older pieces in the synagogue. Lansing did not walk away from this encounter empty handed, disclosing that he obtained from the synagogue 'a Pentateuchal Roll of unusual value on account of its antiquity, preservation and completeness'. A catalogue of the Seminary's Gardner A. Sage Library issued in 1888 listed the scroll among its various Arabic, Coptic and Hebrew treasures as 'a curious scroll of the Pentateuch written in the unpointed Hebrew, dating back probably six or seven hundred years', and as to provenance it stated that 'it was purchased from a Jewish Rabbi in one of the synagogues in Cairo'.[10]

Whether he was already in communication with Adolf Neubauer, or somehow connected to him through other channels, Lansing sent two photographs of the Codex Cairensis over to Oxford for Neubauer to consult as part of his research into the development of Hebrew paleography. The photographs were included in Neubauer's article on the subject, written in September 1889, and published two years later.[11] Using Lansing's facsimile, and a system of analysing accentuation marks developed by Seligman Isaac Baer, together with his own analysis of the handwriting in the colophon, Neubauer concluded that the Codex Cairensis was later than its colophon claimed it to be. Instead, he posited that Firkovich's codex in St. Petersburg (B19a) remained the oldest manuscript, an assertion that continued to be debated through to the late twentieth century.[12] But for now, feeling assured in his arguments about the age of the few known 'ancient' Bible manuscripts, and lamenting the lack of earlier, pre-Masoretic copies, he put forward in his article the following hopeful (or prophetic?) suggestion:

> Did they all perish in the frequent persecutions of the Jews, or were they destroyed when the vowel-points were introduced, or do fragments of them still exist in some old synagogue, hidden away in remote corners? We hope that the last suggestion may prove to be the correct one, and that after thorough searching in the East, some of these fragments may be brought to light.

JAMES RENDEL HARRIS OF HAVERFORD COLLEGE, PA, was about to embark on a thorough searching of the East. Harris, who would later become tangentially, if not concretely, linked to the genizah fragments was a professor of biblical studies at Haverford, and between 1888 and 1889, he and his wife, Helen, took an extended leave to travel in Palestine and Egypt in search of ancient copies of the Gospels. During his trip, he acquired forty-seven biblical and liturgical manuscripts in various languages, including Arabic, Hebrew and Syriac. One of the Hebrew Bible manuscripts can be traced to the Karaite synagogue in Jerusalem, and a Samaritan Pentateuch to the Samaritan synagogue in Nablus.

Harris also spent a good deal of time at the sixth-century St. Catherine's Monastery on Mt. Sinai, the site where Constantin von Tischendorf had made his great discovery of the Codex Sinaiticus. Tischendorf's ultimate betrayal of their trust –manipulating the monks to turn their loan of the codex into a permanent donation to the head of the church in St. Petersburg – made them understandably wary of Harris. Nevertheless, through careful diplomacy and reassurances that, unlike Tischendorf, he would not be taking off with their precious ancient books, Harris developed a good relationship with the keeper of the monastery library, Father Galaktéon, who eventually gave him access to a hidden dark cupboard inside the archbishop's office, where all the ancient Syriac manuscripts were packed away in chests. Here Harris made his most famous discovery: a complete version of the lost second-century Christian work, *The Apology of Aristides*. Working to carefully copy *The Apology* left him no time to examine the other manuscripts, and he had to leave the monastery reluctantly in the knowledge that other treasures for certain still lay inside. His desire to see the project through, however, would eventually lead to a joint venture with two sister scholars that would have a knock-on effect on genizah discoveries.

When they returned to America, he gifted his collection of forty-seven Arabic, Hebrew and Syriac manuscripts to Haverford College in Pennsylvania but, as to providing provenance, Harris would not divulge his sources. He explained that they had all seen 'the dust of Holy Lands and Holy Cities', and he asked anyone who would examine them to 'have the grace to believe that they were all acquired by the lawful, though sometimes, tedious, processes of Oriental commerce'.[13] Harris further claimed, as Shapira had done before him, that he was protecting the sellers' anonymity. More likely, he preferred to keep this information to himself in the hopes of future purchases. While deigning to divulge his own sources, he cautioned other collectors that to 'hide more than one tells of the quarters from which manuscripts come will, in the end, result only in the development of suspicion as to the methods by which books or fragments were acquired'.

From subsequent trips he added another thirty-three items, including medieval Hebrew fragments, some of which were Yemenite. Harris did not buy any Coptic manuscripts until much later. Back in 1889, he had managed to connect with an unnamed *sheikh* in Giza who claimed to know Flinders Petrie, as well as 'something about Coptic monasteries and manuscripts', but not trusting the high prices set on them and facing fierce competition from wealthier buyers, all his attempts to purchase Coptic works prior to 1917 failed.[14]

THE SON OF ENGLAND'S CHIEF RABBI, Elkan Nathan Adler, was about to be bitten by the bug of 'thorough searching in the East'. As a lawyer, Adler was well situated to serve the Anglo-Jewish community and its interests abroad. His much older half-brothers, Hermann (also future Chief Rabbi) and Marcus Nathan Adler, had both visited Palestine before him: Marcus helped establish the Yemen Refugees Relief Fund in 1884 to finance a new housing project for the Yemenite Jews in Jerusalem; Hermann visited with Baron Louis Benas in 1885 to report on the condition of the Jewish population in Jerusalem for the Anglo-Jewish Association, a partner organization of the Alliance Israélite Universelle. Hermann, who had earned his PhD from Leipzig in 1862 and served as a principal at Jews' College London, had also built up a substantial private library, which included several Yemenite manuscripts.

In the autumn of 1888, Adler was sent as a legal consultant by the Holy Land Relief Fund, following the death of its benefactor, Sir Moses Montefiore, to investigate the case of the impoverished Jewish squatters on his estate in Palestine.[15] After arriving in Jerusalem, in addition to dealing with this problem, Adler paid visits to dignitaries such as Renuf Pasha, the governor of Palestine, and the British consul, as well as the heads of the Ashkenazi and Sephardi communities. He also visited the schools and hospitals in preparation for a report to the Anglo-Jewish Association in England and to share with a Jewish organization in Frankfurt on his way home. It is unclear what exactly fired up the 27-year-old with his subsequent lifelong book-collecting zeal. The seeds were probably sewn in his youth growing up in the book-rich environment of his deeply learned father's home in London, and perhaps encouraged by the manuscripts he inherited as a child from his uncle, Benjamin Adler. But he certainly admitted that he found his first visit to Egypt and the Holy Land 'exciting and stimulating'.[16] The journey back home through Europe, where he stopped in Budapest and established a friendship with the prolific scholar and collector, David Kaufmann, was no less inspiring. It may have been among the inducements that led to his many subsequent visits to search for Jews in ancient lands and their books.

Adler would eventually gain expertise in knowing how to gain inside information about books and manuscripts across diverse communities. In some cases, he would have to make connections to individuals with treasures in their homes; in other cases, he would have to gain the trust of the rabbi by attending services. To begin with, however, he, like most other tourists, relied on the local markets and the dealers in antiquities.

A DRAMATIC RISE IN THE NUMBER OF ANTIQUITIES DEALERS operating in Egypt and the Holy Land occurred in the 1880s. In addition to the existing consular agents, greater numbers of independent traders established themselves in the main tourist areas of Alexandria, Cairo, Jerusalem and Jaffa. Even so, the travel guides published in this period did not list such resources; thus, all travellers, from the souvenir hunter to the serious collector, were left to discover them, either on their own or through personal contacts. At the start of the decade, the sixth edition of Murray's *Handbook for Travellers* recommended the help of the consuls, in particular Mustapha Agha or the German consular agent, Mohareb Todros. By the end of the decade, the seventh edition of the *Handbook* printed a new warning that 'really valuable articles are not produced for the inspection of ordinary travellers', while a new vocabulary list offered travellers guidance on how to ask for *anteekas* in Arabic.

The first law prohibiting the export of high-value antiquities without an export licence was passed in 1835 by the Ottoman Khedive of Egypt, Muhammed Ali. The same ordinance instituted an Egyptian Antiquities Service (Service des Antiquites) and proposed the creation of a national museum. In practice, the ban on exporting antiquities was not evenly or uniformly applied: objects could still be smuggled out or moved around under diplomatic cover, or else they were used to curry favour among high-ranking officials.[17] As the despoliation of Egypt's cultural heritage continued apace, Muhammed Ali's successor, Ismā'īl Pasha, issued further regulations regarding the ownership of objects discovered through excavation. With their greater emphasis on objects of high value, the regulations excluded coins, as well as any objects discovered on private land which were decreed as belonging to the landowner. An overarching Ottoman Antiquities Law, passed in 1874, likewise sought to control the movement of objects throughout the Empire by dividing the discoveries between the government, landowners and foreign teams of excavators. Coins, for which there were growing numbers of collectors and dealers, were added to the list of Egypt's regulated objects by the Khedive Muḥammad Tawfīq Pasha in 1880.[18] Notwithstanding these various rulings, the markets of the East flourished: everyone, it seemed, wanted a share in ancient *anteekas*.

Throughout the last two decades of the nineteenth century, hundreds of guests were checking in daily at the Shepheard's Hotel, leading one visiting journalist to describe it as a 'caravansary through which the world flows'.[19] For these visitors, antiquities stores ranged from establishments in Cairo that catered to a richer clientele, such as Paul L. Philip's store opposite the Shepheard's Hotel (from at least 1891), to the numerous small shops and stalls opening up, in addition to those already present, in the streets adjacent to the hotel and along the nearby Sharia al-Muski and the intertwining lanes of the Khan el-Khalili bazaar. After years of travelling to Egypt, a collector like Reverend Greville John Chester was better able to discern 'objects of value' among the highly priced melee of goods on offer. In the bustling marketplace of the *wikala* of el-Ghuri he even took notice of (and probably bartered for) the medieval Arab coins and glass weights being used by the merchants to measure out their wares, as well as a 'well-thumbed manuscript' of the Quran from which a shopkeeper intoned his verses.[20] Discerning collectors could also acquire antiquities from private dealers who operated discreetly out of their homes or offered their homes as spaces in which to view other dealers' wares.[21]

Gaining insider knowledge about where to find antiquities often took place at gatherings like Dr Grant's soirees, or while dining with fellow travellers at the Shepheard's Hotel, or during evening drinks at the Hotel du Nil. The Hotel du Nil, situated near the Muski, was the favoured haunt of Egyptologists and scholars due to the feeling it gave them of 'oriental seclusion' away from the throngs of tourists and the European trappings of the mainstream hotels.[22] Here at the Hotel du Nil, as Sir E. A. Wallis Budge, keeper of Egyptian and Assyrian Antiquities at the British Museum, later related in his memoire about travelling on behalf of the museum, an evening spent with fellow collectors and Egyptologists could teach one 'many things about the "antiquarian politics" of Cairo'. In fact, Budge's first evening in Cairo was spent in the company of the writer, Reverend W. J. Loftie (who had taken him to the hotel); Mr Walter Myers, a collector and fellow of the Society of Antiquaries; Henry Wallis, artist, and collector, and Greville Chester. Chester, who so often gave help to other British Egyptologists, even lent his help to navigate the Cairo markets. As Budge recalled: 'Guided by Greville Chester, I went about Cairo and made the acquaintance of several dealers, and also visited a number of private houses where antiquities were stored.'

For visitors taking the inevitable trip to see the pyramids of Giza, an increasing number of antiquities dealers, mostly Bedouin, established family-run enterprises in the village of Kafr el-Haram opposite the pyramids. The largest of the Giza shops was owned by Ali Abd el-Haj el-Gabri (*aka* Ali el-Arabi), who would later be connected to genizah manuscripts, and next largest by his former partner, Farag Ismaïn, who bought antiquities wholesale from smaller dealers. Ali el-Arabi's business continued through several successive generations and across several branches of his family, with one family member eventually establishing a shop near the Shepheard's in the 1930s.[23]

In addition to native Egyptian dealers, the number of foreign dealers establishing enterprises in Cairo and Alexandria grew during this period. Some were from Italy, such as the numismatist Giovanni Dattari who offered private sales of coins and other antiquities out of his home. In the Arab quarter of the Muski, a Swiss dealer André Bircher bought and sold substantial amounts of antiquities from within a 450-year-old Mamluk Palace he called home. And hailing from Austria, someone with an acknowledged connection to genizah manuscripts, was the Viennese dealer Otto Theodor Graf. Graf's first business in Egypt primarily focused on the carpet trade, but he soon expanded into the antiquities trade and enjoyed massive success with his acquisition of thousands of papyri from the Fayum, the Fayum mummy portraits, Late Antique textiles and the Armana tablets.[24] After opening stores in Alexandria, Vienna and Cairo, his successful enterprise supplied the Austrian National Library with around 10,000 fragments of papyri and hundreds of mummy portraits from the Fayum.[25]

However, of the well-known foreign-born dealers, a great many more were of Greek origin, having arrived with the cotton boom of the 1860s. Greek merchants were involved in all levels of cotton production and sale, and within a few decades upwardly mobile members of the Greek community became heavily involved in other aspects of the Egyptian mercantile world, with some developing into Egypt's leading financiers and bankers.[26] The Tanos were among the most prominent Greek dealers in antiquities. The business was founded by Marius Panayiotis Tano, a Greek Cypriot, who established one of the longest-running family antiquities enterprises in Cairo. Tano's shop was on Sharia Kamel in a key position for attracting the tourists being located directly opposite the Thomas Cook & Son building and diagonally across from the Shepheard's Hotel. Another store, situated in the mirror opposite position – opposite the Shepheard's and diagonally across from Thomas Cook & Son – was established by the Greek-born dealer, Panayotis Kyticas. His store was described as a place where collectors and others went at closing time to get good information on the state of the trade. Around the corner from the Shepheard's at Haret el-Zahar, near the American Mission, was a store owned by the dealer, Michel Casira, who sold objects and papyri to foreign collectors, and Coptic ostraca to the Greco-Roman Museum in Alexandria. Unlike the other major dealers of Greek origin (although he may have been Maltese), Alexandre Dingli, a former ostrich feather dealer, operated his business out of his home. He is known to have supplied objects and a papyrus roll to Wilhelm Fröhner, the curator at the Musée de Louvre between 1893 and 1894; Roman busts to the collector Carl Jacobsen, through Valdemar Schmidt, and he helped connect Dr Daniel Marie Fouquet, a collector of Egyptian antiquities and ceramics based in Cairo, with a local Arab who helped him search for objects found by the *sebakh* merchants.[27] All of these dealers were involved in sales of papyri and Coptic manuscripts, but most importantly for the Cairo Genizah discovery story, one of the Greek dealers had a mysterious connection to the genizah fragments and was later accused of trying to poach items already selected and paid for by another soon-to-be famous buyer.[28]

Many of the immigrants from Greece were Jews who, together with Jewish immigrants from Italy and others from across the Ottoman Empire, became involved in Egypt's business and financial world and went on to constitute most of the middle and upper classes in Egyptian Jewish society. In Cairo, most Jews still lived in the labyrinth-like Harat al-Yahud adjoining the Harat al-Yahud al-Qara'in. This area, off the Sharia al-Muski, had been continuously occupied by Jews since the twelfth century. Along the main thoroughfare were the shops and stalls of a wide range of tradesmen, from tobacconists and goldsmiths to moneychangers and book vendors. Although there must have been shops selling *anteekas* within the Jewish quarter, the Jewish antiquities dealers from this period are not as well documented as their non-Jewish counterparts. One reputable dealer, Moses Isak, is only recalled in a letter written in 1892 by the Danish Egyptologist, Valdemar Schmidt, who noted that Isak had been recommended to him by the German Egyptologist, Emile Brugsch.[29] Likewise, of Michael Abemayor, whose forebears came from Turkey and who established an antiquities store opposite the Shepheard's Hotel in the 1880s, little is known. The store rose to great prominence under the management of his sons, Ellie Albert and Joseph Abemayor, and the business was re-established in New York by his grandson, Michel, after the family left Egypt in the 1950s.[30] Elias Hatoun (or Ilyas Hatun), a Syrian Jewish dealer, established an Islamic furniture workshop in the Muski in the 1890s. Hatoun also dealt in antiquities, particularly Oriental wares, and his store, which was recalled by at least one visitor as being museum-like, continued into the 1930s when it began to operate as 'E. Hatoun & Sons' until at least 1963.

Joseph Cohen's large carpet and antiquities store in the Khan el-Khalili bazaar is more fortunate in having been retained in popular memory. Once described by a visitor in the 1890s as the 'carpet groves of ceremonious Mr. Cohen', a place where one can 'drink a diminutive glass of tea' and smoke a cigarette while browsing,[31] Cohen's store eventually garnered international recognition through his dealings with the major museums, and a reputation for fixed prices and fair dealing despite the expense of his goods.[32] A sign above an old, undated photograph of the store suggests that the shop was established in 1891.[33] There is evidence, however, that Cohen started trading goods in the bazaar in the early 1880s; at least according to one traveller who examined his wares, drank his coffee and smoked cigarettes with him at some point before 1884, and another tourist who purchased saddle bags from him in 1886.[34] Beyond these details, supplied by some of his clients, nothing more is known about Cohen's life.

Among the handful of named Jewish antiquities dealers whose careers began in the late nineteenth century, it was Maurice Nahman who would rise to the greatest prominence. According to Maurice's nephew, Robert, the Nahmans originally hailed from Greece. The family's patriarch, Matatias Nahman, moved from the northern part of Greece in the early nineteenth century to establish a successful banking business in Cairo; he eventually owned an impressive mansion in the commercial district where he entertained members of the Austrian Habsburg dynasty.[35] The family gained numerous relatives through marriage with members of the other leading Sephardi Jewish families, such as the Rolos, Menasces and Aghions, who also originally hailed from various countries across the Ottoman Empire.[36] Matatius's grandson, Maurice Nahman, like so many members of the family, entered the banking business and eventually became head cashier but, for reasons unknown, he also developed a side-line in antiquities dealing in 1890. By 1908, he had become one of two principal suppliers to the American industrialist and art collector, Charles Lang Freer, who was building up his private collection of antiquities, and by 1912, Nahman was listed as an officially licensed antiquarian in the Baedeker guide.[37] Eventually he became one of the best-known antiquarians in Cairo.

Yet, at the time of Adler's visit in 1888, Nahman was working in Cairo's oldest bank, the Crédit Fonciér Égyptien and, based on the sign that eventually adorned his palatial antiquities house, he still hadn't entered that line of business.

The bank itself was founded partly by members of the Suarès della Pegna family who originally hailed from Livorno, Italy, and who, over time, would come to be regarded as Egypt's Rothschilds. Among their many achievements, the Suarès family instituted Egypt's first regular public transport service in the form of horse-drawn carriages, popularly known as 'sawaris'.[38] Together with other leading Alexandrian and Cairene Sephardi Jewish families, including the Cattaouis, Mosseris, Rolos and Menasces, they also initiated multiple joint ventures in road and railway construction, water supplies, sugar refineries and manifold other agricultural, manufacturing and commercial enterprises.[39]

JEWISH COMMUNITY LEADERS IN CAIRO assured Elkan Adler that he was the first foreign Jewish visitor to take a deep interest in the condition of Cairene Jewry. His attentions to them, combined with his own connections to England's Jewish elite, led to his being feted by the Cattaouis and Mosseris and being invited to their homes and private synagogues. The synagogue of Moïse Cattaoui, Egyptian entrepreneur and president of the Jewish Community, was adjoined to his palatial residence and park-sized gardens. According to Adler, Cattaoui had once given over his property for three months to Frederick Hamilton-Temple-Blackwood (Lord Dufferin), England's Special Commissioner. Dufferin had been sent to assess the situation in Egypt in the aftermath of the Urabi Revolt, and Cattaoui, whose young son was murdered during the uprising, was keen to help. Queen Victoria had sent a portrait of herself to thank Cattaoui for this service and, according to Adler, it was something he treasured 'with no little pride'. The Cattaouis, he concluded, were 'great benefactors of their brethren and surpassed by none in their public spirit and intelligent liberality'.

In addition to multiple invitations to dinners and services, Adler was also given a tour of the historical sites, including the Bassatine Cemetery: one of the oldest Jewish cemeteries in the world. From its founding in the ninth century, the cemetery provided the final resting place for many of Egypt's notable Jewish figures, and although it became the main burial ground for Cairo's Rabbanite Jews, it had originally been shared by both Rabbanites and Karaites. Adler, like many others before and after him, also visited the Karaite synagogue and was allowed to view their manuscripts. He too examined the famous Codex Cairensis and its colophon, and noted the curses attached to their other codices warding off potential buyers and protecting them from trafficking. Following the advice of his guidebook, Adler then found himself inside the Ben Ezra Synagogue and he soon convinced his chaperone, the beadle's son, to let him see the so-called scroll of Ezra. After climbing up to the 'about' sixteen-foot-high alcove on a 'very shaky ladder' and swaying on its top rung 'like Mahomet, 'twixt heaven and earth', he found inside 'a door closing a small aperture', a torn and slightly mouldy scroll. But the script inside 'was easily legible', and Adler concluded that to his inexperienced eyes it was probably less than 300 years old.[40] This would concur with Edith Butcher's claim that the old scroll had been removed after the 1881 incident with Reverend Gulian Lansing's visitors and replaced with a comparatively modern one.

Adler spent the rest of his time in the old Ben Ezra Synagogue deeply engaged with a 'genuine antiquity': the medieval woodwork inscriptions around the synagogue walls. After he spent time carefully transcribing them, he was upset to learn that the community was planning to renovate and whitewash the old building. He later disclosed that he 'brought back mostly Karaite MSS' from this trip, but how many, what they were or exactly how he obtained them, he never divulged. He was told (although he did not say by whom) that the community had buried 'many old Sepharim [books] in the Beth Chaim [cemetery] of the Perushim, or orthodox Jews, at Bâsâtin' some months prior to his arrival there. The news of these buried books clearly piqued his interest, but he was assured by the authorities that they were 'only ragged printed books and modern Scrolls of the Law'. Thus, by the end of his first visit to a city rich in hidden genizot, the man who would one day acquire thousands of manuscripts from these hiding places, for whom no sport could ever equal 'the hunt for a buried manuscript', confidently declared to others keeping a watchful eye on the East: 'Nowadays there are no Hebrew manuscripts of importance to be bought in Cairo.' As the end of the 1880s approached, however, he was about to be proved wrong.[41]

A hidden room laid open (1889–90)

SOMEONE SINKING A WELL NEAR THE BEN EZRA SYNAGOGUE several months prior to Elkan Adler's visit to Cairo suddenly unearthed some fragments of Hebrew manuscripts. The anonymous well-sinker, a German, took the fragments to show Archibald Henry Sayce. Either the German knew Sayce well enough to realize that the pieces might be of interest to him, or perhaps they met over a discussion of antiquities at one of Dr Grant's Wednesday night soirees, but by the time Sayce came to recall the discovery over fifty years later, he had to admit that he had forgotten the man's name. At any rate, according to this indistinct recollection, Sayce took the fragments to show his close friend in Oxford, Adolf Neubauer. With little to do, it seems, Neubauer dismissed them out of hand as having no importance.[1] Perhaps these fragments were also connected to the 'ragged printed books and modern Scrolls of the Law' that the community had told Adler they had recently buried in the Bassatine, or perhaps they were an altogether different cache. Whatever the case, the exact nature of these unearthed fragments and their fate, together with the German's name, is still unknown.

As to the German's well-digging activities, they may have been connected to impending changes to the structures in the synagogue compound. Hand-dug wells were also appearing elsewhere in the environs of Old Cairo for a different reason: in preparation for the new railway line and the regular water stops needed by steam locomotives. The extension of the railway line, thanks to Frederick Harvey Trevethick's new reorganization and expansion of Egypt's national railway system, was a mixed blessing. Additional lines opened up the country and facilitated industrial growth, but this new line, which ran parallel with the Fortress of Babylon, altered the topography of the region by cutting the fortress off physically and visually from the Nile. In addition, it facilitated the arrival of increased numbers of antiquities hunters and tourists to see for themselves the ancient buildings described in the travel accounts of Greville John Chester in the 1870s and in the monograph produced by the English historian, Alfred J. Butler in 1884.

When Butler visited Old Cairo, following in Chester's footsteps, and using his account as a point of comparison, he encountered the restoration work being carried out on the medieval al-Mu'allaqah Church (*aka* the Hanging Church). The fourteenth-century sanctuary screen doors described by Chester in 1872 were now gone, having been sold to the British Museum in 1878. Aside from missing ecclesiastical furniture and a few minor changes to the internal configuration of the building, Butler reported that the restoration had been 'carried out with more care and truthfulness than seemed possible'.² This was not the view of Somers Clarke, an English architect and Egyptologist, who inspected the church in 1896: while Clarke praised the motives behind such restorations, he criticized the appearance of the whitewashed walls, which looked entirely new, and the complete re-arrangement of the interior.³ The same was true of other areas in Old Cairo, including the Roman fortress: Butler found changes from Chester's early account, and visitors coming after Butler, like Chester on a subsequent visit in 1889, and like Clarke and others in the 1890s, recorded other substantial alterations to historical structures.

Such changes were not new, of course. The Egyptian climate, with its strong desert winds and dark dust storms from the clay soil, sporadically covered buildings with dirt, gradually eroding them. The natural environment, with its high, salt-loaded, groundwater table, caused intermittent flooding. And the unnatural environment: clean looking, but cheap, short-lived whitewashed exteriors made dirtier from accumulated street rubbish and debris, meant that building maintenance and repair was a vital, ongoing and potentially costly chore.⁴ As old mosques, churches and synagogues were altered or came down, many of the pieces of ecclesiastical furniture that weren't reused or deposited in museums were sold off. Unsurprising then, that medieval ecclesiastical furniture, such as the engraved cedar doors from the Hanging Church, and arks, doors and plaques from the Ben Ezra Synagogue would eventually turn up in museum and library collections in Europe and America, as well as in private collections around the world. European observers like Chester, who was particularly stinging in his criticisms of the changes, did not appreciate the local practices that prioritized structural maintenance over the preservation of what they considered purely decorative elements. When funding was in short supply, the building owners determined that ornamental materials made from marble, copper and wood could be removed and sold to raise the necessary funds for structural repairs.⁵

LARGE RUBBISH MOUNDS IN AND AROUND OLD CAIRO created by such domestic debris had accumulated there for centuries. The mounds stood in the ruins of al-Fustat along the east side of the Roman Fortress of Babylon to the left of the *Qarafa* necropolis and the Muqattam hills. As W. J. Loftie noted during his tour of Egypt in 1879, the English residents took expeditions to hunt in the mounds for 'old Arab beads and beautifully coloured fragments of pottery'. He also noted that no digging was necessary as 'Every wind lays bare a fresh stratum', and that each day brought something fresh to light.⁶

The Ashmolean Museum in Oxford had been among the many beneficiaries of such finds from at least as early as 1881 when Chester compiled the museum's *Catalogue of the Egyptian Antiquities*. Among the items described, there were five green pottery lamps, fragments of porcelain pottery, fragments of ancient Arabic glass, beads of blue and coloured glass, and a fragment of white marble that he had uncovered from the mounds during his excursions to the city.⁷

Henry Wallis, artist and collector of pottery ware, had developed an interest in Islamic vases and ceramics after several years of collecting and selling Greek and Persian wares. But unlike previous collectors, whose serendipitous discoveries were made through random selections from the mounds, Wallis campaigned for a formal excavation on behalf of the British Museum in an organized attempt to boost that institution's collections of Islamic art. Together with Augustus Wollaston Franks, whose department partly funded the mission, Wallis approached the Egypt Exploration Fund for additional help in excavating the mounds.[8] At their July meeting in 1889, they agreed to support an excavation to be led by one of their officers, Count Riamo d'Hulst.

COUNT RIAMO D'HULST, AN OFFICER OF THE EGYPT EXPLORATION FUND, had been on the archaeological scene since 1887. A first public mention of him occurred that May when *The Times* reported his discovery of some Christian tombs hidden under the rubbish mounds close to the Roman wall running parallel with the railway line from Ramleh and near the Sidi Gabr Mosque in Alexandria.[9] The details of the Count's life before he lived in Egypt are shrouded in mystery.[10] Whatever elements of his past d'Hulst kept to himself, by the time his name started to appear in the leading newspapers and literary magazines of the day, he was a permanent resident in Egypt who could speak modern Arabic fluently. Two months after his discovery of the Christian catacombs, the Egypt Exploration Fund hired him to assist Édouard Naville with his excavation of the Great Temple of Bubastis in Lower Egypt. D'Hulst was a welcome addition to the team, particularly given his ability to converse easily with the local men hired to excavate and his willingness to oversee the logistics of moving heavy blocks.[11]

The Fund employed d'Hulst as an excavator and site supervisor from 1886 to 1893, during which time he played a significant role in the recovery and transfer of large monuments for institutions and museums around the world (the 17-foot red granite column from the temple of Herishef, excavated by Naville in 1891 and donated to the British Museum, is a noteworthy example). Despite his supposed aristocratic origins, d'Hulst did not shy away from hard work or trying conditions. Naville related how they had both waded into a boggy pit, blindly waving their hands underneath to recover a near-perfect Hyksos head. At the end of the excavation season when d'Hulst was left in charge of transport, he wrote to Naville about the difficulties involved and the injuries sustained, including two broken fingers after his attempt to lift a large Hathor head onto a cart resulted in it falling on his hand. After being told by the doctor that his fingernail would never grow back, he stoically quoted the popular colloquial Arabic phrase: '*malesh* (no matter)'. It mattered to him somewhat: d'Hulst's private letters to both Naville and Amelia Edwards recount the debilitating work involved in moving and shipping the large objects to London: the scorching Egyptian summers in a malarial region, the need to find replacement workers when those in place refused to work under such conditions, the dogged pursuit of government inspectors from town to town in seeking permission to use a locomotive engine, and the lengths to which he went to protect the shipments from further damage, such as sleeping on top of the boxes as they waited on board the ship.[12]

As to his archaeological aspirations back in the 1880s, all looked set for success. In the early days of the Fund, when the pursuit of monumental objects was deemed essential to their outreach and fundraising campaigns, d'Hulst's contribution to the excavation work was highly regarded. When the season closed at Bubastis, the Fund was happy to extend its services to the British Museum to boost their Islamic art collection and thus dispatched their trusted man in Cairo to supervise Wallis's proposed excavation of the rubbish mounds.

D'Hulst's excavations for the British Museum mostly took place in the vicinity of the ancient Roman walls of the Fortress of Babylon. Some of his searches even extended out as far as Bab el-Nasr, in the old Islamic city of Cairo, and the mausoleum of El-Imam El-Shafei, near Cairo's *al-Qarafa* (City of the Dead), all of which d'Hulst promised to indicate with the help of Grand Bey's map of Cairo. Among the diverse objects uncovered (including materials from an archaeological site at Tel Tinnis) were Kufic stelae, coins, weights, a small sphinx of black granite with the cartouche of Rameses II and, of course, the much-desired medieval Islamic pottery.[13]

D'Hulst's sudden encounter with Hebrew MSS was most unexpected. Even though he did not record the exact location of his find, based on the letter he sent to the Fund describing which pottery pieces derived from which locations, it's clear that he was searching at one point near the old Roman wall. He even mentioned his failed attempt to excavate near the southern Roman gate. Either these scraps of writing had been buried in the vicinity of the Roman wall at some point before he came across them (like those discovered by the unnamed German in 1888), or they were among the piles of debris recently thrown out from the nearby Ben Ezra Synagogue.

When d'Hulst visited the site in 1892 at Sayce's behest, he would have witnessed many changes: the Roman wall and bastion tower had been pulled down, the land where the garden was once situated was being cleared out for future building works, and the synagogue itself was almost entirely new.[14] When he returned to excavate there on behalf of the Bodleian in 1898, he came to believe that the fragments he had first encountered in 1889 were among those that had been thrown out of the synagogue. Nevertheless, as he later pointed out, any one of these piles of fragments could have contained items of another provenience underneath. Sayce also divulged, much later still, that 'a certain portion of the MSS. had been thrown out of the Synagogue and buried in what was then a whole piece of ground. On this piece of ground the garden and some new buildings belonging to the Synagogue were afterward constructed, while a public road was made over another part of the ground.'

Comparing Sayce's testimony to an architectural survey from the 1990s suggests that back in 1889 d'Hulst was excavating in the area east of the synagogue where the compound was bounded by a section of the Roman wall and a bastion tower. In Alfred Butler's 1884 map of the area, this eastern section was designated as a palm garden. From his position in or near the palm garden, d'Hulst had been digging in very close proximity to the dramatic changes occurring to the Ben Ezra Synagogue.

A complete rebuild of the Ben Ezra had been deemed necessary not long after the repair project had been started. Decades later, a prominent community member, Jacques Mosseri, stipulated that the old building was simply 'falling to pieces, and could not possibly be restored'. Thus, in line with other dramatic interventions, like the restoration in 1880 of the medieval al-Amshati Synagogue in al-Mahalla al-Kubra, the community decided that it needed a complete rebuild. Based on his memory (although he was just a child at the time), together with the testimony he gathered from others who remembered the venerable building, Mosseri claimed that the new structure was an exact replica of the old.

The community tried hard to make the restoration as faithful to the original as possible. The only notable change was to the foundations which were raised up so that the former descent down several steps into the interior no longer existed and the entrance was now level with the ground. Later archaeological investigations confirmed these changes as well as the addition of a basement under the newly raised foundations.[15]

WHEN GREVILLE JOHN CHESTER ARRIVED ON THE SCENE that same December of 1889, he was outraged to witness the demolition of this 'most curious & interesting old building'. His ire was no doubt increased by his mistaken belief that the synagogue had once been a church. Chester was currently on his twenty-fourth annual visit to Egypt. The journey had included a first stop at the port of Jaffa, where he obtained 'a quantity of fragments of Samaritan MSS on paper & parchment' purportedly found on Mount Gerizim in Nablus. Having a strong partiality for his *alma mater*, he sent the pieces on to the Bodleian librarian, E. W. B. Nicholson, with whom he had established a prior relationship over his sale of papyri fragments to the Bodleian in 1878, and to whom he had sold some *mezuzot* (doorpost prayers) for the Bodleian's Hebrew collection in 1888.[16] After visiting Beirut, Chester travelled on to Egypt via Jerusalem. Shortly before his pending trip on the Nile, perhaps hearing that changes to the area were underway, he paid a visit to Old Cairo.

In a letter swearing Nicholson to secrecy, for 'the matter must not be *talked about* at present', Chester reported on the synagogue's demise and the use of materials from the 'splendid Bastion tower of the Old Roman fortress of Babylon' for the refurbishment. Several years later, when he witnessed the synagogue newly rebuilt, he would publicly denounce the community's actions in a British magazine but for now, when treasures were to be had, some discretion was required. From the two messages he sent to Nicholson that day, it seems that he had first come upon some of the manuscripts, lying in a discarded heap, and then later inside the synagogue itself. The first set of manuscripts he quickly dispatched to England with a hurried note: 'I sent some portions of ancient Hebr. MSS. Please tell me *as soon as possible* if you want them, what you think they might be worth, & whether you would like more, as they might be had.'

He was due on board his *dahabiyeh* the next morning, but he could not resist the urge to obtain more of the manuscripts. In a second letter to Nicholson, he confided, 'Since I sent off the Hebr. MSS fragments this morning I have obtained a *quantity* more.' The source of the pieces, he divulged, was a room 'laid open whose floor is literally *covered* with fragments of MSS & Early printed Hebr. books & MSS of leather'.[17]

Inside the recently opened genizah, he battled dust and fleas to rummage among the pile of manuscripts, to make his selection, and to buy the best he could find. It troubled him to leave behind the 'numbers of others worth having' and so he tried to find out what the community planned to do with the remainder. He feared that while he was away on the Nile they might be destroyed or buried. The custodians were not forthcoming. They may have been caught unaware by the discovery and equally surprised at the sheer number of manuscripts in the newly exposed room. Most likely they had no plan.

Chester enclosed some of the fragments he had purchased in with his letter to Nicholson. Intrigued by these treasures, he added a postscript: 'I suppose most of the bits are earlier than AD 1400 & some *much* more so?' He took the rest away with him with the intention of sorting, cleaning and straightening them out before sending them off in batches. True to his word, he sent four packets to Nicholson three days later on 23 December 1889. His message was short: he and Sayce had heard a rumour about an Arabic manuscript, and they were in hot pursuit. Twelve days after that, he let Nicholson know that he had mailed the remaining Hebrew manuscripts from Assiut.

Even though he could not read the texts, Chester guessed accurately at their age: of the 213 pieces (1,197 pages) he retrieved that day, all the dated and datable manuscripts were written before the fifteenth century. With an average of six pages per manuscript (although some were just a few pages long, while others extended to over sixty pages), most of them were still in reasonable condition. Many of the pieces were medieval copies of biblical, rabbinical and liturgical works written on large, multi-folio pieces of vellum. One of the manuscripts, the Bodleian would later boast, comprised an 82-page prayer book, an almost complete copy 'according to the Egyptian rite . . . of which no other copy is known'. Other near-complete books, or parts of books, included a 67-page rabbinic polemic against the Karaites from 1112 CE, and a 29-page register of books from Cairo compiled between 1155 and 1160 CE.[18]

OVER IN OXFORD, ADOLF NEUBAUER'S ATTENTION was firmly caught. By now, he was a well-established and highly regarded scholar, having been appointed Oxford University's first Reader in Rabbinic Literature in 1884. In addition to his own manifold publications in the major Jewish scholarly journals of the day, he read widely in numerous languages and compiled extensive reviews of current Judaic scholarship.[19] Serving as a Bodleian sub-librarian over the course of the past sixteen years, Neubauer had carefully developed the Library's Oriental collections and spent copious hours meticulously classifying them. As a scholar, he regularly engaged with correspondents from across the world to discover and identify Hebrew manuscripts of note, and as a bibliographer he was keen to ensure the discoverability of such sources. Yet the ever-increasing number of scholarly articles and books across a vast array of periodical literature later drew him to express frustration at the impossibility of keeping track of it all.

Neubauer was also highly critical of scholarship that did not allow other scholars to easily find and use the same sources through proper citation or indexes, and he reproached the prolific scholar David Kaufmann for failing to provide an index to the exhaustive biographies and notices in his recent 228-page monograph, *Die letzte Vertreibung der Juden aus Wien und Niederösterreich* (The last expulsion of the Jews from Vienna and Lower Austria).[20] In addition to criticizing the recent appearance on the scene of 'meagre' Jewish periodicals such as *Das Jüdische Centralblad*, which supplied material of worth but also 'second-rate documents', Neubauer recommended that 'Jewish literature should have a central and international organ' as not even 'rich scholars' (in which category Kaufmann also fell) could manage to follow the fast-flowing 'current of Jewish literature'.

Added to this mountain of printed matter, Neubauer's reading list was about to get even longer. The bundles of manuscripts that Chester sent through the mail were indeed noteworthy. Not to the extent that he thought it worth recompensing him handsomely for the pieces (Chester was paid the equivalent of seven pounds per item), but to the extent that the discovery of such substantial pieces of medieval literature meant that his previous attempt to draw attention to the 'Genizoth' in the East was finally being realized. And now the Bodleian had its very own scout.

A SEPARATE CROP OF HEBREW FRAGMENTS was about to reach Neubauer from another source. In early January 1890, Reginald Stuart Poole of the Fund received a report from d'Hulst on his excavation work and a list of what to expect to find in each container being shipped to England. Among the materials d'Hulst enclosed in box number nine were a mixture of vellum and paper fragments of Hebrew manuscripts, most just one or two pages in size; many with physical damage such as tearing and staining. Numerous pieces were documents bearing dates from the eleventh and twelfth centuries: some had been written right there in al-Fustat; others had been written in Alexandria, Damietta and Ramleh. The earliest piece unearthed in the rubbish mounds was a letter from 922 CE written in Palestine and sent to Baghdad. A few of the fragments have since been matched to fragments in other collections, including those Chester would subsequently purchase from an unknown supplier.

Just how long d'Hulst's fragments had been exposed out in the open is unknown, although the environmental conditions would be unsuitable for the long-term preservation of paper and vellum. Even supposing the fragments came from the Ben Ezra Synagogue, it is now impossible to know exactly where inside the building they had once been stored, under what conditions and for how long. Among the known possibilities were Saphir's roof box, Chester's sealed room or a cupboard or niche like the one hiding the Ezra Scroll. But then there are the unknown possibilities: the site where the unnamed German found buried manuscripts, and the site or sites where manuscripts belonging to the other ancient and medieval synagogues in the region, such as the ancient synagogue of Dammuh, had been placed after transfer. And while the importance of paying closer attention to the situation of small finds was occurring in the nascent archaeological sciences by trailblazers such as Flinders Petrie, even he lamented the present state of museums, which he described as 'ghastly charnel-houses of murdered evidence'.[21] Thus, the idea of noting down exactly where and how old manuscripts (let alone fragmentary manuscripts) were discovered was little practised and certainly rarely considered.

After d'Hulst's box of fragments arrived in London, it was brought to the attention of Edward Maunde Thompson, director of the British Museum and a member of the Egypt Exploration Fund. Given the museum's recent history with Moses Shapira who, despite enriching their Hebraica collection with genuinely old and mostly intact Karaite and Yemenite manuscripts, had caused them considerable embarrassment with his questionable strips of Deuteronomy, it's likely that unprovenanced Hebrew fragments were regarded as potential hotcakes. Furthermore, having such a rich manuscript collection, including magnificent Bible codices, sumptuously illustrated Hebrew liturgies, as well as copies of most of the major Jewish texts, many of which had not yet been published in print, the museum's interest in acquiring pieces of unprovenanced manuscripts was low.[22] Although no record of the transaction has been found, it is not hard to imagine the 'thanks but no thanks' sentiment that led to such fragments being rejected at that time and re-routed elsewhere.

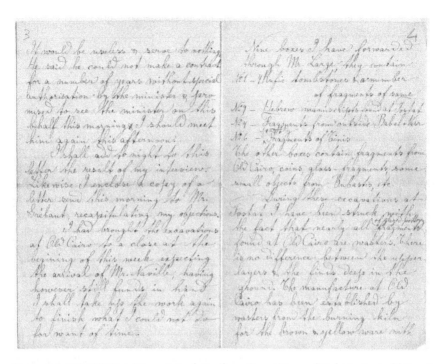

Figure 6.1 MS. EES III, j. 73, pp. 3-4: a letter from Count Riamo d'Hulst to Reginald Stuart Poole detailing his findings during excavations at Fustat.

THE ULTIMATE FATE OF ALL THE HEBREW FRAGMENTS in the half-demolished room may have been impacted by Chester's great interest in them and his willingness to pay high prices to acquire them. The idea that the 'value of the manuscripts appeared to the Synagogue authorities only after they had seen the beadle sell to the dealers' was put forth by the editors of a catalogue of genizah fragments published in the 1920s. This supposition was based on the following information supplied by an anonymous correspondent:

> many dealers helped themselves to small bundles of fragments which they would obtain by bakhshish from the beadle of the old Synagogue at Fustat (Old Cairo), where the Genizah had been discovered in an attic as the result of the work of repairing the Synagogue. The workmen on tearing down the roof dumped all the contents of this attic into the court-yard, and there the MSS were lying for several weeks in the open. During these weeks many dealers could obtain bundles of leaves for nominal sums. They later sold these bundles at good prices to several tourists and libraries.[23]

D'Hulst may have also enquired about the manuscripts lying around in the synagogue courtyard, as he later claimed that the whole lot could have been had at the time for one payment. He also maintained that he had asked for instructions from London, but none were forthcoming. In the meantime, unbeknown to him, the British Museum decided to forward the fragments that he'd sent to the Egypt Exploration Fund to the Bodleian Library. Apart from his private letters to the Fund detailing his discovery, all trace of his connection to them and how they were discovered was seemingly severed and lost.

Thus, from their previously dormant and unknown state of preservation in a genizah or genizot, the newly discovered manuscripts would undergo a dramatic rebirth: parts would be severed and scattered, losing some appendages and accumulating others along the way until, after being widely dispersed, they would eventually find new disjointed existences in libraries around the world. Eventually, nearly half a million scattered fragments – not necessarily from the same source – would be conceptually united as part of 'the Cairo Genizah'. Once the phrase was adopted after 1897, whenever a medieval Hebrew or Judeo-Arabic fragment came on the market, the Ben Ezra Synagogue find spot was assumed and the Cairo Genizah provenance label attached. All that is certain at this point, however, is that a sizeable but indeterminable amount of manuscript fragments created or owned by the age-old Jewish communities of Egypt were about to embark on incredibly convoluted and mostly undocumented journeys.

The Russian archimandrite Antonin may have acquired his collection from the bundles of manuscripts lying in the synagogue yard. Antonin served as the leader of the Russian Orthodox Ecclesiastical Mission in Jerusalem from 1865 to 1894 and, aside from his intensive projects to develop church lands and build schools in the Holy City, he was greatly interested in Byzantine studies, ecclesiastical history and archaeology. In the late 1870s he was involved in creating a Russian Orthodox Orientalists' society modelled on the idea of the Deutscher Palästina-Verein (German Society for the Exploration of Palestine), and by the early 1880s, he was funded to carry out archaeological digs in and around Jerusalem together with Conrad Schick, the German architect and archaeologist, for the Palestine Exploration Fund.[24]

In addition, Antonin undertook the description of the manuscripts belonging to the Church of the Holy Sepulchre and those held by the Patriarchal Library in Jerusalem. He also catalogued the holdings of the monastery Mar Saba in the Kidron Valley, and the manuscripts in St Catherine's Greek Orthodox Monastery at the foot of Mount Sinai. In Jerusalem, he founded a museum at the Russian Orthodox Ecclesiastical Mission where he placed his private collection of Greek, Latin and Hebrew manuscripts, books and coins.

Exactly how or when Antonin acquired his collection of Hebrew fragments remains unknown; nevertheless, they were similar in size, content and state of preservation to those acquired by Chester and unlike the fragments unearthed by d'Hulst. When the Russian Jewish scholar Abraham Harkavy first mentioned the collection in his report on the contents of the St Petersburg Imperial Public Library (now National Library of Russia) in 1899, he described it as comprising 1,189 manuscripts, including '13 complete (or nearly complete) volumes on parchment and paper, all but one in Hebrew . . . 22 Samaritan Bible MSS (on parchment or paper) . . . 1,154 fragments (some large, some small) in Hebrew, Aramaic, and Judeo-Arabic'. Indeed, the contents and condition of the Antonin Collection led the scholar who catalogued his material in the 1960s to speculate that 'being among the first on the scene, [Antonin] was able to acquire a choice selection of the material'.[25] Even if he was not present on the scene in Cairo, it's possible that someone from one of the nearby local Orthodox churches acted as his agent. It is also feasible that some of the manuscripts had been bought locally or even discovered closer to home.

THE JERUSALEMITE DEALER, SOLOMON AARON WERTHEIMER, first appeared on the antiquities scene around this time in the early 1890s. The young and impoverished Hungarian scholar was born near Bratislava on the border between Austria and Hungary in 1866 and descended from an extensive line of illustrious Austrian and Hungarian 'Court Jews' and rabbis.[26] At the age of five, he had moved with his immediate family to Jerusalem, but he was orphaned just one year later. In addition to his traditional religious education, Wertheimer took an independent interest in the study of manuscript sources thanks to his early exposure to the rare books and manuscripts housed in the Sephardi yeshivot (rabbinic academies) where he studied. With a young family to raise – he was married at sixteen and went on to have five sons and two daughters – Wertheimer had to find ways to support them in addition to fulfilling his insatiable curiosity about ancient sources.

At age twenty, he self-published his first book on a tractate of the Babylonian Talmud, supplied with his own commentaries and a critical apparatus compiled from the rare books and manuscripts he was able to consult. As he worked on subsequent publications, he scoured the markets and bookshops of Jerusalem looking for sources, even teaching himself Arabic to read Maimonides's works in their original language and to decipher the *responsa* (scholarly legal correspondence) of the medieval rabbinic authorities.

In Wertheimer's small apartment in Batei Ungarin, a Jerusalem enclave established and inhabited by religious Hungarian Jews, old books and manuscripts were crammed in between the spaces not inhabited by children and the paraphernalia of family life. At some point very soon after manuscripts in the Ben Ezra Synagogue came to light, Wertheimer acquired his own batch. Unfortunately, this acquisition, like so many others from that source, is shrouded in mystery.

Given the close ties between the rabbinate in Jerusalem and Egypt – the chief rabbis in Egypt were all Sephardim from Jerusalem and other parts of the Ottoman Empire – and his own ties to the Sephardi yeshivot, it is possible that news about the Ben Ezra Synagogue spread across these networks. However, the most likely scenario is that a local dealer seeking Wertheimer's expertise in deciphering manuscripts brought them to him for evaluation. Some of the pieces may even have been found by the dealer or dealers right there in Jerusalem or else from some other source.

At any rate, Wertheimer was hooked. It did not take him long before he was publishing works based on these fragments and hankering to read, study and publish more. Financial need, however, would soon force him to sell what little he had in the way of these precious medieval sources. Now he would have to work out a way to buy them, cram their contents and then sell them on to fund his continued scholarly work.[27]

CHESTER'S CAREFULLY SELECTED BATCH OF MSS, sourced directly from the Ben Ezra Synagogue, had all been mailed off to Oxford. On board his *dahabiyeh*, the humorously named 'Rudder Grange', he waited to hear back about them. Thirteen days later, the post brought the disappointing news that Neubauer had fixed a lower price on the manuscripts than hoped. Not that Chester had sought to make his fortune from them – his greater concern to enrich England's museums meant that he often accepted lower prices for his antiquities sales – but he had thought they might be inherently more valuable than Neubauer's low price suggested.

Chester was also alarmed that Nicholson was writing about the manuscripts so openly on a postcard. He warned him against such behaviour in future as it could lead to 'their being watched for & confiscated in the post!' Even though it would not be legal to do so, he explained, it would not make a difference 'with the powers that be'.[28] The 'powers that be' no doubt referred to the leadership of the French Egyptologist, Eugène Grébaut, who had been appointed head of the Service des Antiquites after Maspero had retired from ill health.

Grébaut's excavation and export policies and his methods of imposing them quickly became unpopular with Egyptologists and local dealers. But Chester, who would later refer to the situation as 'Grébaut's regime of tyranny', always managed to find a work around. To keep his dispatches a secret, he decided that the best method was to send them in discrete consignments along with separate postcards detailing them so as not to raise suspicions.

Secret dispatches from Cairo (1890–2)

CHESTER HEADED BACK TO ENGLAND IN MARCH, 1890, at the end of the winter season. He travelled via Naples, Italy, where from his hotel room he wrote to present additional items for sale: 'fragments of papyri, a beautifully written Syriac book and two great Hebrew Vols'. Unlike most of his other sales, none of the items sent from Italy were provenanced. One of the 'great Hebrew Vols' must have been the Bodleian's 199ff, octavo-sized, paper copy of the Mishnah, with Maimonides commentary, which was purchased from Chester that same year.[1] A known Italian contact was the Cairo-born Italian Egyptologist Rodolfo Vittorio Lanzone, and Chester's letters from before this time and after reveal that they were on good terms. Lanzone had taken a scholarly interest in a Hebrew and Old Italian map that Chester had sold to Cambridge University Library in 1866 and, as a later letter reveals, he advised Chester on the importance of the pieces of papyri that he was now offering to the Bodleian.[2]

Over the summer months, Chester spent some time at the Ashmolean Museum cataloguing his donation of Hittite and Phoenician seals. He took the papyri over to the Bodleian for Nicholson to inspect and was introduced to Neubauer. They surely discussed the fragments found in the Ben Ezra Synagogue and, despite the low prices offered for the first batch, Neubauer must have explained why others were worth pursuing. Thus, when Chester returned to Cairo in November 1890, he quickly sent news that he was dispatching a consignment of two small packets of Hebrew manuscript fragments. One piece he noted 'looks very old & curious', and he gave notice that he expected to 'send more soon'.[3]

Undoubtedly, after arriving in Cairo, Chester must have used his established connections to help him find out what the community had done with the many other materials he had seen lying on the floor of the 'laid open' synagogue room. To this end, a well-connected local resident and someone familiar with affairs in and around Cairo would be needed. Such help may have been received from the Reverend Gulian Lansing, whose missionary work in al-Fustat, combined with his Hebraic interests and known visits to the Ben Ezra Synagogue, gave him perfect insider knowledge. However, Lansing may have been otherwise engaged: his wife, Sarah Dales, had died in November 1889 and exactly one year later, he temporarily relocated to the United States on account of his own declining health.[4]

Whether he gained help to locate the fragments from a trusted dealer, or someone at the American Mission, or from someone entirely different, such as the well-connected Dr Grant, Chester needed to find a way to buy and mail batches of them without alerting the authorities and in line with his own travel plans. Given Neubauer's prevailing interest in finding early manuscript editions of important Hebrew works, multi-folio manuscripts over fragmentary pages, and vellum above paper, the supplier would need to have the ability to sort through and select from the recently discovered materials wherever they were now being stored. The supplier would therefore need key connections on the ground.

In 1890, Cairo was teeming with antiquities dealers, from individuals selling *anteekas* as a side-line to full-scale enterprises with multiple agents. Of the named dealers operating at that time, six are known to have dealt with genizah fragments either before or after Chester's time: Count Riamo d'Hulst, Haggi Mahomedo, an obscure dealer working as an agent of 'Ali Abd el-Haj el-Gabiri (Ali el-Arabi), Otto Theodor Graf, Giovanni Dattari and Maurice Nahman. The Count, despite his extensive later involvement with genizah fragments, could not have been Chester's supplier. Chester and d'Hulst were certainly known to one another: Flinders Petrie recalled their joint attendance at one of Dr Grant's soirees, and d'Hulst even described Chester as a friend. But they could not have encountered each other when Chester first discovered the fragments in 1889; in fact, Chester hid his connection to the genizah fragments so well that d'Hulst fully believed that he was barely involved with them, if at all.[5] Otto Theodor Graf's papyri sales to Austria included several hundred Hebrew paper and vellum fragments. Since he most likely acquired them through an agent or scout, the pieces were probably bundled up as part of a wholesale purchase and became mixed up with his existing inventory.[6] With his prominent dealings in papyri, mummy portraits and ancient tablets, which were large scale and highly profitable, it is unlikely that Graf would have engaged in an ongoing effort to seek out and acquire comparatively low-profit bundles of Hebrew fragments for Chester.

Of the six dealers later linked to genizah fragments, it can be assumed that Chester had some connection with Ali el-Arabi. In addition to the many artefacts he purchased from the Giza region, his own earlier collection of papyri must have come from Ali el-Arabi who, working in partnership with another major supplier, Farag Ismaïn, sold thousands of papyri from the Fayum to private collectors and institutions around the world.[7] Ali el-Arabi was also associated, through his agent Haggi Mahomedo, to the supply of a small collection of genizah manuscripts (largely epistolary fragments) purchased in 1908 by Charles Lang Freer. Arabi had asked Haggi Mahomedo to locate the mysterious 'digger', who had previously unearthed a fourth- or fifth-century Greek Bible manuscript now known as the Washington Codex. The codex had been purchased by Freer in 1906, and, two years later, he was seeking to recover additional manuscripts, as well as the wooden table upon which they had been written. When he met with Freer in Cairo, in addition to a small, ivory inlaid table and an Isis figurine, Haggi Mahomedo brought him 'fifty single sheets of "Hebrew Arabic" manuscript fragments'. He claimed that they had all been found by the 'digger' in the same location as the Bible manuscripts. The much-contested find spot may have been near the White Monastery in Saqqara or the monastery of St. Jeremiah near Giza or the monasteries of the Nitrean Desert, but Freer did not believe that 'Hebrew Arabic' fragments came from the same find spot as the other manuscripts or objects and, knowing about the history of the so-called 'Cairo Genizah', he determined that they must have come from the Ben Ezra Synagogue.[8]

Beyond this incident, no other firm evidence exists to prove that the Giza dealers were involved with genizah manuscripts at an earlier stage although, in terms of logistics, Giza was the perfect spot for uncovering manuscripts that might have been buried near the former synagogue in Dammuh, and it was also conveniently close to al-Fustat. Wherever his supplier was based, Chester clearly stated in the letters he dispatched to Oxford from the Nile that he could only obtain Hebrew fragments in Cairo.

Still, there was little demand for medieval fragments of known works, and fragments containing evidence of medieval life could hardly appeal to scholars whose main interests lay in uncovering texts and languages from more ancient times. Given the lower demand and the small profits to be made on such sales, it is likely that Chester's intermediary was someone for whom antiquities dealing was either a side-line, or someone who was in the early stage of their antiquities career. One dealer who fit this bill was the Cairo-based Italian antiquarian and numismatist Giovanni Dattari. In the 1890s, Dattari was working for Thomas Cook & Son near the Shepheard's Hotel while slowly building up his collections of antiquities and coins, which he would sell from his private apartment. Chester was deeply interested in collecting coins too, supplying large collections of them to both the British Museum and the Bodleian, and he may have purchased some from Dattari, although the budding numismatist did not acquire his first major collection of coins until 1891.[9]

Dattari can be linked to sales of genizah manuscripts in 1896 when he sold 350 fragments encased in a metal tin to Albert Nicole, son of Jules Nicole, the Geneva scholar and collector of Greek papyri. Undoubtedly, it was an accidental purchase since Nicole had asked Dattari to find him some papyri fragments like the ones he had already acquired from his store. The mix-up was not unexpected since Dattari had confided to Nicole that miscellaneous items were often bundled up together to increase the value of the sale. For Dattari to buy a much-coveted item, like medals or coins, he often had to purchase them together with other items as a bundle.[10] Furthermore, the ubiquitous tin box – hundreds of which were produced during excavations at Oxyrhynchus to store the massive amounts of papyri recovered, as well as other 'miscellaneous *anticas*' – may have been another misleading factor.[11]

Chester's purchases were not made at random. He clearly made every effort to obtain substantial-looking manuscripts he thought would be of interest to Neubauer, which included paying higher prices for subsequent instalments. Of all the genizah fragments that would come the Bodleian's way, Chester supplied the greatest number of multi-folio items on vellum. Chester's supplier must have been granted the ability to select quality fragments himself, or to request the selection of certain types of fragments from whoever had hidden away the piles of fragments or from whoever was now guarding them. And he would have needed the right contacts and/or the ability to communicate these needs in either Hebrew or Arabic.

Good connections in the Jewish community were certainly possessed by Maurice Nahman, who could speak fluent French, English and Arabic and had at least a rudimentary knowledge of Hebrew from his youth. Like his older friend and associate

Dattari, Nahman began dealing in the 1890s from his private apartment, which was located on Sharia Sheikh Abu el-Sibâ close to his workplace at the Crédit Fonciér Égyptien. Dattari and Nahman may have become known to one another through shared Italian connections – Nahman married two Italian women during his lifetime – or simply through their mutual interests. Both were associated with Ali el-Arabi, making regular purchases from him. But it was Nahman, also being the longer lived of the three, who eventually became the best known, gaining a broad international reputation and impressive clientele list.[12] Yet as to his first activities in the field – what he was buying and selling and to whom – little to nothing is known. For certain, in the days before official licensing, and as 22-year-old starting out under the watchful eyes of Grébaut's officials, discretion would have been the better part of valour. As the Belgian Egyptologist Jean Capart noted in the obituary he prepared for Nahman: if Maurice Nahman had ever kept a diary, Egyptologists would have learnt many secrets that were closed to them.[13]

A firm connection between Nahman and the sale of genizah fragments can be established in the 1920s through his papyri sales to the Egyptologists Bernard Pyne Grenfell and Francis W. Kelsey. The inventory of these purchases in the University of Michigan Library (P. Mich. Inv. 531–3) includes three Hebrew manuscript fragments, one of which matches up with fragments in other genizah collections.[14] With sellers failing to disclose provenance and eager buyers snapping up desirable objects whenever they could lay their hands on them, it is not surprising to encounter greater numbers of such motley assemblages. Over time, Nahman clearly developed a marketing strategy of offering assembled 'hoards' of antiquities for sale over individual items.[15] Aside from his connections and method of assembling collections, Nahman's long history of dealing in Coptic books, papyri and fragments could be the smoking gun that ties him to Chester's genizah purchases.

In addition to the Coptic and Syriac manuscripts already floating around the Cairo markets, thanks to those who had rummaged through the monasteries in prior decades, including Chester himself, some of the old Coptic books appearing on the markets for sale may have come about indirectly through the work of the American Mission. In their ongoing efforts to convert the Copts to Protestantism, the mission provided them with a steady stream of newly printed copies of the New Testament in modern Arabic to replace their orthodox copies in the Coptic language. In 1891, Andrew Watson, Lansing's colleague in the Cairo mission, reported their success with the Copt children who 'have in large numbers attended our schools' and with the adults who 'have eagerly purchased our books'. He also noted that, thanks to the work of the mission, some churches had removed the pictures they worshipped to a private room, and large portions of the Coptic Church services were now being conducted in Arabic rather than the 'dead Coptic'.[16] As the Mission gained ever greater success in converting the services to Arabic, some of the community's 'dead' old Coptic books and manuscripts may have been sold off.

CHESTER LISTED HIS RECENT HEBREW MSS CONSIGNMENTS in a long letter sent to Nicholson on 29 November 1890.[17] He was worried about registering too many of his packages, having heard on 'pretty good authority' that officials could stop and search parcels at the post office. The list included two unregistered packets of Hebrew manuscripts sent nine days earlier on the 20th, and five unregistered sent three days after that. After allowing another three days to pass, and hoping that his previous dispatches had gone unnoticed, Chester mailed off two unregistered Arabic books. On the next day, the 27th, he placed four Coptic books in the mail, registering two of them together with a postcard noting: 'The Vocabulary is, I believe, very scarce, & the Revelations rare too.' He also let Nicholson know that he was expecting to receive additional Hebrew manuscripts, but he would not send them until he had heard that the others had arrived safely. On 28 November, he dispatched five registered packets of Hebrew manuscripts, noting that one was a palimpsest (a manuscript whose text has been scraped away and written over by another), and that 'the under writing looks very old'.

Chester wasn't mistaken about the under writing. The Oxford Aramaic and Hebrew scholar G. H. Gwilliam subsequently hailed the palimpsest as a great treasure after he realized that underneath the Hebrew script (sections of the Mishnah) lay traces of rubbed out words from an ancient Palestinian Syriac (Christian Palestinian Aramaic) translation of portions of the Old and New Testaments. A note in the Bodleian archive of Chester's letters, records the payments that were made to him for the packets he sent late in 1890, including a more generous payment of £2 6s. 0d. for the palimpsest.[18]

Before signing off his letter, Chester informed Nicholson that he was 'in treaty for 2 large Arabic MSS, with Coptic illuminations resembling the curious designs in some of the textiles'. He also expected to receive another batch of Hebrew fragments, which he would refrain from sending until he heard that the others had arrived safely. On 9 December, the date of his next postcard, Chester divulged that he had mailed off two registered packets of manuscripts during his visit to Zagazig. In the same postcard, in addition to giving notice that he was sending along more packets, he also disclosed that he intended to 'divert the next batches to Dr Neubauer'. No doubt the fear of getting caught led him to try mailing the manuscripts from alternative locations and to different postal addresses. On the 14th, he sent five packets to Nicholson from Cairo, disclosing his hope that 'some of this batch will be more valuable, as I have paid more for them'. The supplier had also sold him another leaf of the Palestinian Syriac palimpsest with Hebrew upper writing. Chester's connection to these palimpsests would later be forgotten, however. When Gwilliam published the pieces in 1893, he recalled that the Bodleian had received them from Chester, but by the time the leaves were catalogued, they were simply designated as 'from the Genizah (1892?)'[19]

In early January 1891, Chester was on the Nile and, after having sent several urgent messages worrying about the receipt of his letters and parcels, he finally heard back from the Bodleian. He was surprised and disappointed in the price offered for the Coptic vocabulary: 'I know they are <u>very scarce</u> in Egypt & although I have been on the look out for years, it is the first I have met with. I should not like to take less than £2 for it.' He had additional Hebrew fragments for them too but, having been asked questions at the post office on the previous occasion, and having had to certify that the items were not Arabic or Egyptian, he preferred to wait a while before sending them.

Even though he was happy to wait to get back to Cairo before acquiring any more Hebrew manuscripts, the Bodleian, apparently, was not. The Bodleian side of the correspondence is now missing but, based on Chester's responses to Nicholson, they were keenly interested in receiving additional Hebrew manuscripts. The increase in demand may have been due to the better quality of the supply, which recently included the ancient writings in palimpsest form.[20] In one of his postcards, sent on 4 February from Girgeh near Luxor, he further placated Nicholson: 'I cannot move in the matter of obtaining more mss until we reach Cairo which I earnestly trust will be in less than 3 weeks. I will then lose no time & will forward what I get as soon as possible.' By the time he reached Cairo in late February, he informed him right away that he was sending 'two little harbingers of a larger flight in the week' and to let 'Dr. N' fix a fair price.[21]

Before leaving Egypt in early March, Chester mailed two packets of Hebrew manuscripts from Alexandria by registered post. These last two batches, he told Nicholson, 'must contain something curious'. It is unclear why he believed this batch contained more interesting items than previous consignments, but the materials in the Bodleian attributed to him from 1891 certainly comprise a greater amount of vellum, as well as a greater number of grammatical works, Arabic theological and astrological treatises, medieval philosophical, mystical and medical works than the materials he had hand-picked from the newly exposed room in the Ben Ezra Synagogue.

By the end of March 1891, Chester was back in Italy on his return journey to England. Writing from Rome, he confirmed to Nicholson that he had 'no more manuscripts to send'. Yet, one month later, and back in London, he sent him another message with an odd and unexpected admission: 'I am sorry to say I failed to get off the 3 accompanying packets of MSS from Egypt.'[22] Since he also promised to send the Bodleian '2 books & some Coptic Papyrus fragments soon & some coins', it seems that everything must have been packed up with some of his luggage and shipped off to England before he visited Italy. This may have proved another effective way for Chester to disguise his exports.

According to E. A. Wallis Budge, whose account of Chester tended to overplay the picaresque and downplay his expertise, Chester was someone who

> got into difficulties with the officers of Customs in every port and baffled them by feigning ignorance of the language and making a judicious use of *bakhshish*. His friends never understood how he managed to persuade the officials that his heavy leather bags contained nothing but 'wearing apparel' when they were filled with pottery, bronze statues, stone stelae and even parts of coffins.[23]

Of the over 8,800 objects, including fragmentary coffins, that the British Museum acquired from Chester, museum records show that, in 1891, 292 objects came from Egypt. That same year, Chester also sold a small selection of Hebrew fragments to Cambridge University Library. These pieces formed a few non-consecutive folios that had come loose from Hebrew prayer books and other liturgical works.[24] They may have been items that Neubauer rejected. Otherwise, no records exist to show that any of Chester's offerings to the Bodleian were sent back to him or sold on to someone else. In fact, the Bodleian's keen interest in the fragments may be deduced from Chester's response to Nicholson that he was pleased to be able to get to the Bodleian 'what cannot often be obtainable', as well as from the comparatively higher prices paid to Chester than the prices paid to other later fragment sellers.

HEBREW FRAGMENTS WERE BROUGHT TO AMERICA BY CYRUS ADLER between March and April 1891. Since becoming America's first PhD in Semitics in 1887, in addition to teaching the subject at John Hopkins, Adler had gained the position of assistant honorary curator in the Department of Antiquities at the United States National Museum. The position had come about thanks to Adler's proposal to form a collection of casts of Near Eastern antiquities, which led to the creation of a section of Oriental Antiquities within the department. Alongside his abiding interest in biblical archaeology, Adler had developed an equal enthusiasm for museums and a keen appreciation of the power of the exhibit to inform and instruct. According to one biographer, Adler regarded 'exhibits and exhibitions as carriers of international good will and as a means of strengthening and improving the political and cultural ties among the nations'. Behind this notion, no doubt, Adler discerned how exhibits could be a force for good in assisting the ongoing exertions of the *Wissenschaft* scholars to defend and promote accurate knowledge of Judaism.

The first exhibition of Oriental Antiquities inside the National Museum opened in February 1889, and as a vindication of his sense of popular interest, over 100,000 visitors came to see it. Included in the exhibit were Jewish ceremonial items, many of which Adler had obtained through his family and family connections, including the Sulzbergers and Friedenwalds, who would also eventually be involved in collecting genizah fragments. The creation of a collection of Jewish ceremonial objects was a first step in instituting a Section of Religious Ceremonials in the National Museum, which was fully established after the World's Columbian Exposition. Adler was appointed as the Exposition's Special Commissioner to Turkey, Egypt, Tunisia, Algeria and Morocco in 1890. For the next fifteenth months of his life, he travelled around these countries, meeting with government officials, industrialists, merchants and private financiers to elicit their support through funding and through actual physical participation. In acquiring pieces for the Exposition, the museum stressed the importance of obtaining with each piece the object's history and provenance.

Even so, Adler was not above attempting to acquire pieces whenever and however he could do so. In between meetings with potential supporters and partners for the project, Adler also purchased artefacts and manuscripts for the Exposition and future museum exhibitions. In the Cairo markets, he purchased a bundle of Hebrew and Arabic fragments from an antiquities dealer. When he reflected upon this purchase in 1916, he emphasized the fact that the manuscripts' origin (i.e. their findspot) was not then known to him. Twenty-five years later, he shared more details about the discovery in his memoir. Here he recalled wandering often around the shops in Cairo and how he one day noticed:

> several trays full of parchment leaves written in Hebrew, which the merchant had labeled anticas. I saw at a glance that these were very old . . . indicating an interest in the whole lot I purchased them, big and little, some of the pieces only one sheet, some of them forty or fifty pages, at the enormous price of one shilling per unit.[25]

With the passage of time and the advent of the Cairo Genizah discovery, Adler later declared his pieces to have been among the first to have come from that source.

Adler acquired forty-nine manuscripts in all. Many of them, like Chester's pieces, were multi-folio items on vellum; a few were well-preserved sections of codices bound with string; most held biblical, rabbinic or liturgical content and hardly any were documentary or epistolary in nature. One of Adler's manuscripts belongs with leaves that Chester retrieved directly from the Ben Ezra Synagogue. Both portions of the manuscript were still in excellent condition. Fragmentary leaves from the same manuscript were also discovered in collections acquired at a later period, although these later fragments had suffered tears and staining. Apart from this match, and a few others, it is impossible to determine whether all originally came from the same find spot; some of the more substantial pieces, and works of a later date, may have become mixed up with pieces already in the shop's existing inventory.

CHESTER RESUMED BUYING HEBREW FRAGMENTS IN CAIRO after he returned there in November 1891. In trying to outwit the authorities, he disclosed that he would number the consignments rather than label them. He did not know it, but this was to be his last season in Egypt. An influenza pandemic, the so-called Russian Flu, had raged across Europe and the United States starting in 1889 and, thanks to the international expansion of shipping, road and rail networks, a second wave of the disease reached other parts of the world much faster, including the Middle East.

Chester was not about to let anything curtail his travel plans: despite having a respiratory illness that had caused him to quit his ministerial post twenty-seven years earlier, he had become a traveller and explorer par excellence. Still, signs of his deteriorating health regularly cropped up in his letters to the Bodleian. Writing to Nicholson from London in April 1890, he had included a postscript about his 'bad cough' and, after returning to Egypt in November 1890, he mentioned again his 'very bad cough'. The following November, he told Nicholson that he had a 'dreadful cough' and finally, in December 1891, he confided: 'My cough is very bad, but I hope to reach my dahabeyeh at Siout tomorrow, & to be better on the Nile.'

In between waiting for a houseboat and longing for the famous restorative powers of the river, Chester still managed to dispatch some packets of manuscripts that December. The packages also contained a papyrus fragment that he had discovered with Sayce in the Fayum.[26] While Chester was finally getting some respite on the Nile, two female scholar-adventurers from Cambridge arrived in Cairo searching for ancient Syriac manuscripts.

AGNES SMITH LEWIS AND MARGARET DUNLOP GIBSON would later become pivotal figures in the story of the genizah manuscripts. But in 1892, the Presbyterian twin sisters had their sights set on uncovering ancient Christian texts. It was Margaret's second trip to Egypt and Agnes's third. Agnes had visited without Margaret while on a trip to Cyprus with her friend, Grace Blyth. Before going on to Cyprus, the friends spent several months in Egypt so that Agnes could develop her Arabic language skills by attending the American Mission school in Cairo for four hours each day and the Arabic services on Sundays.[27]

Arabic was not the only language that Agnes knew. Growing up, the twins had accompanied their father (their sole living parent) on trips abroad. These special holidays were granted to them only after they had learnt the language of their country of destination. In this way, the twins gained fluency in French, German, Spanish and Italian. At the age of twenty-three, the death of their father left them with a large inheritance, and not being inclined to wallow in unproductive mourning, they made a fitting tribute to him by embarking on a tour of Europe and the Middle East. Their linguistic abilities enabled them to see and do things normally barred to unmarried British women, and their unusual adventures were captured by Agnes in a fictionalized account, which she published under the title *Eastern Pilgrims*.

Following the death of Agnes's husband, the Reverend Samuel Savage Lewis, in 1891, the sisters began to plan a trip to St. Catherine's Monastery in the Sinai Peninsula. As the site identified with Moses' vision of the Burning Bush, a symbol of the twins' Presbyterian Church, it had long held great appeal to Agnes. The sisters had recently begun to study Hebrew and Arabic, and Agnes's great interest in James Rendel Harris's discovery of *The Apology of Aristides* in St. Catherine's Monastery made her determined to learn Syriac. The young Revd Robert Kennett (later Cambridge Regius Professor of Hebrew) tutored her, and the equally young Francis Crawford Burkitt (later a world-leading Syriac scholar) instructed her in the writing of the Estrangelo script. Through a chance meeting with his wife, Helen, Agnes was introduced to Harris and the four became friends. Harris confided to the sisters the fact that important manuscripts were still to be found at Sinai, and he entrusted them with the secret of the chests of Syriac manuscripts in the monastery's dark closet. Hoping that they could somehow gain access to them, he also taught them how to use a camera.

The twins' remarkable journey to St. Catherine's Monastery between January and February 1892 was recounted in detail by Margaret in *How the Codex Was Found*, using Agnes's journals.[28] Their friends had advised them that the monks would not welcome women at the monastery, much less give them the opportunity to view manuscripts. Undeterred, they were led through the desert by a dragoman recommended to them by Andrew Watson of the American Mission. Fortunately, at the end of the gruelling journey through the desert on camel back, the sisters were greeted warmly by the monks. The monastery's librarian Father Galaktéon, according to Agnes, was 'delighted at being able to converse with us in their own tongue, and to read descriptions of their own birthplaces in the Greek edition of my book *Glimpses of Greek Life and Scenery*'.

In a much later account of their trip, partly written to quell false reports circulating about her manuscript discoveries, Agnes reported that she had boldly asked to see the 'oldest Syriac manuscripts, particularly those which Dr. Harris had not time to examine' so that she could take a report to him. Thanks to Galaktéon's regard for Harris, Agnes was allowed without reserve to explore the highly anticipated 'dark closet'. The second manuscript that she took into her hands revealed itself to be a great treasure: a 358-page Greek codex with traces of Syriac script lying rubbed underneath.

Agnes was undoubtedly the first person to examine this manuscript in a long time: its state of preservation was so poor that only a steam kettle could separate its leaves. The upper script of the palimpsest comprised a Greek martyrology of female saints written in the eighth century by John the Recluse of Beth-Mari. The lower script, discerned thanks to Agnes's keen eyesight and knowledge of Syriac, was from the Gospels. As she examined the codex more closely, she found a date in the colophon of the upper text, making her realize that the lower script was at least several centuries older. It would, in fact, prove to be the earliest Syriac version of the Gospels ever discovered.

CHESTER WAS STILL RECOVERING ON THE NILE while the twin sisters were photographing their amazing discoveries in the dark closet of the Sinai monastery. When he arrived at Luxor in late January 1892, he promised to send Nicholson additional manuscripts from Cairo in March. He also reported that the influenza epidemic was 'raging in Cairo'. The following month, however, in a postcard dated 23 February 1892, sent from 'Near Cairo', Chester also let Nicholson know that another four packages of manuscripts were on their way.

This information suggests that Chester's supplier was either someone who was located near Cairo or that it was someone willing to deliver or courier packages to him. With the influenza complicating travel arrangements, Chester could not supply the Bodleian with a Cairo mailing address for the time being, but he added that he was 'progressing favourably though very slowly' and that he was 'very weak and emaciated'. Despite his poor health, he continued to negotiate the purchase of manuscripts, informing Nicholson that: 'There may be one more batch in a week's time; that will be the last'. The following week, in a postcard stamped 'Guiza' (Giza), he sent news that he hoped to send 'another batch on Friday'.

By the time Friday came around, Chester was obliged to send a short missive from his room at the Shepheard's Hotel that he had been 'unable to get any more Hebr. MSS'. No further explanation was offered. Chester quickly digressed to inform Nicholson that he would be in Naples by 18 March, and that he was slowly improving. Chester's brief note suggests that there was nothing untoward about his inability to acquire the last batch of manuscripts. However, a letter sent the very next day to *The Academy* journal from his hotel in Ramleh casts a different light on the situation. In a dramatic opening, he declared: 'Permit me to draw public attention to an almost incredible act of vandalism which was perpetrated during the last year in Egypt'. With the reader's attention caught, he proceeded to describe the Roman Fortress of Babylon in Old Cairo and its ancient synagogue, followed by the announcement:

> All this is now a thing of the past. The Jews – and I suppose they had a legal right 'to do what they would with their own' – have razed the ancient church and synagogue to the ground, and in its place have erected a hideous square abomination, supported literally on iron pillars.[29]

If he was outraged by the synagogue's renovation, he was even more excised by the idea that both the French and English authorities could have allowed 'the simultaneous destruction of the fine Roman wall which bounded the property, and with it the bastion-tower'. Of both structures, he reported, 'not a vestige now remains'. A similar report was provided one year later by the Count d'Hulst in a letter to *The Academy* lamenting the various restorations to Islamic monuments:

The beauties of the Mu'allaka ... have largely disappeared since a recent 'restoration'. The Jewish Synagogue, the desecrated Church of St. Michael's, two towers and part of the wall of the Kasr Esh Shemmah, have also been pulled down, to make place for a new synagogue. Apparently, nobody interfered.[30]

Chester's letter provides an end-date for the completion of the Ben Ezra Synagogue rebuild about which, little else was recorded. The surprise and condemnation expressed in the letter suggest that his discovery of the newly erected 'hideous square abomination' had taken place only recently. Had he seen it earlier, it would have been out of character for the outspoken Chester to have waited to express his incredulity, even privately to Nicholson, as he had done when he first saw the synagogue being dismantled back in 1889.

Seen in this light, Chester's inability to get 'any more Hebr. MSS' may have been brought about by the relocation of the manuscripts to a new hiding place. Chester's supplier may have shared the news about the Ben Ezra Synagogue prompting him to take an impromptu visit to see it for himself. Horrified by the loss of the former church and the Roman buildings, he made sure to fire off a letter to *The Academy* as soon as he was comfortably settled in Ramleh. After leaving Egypt in a state of annoyance, the added stress of the journey home must have exacerbated his underlying health condition already weakened by his exposure to the flu. By the time he reached Italy, he was hospitalized in Naples with a suspected case of angina pectoris. As Henry Wallis confided to A. W. Franks, who no doubt was waiting to see what Chester was bringing him for the British Museum, the medical staff thought 'he might be carried off at any moment'. Chester made it back to London, but on his postcard sent from Egypt back in March, Nicholson added a small historical note: 'The last he ever wrote us. He died in a London private hospital a month or two later.'[31]

In Egypt, the Khedive Muḥammad Tawfīq Pasha, the first ruler to have governed under British control, also succumbed to influenza. His young son ʿAbbās Ḥilmī II would hold the position for the next twenty-two years, navigating a difficult path between the rising nationalist movement and the continued presence of the British in the hope of restoring the Khedivate and the special autonomous status that had previously been granted to Egypt by the Ottoman Sultan.[32] In this new era, with the ancient Ben Ezra Synagogue 'restored out of all knowledge', and most of the figures who had once seen manuscripts within it now gone, any possibility of locating the original find spot, or find spots, for the various Hebrew fragments that had emerged out of Egypt prior to 1892 was apparently lost forever.

Lost provenance (1892–3)

ADOLF NEUBAUER KEENLY FELT THE LOSS of such a reliable and knowledgeable agent in the field as Greville Chester. When the steady flow of medieval Hebrew manuscripts arriving in the Bodleian's mail came to a halt, it may have prompted him to mention the loss, and the potential finds still out there, to his good friend Archibald Henry Sayce during one of their regular Sunday walks.[1] With his key connections to the Egypt Exploration Fund, the Antiquities Service, local dealers, annual visitors like himself, as well as to Dr Grant (his physician in Cairo), Sayce was perfectly placed to make subtle enquiries on Neubauer's behalf.

The exact sequence of events that led Sayce to commission the Count d'Hulst to this task is unclear. Yet given the unexpected donation of Hebrew fragments from the Egypt Exploration Fund two years prior, it might have seemed a wise place for him to start asking questions. At any rate, this scenario corresponds to information sent six years later from d'Hulst to the Bodleian librarian, E. W. B. Nicholson:

> Years ago, when I carried on some excavations for the Egypt Exploration Fund at Old Cairo, I gathered some of the fragments they cast out as worthless. As they appeared to me of some value, I forwarded them on to our committee, all the papers could have been had at that time for £20. Unhappily these fragments were kept in London for a year or two before being forwarded on to you. After you had obtained them, Prof. Sayce asked me to try & find out what had become of the Cairo MS. & I have been connected with the matter ever since.[2]

With the Ben Ezra Synagogue rebuilt, and the fate of the manuscripts being kept secret by one or more of the synagogue's guardians, d'Hulst would have many conversations ahead of him before he finally encountered a hoard in a subterranean storage place late in 1894. His ultimate discovery, he later recalled to librarian Falconer Madan, involved 'many and great difficulties in the way of their acquisition'. However, his visit to Old Cairo at some point late in 1892 could have only left him with unanswered questions with regards to the manuscripts' whereabouts. That he saw the new synagogue building is evidenced by the notice he sent to *The Academy* about the restoration work. But if he had spoken to a custodian, he or she must have been unforthcoming about the genizah fragments, for the most d'Hulst was able to acquire at that point from an unknown source and location was, in his own words, a 'small lot of MSS'.

Writing to him in January 1893, Sayce assured d'Hulst that Neubauer would like to have the MSS, and he promised to send a cheque once he knew where to send it. However, d'Hulst's personal connection to these fragments was not recorded in the Bodleian's records. The only record that remains of their purchase is a payment of £10 given to Sayce in June. The fragments must have been deemed worthy of this relatively high amount; in fact, it was the highest amount recorded in the Bodleian Ledger for Hebrew manuscripts that year.[3]

By tracing the fragments back through subsequent publications and through the errors made in cataloguing them, it is highly probable that d'Hulst's 'small lot' of manuscripts contained ancient copies of the biblical books of Numbers and Wisdom texts written in Palestinian Syriac, rubbed out and overwritten by sections of a rabbinic text known as *Sifra*. Even though the link to both d'Hulst and Sayce was later obscured by the librarian, Arthur Ernest Cowley, who only noted in the index to the published catalogue that these fragments were 'from the Geniza (1892?)', the firm connection to Sayce was established when George Henry Gwilliam first published them in 1896. In his introduction to the work, Gwilliam noted that 'Shortly after the publication [1893] of the five fragments of Palestinian Syriac [from Chester in 1891] . . . two more fragments were procured for the Bodleian Library by Professor Sayce'. Gwilliam had not published Sayce's fragments right away in 1893 as, in the meantime, he had heard that important Syriac palimpsests from other quarters were coming to light and that it was prudent to wait.

Nevertheless, the fact that d'Hulst had visited the new synagogue late in 1892 does not mean that his 'small lot of MSS' was from the same location. He could not even be sure if any of the manuscripts he had witnessed being thrown out in 1889 had been placed back inside. Structurally, the new building contained two hidden spaces at the back of the women's gallery on the second floor. Later testimony confirms that the one on the right had a door, and the one on the left was sealed off, apart from a small, window-shaped opening near the ceiling. Both spaces, and the synagogue's newly formed basement area, could potentially be used as genizot. Yet, back in 1889, while the structure was being rebuilt up from its foundations, given the choice between burying the manuscripts or finding another temporary storage area prior to the building of the new genizah chamber, burial would have presented an easier solution needing fewer long-term resources regarding storage space and manpower. Chester's great interest in the pieces, as well as the interest shown by other dealers in buying the bundles left out in the yard, however, probably induced someone to bag up and set aside the most saleable-looking pieces while the rest were tossed into the nearby rubbish mounds, buried or interred elsewhere.

One of the synagogue beadles, named Bechor, later 'betrayed' such a secret, claiming that he had buried ten bags of manuscripts in a graveyard far from town.[4] This graveyard may have been the large Bassatine Cemetery whose mausoleum-style tombs and natural caves offered numerous accessible places for internment and retrieval, as well as hiding places not easily discovered by others. The decision to discard or bury scraps and keep aside whole sections could explain the difference between the manuscripts retrieved by d'Hulst in the rubbish mounds to those acquired by Chester through his agent. The fact that substantial sections of manuscripts are now to be found spread across collections around the world suggests that, over time, the larger book structures that had been kept aside were broken down into smaller pieces for sales purposes.

ARCHDUKE RAINER OF AUSTRIA ACQUIRED HEBREW FRAGMENTS at some point between 1889 and 1892. The Hebrew fragments, several hundred pieces, were purchased as part of a massive collection of papyrus fragments from the Viennese dealer, Otto Theodor Graf, who had started to gather papyri for Austria in the early 1880s at the urging of the orientalist Josef von Karabacek. In fact, Graf was so successful at gathering papyri and manuscripts, that other antiquarians, like the Count d'Hulst, were led to assume that he had 'very good agents in the country' scouting out the latest finds.[5] They were not wrong: Graf commissioned countless local small dealers to scour the Fayum and other sites in Lower and Central Egypt, such as El Ashmunein and Ihnasiya el-Medina, to find the papyri on his behalf. Archduke Rainer Ferdinand, an Austrian politician and member of the Imperial family, purchased the papyri and other fragments and eventually presented the entire collection to Emperor Franz Josef I. The collection was housed in the Austrian Imperial Library (today the Austrian National Library).[6]

Scholarship on the Rainer collection took place almost immediately: a first volume was published in 1886 dealing with various notable papyrus fragments in Greek, Arabic and Coptic. Several of the papyri fragments containing portions of early Hebrew liturgy were described by the Austrian Jewish scholars, David Heinrich Müller and David Kaufmann. When Josef von Karabacek published a fifth volume of Rainer's fragments in 1892, it included another article by Müller and Kaufman: the transcription, translation and description of an eleventh-century letter addressed to the Palestinian Jewish leader Solomon ben Judah. These pieces, and the other Hebrew fragments, they declared, 'probably came from a synagogue in Old Cairo'. Beyond this assertion, they did not provide any further explanation as to why they thought or knew this to be the case.[7] The Viennese Jewish scholar, Abraham Epstein had also examined fragments in the Archduke Rainer collection, and in reviewing Müller and Kaufmann's work, he concluded that the fragments must have come from the same genizah chamber above the synagogue in Old Cairo that Jacob Saphir had once seen and described. Epstein also supposed that Müller and Kaufmann had followed the same process of deduction, leading them to determine that the fragments were from a 'synagogue in Old Cairo'.[8] In fact, Epstein was so sure of the connection himself, he erroneously attributed the same level of conviction (*sans doute*) to Müller and Kaufmann, whereas they had used the term 'probably' (*wahrscheinlich*). Kaufmann only made the connection to Saphir and the Ben Ezra Synagogue some years later in an attempt to posit the same provenance to the many fragments, including his own, that had come out of Egypt. But at this point, he had either not made the connection, or he was being purposefully vague in order not to expose the source from which he too was beginning to acquire fragments for his own collection.

ANOTHER PACKAGE OF MSS ARRIVED IN OXFORD LATE IN 1892 while Neubauer was waiting to hear news from Sayce. The package consisted of 68 items (608 manuscript leaves), most of which were vellum pieces in good condition. Many of the manuscripts were liturgical or biblical; none of them (or at least none of the ones Neubauer kept) were documents. The source was Rabbi Solomon Aaron Wertheimer in Jerusalem who, still struggling to support a family while financing the publication of his research, was forced to relinquish ownership of his precious scholarly scraps. The letter accompanying the consignment has not been identified, but in letters sent with the pieces he later sold to Cambridge, Wertheimer claimed that his fragments came 'from one of the genizahs of old Egypt'. In addition to fragments, he sent Neubauer a biblical commentary by the medieval commentator Nachmanides: a quarto-sized volume consisting of 169 pages. This item was not supplied with any provenance.

That same year, Wertheimer expanded his network to include Cambridge University Library.[9] Neubauer may have recommended that he offer them the manuscripts he did not want, given that their Hebrew manuscript collection was still relatively small at around 800 items. Even though Cambridge owned many valuable pieces, including the manuscripts donated by the Reverend Buchanan from the storage chests in India, the library's Hebrew purchases had not, overall, amounted to anything spectacular.

By comparison, the Oxford Hebrew manuscript collection had already reached world-class status. Stretching back to the founding of the Bodleian Library itself, it included magnificent holdings, such as the Pococke, Huntingdon, Kenicott and Oppenheim collections, and outstanding items like the Kennicott Bible. Neubauer published the first catalogue of the Bodleian's 2,600 Hebrew manuscripts in 1868: his careful, judicious descriptions of each one provided an important research tool that is still used today.[10]

Meanwhile, the collection at Cambridge, languishing under the superstition of a 300-year-old curse, finally received attention from the keen and critical eye of a Hungarian-born scholar and Rabbi, the university's first Reader in Talmudic and Rabbinic Literature, Solomon Marcus Schiller-Szinessy. Schiller-Szinessy's work, conducted at first in a private capacity, eventually produced a series of six catalogues, but the meticulous detail to which he treated each item (each description ran to an average of thirty-three pages), combined with his subsequent scholarly endeavours at Cambridge, meant that most of his work was left unprinted.[11] After Schiller-Szinessy's death in 1890, his position was taken up by the outstanding Talmudic scholar and larger-than-life personality Solomon Schechter.

SOLOMON SCHECHTER WAS BORN IN 1847 IN ROMANIA to a Hasidic family and raised with a traditional, orthodox education. Thanks to the influence of a local *maskil*, he gained an early appreciation of the wider world of Jewish scholarship. His thirst for greater knowledge eventually led him to undertake further study in Vienna and Berlin in programmes of higher learning led by proponents of the *Wissenschaft des Judenthums* movement. At these institutions, he advanced his already prodigious grasp of the Jewish sources by gaining additional expertise in the scientific, historical and modern exegetical approaches to their study and decipherment. Even though he had left the world of Hasidism behind him, he still adhered to Orthodox Judaism, and he longed for a social setting wherein his love of scientific Jewish studies could be combined with traditional practice, in fellowship with a group of like-minded people.

Thus, a growing feeling of being 'out-of-place' in the progressive milieu of the Berlin schools, combined with his loathing of rising German intellectual anti-Semitism, led him to follow his friend Claude G. Montefiore to England when he returned there in 1882.[12] Over the next eight years, in addition to serving as Montefiore's personal tutor, teaching at Jews' College, and involving himself in Jewish high society in London, Schechter spent many hours deeply immersed in the manuscript treasures of the British Museum and Oxford. The deep connections he made in the London community, which included writers, journalists and editors, enabled him to begin publishing his research in English journals.[13] Likewise, Schechter's circle, whose members had previously deemed themselves 'the wandering Jews' because their former haphazard meetings had wandered from house to house and from topic to topic, quickly benefitted from the unifying presence of this 'blazing comet in the intellectual sky'.[14]

Moses Gaster, future Sephardi chief rabbi in England, was among Schechter's new friends in London. Like Schechter, Gaster was born in Romania and had Hasidic roots on his mother's side of the family. Unlike Schechter, Gaster was also descended on his father's side from a well-to-do family of merchants and community leaders; his father was the commercial attaché to the Dutch consulate and of possible Sephardi descent. In terms of their education and their path to England, however, both men had similar experiences. Gaster was educated by some of the leading proponents of the *Wissenschaft* movement in Germany, and his disgust at rising anti-Semitism motivated him to become more involved with Jewish nationalist movements, particularly a group known as *Hovevei Zion* (Lovers of Zion). To this end, he was instrumental in helping a Romanian branch of the group build a colony in Zikhron Yaakov in Palestine; a member of the group was Schechter's brother, Isaac. Gaster's other political activities, including his demands that the Romanian government grant full citizenship to the Jews, led to his expulsion from the country in 1885.[15]

Not long after moving to England, Gaster was appointed as the *Haham* (chief rabbi) of the Sephardi and Portuguese community in London and to the Ilchester Lectureship in Greco-Slavonic studies at Oxford University. His scholarship was overall more broad ranging than Schechter's, encompassing Jewish history and folklore, magic and mysticism, Romanian literature, Samaritan history and language and biblical studies, but often less meticulous. Neubauer, for one, criticized his tendency to be 'inclined by nature to make everything old'.[16]

In time, Gaster accumulated his own enormous private library of books and manuscripts, including around 18,000 genizah fragments. His preferred method of collection building, he divulged, was to swoop up books and manuscripts in large batches so that he would receive favourable rates from booksellers. He also encouraged his contacts to be 'bookdealers' on his behalf by giving them money in advance so that they could at once purchase items of interest, particularly in the 'Orient'. As letters in his personal archive reveal, one of Gaster's suppliers was Wertheimer in Jerusalem. By his own admission, his role as *Haham* of the Sephardi community enabled him to gain key contacts with Jewish communities in the East, to the extent that he would later boast: 'much of that which was brought from the Orient to Europe in the last forty years is the result, directly or indirectly, of my initiative.'[17]

SCHECHTER WAS BECOMING A RISING SCHOLAR IN ENGLAND as he set about making the most out of the fruits of other collectors' efforts. In the Bodleian, he was helped by Neubauer to access both the known and the little-known copies of post-biblical texts held at the library. The results of Schechter's intense research efforts included the publication in 1887 of the first-ever critical edition of a significant post-biblical rabbinic work known as *Aboth de R. Nathan* (Rabbi Nathan's 'Sages'), which contained quotations from the earliest rabbinic writings. In reviewing his work, Neubauer praised Schechter's 'profound knowledge of the Talmudic literature, his critical method and his patient investigations'.[18] In addition to helping Schechter discover manuscripts for his research, Neubauer engaged deeply with his colleague's work: together they discussed textual readings, exchanged ideas on the interpretation of texts and, thanks to his ability to read Arabic, Neubauer was able to provide Schechter with additional valuable insights into his research.[19] Schechter likewise demonstrated a great appreciation for Neubauer's scholarship, offering unqualified praise for his work and erudition in an article lamenting the otherwise parlous state of Jewish scholarly literature.[20] He also allowed Neubauer to purchase for the Bodleian his own personal copy of a fifteenth-century commentary on *Aboth* (341 folios) out of which he'd made 'ample use' in his publication. In choosing Oxford, Schechter signalled that in addition to regarding the library as a major repository for important Hebrew manuscripts, he also trusted its curator.

By 1890, his highly respected status in Jewish scholarly circles, together with his recent publications, enabled Schechter to secure recommendations from luminaries such as David Kaufmann for the post of Reader in Rabbinics at Cambridge.[21] In their new Cambridge home, Schechter, with his intelligent wife and helpmeet Mathilde, entertained an expanded group of friends which, in addition to the Londoners, now included Cambridge dons and students. The Schechters also gained friends outside of the university, like Agnes Smith Lewis and Margaret Dunlop Gibson, who, thanks to their gender or religion or both, were excluded from mainstream university life.

Schechter continued to visit Oxford on a regular basis, reviewing and collating important rabbinic works in the library, and often staying at Neubauer's house. Mathilde would bring along food and other provisions as the parsimonious bachelor rarely provided adequate sustenance for his guests. Neubauer often called upon Schechter to pay him a visit when he acquired new manuscripts for the Bodleian, or he took him news of the latest finds when he stayed in Cambridge. Even though his personal existence was solitary and austere, the Oxford scholar was known to his friends as someone who in public settings was 'gifted with all the qualities for social popularity' – he was handsome, droll, an excellent conversationalist and unstinting in feeding minds.[22] Among the many finds that Neubauer shared with Schechter was 'a very old fragment' of a book known as *Sefer Hagalui* (*Book of the Exiled*) by the medieval polymath, Saadiah Gaon, which was being prepared for publication by Abraham Harkavy. The piece provided Schechter with important comparative information for his work on identifying portions of the lost Hebrew version of Ecclesiasticus (the Book of Ben Sira) within rabbinic works.[23] Neubauer complemented his work by publishing some evidence of Hebrew sentences of Ben Sira found in other manuscripts.

Both scholars were moved to work in tandem to combat increasing attacks on post-biblical Jewish literature by the proponents of 'Higher Criticism'. Indeed, as early as 1885, Neubauer had published a lengthy article on 'the Dialects spoken in Palestine in the time of Christ', which traced the development of Hebrew and affirmed the arguments of 'the best critics' that Ben Sira's book was originally written in Hebrew. As the ideas of Higher Criticism continued to grow and spread, Schechter confided his angry feelings to his scholarly friend, Richard Gottheil: 'They now have the opportunity and want to undo the history, but let them say so frankly . . . are there not such things as truth and untruth, and is it not the duty of the teacher to expound the former and warn against the latter?'[24] Sayce likewise felt moved to write a tract on the subject. Using the example of an eighth century BCE inscription that he had deciphered together with Neubauer, he revealed that the physical evidence had been outright denied by the Higher Critics in favour of their own prepossessions. Even as an Anglican Priest, he told his readers, he felt an imperative to follow the 'archaeological evidence withersoever it may lead'.[25] Sadly, instead of continuing to unite against the critics, Neubauer and Sayce would eventually get caught up in a race against Schechter to find the 'archaeological' proof of the original Hebrew of Ecclesiasticus.

In the early 1890s, however, the spirit of collaboration still prevailed. Neubauer, in addition to praising Schechter's 'profound knowledge of the Talmudic Literature', publicly declared that only a scholar such as Schechter could undertake the arduous task of collating all the existing manuscripts of the Babylonian Talmud.[26] This worthy endeavour, he proposed, would include the fragments of Talmud recently received at the Bodleian, as well as manuscripts from Yemen newly placed at Columbia University in New York. As medieval copies of major Jewish works began to trickle into various institutions around the world, Neubauer became ever more aware that significant manuscripts were still out there waiting to be discovered, and while he was on his own secret mission to acquire the spoils of Egypt, he issued a rallying cry for intensified efforts to acquire ancient manuscripts from Yemen and Persia. He cast doubt on the idea that Saphir, Halévy and Shapira had taken everything from these quarters, and he recommended that 'influential Rabbis should communicate with the richer Jews in Yemen, offering remuneration to induce them to exchange their MSS. for printed books'. With printed books being scarce in Yemen, he was sure that they provide a sufficient inducement and worthy exchange. At the very least, he opined, the Yemenite Jews should be persuaded to 'allow copies to be made of MSS. of the Talmud, Midrashim, and other early productions'. He further suggested that 'these communications could reach the Yemen Jews through either the medium of the Alliance Israélite Universelle in Paris, or from Jerusalem, where some Jews from Yemen are resident', and he ended with an urgent plea 'But this ought to be done soon, or it may be too late.'[27]

Schechter may have been prompted by similar interests and concerns to pay greater attention to the manuscripts held in Cambridge. Soon after his arrival there, he visited the University Library's Hebrew collection, where he discovered and published items of importance to his own research. He also surveyed the collection and reported on some of its unique contents in a series of articles published in numerous issues of *The Jewish Quarterly Review* between 1891 and 1893.[28] His regular presence at the library, together with his notable expertise, prompted the recently appointed librarian, Francis Jenkinson, to turn to him for ongoing advice regarding the purchase and cataloguing of Hebrew manuscripts. In the summer of 1892, he examined some of the 'collection of fragments of Hebrew MSS. from Egypt' that Greville Chester had presented to the library the previous year, and he helped classify them.[29] In 1893, he was awarded a Studentship to fund his travel to examine Hebrew manuscripts in Italy. He returned from his several-months-long trip, which included gaining privileged access to the Vatican's Hebrew treasures, even more alive to the possibilities of collecting. When a package arrived at Cambridge University Library from Solomon Aaron Wertheimer that same year, Schechter assisted Jenkinson in determining that four of its contents – three medieval documents and a Talmudic commentary – should be added to the library.

WERTHEIMER WAS ENCOURAGED BY HIS FIRST SALES abroad, and they must have given him hope that he had found an effective way to fund his own research and publications. His optimism was such that he had formalized a partnership with an intermediary to acquire and sell a selection of Hebrew manuscripts. A receipt of payment, signed on 26 February 1893, reveals that his middleman had handed over an amount of 'ancient writings' for which he agreed to pay him 'two English pounds'. Thereafter, the partners agreed that the manuscripts would be sent abroad and that both men would then split any profits from their sales. A signature at the bottom of the receipt has been identified as a Yakob Megas Kasurelka who became known to subsequent generations of Wertheimers as the 'Yemenite'.

Yet the name 'Kasurelka' is neither a typical Yemenite Jewish surname nor an appellation found in any other records of known Jewish names. Reading the signatory's name as Yaakov Moshe 'Kasorla', however, results in a Sephardi name well known among Tunisian and Greek Jewish families. And if of Greek origin, then he may have been known locally as 'the Yevani' (rather than by the similar sounding 'Temani' for Yemenite). No other information about this partner has surfaced.

The only trace of anyone with a remotely similar sounding name from that period and that region is a 'Kasorla' who appears in a brief report in the Jerusalemite newspaper *Haòr* (aka *Ha-Tzvi*) in January 1892. The report reveals that the Talmud Torah seminary of the Jerusalemite Sephardi community was sending a young rabbi Yaakov Kasorla as one of its emissaries to Egypt to raise funds. Given Wertheimer's ties to the Sephardi community in Jerusalem and the timing, this Kasorla was someone easily placed to acquire and hand over a quantity of manuscripts sourced in Egypt. Even so, Wertheimer's offerings to clients abroad included a substantial number of Yemenite materials and, in this regard, support the family's claim that he had at least one key Yemenite contact within the Jerusalem community.

YEMENITE CONTACTS IN EITHER JERUSALEM OR CAIRO were also acquired by the German theologian and orientalist Adalbert Merx and by the French Jewish orientalist Joseph Derenbourg. In his monumental book *Documents de paléographie hébraïque et arabe*, Merx praised Neubauer's earlier publication on the palaeographical analysis of Hebrew manuscripts, including those of the Karaite synagogue in Cairo, and he lauded his method of establishing geographical criteria for the study of Hebrew script. In his own work to develop the science of Hebrew palaeography further, Merx analysed four additional medieval documents written in al-Fustat, which he believed had been previously stored in private homes. The documents, he explained, had come into his possession thanks to the good fortune that he had found them with a Yemenite Jew. Beyond this crucial information, however, no other provenance for his manuscripts was supplied.[30]

In 1892, Joseph Derenbourg was asked to lead a French scholarly effort to celebrate the millennium of the birth of the medieval polymath Saadiah Gaon through the publication of an edition of all his writings. At some point, while he laboured at this effort between 1892 and 1895, Derenbourg 'procured from Jerusalem' a Yemenite manuscript of Saadiah's translation of the Pentateuch along with 'some minor fragments'.[31] Whether this was the same source as the one mentioned by Merx is undetermined. While Merx's fragments ended up in Heidelberg, Derenbourg's eventually found their way to the Bibliothèque de l'Institut de France.

WERTHEIMER BOUGHT FROM HIS MIDDLEMAN an unspecified number of manuscripts. Apart from his mention of genizahs in 'Old Egypt' to his buyers, and a few matches between his fragments and those in other genizah collections, it cannot be determined whether all of Wertheimer's fragments came from this same source, let alone from inside the Ben Ezra Synagogue. His correspondence, analysed together with institutional catalogues, reveals that included among the materials he sent were numerous books, palimpsests and documents of either Yemenite, Jerusalemite or some other provenance, or they were from so late a period (eighteenth to nineteenth century) that they were unlikely to have been stored in a genizah of the old Ben Ezra Synagogue. Based on his scholarly activities, Wertheimer initially kept aside and studied manuscripts of interest to him and sent on those of no interest or pieces he had already copied down for his own use. He was well aware of the content of his sales and could trace easily what he sold and to whom.

The day after he paid his 'two English pounds' for the collection of ancient writings, Wertheimer wrote a postcard in German addressed to 'The Magnificent University Library' in Cambridge listing thirteen items for sale at the total cost of six pounds and three shillings. In Hebrew script, on the side of the postcard, he sent greetings to the great wise rabbi Dr Schechter. He asked if Schechter had received his book *Darke Shel Torah* (Ways of Torah), noting that he had written to him previously about it and that the cost was two shillings. After he had self-published the volume in 1891, Wertheimer reached out to leading rabbinical scholars to make them aware of his scholarship, and he no doubt hoped that his manuscript sales would also help him to sell and promote his work.[32]

The word 'taken' was afterwards written in pencil on the postcard, but by April he was still unpaid, even though Schechter had privately expressed interest in the items. In his follow-up postcard to 'The University Library', written this time in English, Wertheimer enquired after the thirteen manuscripts and the two shillings for his book, and he ended with what he must have hoped was a tantalizing offer: 'an ancient "Sefer-Tora" found in one of the "<u>Geniza</u>" [*sic*] of Cairo (Egypt) written on leather of Roebuck "<u>tsvi</u>".

According to Jenkinson's short, pencilled note, a response was finally sent to Wertheimer towards the end of May. In June, Wertheimer informed Jenkinson that he was sending along another 'thirty M.S.S.' at the cost of 'only' three pounds. He politely asked him to send this new sum together with the still unpaid monies. Exactly as in the last postcard, he repeated what he must have believed was surely a most tempting offer, particularly as this time he made sure to stress its age, material and provenance: 'I have also with me a very ancient <u>Sefer-Tora</u> written on <u>Kelaf Roebuck</u> & is found in one of the <u>Genizas</u> of old Egypt & is quite old.' Ever hopeful, he signed off: 'awaiting an early reply'.

Nevertheless, the exigencies of the self-financing Jerusalemite scholar did not align with the pace of Cambridge life and, by August 1892, he found himself still waiting for the cash. This time he pleaded with Jenkinson to send the money or return the packets, and he vowed to wait another month but no more. The ancient Torah scroll from 'the genizahs of old Egypt' was no longer mentioned, and it is unknown whether it ever got sold on either as a whole or in parts. Payments from Oxford were still forthcoming, however. His sales to that quarter amounted to 172 items (783 leaves). The items included a significantly larger proportion of Judeo-Arabic fragments, as well as pieces that Neubauer identified as bearing the hallmarks of Yemenite script. A Kabbalistic prayer text from 1839 was also bundled up with the fragments in a volume later classified as 'from the Genizah'. In addition, the Bodleian purchased from Wertheimer an eighteenth-century copy of an Arabic medical treatise by Dawud al-Antaki, a leading physician in fourteenth- to fifteenth-century Ottoman Cairo.

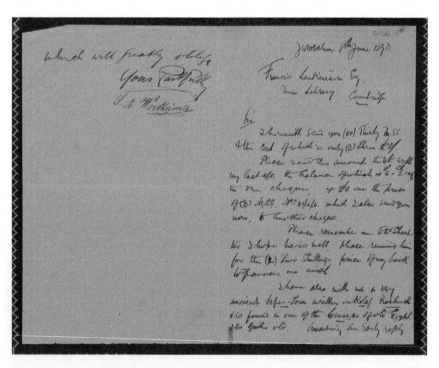

Figure 8.1 CUL MS. Or.1080.13, a letter from Solomon Aaron Wertheimer in Jerusalem to Cambridge University Library, June 1893.

WERTHEIMER MAY HAVE BEEN THE SOURCE for three volumes of fragments in the Bodleian collection simply attributed as 'from the Geniza, 1892'. The fragments are largely liturgical and rabbinical, and two are written in Yemenite script. One of the fragments (MS. Heb. d. 54, f. 1) is a folio comprising text from the Jerusalem Talmud; it is also a palimpsest with faint underwriting in Christian Palestinian Aramaic.[33] The folio matches a piece held in Paris (MS. Heb 1489. 1) with its own hidden provenance history. The Parisian fragment only came to light in 2013 with eleven other fragments that were hidden within an outer wrapping of various papers belonging to or connected with the Mayor family of Neuchâtel and Lausanne in Switzerland.

One of the papers is a letter from William Charles Auguste Mayor, an American-born Swiss architect who was in Egypt in 1872. Mayor's visit to Egypt was part of a two-year tour of the Mediterranean during which time he produced many sketches and drawings of the places he visited that were later exhibited in his hometown of Neuchâtel. A letter from Mayor to his son relates some of his tourist-type activities together with a demonstration of his new ability to write his name in Arabic letters. Mayor's letter was written in February of that year from the Hotel du Nil where Greville Chester would have been staying at the time, and close to the time when Grant Bey and Moses Shapira were making forays into the Ben Ezra Synagogue. Beyond this, however, no other connection exists that could place Mayor in the market for fragments, and no other information pertinent to antiquities collecting appears in his letter.

Yet, one of the other papers wrapped around these fragments may confirm that they were purchased in Jerusalem (and maybe even from Wertheimer, given the matching fragment). The paper is a letter from the Swiss scholar and pastor Paul Laufer, who in 1893 spent a year touring the Holy Land and Egypt. His journey was described in his book *Au Pays du Christ* (In the Land of Christ) in 1897. Laufer later became a professor of theology in the Theologischen Fakultät der Freien Evangelischen Kirche in Lausanne, where numerous members of the Mayor family continued to reside. In this particular letter, enclosed with the Hebrew fragment, Laufer also describes visiting the Samaritan synagogue in Nablus.

WERTHEIMER WAS STILL WAITING FOR PAYMENT from Cambridge. After another two months had passed, he sent a letter to Jenkinson. This time it was to issue the mild complaint that Jenkinson had sent the unwanted packets back to him via a 'Mr. A. Zinger Esq.' who was now refusing to forward them on unless he paid the cost of mailing them from Jaffa to Jerusalem. Zinger was Albert Singer, a Hungarian Jew, who served as the Jerusalem forwarding and commissioning agent. Singer's shipping and banking business had branches in Jaffa, Haifa and Acre, and later Egypt and the Sudan. The packet sent from Cambridge had arrived to him through the London shipping agency Pitt & Scott.[34] Wertheimer's suggested solution was to ask Pitt & Scott to instruct Singer to forward the packet without payment and to place a credit on the library's account towards the cost of a future purchase. Wertheimer remained polite, possibly because he hoped to continue the relationship to fund and make sales on his planned multi-volume work *Batei Midrashot* (Houses of Study), the first volume of which had just been printed in Jerusalem by Moses Lilienthal, and thus he added a note that copies of his new book, published 'from a very old handwriting [*sic*] book' could be had for the price of three shillings each. Wertheimer could not afford to have his work bound and covered, and so he sent the printed folios abroad folded up in such a way as to keep them together.³⁵

Unfortunately, the sorry circumstances of Wertheimer's fragments did not end there. In December 1893, having received a letter from Cambridge informing him that he was not to send parcels 'on approval', Wertheimer was forced to pay Singer to retrieve back the manuscripts. When the parcel arrived, he found that a fragment was missing from his consignment of thirty, as well as all thirteen pieces sent in February. To avoid further payments to the forwarding agent, Wertheimer pleaded with Jenkinson to send the manuscripts over to Dr Neubauer in Oxford. The cost of 67 cents may have seemed low by Cambridge standards, but it was hard for Wertheimer, who reminded him: 'you know a man like me does not afford such expense.' While he did not want to lose his potential new customer, he wondered how to send manuscripts to them and 'in what way' if they would not receive them on approval.

Moses Gaster was happy to buy bundles in advance of seeing them. As he related in his memoir, 'The Story of My Library', he was able by this method to obtain no less than fifty manuscripts at once. His first acquisition of such a bundle was, he recalled, 'a mixed bag: old and new, valuable and worthless, all together'.³⁶ This way of buying enabled him 'in less than thirty years to purchase more than 1,500 manuscripts'. While this recollection did not mention fragments (he would eventually sell 3,000 fragments to the British Museum in 1924, and 15,000 were sold to the John Rylands Library 15 years after his death), it stands to reason that this is how he came by so many. Yet, by obtaining bundles of materials sight unseen, there was no possibility of recording the exact provenance of each piece.³⁷

In 1893, the antiquities market was flooded from another source, this time the Qubbat al-Khazna mosque in Damascus. The Dome of the Treasury in the mosque held a cache of medieval manuscripts. Most of the pieces were in Arabic; most were literary, but there were also Hebrew and Judaeo-Arabic pieces and documents. How they were discovered and dispersed is still under investigation.³⁸ The idea that the catalyst for this was a fire in the treasury is now disputed. Most of the manuscripts found their way to Istanbul. Of relevance to the genizah story, however, is that some of the pieces are still unaccounted for, and this makes it highly likely that they fell into the hands of various dealers and through them into the marketplace for fragments.³⁹

The fact that the Oxford scholars likewise provided only minimal clues, if any, as to the suspected provenance of the Hebrew fragments 'found lately in Egypt' suggests that they were unsure of the ultimate source. Neubauer's nephew, the scholar, Adolf Bücher, provided a hint earlier in 1893, when he published fragments from the little-known three-year liturgical cycle of the Palestinian Jews. The practices revealed by the fragments led him to recall earlier historical descriptions of the synagogue in Cairo that had once belonged to the Jewish community from Palestine, and he surmised that it was 'extremely probable' that such fragments as these must have originally come from that place.

From the genizah of an Egyptian
synagogue (1894)

TWO YOUNG SCHOLARS FROM OXFORD WERE VISITING EGYPT in early 1894. One was John Frederick Stenning, a scholar of Aramaic and future Oxford college Dean, and the other Arthur Ernest Cowley, a scholar of classical and Semitic languages, future assistant to Neubauer and, much later, Bodleian Librarian. The main purpose of their publicly funded trip was to examine important manuscripts in the monasteries. Stenning had also been privately asked to check and follow up on a recent transcription of the Sinai Palimpsest discovered at St. Catherine's Monastery by Agnes Smith Lewis back in 1892.[1] Cowley was tasked with checking manuscript versions of liturgical texts on behalf of the liturgy scholar and librarian, Frank Edward Brightman. While in Egypt, he also acquired eleven pages of a torn Hebrew vellum manuscript with parts of the biblical book of Exodus unusually written in shorthand, as well as part of a liturgical work quoting Exodus. Exactly how and where he got hold of them is not known, but he donated the manuscript fragments to the Bodleian the following year, and when he came to catalogue them many years later, he provided them with the provenance description of 'from the genizah'.[2]

While all the liturgical fragments published by Bücher and Neubauer had come from Egypt via Greville John Chester, others had been steadily arriving at the library through or directly from Jerusalem. That same year, Neubauer also received another palimpsest: a fragment with parts of the Jerusalem Talmud in the upper writing and parts of a Georgian liturgy in the hidden text beneath. The supplier of the manuscript was not credited in the catalogue, possibly because the manuscript was later bound up by mistake with an unrelated Armenian manuscript. The Georgian-Hebrew piece was only properly studied in 1921 by the American Byzantinist scholar Robert P. Blake who was informed by Cowley that 'the fragment had been acquired in 1894 along with several others from Rabbi S. Wertheimer in Jerusalem, and that its provenance from the Geniza collection was almost certain'.[3] Blake's subsequent investigations found that the fragment was a match to other pieces in Cambridge and the British Museum that had also been designated as having derived from *the* Genizah (i.e. the Ben Ezra Synagogue), which he felt satisfied settled the matter of provenance. However, Blake also concluded that the rubbed Georgian text had been produced in Palestine 'where literary work in Georgian monastic circles began early'. Since Palestine was also the birthplace of the Jerusalem Talmud and the home of the suspected supplier, it rather than Egypt may have been the country of origin for all three pieces, a possibility unfortunately obfuscated by the tendency to ascribe all Hebrew fragments to a single find spot.

The Bodleian sent a total of £28 in four payments to Wertheimer in 1894, but nothing is attributed to him in the library's catalogue for that year. While he received payment but no recognition from Oxford, some sort of understanding seems to have been worked out with Cambridge, thanks to Schechter's intervention. In July, Wertheimer sent a bundle of thirty-two manuscripts to Jenkinson and from his brief description of some of the highlights and prices, one must have surely caught Schechter's eye. The piece was a copy of the *Midrash Ha-Gadol* to Exodus, which Wertheimer claimed was missing only its first page. On the side of the postcard, he added a note about the books in his own *Batei Midrashot* series which he had sold to Oxford and was now offering to Cambridge at the price of four shillings. He also asked whether the librarian was interested in silver and copper antique coins.

When the *Midrash Ha-Gadol* arrived along with the other items, Schechter may have been disappointed to find that it was a seventeenth-century Yemenite version rather than a much-coveted older version. On a handlist of the items he examined, he noted that the library should offer £6 for the Midrash and not the £15 posited by Wertheimer. He also noted that a few items were unique and that others, mostly biblical fragments and a Passover Haggadah, were 'unwanted'. In September, Wertheimer sent a postcard accepting the amounts offered on the first package and the news that he was forwarding a second package of sixty-two fragments. Schechter quickly reviewed the manuscripts, accepting some and rejecting others as 'worthless' or 'not wanted at all'. In a similar way to his Oxford sales, Wertheimer's offerings included items of mixed provenance, such as several sixteenth- and seventeenth-century Yemenite legal documents and letters. These pieces were also accepted at Cambridge and, due to the lack of documentation, eventually designated as 'probably' or 'possibly' from 'the Cairo Genizah'.[4] Despite Schechter's rapid assessment of the list's contents and his recommendations for purchase, the wheels of library bureaucracy turned slowly, leaving Wertheimer waiting again for payment.

ANOTHER JERUSALEMITE DEALER may have prompted Wertheimer's query about antique coins. The dealer, a former member of the Etz Chaim Yeshiva in Jerusalem, and a possible source or connection for Wertheimer's Yemenite manuscript offerings, was someone by the name of Samuel Raffalovich (aka Samuel Raffaeli). Raffalovich eventually became involved in the supply of genizah fragments, but in 1894, he was earning a living as a moneychanger near the Jaffa Gate in Jerusalem and building up considerable expertise in numismatics thanks to the antique coins being offered to him by Bedouin and local Arab peasants. Born in the Russian region of Podolia in 1867, and descended from a line of wealthy merchants, Raffalovich moved with his parents and brother to Palestine at the age of sixteen. Two years later, he married the granddaughter of a leading Jerusalemite Nissan Bak. Bak ran the historic Hebrew printing press that his father, Israel, with the help of Moses Montefiore, had established in 1841. Bak was also involved in the building of a new synagogue and the founding of several new neighbourhoods in Jerusalem, including one for the community of Yemenite Jews who had recently migrated there. In 1845, at Montefiore's invitation, Bak had visited Preston in England and established contacts to promote cotton manufacturing in Palestine.[5] Later, Bak's son, Meir Chaim Bak, developed business interests in England, and Raffalovich, who was Meir's son-in-law, worked with him there for five years before returning to Jerusalem to set up his own money-changing business. As fascinating old coins came his way, Raffalovich quickly discovered an overriding passion that led him into the antiquarian world. In Palestine, at the urging of his friend Eliezer Ben-Yehuda, he became known by the Hebraized surname Raffaeli, but for his dealings in Europe, he remained Raffalovich. In time, Raffaeli was recognized as a leading authority on Jewish coins and celebrated as a tireless advocate for establishing museums in Palestine dedicated to Jewish history and archaeology.[6] As Raffalovich, he would become a mere footnote to genizah history: regarded by those in the ivory towers of academe as a shady Oriental bookseller and remembered only as someone who peddled 'rubbishy' leftover manuscript scraps.

HEBREW FRAGMENTS FROM AN AMERICAN SOURCE were also brought to Schechter's attention in 1894. The source was someone who would be of great future significance to Schechter's life, the American Jewish scholar Cyrus Adler. In preparing to mount an impressive exhibition of biblical artefacts at the Cotton States International Exposition in Atlanta, Adler was ambitiously trying to bring together as many geological samples, items of flora and fauna, antiquities, coins, stones, costumes and religious objects as the twenty- by twenty-foot space would allow. In one section, a display of Bibles, he intended to display facsimiles of the major Bible manuscripts, such as the Aleppo Codex and Codex Sinaiticus, and in addition, he decided to include a few of his own original thirteenth-century vellum fragments of Psalms and Deuteronomy purchased as part of a bundle of manuscripts in Cairo in 1891.[7] Upon his arrival in London in September 1894, as part of his second tour of Europe and the East, Adler wrote to his wife, Sarah Sultzberger, to let her know his whereabouts. He intended to visit Neubauer in Oxford to finally show him his MSS and he was also heading to Cambridge to spend the Sabbath with Schechter.[8]

Adler first established his close friendship with Schechter during his tour of Europe and the East for the Columbian Exposition in 1890. While in London, he became friends with the editors of *The Jewish Quarterly Review*, the scholar Israel Abrahams, another individual later connected to genizah fragments, and Schechter's pupil and benefactor Claude Montefiore. He also became acquainted with two other characters in the Cairo Genizah story: Moses Gaster, who he declared was 'certainly not a Sephardi' and Elkan Nathan Adler, 'who insisted on giving me a card to some Pasha in Constantinople'. On his first meeting with Schechter, Adler remarked to his wife that he was 'a fine scholar with a good library . . . a devout Jew in his practice with a most liberal construction in his ideas' and that he was quite taken with him. In fact, the impression was so deep that Adler was inspired to find ways to bring such an illustrious scholar to live in America. Two years later, on his way back from his first trip to the East, Adler had fully intended to stop off in Cambridge to see Schechter again and show him the manuscripts he had acquired in Cairo, but he had caught a severe cold and had to cut short his stay in England. In his apology note, Adler reminded

Schechter about the Midrashic manuscripts in the possession of Mayor Adolph Sutro of San Francisco. Having bought Moses Shapira's estate after his suicide, Sutro now owned twenty-seven copies (some substantial; some fragmentary) of the *Midrash Ha-Gadol*.[9] Adler asked Sutro if Schechter could borrow his Midrashic manuscripts, and Sutro responded that he was willing to help send descriptions and extracts of the material, but he 'most decidedly' objected to sending over the manuscripts themselves. He had almost lost a manuscript once when the ship due to convey it to Europe sank; the manuscript was only saved because it had been delayed in the mail and not placed on board the ship.[10] Despite Sutro's willingness to help supply information, the incident must have underscored for both men the challenges to scholarship posed by private ownership of rare materials. The inaccessibility of Sutro's Hebrew collection and the scattered holdings of Hebraica and Judaica across just a few of America's institutions further spurred Adler's desire to establish a major Jewish library for his country.

In Cairo during the winter of 1894, while Cyrus Adler was showing his fragments to Schechter, some unknown but important connection was being made by the Count d'Hulst in the effort to locate the source. Of the details, nothing is known; the only vague clue comes from a letter he later quoted from his close friend, the Reverend William MacGregor of Tamworth. According to d'Hulst, MacGregor had written to him on 22 November 1894 regarding his searches for the source of the genizah manuscripts with the following words: 'I hope you charge the Bodleian something for your trouble and your connection?'[11] Two years had gone by since Sayce and d'Hulst had corresponded on the matter of a 'small lot of MSS'. In the meantime, d'Hulst had experienced many personal troubles, having been let go from the Egypt Exploration Fund.

In the past few years, his excavation work with Naville had drawn increasing criticism from Flinders Petrie. Petrie, in his new position as the Amelia Edwards Professor at University College London, was soon able to establish an 'Egyptian Research Account' through which to train new generations of archaeologists in careful site mapping and the recovery of small finds. As he set about shaping the future of archaeology, his complaints to Edwards about Naville and d'Hulst and their methods of excavation that he had once expressed privately were now articulated more openly. When he heard late in 1892 that the Egypt Exploration Fund intended to deploy them to excavate the magnificent temple at Deir el-Bahri on the west bank of the Nile, he issued a stern warning to Edwards's close friend and Fund committee member Kate Bradbury, that, in addition to Naville's careless treatment of excavation sites, his and d'Hulst's forceful methods of applying wet paper squeezes to copy ancient inscriptions would damage the temple's delicate reliefs. At Bradbury's request, Petrie repeated his confidential accusations in an official statement to Maunde Thompson, the committee chairman.[12] That same year, d'Hulst also had a run-in with the newly appointed director of the Service des Antiquités, Jacques de Morgan. Having grown used to negotiating unofficially with the heavy-handed Grébaut over site preferences and all manner of other excavation needs on behalf of the Fund, he was surprised to have the same casual approach to de Morgan backfire. When de Morgan expressed unwillingness to allow the Fund to have access to certain sites, d'Hulst had told him that 'it would make a bad impression in England if he began his official career by refusing us a good site to work', a statement that de Morgan interpreted as menacing. The Fund committee members were alarmed that the delicate entente cordiale between the French authorities and the Fund (by now a prestigious organization with renowned figures on its board and in its national and international membership) could be upset through such unsanctioned conversations. They suspended d'Hulst's activities while they investigated and repaired the damage with de Morgan. The following year, de Morgan was unanimously recommended for election as a new member of the Fund's committee.

These incidences, combined with their assessment of d'Hulst's recent work at Behbeit el-Hagar, the results of which, the committee members felt were 'not adequate to the cost', enabled them to sanction the dismissal of the officer who had assiduously served them for the past seven seasons. An official letter of dismissal was sent to d'Hulst at the bottom of which, an apologetic Poole added in pencil: 'I write with the utmost regret knowing your loyalty & hard work.'[13] In the end, as a non-scholarly, private individual lacking any formal training or institutional affiliation, d'Hulst was an outsider moving in the wrong circles. The things that had previously recommended him: his energy, hard labour, local knowledge and linguistic skills were no longer crucial to the operations of the now successful and well-established Fund. A leading Egyptologist such as Naville, however, was indispensable to the Fund's publishing activities and his archaeological deficiencies in the field could be reined in with the right assistant. Naville accepted the committee's decision but urged Poole to 'say all that is kind to him from me. The Count has been very loyal to the Fund'. Sayce, another committee member, also acquiesced; his opinion that the Fund was 'much indebted' to d'Hulst was only offered in writing many years later. MacGregor, despite his private protestations to d'Hulst and his promise to resign from the committee, realized that it would be foolish to relinquish his membership and role as local honorary secretary for Tamworth for such a minor cause.

With a difficult year behind him, one that ended with him confined to bed with a fever, d'Hulst had entered 1894 looking for alternative ways to stay connected to the world of archaeology and Egyptology. In addition to his photographic pursuits and part-time antiquarianism, he no doubt realized that a more concerted effort to find the Hebrew manuscripts being sought by Sayce on behalf of the Bodleian provided a good opportunity to act as a representative in the field for a revered British institution. Yet, it would take him eleven months before his 'trouble' and his 'connection', as recorded in MacGregor's enigmatic note, would enable him to fulfil Sayce's request.

OVER IN HUNGARY, A SCHOLAR, who had already published a Hebrew fragment from 'an old synagogue in Cairo' in 1892, was receiving bundles of fragments from an unknown supplier to his home. This scholar was David Kaufmann, and not only did he amass his own private collection of over 500 genizah fragments, he would also soon shape the way future scholars would refer to the provenance of all the fragments.[14] Kaufmann never disclosed the exact details of how he acquired them, except for a brief mention in a private letter to Josef von Karabacek written in March 1897 in which he complained that it was due to the 'indolence' of his 'Oriental friend' and the cholera epidemic that he had lost the ability to acquire all of the Egyptian fragments. Much later, one of his students claimed he had heard Kaufmann say that the loss was due to 'the careless Hungarian connection'.

Kaufmann may have inadvertently leaked information by himself to fellow scholars across Europe. One person who could have picked up early insider collecting tips from Kaufmann may have been that regular traveller to the East and visitor to his home in Budapest: fellow book enthusiast Elkan Nathan Adler. The two men had first met following Adler's trip to Palestine on behalf of the Holy Land Relief Fund in 1888. Adler's return journey included stops in numerous European cities where he gave reports to Jewish organizations connected to the Anglo-Jewish Association and the Alliance Israélite Universelle on the state of Jewish educational establishments and hospitals in the Holy City. Many years later, when he later came to eulogize Kaufmann, Adler vividly recalled that first meeting:

> though it was my first visit to Buda-Pesth, I could only stop a few hours. I called on him in the afternoon and fully intended to spend the evening in one of the music halls for which the bright capital is so famous. But it was after midnight before the dear Professor would let me leave his house, and all forgetful of the music I left him most unwillingly.

Adler also recalled his final visit to Kaufmann's home in 1898 and how, after being shown his many manuscript treasures, he gained the conviction that 'the intelligent stay-at-home is a far better collector than the much-travelled *comis voyageur*'.[15]

By the time Kaufmann first welcomed Adler to his home, he had been collecting manuscripts since the early 1880s. At the age of twenty-nine, and already a prodigious scholar with a doctorate from Leipzig University, Kaufmann married into the Gomperz family, an illustrious alliance that provided him with the financial means to pursue his passion for collecting books and manuscripts and to build up one of the best private libraries of Hebraica in Europe. In addition to his already wide-ranging scholarly pursuits, his new family connections inspired him to develop an interest in the genealogical history of notable Jewish families. Through his research into the Gomperz family, he encountered the *Hofjuden* or 'Court Jews' of eighteenth-century Austrian society, and he grew deeply fascinated by the distinguished forebear of a related family: Samson Wertheimer, the former chief rabbi of Hungary and the principal financier to Emperor Leopold I of Austria. In researching the history of the Gomperz and Wertheimer families, he engaged in a regular correspondence with Solomon Schechter and, among other topics relating to Jewish historical and literary texts, the history and state of *Wissenschaft des Judenthums*; they even indulged in a little *lashon ha-ra'ah* (gossip).[16] It's possible that through his genealogical research, Kaufmann gained a connection to the Wertheimer descendant living in Jerusalem, the Wertheimer who was a known supplier of genizah fragments to Schechter in Cambridge and Neubauer in Oxford. Yet, Kaufmann had already established a key relationship with Mordechai Adelmann in Jerusalem, who by this time was helping to build a public Jewish library in the Holy City.

ADELMANN WAS SERVING AS THE PRESIDENT of the Jerusalem Lodge in 1893. The Jerusalem Lodge was one of many established by the International Order of the B'nai

Brith. Two years prior, when the educational pioneer Ephraim Cohen-Reiss was president and Adelmann was still serving as the Lodge's secretary, an appeal had been launched to build a public library in Jerusalem. The appeal went out to the world-wide members of the International Order of the B'nai Brith to coincide with the 400th anniversary of the Jewish expulsion from Spain. The Jerusalem Lodge requested their material support for 'a properly endowed Jewish library which shall bear the name of Don Isaac Abarbanel, the most celebrated man of that epoch'.[17] The committee for the establishment of the Jewish Abarbanel Library hoped to inspire international members to supply gifts of books and other publications. In November 1892, Cohen-Reiss reported to the International Order that the Jerusalem Lodge was making great strides in all its activities with the addition of another evening school and 700 volumes added to the Abarbanel Library. Under Adelmann's presidency the members of the Lodge, reported Moritz Ellinger, editor of the B'nai B'rith journal *Menorah*, were succeeding in managing all institutions of importance in the 'Holy City' as well as endeavouring to establish closer ties with other lodges in the 'Orient'. As part of this endeavour, Ellinger noted: 'We have sent out two of our prominent members to the lodges in Jaffa and Beyrouth and will call upon the lodges in Alexandria, Cairo and Tanta and submit, to consider with us, the plan of a union.' Ellinger also mentioned the success of the Abarbanel Library and plans for its growth: 'as the demand for books is constantly growing more urgent, and our supply of books does not meet fully the demands made upon our collections. . . . A special committee of four members, recognized scholars of Hebrew and Arabic, is charged with the two-fold task of providing material for the learned as well as the self-trained.'[18] These twofold endeavours, establishing ties with other Jewish lodges and seeking out materials for the building of a great national Jewish library, may well have coincided with the hunt for genizah manuscripts by European Jewish scholars. Members of the committee and other local dealers and collectors may have added manuscripts in the early days of its founding. The largest recorded donation of materials (10,000) reached the library in 1895; they had come from Joseph Chasanowitz, a physician, bibliophile and ardent Jewish nationalist living in Bialystok. But the library also increased its holdings thanks to the support of many leading Jewish scholars in Frankfurt, London and Paris (including those who would become connected to the Cairo Genizah story) who lent both material and financial assistance. The benefit appears to have been mutual: as part of this effort, starting with Chasanowitz, the Jerusalem Lodge granted library membership to non-resident supporters, and it welcomed and entertained the many scholars who visited it.[19] According to an article written by Avinoam Yellin, son of David Yellin (one of the library's founders), genizah fragments purchased from a 'Rabbi S. Wertheimer' were added to the Jewish National Library in 1893.[20] Since Wertheimer was the source of so many genizah sales, it's possible that Kaufmann's fragments also came to him indirectly from Wertheimer through Adelmann.

Discord between Kaufmann and Neubauer became more apparent between 1893 and 1894, with half-veiled disapproval of aspects of each other's work, and possibly of each other, appearing in print. The clash appears to have prompted Neubauer to divulge the source of the Bodleian's fragments. The discord was first sewn in 1891, when Kaufmann, as part of his research into Anglo-Jewish history, had come across a liturgical manuscript, titled *Etz Chaim* (tree of life), held in Leipzig. He noticed that it had been incorrectly described, leading Leopold Zunz, the father of Jewish liturgical scholarship, to overlook it. Kaufmann knew, however, that it had not been overlooked by Neubauer, who in 1887 had brought its author to the attention of Dr Hermann Adler, the delegate Chief Rabbi of England, for a paper he was preparing for the Anglo-Jewish Historical Exhibition in 1888.[21] In an article about the piece, Kaufmann expressed surprise that the manuscript hadn't been fully exposed at the time, as the exhibition exactly coincided with the 600th-year anniversary of the composition's creation. Had it been publicized, the piece would have 'attracted universal attention' and facsimiles given to the exhibition participants would have provided 'appropriate mementoes'. He continued to discuss the manuscript's importance, claiming it held key evidence of the English Ritual before the Jews were expelled from England in 1290.[22] Kaufmann followed up with another article on the same subject two years later to provide a full history of the transmission of the manuscript and its significance to Anglo-Jewish history. Again, his silence on the matter of it having been overlooked by Neubauer spoke volumes.[23]

Neubauer responded in 1894 with an article whose title appeared to put the *Etz Chayim* back in its place by labelling it as one of many 'Miscellanea Liturgica'. He acknowledged the tacit blame assigned to him for ostensibly not recognizing the importance of the work. At the same time, he took a sideswipe at Kaufmann for his idea that a mere handful of compositions by a few medieval English liturgists could be described as 'successfully cultivating the Hebrew muse on England's soil'. He continued to debate the validity of his claims with regard to the text's language and significance, and he concluded that the main influence of the piece had come from France. He finished off his rejoinder by correcting Kaufmann's typographical errors. More importantly, for the Cairo Genizah story, however, Neubauer used the article to state that going forward he would move liturgical research beyond its stagnant state by writing a series of articles on the liturgical fragments in the Bodleian that had come from 'a *Genizah* at Cairo'.[24]

Kaufmann's own manuscript acquisitions continued to increase at an average rate of twenty each year, gradually filling his three-story house with dust. Whether his contact had continued to be Adelmann, or whether it was Wertheimer or someone else entirely may never be known. Only on the one mysterious box of fragments did he reveal in his scrawled handwriting: 'Aus der Genisa einer egyptischen Synagoge. Di[enstag]. 11. Dec. 1894.' The date coincides very closely with the time that d'Hulst was making his important connection, a connection that would lead him to discover fragments hidden in a subterranean place near the Ben Ezra Synagogue.

A subterranean hoard (1895–6)

Sayce made a dramatic announcement to Neubauer three months after Kaufmann marked his box of fragments with the enigmatic provenance note. Writing from Assiut on 26 March 1895, he shared the long-awaited news that d'Hulst had finally 'succeeded in discovering & entering the old subterranean place from wh[ich] the Hebrew MSS have all come'. The subterranean place, he revealed, was still full of manuscripts and books. Although, somewhat confusingly, he claimed that the lower and more accessible books had been torn to pieces to generate the manuscript pages that had been sold to Europe. The mysterious subterranean area must have held different levels within it whereby something lower could somehow be more accessible.[1]

The site where the Roman fortress wall and bastion tower once stood was most likely where d'Hulst excavated back in 1889. This is the point to which he must have returned in 1892 when he reported the changes to the synagogue and the loss of the wall. It may have been the location from which he recovered the 'small lot of MSS', including the palimpsest, that were passed on to the Bodleian through Sayce in 1893 and afterwards to the scholar George Henry Gwilliam. When Gwilliam finally published these palimpsests in 1896, he declared that all seven leaves (Greville Chester's from 1891 and Sayce's from 1893) were found in an underground chamber beneath a synagogue in Cairo after the site was cleared to make room for new buildings. This find spot, however, could only have been applied retroactively to Chester's 1891 fragments and Sayce's 1893 fragments, as d'Hulst did not locate the underground find spot until 1895.

When the Reverend William MacGregor asked d'Hulst about the trouble he was taking on behalf of the Bodleian and his 'connection', it can only be assumed that the connection he mentioned must have been the key to unlocking the manuscripts' mysterious whereabouts. Whether that connection also related somehow to Kaufmann's box is undetermined. The exact location of the subterranean hiding place is also unresolved at this time. Added to a lack of detailed information in the archival record is the problem posed by the many physical changes over time to the space in which the Ben Ezra Synagogue and its compound stand.

An archaeological survey of the site, conducted in the 1990s, revealed several buried structures in and around the Ben Ezra Synagogue and its compound. A space under the synagogue had been created after the ancient synagogue foundations were raised to the ground level. The survey corroborated this fact by proving that the masonry styles of the 1892 building and the basement were the same. The new space allowed for a basement that was entered by descending a set of stairs into a passage. Two-thirds of the way along the passage, a second set of stairs led down into an area identified as a *mikve* (ritual bath), which then connected out via another passage to a well in the synagogue courtyard. By the time of the survey, the well appeared to function as a light shaft, and it was covered over by a nineteenth-century iron grille. Among the other subterranean structures discovered around the synagogue was a cistern underneath one of the synagogue's twentieth-century buildings (Annexe I). The cistern extended northwards underground towards the far northern end of the synagogue compound where the land meets the boundary wall of the Church of St. Barbara, and where a second building (Annexe II) was eventually erected in the 1940s to house the custodian. According to the architectural drawing, the cistern had a deep thin upper section and a wider square-shaped lower basin.[2] It may have fallen into disuse after the severe 1883 cholera outbreak. In some Egyptian towns, like Damietta, private cisterns were replaced with large city-administrated and cemented ones. The survey of Annexe II likewise revealed 'substantial subsurface evidence' of earlier domestic structures, including the remains of steps.[3]

The land outside of the synagogue compound had also changed since d'Hulst had first conducted his excavations in the area. At the far eastern end of the synagogue stood the rubble from the old Roman wall and bastion tower, the dismantling of which had deeply upset Greville Chester. Beyond the rubble to the east lay empty land where community housing for the poor was built in around 1911. Another wall once bounded the far end of this piece of empty land, and a gateway made within it offered access to a second lot of empty land. This second piece of empty land joined to the main road, *Bani el-Adyera* street, at its far end. The wall and gate were gone by the 1960s, and another building (Annexe III) was built near *Bani el-Adyera* street. The wall and gate proved of great interest to Solomon Schechter when he visited there in 1896, as it is the subject of the only photographic image he appears to have taken of the entire place.[4]

BUYING AND SHIPPING THE SUBTERRANEAN HOARD would prove a logistical nightmare for d'Hulst and Sayce. The synagogue custodians agreed to sell everything for fifty pounds with five pounds *bakshish*, but the problem of how to get the manuscripts out of the country remained. Sayce queried Neubauer whether the Bodleian could enlist the help of the British Government or Lord Cromer. While Sayce himself was a friend of the former English prime minister William Ewert Gladstone, he had little connection to the incumbent leader Lord Salisbury. He had some friendly ties with Lord Cromer, but he knew that he was unlikely to get involved. Cromer only tolerated matters connected to the Service Des Antiquités while ever it proved a useful bargaining tool with the French, and he had once confided to Sayce his feeling that Egypt's antiquities were 'more trouble than anything else'.[5] Thus, despite his own deep involvement with the antiquities department, his friendships with most Egyptologists in the field, and his own experiences in exporting antiquities, the sudden discovery of a large cache of Hebrew manuscripts, combined with the need to keep them secret, clearly had Sayce flummoxed. In his congratulatory note to d'Hulst, sent the following day, he posed the same question: 'I think that the Bodleian Library would agree to the terms, but how are the MSS. to be got out of the country? If that could be arranged, I would telegraph to Oxford for the money could be paid over at once.'[6]

The following week, on 2 April 1895, Sayce responded to d'Hulst who, it appears, had outlined a plan to move and ship the materials:

> How many boxes do you think will be necessary [?]. If there is no difficulty about sending them out of the country, your plan would be the best to adopt. I hope to reach Cairo about the 15th, and I should be much obliged if you could come and have lunch with me, when we could settle everything about the Hebrew MSS. I hope by that time to have had an answer from Oxford about them. If there were no difficulty about sending them out of the country, your plan would be the best to adopt.

Despite their best-laid plans, efforts to acquire the manuscripts for the Bodleian were delayed until the winter season. Whether the delays were caused at their end, or the Oxford end, is unclear. Certainly, by September, a major cholera epidemic had erupted in Egypt. The spread of the disease was exacerbated by the low level of the Nile and contaminated water supplies. Measures to contain the spread included isolation or treatment in cholera huts, and the disinfection of buildings and their surroundings. The towns and villages in Lower Egypt were the worst affected, but Cairo was also hit hard with both the disease and the knock-on effects of stringency and precaution.[7] The mortality rate was far less than a previous outbreak in 1883, proving that lessons had been learnt and conditions improved, but the British regime was still falling short in its medical and sanitary administration of Egypt. Old Cairo, with its notoriously inadequate water and sewage systems, was particularly hard hit the following year, leading medical administrators to realize that containment efforts had to begin there to stop its further spread to Cairo.[8] At any rate, the outbreak, combined with the measures to contain it, may have complicated attempts to recover the manuscripts from their underground hiding place.

In October, Neubauer's letter to d'Hulst stressed the need to establish whether the hoard contained whole books or at least considerable portions of books. No doubt the Bodleian Curators needed to be convinced of the rationale behind the purchase. And, according to Sayce, Nicholson had some concerns about 'the mode of getting them' as well as 'fears about their ownership'. Neubauer was equally anxious that others would get to the prize before him, and so he urged d'Hulst to try to finish the work before the winter's end. At some point during the months of October and November, the underground stash was moved, and most likely placed in the space behind the wall on the upper floor of the women's gallery. By 29 November 1895, Sayce was finally able to announce that 'At last, the MSS are coming in'.

In addition to sharing this momentous news, Sayce revealed that the three heads of the community had sold the manuscripts, but the operation was impeded because 'the one with whom the bargain was made is perpetually drunk'. The manuscripts, which included some portions of manuscript books, together with several large, printed works, were packed tightly into a box with dimensions of over a metre in length, half a metre broad and nearly a metre high. Sayce estimated that the remainder of the hoard would require another three boxes of similar size and that they should be shipped together to save on costs. In the meantime, the first box was being sent on ahead, and

Sayce quipped that Neubauer's new assistant Arthur Ernest Cowley would receive it as a 'Christmas box'. In fact, only one box, or at most two boxes, reached Oxford as plans to ship the rest were disrupted.[9] These disruptions may have been caused by the cholera outbreak, which necessitated restrictions on certain types of transportation, or they may have been exacerbated by the delicate interactions with the person in charge of selling the items.[10] Sayce reported on the holdup the following month, and he claimed that 'as soon as any money is paid to the old Rabbi & his colleagues they immediately get dead drunk upon it, & nothing can be done with them until their funds are exhausted'. Given the lack of any other corroborating evidence as to the drinking habits of community members, Sayce may have meant that they became figuratively drunk on the money. But whether he meant literally or figuratively drunk, news of the discovery or at least of the payments, must have leaked out and may have reached the ears of agents and dealers and their extended networks elsewhere. Thus, the operation to pack and ship four boxes was probably impeded by the arrival of several other manuscript hunters on the scene, or in the locale, who may have offered higher prices.

WHEN ELKAN NATHAN ADLER ARRIVED IN CAIRO IN JANUARY 1896, he was taken on a tour of the Ben Ezra Synagogue. Adler's ongoing involvement with the Anglo-Jewish Association and its operations abroad gave him additional reasons to travel and keep the Council updated with his reports. While making efforts to observe the condition of Jewish communities in various countries, specifically the state of Jewish education, he was also amassing a large and magnificent private collection of books and manuscripts by acquiring pieces at every stop. Not having a dedicated agent on the ground, Adler used the Hebrew lingua franca and his rabbinic connections to open doors. As he recounted in 1905:

> Hebrew, a *lingua franca* which, however badly spoken, is a sure proof of one's Judaism, enabled me to be understood and accepted as one of themselves. So, after service and a few preliminaries, one asks 'where is the Genizah', and is told 'it is under the floor beneath that stone'. The stone is easily removed and one goes down into a sort of damp cellar and finds the scraps of yesterday's letters mouldy and illegible. Still the search has stimulated curiosity, and I can explain that I am prepared to offer money, good money, for worthless old books.[11]

In Spain and Portugal, he purchased Inquisition records, and in other parts of Europe he mostly acquired important incunables and exceptionally rare early printed works, such as the famous Prague Haggadah of 1526, as well as significant non-Judaic works like a Shakespeare folio and Rembrandt etchings. In Egypt, he bought Karaite manuscripts, and additional Hebrew manuscripts were obtained in other parts of North Africa. Adler also recalled how he eventually learnt to adapt his approach depending on the community and, he admitted that in places such as Frankfurt and Vienna, where people were accustomed to dealing with booksellers' agents, it was harder to 'get the advantage over them'.

However, prior to 1896, a major manuscript discovery still eluded him. An awareness that materials were coming to light in *genizot* in Egypt might have been something he picked up from his correspondence with David Kaufmann, particularly if Kaufmann had inadvertently revealed to him information about acquiring a special box from Egypt in December 1894. Adler would have read the increasing number of scholarly articles pertaining to manuscript discoveries, particularly the ones that concerned his brother, Hermann and the *Etz Chayim,* and also Neubauer's recent piece about the Bodleian fragments 'found in a *Genizah* at Cairo'. Nevertheless, for the past few years, Adler had focused his attentions on Morocco, Algeria and Tunis.

Before embarking on his return trip to Palestine and Egypt in December 1895, Adler attended the monthly meeting of the Council of the Anglo-Jewish Association, during which the members agreed to fund a new building for the Evelina de Rothschild School for girls.[12] In addition to visiting that school, the Jerusalem Technical School and a school in Jaffa, Adler spent the first weeks of his December holiday with friends, especially Nissim Behar, the director of the Lionel de Rothschild School and founder of modern Hebrew education. Adler had formed a close relationship with Behar back in 1888, and with his sister Fortunée Behar, the headmistress of the Evelina de Rothschild School.

The Behar siblings had been born in Jerusalem but raised in Constantinople. Nissim Behar was an early champion of the Alliance Israélite Universelle schools and the cause of Sephardi education, helping to establish Alliance schools in Aleppo, Syria, Bulgaria and Constantinople. Although he was not an avid collector himself, while working for the Alliance in Aleppo, Behar appears to have been involved in taking photographs of the famous Crown of Aleppo on behalf of his superior in Paris, Isadore Loeb.[13] Upon his return to Palestine, Behar founded the first Alliance school in Jerusalem, and he established the method of teaching Hebrew through Hebrew.[14]

When Adler reached the Holy City, talk of book collecting was very much in the air. Joseph Chasanowitz's 10,000 books had arrived in Jerusalem that autumn destined for the new national library. Behar himself was one of seven members of a 'General Jewish Library of Jerusalem' committee established in January 1894 to promote the interests of the national library.[15] Kaufmann's close associate Mordechai Adelmann, a seasoned collector who was still serving on the B'nai B'rith Jerusalem Lodge committee, and later served as a member of the renamed 'Local Committee of the Jerusalem Central Library', was likewise closely involved in all these matters.

Adler returned to Cairo in late December or early January. He may have gone there partly to inspect the Alliance school since it had recently petitioned the Anglo-Jewish Association for funding for an English teacher, but no record of such a visit was reported. Unlike his first visit to Cairo in 1888, which he described in detail over two columns in *The Jewish Chronicle,* Adler did not rush to publish an account of his experiences there in 1896. Given that this was an equally if not more momentous trip, the silence is surprising. In fact, his encounter with 'the Genizah' on 3 January 1896 was only shared publicly one year later, and then only after the news of a major genizah discovery in the Ben Ezra Synagogue had already broken.

When he finally wrote about it, Adler described returning to the scene in the company of the chief rabbi: a circumstance which is interesting, given that his first tour was taken alone. The sight that greeted him was unexpected: the ancient synagogue, he noted, was 'restored out of all knowledge'. Inside the new building, Rabbi Raphael

Ben-Simeon guided him to the end of the ladies' gallery where he entered 'the secret chamber of the Genizah through a hole in the wall'. During the three or four hours he was allowed to spend there, he took away with him a sack full of paper and parchment writings (although, he later recalled that it was a Torah mantle – the only receptacle they could find). That the materials had been placed there only recently, or at least as recently as 1892, was not mentioned. However, when he came to write about his adventures many years later, he crowned himself as 'the first European' to have entered the Genizah.[16]

Given Adler's descriptive powers, it is even more surprising that none of his recollections of the genizah chamber (supposedly filled with over a quarter of a million fragments) record an impression of what such an incredible sight should have made on him. But if, as Sayce told Neubauer in November 1895, the manuscripts had only just begun 'coming in', then it's possible that Adler only caught the middle game of a secret operation to disinter tens of thousands of fragments from an underground location or locations and re-situate them inside the synagogue. The result of tossing medieval fragments into the space behind the wall would eventually create a scene reminiscent of

Figure 10.1 MS. Bodl. Heb. f. 51, a fragment of Exodus in shorthand writing, given to the Bodleian Library by A. E. Cowley in 1895.

a 'battlefield of books'. Exposed to fluctuating environmental conditions underground, many would be discovered stuck together in 'unshapely lumps'. The damp, earthy smell of the fragments was one of the clues that Adler later claimed led to the full discovery of the hoard. And anyone who encountered the hoard in the chamber behind the wall after 1896 would likely gain the impression that it was a 'real old genizah'.

Even though he did not publicly write about the nature of his discovery in *The Jewish Chronicle*, Adler told his friends about some of the contents of his sack, and news began to leak out. Not long after he arrived home, he attended a lecture given by Michael Friedländer, the principal of Jews' College, about the fragments with unusual shorthand notation that Cowley had brought back from his recent trip to Egypt and Neubauer published in *The Jewish Quarterly Review*. Adler was noted as offering remarks at the end of the lecture, which may have related to manuscripts now in his possession.[17] He had certainly set to work on deciphering some of his treasures right away. Just fourteen days after Friedländer's talk, *The Jewish Chronicle* gave notice that he was helping Adler to decipher a fragment from the 'Genisa at Fostat', a dedicatory poem written in honour of 'Jehuda ha-Nagid', an eleventh- or twelfth-century Egyptian leader. Since no other explanation was supplied, and the newspaper had not previously reported on the existence of such a 'Genisa', the casual reference implies that certain members of its readership, which included Kaufmann over in Budapest, were in the know. Indeed, Adler subsequently mailed his fragment to Kaufmann for further elucidation.[18]

KAUFMANN AND NEUBAUER CONTINUED TO BE AT ODDS with each other in the pages of *The Jewish Quarterly Review*. Their veiled disagreements were in relation to the significance and elucidation of certain manuscript witnesses. During the course of these exchanges, Neubauer drew greater attention to Adler's recent acquisitions from Cairo, as well as to his own supplier in Jerusalem, Rabbi Solomon Aaron Wertheimer. The focus of the debate was an Egyptian Purim scroll (*megillah*) discovered by the scholar George Margoliouth in the British Museum. The scroll related an event in which twelve Cairene Jews were saved from destruction at the hands of Ahmed Shaitan, the Ottoman Viceroy of Cairo, during his revolt against the Sultan Suleiman of Constantinople in 1524. According to the seventeenth century Egyptian historian, Joseph Sambari, the reading of the text took place in Cairo every year in a way that mirrored the traditional reading of the biblical story of Esther. Neubauer had published Sambari's historical text back in 1887. Kaufmann followed up on Margoliouth's article with corrections, and he concluded his piece with the wish that a new edition of Sambari's work could be produced that would supplement Neubauer's omissions.

In the next issue of *The Jewish Quarterly Review*, Neubauer introduced a twelfth-century composition in Hebrew that comprised an earlier Egyptian tradition of Purim. The text was reconstructed from a fragment in the Firkovich collection and two in the Bodleian. He used the text to posit some theories about the chronology of the medieval Jewish rabbinic authorities known by the title 'Nagid'. Neubauer then cited several of Adler's fragments that shed light on the office of the Nagid, and some pieces held in Paris, including a twelfth-century marriage contract from Fustat. Moreover, he used the opportunity to point out that the Müller and Kaufmann article from 1888, based on a fragment from the Rainer papyrus collection, was flawed. In addition, he directly responded to Kaufmann's call for a third edition of Sambari to supplement his omissions by calling his attention to another manuscript of the work being held in Paris.

In a postscript, Neubauer explained that when his friend S. J. Halberstam came to review the proof copy of his article, he realized that the manuscripts he was citing had already been published by Wertheimer in his *Ginzei Yerushalayim*. In other words, Wertheimer was preparing fragments for publication and then selling them on without informing the buyer of their publication status. Neubauer then discovered that the same thing had happened with two other manuscripts Wertheimer had sold to him, and he used the opportunity to give him a gentle rebuke.

In addition to publicly upbraiding Wertheimer, Neubauer made it plain that he had a larger message to convey. Not only was the history of the Jews of Egypt still unwritten, the manuscripts by which to write that history were spread across international institutions and he added, most pointedly, that they were also in the hands of 'private possessors' who were 'not invariably inclined to make them accessible'.[19] The accusation was undoubtedly aimed at Kaufmann and designed to contrast Neubauer's more publicly minded collecting work with Kaufmann's more self-centred collecting activities. Yet, when the Purim fragments were catalogued years later, their initial classmarks were changed and they were rebound together with other versions in one volume. The important information about two of their previous owners (Chester and Wertheimer) was forgotten or simply omitted and they were designated as 'From the Geniza, 1891, 1895, and 1896'.

The idea of so many fragments remaining hidden in private hands was something that also plagued Neubauer's new assistant, Arthur Ernest Cowley. In an article for *The Jewish Quarterly Review* offering general remarks on the history of the Samaritans, he reiterated Neubauer's points in relation to Samaritan literature by issuing a plea: 'I beg you therefore, if any one has any such fragment or knows of the existence of any, to give me the opportunity of inspecting it'.[20]

MOSES GASTER WAS A COLLECTOR with an impressive private library of books and manuscripts, who was also considered an authority on the Samaritans. In March, Cowley had presented a lecture on the subject of 'The Literature and Religion of the Samaritans' to the Jews' College Literary Society, and Gaster, who was in the audience, told him of his ties to the Samaritans through the Sephardi *Haham* in Nablus. He also revealed that he owned a copy of the Samaritan work 'Kourban Moshé', which he claimed dated from the fourth century CE, and that it was connected to the 'Egyptian papyri that had lately come to England'.[21] Thus, while Cowley's plea in *The Jewish Quarterly Review* may have been aimed at any individuals inclined to purchase fragments lately emerging from the Near East, it may also have been directly aimed at Gaster. While Gaster himself decried private ownership, he firmly believed that in his own case, his personal library offered the best and safest environment for all manuscripts and to that end bore no scruples in convincing others to give him their treasures:

> In my capacity as Haham of the Sephardic community, I came into close contact
> not only with the members of my congregation but also with the communities

in the Orient. I convinced people that when they keep books in their own house, sooner or later they are lost and consigned to oblivion. I could easily show them that often after the death of the owners, such books, even valuable volumes, are dispersed or destroyed by the heirs out of sheer disinterest. In order to avoid this literary barbarity, I induced people to donate their books to me, in effect to hand them over to the ordered care of my library.[22]

While he claimed that he would reward his donors by adding their name to a bookplate, he was also notoriously silent on the provenance of his manuscripts. Cowley ended his own appeal for greater access to important materials with what turned out to be a prophetic statement: 'Even the smallest and apparently most insignificant fragment may be useful when taken in conjunction with what is already collected.'

Elkan Adler, who was also in the audience at Cowley's lecture, was keen to let other people know about his treasures. Shortly after bringing attention to his 'genisa' fragment relating to 'Jehuda ha-Nagid', he prepared a short article on a four-page manuscript connected to the Palestinian triennial cycle of Torah readings. The manuscript, he announced, had been 'among a large mass of Hebrew and Arabic MS. fragments which, by the courtesy of the Cairene Hebrew community, I have just been permitted to bring away from the *geniza* at Fostat'.[23] On 10 March, Adler sent a fragment as a gift to his good friend in Denmark, the chief rabbi, David Simonsen. The piece, a tenth-century document enclosing a legal query to one of the Jewish leaders in Egypt, was accompanied by a note from Adler informing Simonsen that the fragment was from the genizah 'in the old synagogue in Fostat Egypt'.[24] In fact, Adler's indiscretions as to the Fostat find spot led Sayce to complain later to Neubauer that he 'was spoiling everything'.[25]

PRIVATE COMMUNICATIONS BETWEEN SCHOLARS IN OXBRIDGE may have led to news leaking out through other sources. After Sayce told Neubauer about the delays in purchasing the underground cache, Neubauer must have passed the news on to Gwilliam who had been waiting to see if there was any likelihood that other fragments would be 'offered for sale in the same quarter'. When it seemed an impossibility, Gwilliam and Stenning decided to publish what they had so far. Through Burkitt they learnt that he and Mrs Bensly had edited some other fragments of Palestinian Syriac discovered during their Sinai trip, and the two were invited to collaborate on the publication. Thus, through the Oxfordians, news about fragments in al-Fustat may have leaked to their collaborator Cantabrigians, and through them to other members of the Sinai team: Harris, Lewis and Gibson. Harris would not go chasing manuscripts that year: he and his wife were on a mission to help the victims of the Armenian massacre. Lewis and Gibson, on the other hand, were eager to go wherever the possibility of palimpsests beckoned. According to Lewis's memoir, when news from Cairo (perhaps from their Presbyterian friends at the American Mission) 'seemed to indicate that there might be a chance of our finding something there', the sisters quickly abandoned their plans to stay at home that winter.[26]

However it reached them, and in whatever form it came, the news must have been compelling. So compelling, in fact, that they even decided to risk the cholera epidemic.

Before leaving, they spent time with the Schechters and, as Mathilde later noted in her unpublished memoir, when the sisters asked if they could bring them back a gift, Schechter replied, 'if they could buy Hebrew MSS. from the little antiquity shops, they should do so'.[27] Whether connected to Schechter's request or not, as they set off for Cairo, they decided to 'see the manuscripts at Jerusalem also'.

When they arrived in Cairo, they found, as they had half suspected, that the city was under quarantine. In sympathy with the sentiments of a distinguished surgeon friend, who had pronounced quarantine to be 'more dangerous than the cholera', they were determined to avoid it. Instead, they decided to take the shorter but more gruelling overland passage to Jerusalem through the northern part of the Sinai desert up past the swamps of Lake Bardawil, where Greville Chester had once blazed a trail in search of the route of the Exodus. On they trudged through Gaza and up across the wilderness where, at one point, they and their guides proceeded to get hopelessly lost. After several days of wandering, without food or tents, they found themselves northwest of the Jaffa Gate in Jerusalem, near the Birket Mamilla or Upper Pool of Gihon. Finally, after arriving soaked and bedraggled at their hotel, the sisters were able to spend the next four weeks in comfort.

Their time in Jerusalem was spent mostly photographing manuscripts in the Greek Monastery of the Church of the Holy Sepulchre and touring around the Old City and parts of the new, including the Yemin Moshe neighbourhood. They purchased a 'large Hebrew MS. of the Pentateuch', but remained silent as to the source of the sale. They were equally guarded about a 'bundle of fragments' they mysteriously acquired from 'a dealer in the plain of Sharon'. The anonymous merchant may have been based in Jaffa, then the largest city on the south edge of that area, with its own thriving marketplace, and the sisters' eventual port of departure. Or else he may have been someone for whom the sale of antiquities was a side-line, like Adelmann who owned a store in Jerusalem near the Jaffa Gate and who travelled across the country to help immigrants arriving at Jaffa and those living in colonies across the plain. Equally, the purchase of the bundle could have been made in Jerusalem, perhaps through someone else known to be connected to the supply of fragments at that point or later, like Solomon Wertheimer or Samuel Raffalovich.

Conjecture aside, the use of such a broad geographic area to describe the place of purchase was clearly intended to obscure the trail. In the very next sentence of her travelogue, Agnes Lewis briefly mentioned that a 'similar bundle' had been bought in Cairo and packed away in Mrs Gibson's trunk. Given the short amount of time they spent in the cholera-ridden city, it is hard to imagine how they had time or ability to source such a bundle. Perhaps it was already there waiting for them at somewhere like the American Mission, or perhaps it had never been bought there at all. Furthermore, while an actual place of purchase was mentioned in this instance, it was glossed over so quickly as to again suggest obfuscation on the part of the author.

The details that followed – their expected trip overland to Beirut, which had to be cancelled due to the rain, and their subsequent travails with the Customs House in Jaffa – were, by contrast, described at length. Albert Singer, with whom Wertheimer had experienced difficulties in importing his manuscripts back from England to Jerusalem, was the unnamed Jewish vice-consul at Jaffa who 'raised difficulties' as to the import of the sisters' trunk from Beirut. Not only was Singer suspicious about their activities, the Customs House officials in Beirut had also sent a message to their counterparts in Jaffa 'to be very particular about that box'.

That they were distrustful of its contents is not surprising given the odd circumstance of it being sent up to Beirut from Jerusalem and then down again to Jaffa. Agnes claimed that their guide, Joseph, came to their rescue when the box was opened, and the bundle of fragments was discovered inside. Taking advantage of a law that exempted copies of the Bible from being confiscated, he explained that the pieces of Hebrew writing were used by the ladies for their prayers. Had Vice-Consul Singer been physically present, it is hard to imagine that such an argument would have prevailed, but for the Turkish officials examining the contents of the trunk, as well as the other manuscript and bundle, it sufficed. Nevertheless, the whole story they gave connected to the acquisition of these fragments was distinctly odd regarding both the details omitted and those provided, particularly given the momentous chain of events that followed and the significance of pieces of literature they were unknowingly carrying within their bundles.

The sisters returned to their house in Cambridge on 3 May 1896 and Margaret set about identifying the biblical fragments. Among the pieces, however, were texts that she couldn't decipher and so, assuming them to be rabbinic, they decided to seek guidance from Schechter. Ten days later, Agnes met him walking across King's Parade and she told him of their manuscript purchases. While she continued about her errands, Schechter went hotfoot over to their house. Upon her return she found him there pouring over the manuscripts. One of them, a piece from the Jerusalem Talmud, he pronounced as very rare; another piece, which appeared to interest him even more deeply, he asked to take away with him for further examination. Just one hour later, Schechter sent a telegram to the sisters: 'Fragment is very important, come to me this afternoon.' He followed this up with a handwritten note to let them know that 'the fragment I took with me represents a piece of the *original Hebrew of Ecclesiasticus*. It is the first time that such a thing was discovered'. Swearing them to secrecy on the matter, he requested another meeting so that they could discuss how to 'make the matter known'. Privately, to Mathilde, he declared: 'Wife, as long as the Bible lives my name shall not die.'[28]

SCHECHTER'S DISCOVERY OF BEN SIRA was as consequential as it was serendipitous. He had been engaged for some time in an intense scholarly debate concerning the original Hebrew version and here was evidence on the sisters' dining table to corroborate his theory. The Book of Ben Sira derived from the ancient Near Eastern tradition of wisdom literature and was a similar composition to the book of Proverbs. It was written at some point between the second and third centuries BCE by the Jerusalemite Simeon ben Jeshua ben Eleazar ben Sira. His composition did not become integrated into the canon of the Bible, and the complete original Hebrew version was eventually lost. The only surviving version was the Greek translation made by his grandson in 132 BCE. The Greek text, Ecclesiasticus, became one of a series of non-canonical biblical works known collectively as the Apocrypha and part of the accepted cannon of the Catholic Church.

By the nineteenth century, the dating of the later biblical books became a focus of debate between the leading Protestant scholars of the school of Higher Criticism (biblical criticism) and Jewish scholars, like Schechter and Neubauer, who realized that the Higher Critics' laudable attempts to subject the Hebrew Bible and the Apocrypha to rigorous scholarly analysis were being tainted by their anti-Jewish bias. In contrast to what they regarded as the early and authentic Israelite period of the 'Old Testament', the Higher Critics characterized the Judaism of the later post-exilic biblical period as contaminated by what they deemed as the legalistic and materialistic disposition of the priestly elite. This idea was inherited from earlier German scholars whose theological works had drawn a clear demarcation between the ancient Israelites (their spiritual forebears) and the distinctly separate members of a temporal-bound post-biblical Jewish religion.[29]

In translating Ben Sira's work, his grandson had added a colophon, enabling it to be the one book of the period that can be reliably dated. Whereas most Bible scholars believed that the Greek version of Ecclesiasticus was the most authentic text, and either ignored or were ignorant of the Rabbinic evidence, Schechter and Neubauer had both spent copious hours carefully collating Hebrew quotations from Ben Sira's work found scattered throughout the vast landscape of rabbinic literature from the earliest works through to ninth-century writings to prove the case for a Hebrew original.[30] One major catalyst for their work in this area had been the inaugural lecture of the new Laudian chair of Arabic at Oxford, David Samuel Margoliouth, in 1890. Margoliouth, the son of a Hebrew-Christian missionary who had translated the New Testament into Hebrew, was himself a highly respected Oxford scholar of classical and Oriental languages. His lecture, 'The Place of Ecclesiasticus in Semitic Literature', based on his Kennicott Prize winning dissertation, attempted to reconstruct the Hebrew version from the Greek and Syriac versions, while largely ignoring the rabbinic evidence. Ben Sira's Hebrew, he suggested, agreeing with many in the academy about the quality of post-biblical Hebrew, was a somewhat bastardized and vulgar version of the classical language. A gulf must separate the Hebrew of Isaiah from that of Ecclesiastes, he argued, and 'a yet greater gulf must yawn between Ecclesiastes and Ecclesiasticus'. If there were any merit in restoring Ben Sira's language, he concluded, then it would be to get closer to the language of 'Christ and His Apostles'.[31] When evidence of the original finally came to light, Margoliouth would claim that having consigned to a genizah meant that the original Hebrew of Ben Sira was not lost but deliberately destroyed.

In the wake of Margoliouth's public lambasting of post-biblical Hebrew, Schechter and Neubauer realized that through their attempts to recover the original language and content of Ben Sira they were not only providing comparative tools by which to date other biblical books, they were also demonstrating the vitality and spirituality of later Judaism and the Hebrew language. Thus, when the sisters unknowingly conveyed in their bundles a medieval copy of Ecclesiasticus in Hebrew, they brought back to England key evidence of an authentic chain of transmission from the original Hebrew version through to the medieval period. For Schechter, who knew the rabbinic quotations intimately, it took less than an hour to verify his excited suspicions by checking the ragged-looking fragment against printed works in the library.

After the sisters and Schechter conferred on a plan of action, Agnes wrote to *The Athenaeum* that evening with the following announcement:

All students of the Bible and of the Apocrypha will be interested to learn that amongst some fragments of Hebrew MSS. which my sister Mrs. Gibson and I have just acquired in Palestine, a leaf of the Book of Ecclesiasticus has been discovered to-day by Mr S. Schechter, Lecturer in Talmudic to the University of Cambridge. The Talmud contains many quotations from the Book of Ecclesiasticus, which are not always accurate; and Jewish writers of the ninth century have also preserved some passages for us. But now for the first time we have a leaf, albeit a mutilated one, direct from itself.[32]

In making the matter known, the source of the fragments was declared to be 'Palestine'. Yet fragments from the same manuscript were about to emerge from another source in Cairo. Six weeks after Agnes's announcement in *The Athenaeum,* the 'Literary Gossip' section of that journal provided the following news:

We are now glad to be able to mention that among other Hebrew documents procured by Prof. Sayce for the Bodleian Library, Dr. Neubauer has found other fragments in Hebrew of the same book, containing chapters xl to xlix. The language most closely approaches classical Hebrew, and is in hemistichs, like the book of Proverbs, but apparently without any metre.[33]

While such significant information was sandwiched almost nonchalantly between a notice concerning the upcoming publication of some short stories by a Mrs W. K. Clifford and news of a delay on the secondary education bill, it did not fail to gain wide notice. Schechter was outraged at Neubauer's behaviour which had formerly been so collegial and non-territorial and now smacked of one-upmanship.

NEUBAUER HAD SPENT YEARS TRACKING down the source of the Egyptian fragments, and he had long envisioned great finds emerging from the Near East. Thus, Schechter's sudden, and somewhat lucky, coup could have been too much to bear. It may also have occurred to Neubauer that the sisters had been tipped off to the source of the fragments through their mutual connection with the scholars working on the Palestinian Syriac manuscripts: hence their hurried trip to Egypt. If so, he may have felt resentful that his covert mission to recover the manuscripts had inadvertently led to Schechter's discovery. It must have been a frustration for the 65-year-old whose health was on the decline and whose ability to read such precious manuscripts was severely hampered due to failing eyesight.

When Neubauer and Cowley published their fragments the following year, they caused even greater upset by declaring that their discovery of Ecclesiasticus fragments had taken place 'almost' simultaneously with Schechter's in Cambridge.[34] Agnes Lewis afterwards contended that it was 'natural for us to think that my letter of May 13th, published on May 16th, was of some assistance in guiding Messrs. Neubauer and Cowley to this important result'. She also added, somewhat audaciously, that she heard the Oxford scholars had first spotted the line: 'Let us praise famous men, and the fathers that begat us.'[35]

For certain, Neubauer and Cowley had been busy sorting through the fragments found by d'Hulst since they had first arrived at the Bodleian in January or February. Their selection eventually amounted to 1,108 items, having set aside fragments deemed unworthy of adding to the library's magnificent Hebrew collection. The decision as to which pieces to keep was also guided by Neubauer's close associate, the Regius Professor of Hebrew, Samuel R. Driver, who had been asked by the Bodleian administrators to approve the selections. This effort at weeding out fragments may have been the only way that Neubauer could get the library's administrators to agree to their purchase in the first place. The case to buy the pieces could easily be made on the promise that there were treasures to be found among the jumbled pieces; however, the case to fund the long-term storage, preservation and cataloguing of every tiny, mutilated fragment would not be something readily acceptable to a library whose ability to acquire substantial treasures from around the world was dependent on sound fiscal judgement. Thus, in May, the Bodleian Curators decided to authorize 'the giving away, exchange, or sale of unbound fragments of Hebrew writing recently purchased or in future to be purchased'.[36] With the agreement also pertaining to subsequent purchases, Neubauer was set to continue the negotiations for the Cairo fragments.

As to the hunt for the complete Book of Ben Sira, instead of working together to track down the missing leaves, Schechter and Neubauer each embarked on a secret race against the other to find the rest of the work. From the size of the leaves and the number of hemistichs per leaf, Neubauer worked out that the complete copy of that manuscript would have extended to between thirty and thirty-six leaves.[37] He also knew that his leaves had been found in an underground chamber in or near the Ben Ezra Synagogue in Old Cairo, and despite Schechter's contention in the published edition of his fragment that it had been found in a bundle from Palestine, Neubauer knew that fragments from Egypt had also come to him via Palestine.

SCHECHTER'S APPRECIATION OF FRAGMENTS was probably enhanced by the discovery of the leaf of Ben Sira. At some point during 1896, under his guidance, Cambridge University Library purchased over forty fragmentary manuscripts from Wertheimer, and during the summer, Schechter produced a short article describing some of the pieces in the Lewis-Gibson collection, in which he defended the acquisition of fragments. He also used the piece as a vehicle through which to underline his own reputation:

> They consist, it is true, mostly of fragments, but this by no means diminishes their significance. I need only remind the reader of the Ecclesiasticus Fragment, which by general consent is one of the most important discoveries made within recent decades.[38]

The article, stating the importance of fragments, may also have been a means by which to further promote his proposed quest to find the source to the authorities of the university. Now, with the discovery of additional leaves of Ben Sira at Oxford, Schechter realized that recovering the entire work was a distinct possibility. His growing desire to get to the source, according to his wife, Mathilde, 'almost became an obsession'.[39] In addition, Neubauer's find confirmed that the fragments most likely came from the same location that he had mentioned in *The Jewish Quarterly Review* ('a Genizah at Cairo') and the location recently revealed by Adler ('a Geniza at Fostat'). The only find spot that wasn't directly referred to was the Ben Ezra Synagogue.

Talking over his plans to go to Egypt with friends at Cambridge, he found enthusiastic support from the likes of Professor Henry Sidgwick and Dr Donald MacAlister, who encouraged him to apply to the university for travel funds. Yet, his friend and student, Charles Taylor, the Master of St. John's College, advised him against such an application, for it would no doubt prove to be a lengthy, bureaucracy-bound process with no certainty as to outcome. Instead, Taylor, who was independently wealthy and, in addition to his own specialism in mathematics, an ardent Hebraist, offered Schechter his private financial backing to secure the manuscripts. Not only would it ensure the secrecy of his mission, having immediate access to funds would provide him with the necessary means to guarantee the mission's success.[40]

With an increased impetus to secure the sale of the subterranean hoard, knowing that remaining leaves of Ben Sira could be hidden in the pile, Sayce sent a message to d'Hulst to inform him that he had persuaded the university authorities to send Neubauer to Cairo for the winter season. Neubauer, he felt, stood a better chance of negotiating with the synagogue authorities. All being well, they would send him out there after the autumn term ended. But rumours were also circulating about Elkan Adler's recent visit there and it was unclear just how much he'd hauled away. Sayce was worried about sending Neubauer on a futile trip, and he anxiously enquired about the status of the hoard and d'Hulst's advice on the plan.[41]

ELKAN NATHAN ADLER DISCOVERED FURTHER TREASURES in his sack, and he reached out to numerous scholars for help with the decipherment and publication of a fascinating sixteen-page manuscript. The manuscript turned out to be an eleventh-century copy of the *Sefer Ha-'Ittim* (Book of Times) by one of the leading rabbinic authorities of medieval Spain, Judah ben Barzillai (aka Al-Bargeloni, or 'of Barcelona'). Barzillai was a major codifier of Jewish law, and while his work was highly cited, complete copies were mostly lost. The work provided insights into the state of knowledge of the Masoretic Text among the early rabbinic authorities. In addition to consulting with Friedländer on the transcription of the text, Adler reached out to Schechter about its origins. In early July, Schechter responded to Adler's letter to let him know that the text was most likely by Barzillai. In addition, he offered him advice on which scholarly works and authorities to consult to help with the identification of the text and its author. A copy was also owned by Moses Gaster, and he recommended that Adler consult it. Such crucial help, enabling Adler to fully identify and subsequently publish his manuscript, also left him feeling somewhat beholden to his scholarly friend. In his subsequent publication of the manuscript, he acknowledged 'Mr. Schechter, to whom I am indebted for a great deal of valuable help in connexion with this paper'. Schechter would soon call in the favour and, as Adler pointed out, 'accorded unique privileges'.[42]

Despite discussing individual fragments in his collection with other scholars, Adler had indeed kept the full extent of his haul from Cairo a secret. At some point in October or November, however, he issued an invitation to both Neubauer and Schechter to visit him at his brother's house so that he could show them his sack of fragments. Adler may have hoped that the two eminent scholars would quickly identify items of great significance: perhaps even a piece of Ben Sira that may have evaded him. In inviting both men, he clearly took the middle course, but no doubt fearing that some momentous find would be made without him, Schechter responded to Adler: 'do expect me there do but do not show your treasures till you see me.'[43]

At any rate, no portions of Ben Sira or anything particularly outstanding came to their notice that evening. Yet, the visit to see Adler's sack was a turning point in the fate of the fragments. As Adler later recalled, Neubauer was unusually angry, while Schechter paid a curious amount of attention to the fragments' condition:

> I showed my treasures to Dr. Neubauer and to Dr. Schechter. Neubauer was very angry with me for not ransacking the whole Genizah. I told him that my conscience, which was tenderer then than now, reproached me for having taken away what I did, but he said that science knows no law. Schechter also was keenly interested in the fragments . . . he used his eyes and nose to very good purpose, for it was its characteristic odour and appearance that enabled him to recognise the Gibson fragment as one of the family.[44]

Adler's decision not to haul away everything was perhaps, as he told his friends, a matter of conscience; but more likely, it was because exporting large quantities of fragments out of another country, even under British colonial rule, was a tricky matter. Neubauer's anger at Adler for not having taken away all the manuscripts may well have been a cover to hide the fact that he had someone on the ground trying to do that very same thing, or else it was the realization that by sharing the news, Adler would alert others to the secret stash which would exacerbate the problem of unidentified, unclassified and untraceable fragments spread around the world.

Concerns about the problem of private collectors aside, it seems that after viewing the damp and scrappy state of his fragments, Neubauer nonetheless made a fateful decision regarding Sayce's plan. Combined with some recent advice from d'Hulst (most likely a warning against travel while the cholera epidemic continued to rage through Cairo), he decided to temporarily abort his plan to travel to Cairo that winter. Sayce communicated the decision to d'Hulst:

> I have just received a post-card from Dr. Neubauer, in which he tells me that in consequence of what you told me he has postponed his visit to Cairo, & if you think he can do no good here will not come at all. He says he will be entirely 'guided by the Count's advice'. He further tells me that he has seen Dr. Adler who has brought with him 'a lot of worthless rubbish for which he paid high prices'. I told him, that at present there seems little use in his coming here & that he had better leave the matter in your hands.[45]

The damp, musty odour of Adler's fragments caused, no doubt, by their interment in an underground location for an unknown period of time before being placed inside the Ben Ezra Synagogue, was also present on the fragments purchased by Lewis and Gibson. If Schechter had not known previously exactly where in Cairo he should search for the rest of Ben Sira, now he did. This revelation, combined with whatever else Adler must have related to them about his visit to Cairo that evening, helped him to realize that his relationship with Adler could be advantageous in gaining access to key members of the Cairo community. It was time to call in his chip.

In addition to continuing to take an interest in Adler's Barzillai by guiding him to identify the sources within the text, and providing him with scholarly references on which to follow up, Schechter also asked his grateful friend if he, or his brother Hermann, could supply him with an introduction to Cairo's chief rabbi. Adler came through and furnished him with a glowing letter of recommendation in which he described Schechter using the Hebrew terms '*lamdan*' (meaning someone deeply learned in rabbinic literature) and '*tzadik*' (meaning 'righteous'): virtues that Schechter jokingly questioned owning; but that, of course, Adler knew would hold great appeal for Rabbi Raphael Ben-Simeon.

Just prior to his trip to Cairo, on 14 December 1896, Schechter wrote to Adler to let him know that he planned to stay overnight in London before leaving for Marseilles. He asked him if he could meet up with him to talk about Egypt. He also requested further letters of introduction to 'Catui or some such name in Cairo and Manasseh in Alexandria. Can you give me one or get one for me from a friend[?]'[46] By Manasseh and Catui, he meant the highly affluent Menasce family of Alexandria and the equally well-to-do Cattaoui family of Cairo. Adler's reply to him is not extant. Among the many missing letters in the archives is one that Adler later claimed he had received from Schechter promising 'not to take anything away with him from Egypt'.[47]

While Schechter realized that Adler's letters would help open the doors of Jewish institutions, the question of gaining permission to export manuscripts was addressed, he hoped, by a letter of recommendation from the vice chancellor of Cambridge University and by letters of introduction from other Cambridge professors of note. Armed with the keys to Cairo, Schechter was now ready to embark on a transformative journey.

11

The keys to Cairo (1896–7)

FROM THE GRAND ROYAL HOTEL IN CAIRO, Solomon Schechter penned a hurried letter to his wife. In his odd mix of German and English, he let her know that he had arrived safely the evening before.[1] He was also keen to tell her that he had already made a visit to see the chief rabbi, Raphael Ben-Simeon, that he was well received, and that they had chatted all morning. Indeed, the Rabbi had almost at once agreed to take Schechter to see 'the Genizah' (Schechter underscored the words), where he would be allowed to make a selection. However, it was almost the end of the week, and the genizah visit would have to be delayed until the following Tuesday because the Rabbi had to prepare for the Sabbath, meetings on the Sunday, and a fast day on the Monday.

Thanks to Adler's interventions, Schechter's reputation preceded him for, as he related to Mathilde, the Rabbi kissed his book, the *Aboth de Rabbi Natan*, three times. In addition to his introductory letter, Adler had sent on ahead some printed books as gifts, possibly addressed from his brother's house to lend the appearance of a gift from one chief rabbi to another. Accordingly, Ben-Simeon did not know at first who to thank. It was only a letter from Elkan Adler, mailed on his way to Persia, that made him realize who had sent the books, and he wrote to Hermann Adler to ask him to convey his thanks to the kind traveller, and to assure him that he would be happy to help Schechter. He was not sure, however, whether the ancient writings sought by Mr Schechter would be found in Cairo. Nevertheless, as Adler had cannily realized, the consignment of books, which included Schechter's *Agadath Shir Hashirim*, drew Ben-Simeon's warm and enthusiastic thanks, and they gave Schechter a key to gaining this particular Rabbi's good will and helpful assistance.[2]

Raphael Aaron Ben-Simeon was a near contemporary of Schechter's, having been born in Morocco in 1848. When he was six years old, his family moved to Jerusalem where his father became the leader of the Maghrebi (North African) Jewish community. In addition to a traditional education, Ben-Simeon was taught Arabic and European languages, and afterwards he gained various rabbinic appointments, including the Head of the Magen David Yeshivah. Throughout his lifetime he published numerous works relating to Jewish law and customs, most notably *Nehar Misrayim*, a complete compendium and guide to the customs of the Cairene Jewish community, and *Umi-Sur Devash*, his collected responsa on how to interpret Jewish law in light of modern circumstances.[3] In the 1880s, he was sent as an emissary by the Maghrebi community to France and Germany, and then to Morocco twice in 1888 and 1890, before becoming the *Hakham Bashi* (chief rabbi) of Cairo in 1891.

In Morocco, he discovered his metier, which was advocating for the importance of preserving old works through print. He established the *Doveve Sifte Yeshenim* society to promote and fund the printing of old Moroccan Jewish writings in the printing houses of Jerusalem and Alexandria. The idea was born of seeds planted early in his life by the *Haskalah* and *Wissenschaft* movements and based on his knowledge of an earlier, Western-based literary society, the *Mekitze Nirdamim*, founded by *maskilim* in Berlin, London and Lyck to preserve medieval Hebrew texts. Elkan Adler's father, Chief Rabbi Nathan Marcus Adler, had served on the *Mekitze Nirdamim's* first executive board. Ben-Simeon's activities succeeded in imparting to Moroccan Jews an increased awareness of print culture, and he provided them with a new method of gathering and collating local knowledge.[4] This was particularly important in the face of many recent disasters (both man-made and natural); it also helped preserve Hebrew and Arabic culture in the face of the modernizing educational activities of the Alliance Israélite Universelle, which treated these languages as secondary. On the other hand, while the movement was instrumental in saving many works that would have otherwise been lost, in some circumstances, it may have unwittingly engendered a disregard for the handwritten text, allowing manuscript hunters to take advantage and offer up modern print editions in exchange for ancient copies.

In addition to meeting Rabbi Ben-Simeon, Schechter was introduced to his younger brother, Mas'ud Hay Ben-Simeon (also known as Haim Bensimon). Mas'ud served as the secretary of the Grand Rabbinate of Cairo, and later he was appointed as the chief justice of the Rabbinical Court. He also served as interim chief rabbi for one year in 1920. Mas'ud was fluent in Arabic, with reading and writing knowledge of French, Spanish and Italian, and in the twentieth century he gained recognition for his major tripartite work of Jewish law in Arabic.[5] Schechter quickly realized that the way to the Rabbi's heart ran through his adored brother. Indeed, his intuitive sense was not wrong: Ben-Simeon had raised his brother as his own son after he was orphaned at the age of eleven, and in the wake of Mas'ud's premature death in 1925 at the age of fifty-four, Rabbi Ben-Simeon was reportedly 'forever broken'.[6] To get into Mas'ud's good graces, Schechter quickly agreed to take Arabic lessons with him three times a week during his stay. Mas'ud, for his part, agreed to take Schechter around in search of '*der Genizah*', and Schechter asked Mathilde to send him additional good copies of his books, the *Aboth de Rabbi Nathan* and his *Agadath Shir Hashirim*.

A VISIT TO THE BAZAARS WITH A MR CATTAOUI was the subject of Schechter's next letter to Mathilde on Tuesday, 29 December.[7] Mr Cattuoui's son, to whom he had a recommendation, was exceedingly kind to him and had promised to take him to *der Genizah den wir sehen aus leich funden werden* (the Genizah that can easily be found) the next morning. At this point on, and in his later acknowledgements, Schechter proceeded to muddle the names of the Cattaoui family members who lent him their help. In all his public acknowledgements, he thanked the 'President of the Cairo Jewish Community' and yet, he named this individual as 'Mr. Yussef M. Cattaui' (and elsewhere as 'Mr. Joseph Cattaui') and referred to his son as 'Mr. Elie M. Cattaui'. The only two members of the family fitting this description were Youssef Yacoub Cattaoui (son of the great Cattaoui forebear, Ya'qub Menasce Cattaoui, born in 1845) and his son Elie Menasce Cattaoui. It's possible that this father and son were the first members of the family to greet him and show him around the city. However, trusting his remembrance of the title 'President' to be more reliable than his memory for names, the individual who rendered him the greatest service must have been Moïse Cattaoui Pasha, the president of the Cairo Jewish community, and an important figure in Egyptian commercial life.

Moïse, born in 1850, was the brother of Youssef Yacoub Cattaoui and the son of Ya'qub Menasce Cattaoui, and he was well known to Elkan Adler from his visit in 1888. Another Cattaoui who may have given Schechter some help was Moïse's illustrious nephew, Joseph (or Yussuf) Aslan Cattaoui, who at that time held a position in the Ministry of Public Works, the ministry which oversaw the Service Des Antiquités. Joseph later became the family's most outstanding representative. In 1912, he was given the honorific title of 'Pasha' and gained positions in the Ministry of Finance and in the Ministry of Communications. In 1919, he was sent to England to help negotiate Egyptian independence, and eight years later he was appointed to the Egyptian Senate by King Fuad I. In addition to speaking French, Joseph Aslan Cattaoui was fluent in Arabic and Hebrew, and he authored books on Egyptian and world history, as well as articles on scientific and philosophical themes.[8] In 1924, he took over from his uncle Moïse as the Jewish community's president. Yet, the fact that there were numerous members of the Cattaoui family who served as community leaders, wardens of the synagogue, and facilitated access to the city's *genizot* was also attested by Adler who publicly thanked the 'Messrs Cattaui' for the fragments he brought back from Cairo in January 1896.

But, for now, it was the unnamed 'Mr. Cattaoui' who helped him to move to a more salubrious hotel in a better neighbourhood. Schechter's new hotel, the Métropole, had the advantage of being two shillings cheaper, although it was hidden down an alleyway, and described less than a decade later as an institution that sounded 'finer than it really was'.[9] For Schechter, however, it held some charm in being cleaner and close to the Parisian-inspired el-Azbakeya Garden and its European style cafes, as well as the Place de l'Opéra. It may have been for budgetary reasons that Schechter chose two less well-known hotels away from the buzz of the Shepheard's, or it may have been part of the plan to keep a low profile. But whatever the state of his budget, he spent an additional ten shillings that day to take the Rabbi on his first trip to see the pyramids. The excursion, he assured Mathilde, was the only way to make himself popular. In the meantime, the Rabbi had informed him about another genizah in the cemetery that they would open the following week. With additional *genizot* being mentioned, Schechter realized that his visit would be 'a hard piece of work, but it has to be done'. He reminded Mathilde to *Halte vorlaeufig alles geheim* (keep everything secret for the time being).

SCHECHTER FINALLY ENTERED 'THE GENIZAH' on Wednesday, 30 December 1896. In a shorter, but by no means less significant, note to Mathilde, he told her:

> I have just returned from the Genizah where I have been working since this morning, and I am half dead. I brought back with me two large bags of MSS fragments in which there are many valuable items. I will still need a week for this

Genizah because the workers are very slow. I must take a bath immediately. You have no idea of this Genizah dirt.[10]

He added a postscript to the letter asking her to send him six copies of his *Aboth de Rabbi Nathan*, the distribution of which was clearly proving helpful.

In his next letter, written on the first day of January, sandwiched in-between greetings for the *goyischen* new year, complaints about the mosquitos, his impressions of the pyramids and the 'embarras de richesse' of Cairo, Schechter shared additional news of his forays into two genizot:

> I was back at the Genizah and brought a big sack of fragments. The Genizah is so large and it contains so much rubbish and printed matter that I have to forego any selection. I take all that is MS. Two people work for me, the Beadel and some Arab. Of course, I give enough bakshish. Next Tuesday I will get some things again. The examination will have to take place at home first. M. G. H. [*Mitt Gottes Hilfe*] I will find some good things. My main occupation next week will be the second Genizah, which I am very curious about because it seems that it has hardly been touched so far.

Two days later, Mathilde wrote a letter to Mayer Sultzberger to let him know about Schechter's 'secret mission'. She disclosed that the university planned to report about Schechter's trip at the end of the month because 'otherwise his plans might have been defeated, caused by his discovery of the Ecclesiasticus fragment'. Mathilde also shared the information that Charles Taylor had presented '£200 to the University for the said purpose', and she asked Sultzberger to inform Cyrus Adler but to likewise swear him to secrecy.[11] At the same time, Schechter, who was fully realizing the great benefits brought about through the gift of fine books, penned a letter to his good friend in Breslau, Markus Brann, asking him for the price of a 'Vilna Shas on excellent paper' (a highly regarded copy of the Talmud printed in the 1880s), and the cost of sending it to Egypt. He also informed Brann that he had visited the Maimonides Synagogue and the synagogue of the Karaites, and he enquired whether their mutual friend, Rabbi Jacob Guttman, had received 'a packet of manuscripts and notes'.[12] Brann, a professor at the Jewish Theological Seminary in Breslau, was closely connected to scholars at the Jewish Theological Seminary in Budapest, particularly David Kaufmann, his co-editor on the scholarly journal *Monatsschrift für Geschichte und Wissenschaft des Judenthums*, and it's possible that this is how Kaufmann first received the news of Schechter's visit to Cairo. His colleague at the Jewish Theological Seminary of Budapest, the Talmudic scholar, Ludwig Blau, later revealed that Kaufmann had been bargaining to buy the whole genizah, and that he had become 'as pale as death' when he learned that Schechter, who had travelled to Cairo for this same purpose, had overtaken him.[13]

On 5 January, Schechter complained to Mathilde that his work had been disturbed by the death of 'a great Parnas (a brother-in-law of Cattaui)'. The Parnas (leader) was Nissim Mosseri, founder of the banking house of J. N. Mosseri et Fils Cie. He was Elena Yaʾqub Cattaoui's husband and father to Jacques Mosseri. Jacques later acquired his own large genizah collection, but at the time of his father's death he was just twelve or thirteen years old. Schechter, unaware of Nissim's importance to the community, grumbled about the excesses of the funeral and about the closure of the shops in the Jewish quarter. He mentioned having dined with the Rabbi the previous Sabbath evening: 'it is quite a different world', he observed, 'and with its good points'. He also shared his plans to meet with the Archdeacon Butcher to visit the Coptic churches.

A professor Gardner had given him a letter of introduction to Lord Cromer, and he had left it with a Mr Rodd at the embassy. Rodd had since been to see him at the hotel to discuss meeting with the consul-general at the end of the week. Schechter's first connection at the embassy, it turns out, was James Rennell Rodd, secretary to Lord Cromer, and future first Baron Rennell. Professor Gardner was Ernest Arthur Gardner, an archaeologist at Cambridge – brother to Percy Gardner, archaeologist at Oxford. Ernest had met James Rennell Rodd in the late 1880s while working as an archaeologist for the British School at Athens when Rodd was serving in the Athens British Embassy. Rodd was a published poet and scholar who shared Gardner's interest in Hellenic studies and in future supplied him with an introduction to his work on *Greece and the Ægean*. Ernest was also brother to Alice Gardner, historian at Newnham College, and a close friend of the Schechters.[14]

During the next couple of days, while he waited for his embassy interview, Schechter spent time examining the contents of the second genizah'. The initial result was a 'small yield', but he was determined to search again. At the same time, he admitted to Mathilde that he found the sight of the 'long, wide fenceless cemeteries' in the Egyptian desert sand, which suggested to him an 'aspect of the Infinite without a spark of hope', to be truly 'frightful'. At that point, fourteen days after his arrival in the city, he had amassed nine sacks full of fragments, and he expressed the hope that 'a certain percentage' was valuable. By the 7th, he was back at the cemetery again, and reported to Mathilde on the cold weather in Cairo, and the cutting dessert wind that was only helped by a winter coat. At the hotel, he met other people with connections to his scholarly friends: a Mr Craig, who was going to marry Mrs Ernest Gardner's sister, and another man who he described as Richard Gottheil's brother-in-law. He also met Andrew Watson of the American Mission, who instructed him on the proper way to wear an overcoat in Cairo.

In his spare time, Schechter took a tour of the Coptic churches with Dean Charles Butcher, the Anglican chaplain in Cairo, and his new wife, Edith Louisa Butcher. Schechter was taken with both, and the feeling, it seems, was mutual. In describing Mrs Butcher to Mathilde as 'the greatest bluestocking I have ever seen', it is not clear whether he meant the term in its less than flattering sense, as he went on to praise her knowledge of a dozen languages, including Arabic, and her book writing. No doubt as they toured around Old Cairo, she shared with him information from her work on a two-volume history of the Coptic Church, which later reviewers praised for its readability but criticized for its accuracy. The information sharing during the Butcher's guided tour may have only gone one way: when her book was published much later that year, her description of the Ben Ezra Synagogue was silent on the matter of a genizah.

On Sunday, 10 January, he wrote directly to his close friend, Mayer Sultzberger, primarily to enquire after the health of his ailing younger brother, Jacob. He shared the news that he had spent the past three weeks mostly occupied in genizot. The letter was brief: Mr Cattaoui was waiting to show him the sights.[15] In his letter to Mathilde, sent two days later, Schechter revealed that he had been to the embassy, but as it was the Khedive's birthday, Lord Cromer was otherwise engaged and could not receive him. Fortunately for Schechter, he was received by Cromer's trusted right-hand man: Harry Boyle.

HARRY BOYLE WAS THE VICE-CONSUL AND ORIENTAL SECRETARY during the Cromer administration and a self-taught man who could speak twelve languages, including fluent Arabic. Thanks to his abilities in the language, and his modest way of living, he interacted closely with native Egyptians. In time, he built up a deep local network and as a result became known as 'the man who helped Cromer rule Egypt'. Years after he left Egypt, he married a Polish-Jewish woman, Clara Asch, who eventually wrote a memoir about his life and work. In summarizing the extent of his influence in Egypt, Asch quoted the obituary in the *Al Ahram* nationalist newspaper: '[Boyle was] the source of all favour and disfavour; a look from him sufficed to bring all the happiness in the world, and a turn of his back would cause the deepest sorrow.'[16] Schechter must have made a favourable impression: he reported that the vice-consul was 'exceedingly kind' to him and that Cromer sent him a letter of introduction to the *Hakham* (in this case *hakham akbar* or president) of the Karaite Jews.

Eliyahu Mangūbī had been serving as the Karaite president (*hakham akbar*) since 1876. Thanks to his efforts to establish good relations with Egyptian heads of state and with the British administrators after 1882, he eventually formed strong ties with Lord Cromer. In 1890, Cromer worked with him to get the Karaite community recognized as a separate religious community (*millet*) so that they could acquire their own funds and be more self-governing. The recognition of the Karaites as a distinct entity also led to better relations between the Karaites and Rabbanites.[17] As for Schechter's visits to the Karaite synagogue, it remains unknown what interactions he had with their genizah. Yet, it must be supposed that he, like every other manuscript hunter before him, did not leave empty handed. Certainly, the amount of Karaite material in the Taylor-Schechter Genizah Collection suggests that some of the material came directly from that source.

In addition to meeting Harry Boyle at the embassy, Schechter made friends with a Jewish businessman from Manchester by the name of Reginald Henriques. Boyle and Henriques had known each other since 1894, possibly in connection to Henriques' business exports, and as permanent residents in Cairo, they were both members of the English Turf Club. Situated inside the old British Agency building, the Turf Club provided its members with an exclusive place of 'refuge' away from their foreign surroundings where they could relax and network with fellow Britons at any time of the day. Schechter described Henriques to Mathilde as 'a young delightful fellow' and hinted that he had rendered him some sort of helpful service, which may have been in the form of introductions.

Born in Manchester in 1868, Reginald Quixano Henriques became a resident in Egypt in the early 1890s and remained there until his death in Maadi in 1916. The Henriques family could trace their Sephardi ancestors back to Spain and Portugal and through to Jamaica. The Quixano Henriques line came from Moses Henriques of Kingston, Jamaica, and his wife Abigail Quixano. Moses's grandson Edward Micholls Henriques, part of the English branch of the family, moved to Manchester to take advantage of the booming cotton trade in the mid-1800s. With his brothers, he established the firm Henriques and Co., and he and his wife produced a family of eight children, including Reginald.

After attending the Manchester Grammar School, Reginald Henriques went into the family business to help manage their large lining and velveteen manufacturing company. Following his father's retirement in 1896, Reginald, his brother, Frank Q. Henriques, and their cousin David Leopold Quixano Henriques were placed in charge of the firm. In addition to offices in Manchester and London, branches of the business were established in Cairo, Tanta and Alexandria under the name 'Henriques and Henriques'. Reginald assumed sole management of the Egyptian branches after 1891. In December 1897, when the family partnership was dissolved by mutual consent, he established the Egyptian branch as a separate firm, although under the same name.

Reginald Henriques's business acumen was greatly appreciated by members of Egypt's Jewish business elite, the Suarès Group. The group included members of the leading Sephardi Jewish families in Alexandria and Cairo: the Suarès della Pegna family, the Cattaouis, Menasces and the Rolos. Their close alliance grew out of their mutual investment activities and through intermarriage among their members. Raphael Suarès led the coalition, and together they financed major business ventures in partnership with French and British financial syndicates. These included large-scale rural land-development, real estate development, banking and manufacturing. Members of the group were also involved in the creation of the British-run Egyptian Delta Land and Investment Company Ltd. Henriques was elected as the company's second managing director three years later, and he helped lead the project to develop the exclusive suburb of Maadi. Before his premature death at the age of forty-eight, he had also served on the executive board of the Salt and Soda Company and the Anglo-American Nile Steamers and Hotels Company.

It was probably in the Turf Club that the 29-year-old Henriques first heard about Schechter. As Schechter reported to Mathilde, an unnamed wealthy Jewish individual told him that he was generating great interest among the club members and there was 'much talk . . . about the great Jewish Savant'. The combination of Schechter's engaging personality and obvious erudition, together with some good self-promotion thanks to the distribution of his books, most likely helped spread the word. Henriques, like others, was immediately attracted to Schechter's magnetic personality and his 'remarkable capacity for friendship' with people from all walks of life, and he willingly offered him help. Schechter may have also impressed upon his younger Jewish acquaintance the importance of his mission.

By the second week of January 1897, Schechter's mission was mostly going well: his network had expanded, and the sacks of fragments were piling up. At the start of his third week in Cairo, he reported a full day's work in the Genizah without a lunch break. He retrieved an additional four sacks of fragments, bringing the total to thirteen. Even though he didn't have the time to examine them properly, Schechter confidently expressed his certainty that they contained 'many glorious things'. Nevertheless, he still felt the need to have gifts to hand, and he confided to Mathilde that he badly wanted six copies of his recent work, *Studies in Judaism*. Frustratingly, his publisher A. C. & Black had still not responded to his request.

He also wrote to Francis Jenkinson and shared information about his work on the 'Genizas'. To Jenkinson he expressed annoyance at the 'beadel & other infernal scoundrels' who were helping him clear away the rubbish and printed papers. Despite giving them copious amounts of '*bakeshish*', he claimed that they were 'stealing many good things' and selling them on to the dealers in antiquities.[18] Schechter tracked down the dealers connected to these sales, and he purchased the pieces of interest to him. One dealer in particular had some mysterious connection with the Genizah that enabled him to obtain fragments from the site and attempt to sell them to Schechter. He remained anonymous in an account Schechter wrote of his adventures for *The Times* of London, but in a near-identical article written for *The Sunday-School Times* of Philadelphia, published around the same time, he was identified as a Greek dealer. Schechter complained about him to the Jewish community authorities, and the 'plundering' was put to an end, but not before the 'worthy Hellene' had managed to get Schechter to buy a selection of fragments that Schechter maintained were his 'by right'. While he appreciated the irony that a 'descendant of Antiochus Epiphanes' would be 'so eagerly active in the diffusion of Hebrew literature', he wished that he would 'carry on his enterprise at some other place', since it created an unfortunate clash with his own 'claims' on the Genizah.[19]

Well-known Greek dealers of the period included Nicholas Tanos, Panayotis Kyticas and Michel Casira. All three were listed in the Baedeker travel guides; they all were connected in some way to the trade in papyri, and all were regarded as reputable dealers who sold at high prices. The Greek dealer with a mysterious connection to the Genizah could have been any one of these figures. Maurice Nahman, the well-known Jewish antiquarian, who was later involved in genizah sales, was likewise of Greek origin. It's unlikely, however, that Schechter would have described him as a descendant of the wicked Hellenistic king who despoiled the ancient Jewish Temple in Jerusalem. Another dealer of Greek origin was Alexandre Dingli. Dingli, who seems to have operated a business out of his home, was connected to the discoveries of lustre ware in the rubbish mounds of al-Fustat in the 1880s and to the supply of papyrus fragments in the 1890s, as well as to Egyptian antiquities in general. Evidence in a diary written by the British archaeologist, Percy Newberry, connects Dingli to two other characters involved in the Cairo Genizah story: Count Riamo d'Hulst and Giovanni Dattari. Newberry's diary records that on 2 January 1899, he visited antiquity shops in Cairo and saw 'Dattari, d'Hulst & Dingli'.[20] In addition to their indirect connection to the excavations for pottery in al-Fustat, Dingli and d'Hulst were also both tangentially linked to sales of the famous black head of Amenemhat (Amenemhet) III: Dingli sold a piece to Valdemar Schmidt in 1894, and d'Hulst sold one to MacGregor in either 1894 or 1895 (Sayce recalled in his memoir seeing it displayed at MacGregor's in 1896).[21] Nevertheless, no other evidence has been found at this point to link Dingli directly to the sale of genizah fragments. Dattari, on the other hand, is firmly tied to sales of genizah fragments to a Jules Nicole, although somewhat incidentally.

JULES NICOLE HAD ARRIVED IN CAIRO IN DECEMBER 1896 with his 23-year-old son Albert. A professor of Greek language and literature at the University of Geneva, Nicole recently started a collection of Greek papyri from Egypt thanks to the help of his friend, Édouard Naville. He was now headed to the source to find additional papyri for himself. He may have had word from Naville, through the Egypt Exploration Fund, that Bernard Pyne Grenfell and Arthur Surridge Hunt were being sponsored by the Fund to search for papyri in the ancient city of Oxyrhynchus (modern-day al Bahnasa) and that the expedition, set to begin in December 1896, held out great promise. Albert recalled the details of their visit many decades later in a handwritten memoir of his life.[22]

While staying at the König Pension in Cairo, which was close to the Place de l'Opéra and largely frequented by German papyrologists and archaeologists, Nicole began to make enquiries about papyri and was promptly directed to Ali el-Arabi in Giza. During one of their visits to el-Arabi, they met Dattari who invited them to visit him. In order to purchase important coins for his Roman coin collection, Dattari had been forced to acquire papyri as part of the bundle. The bundle, Nicole discovered, contained two fragments that appeared to comprise the work of the ancient Greek dramatist Menander. Dattari went to check how much he'd paid for them as he usually took a 10 per cent profit on his sales, but he discovered that someone had given them to him and so offered them freely to Nicole. But Nicole could not take them without making it known that they were rare and possibly priceless. In order to stand by his principle of not selling an item that he hadn't bought, Dattari asked Nicole to purchase something else to make it worth his while giving away the Menander as a gift. Albert spotted a scroll of Esther and begged his father to buy it. Nicole consented but only on the condition that if it proved to be valuable it would become the property of the Geneva University Library. A few days later, Jules Nicole found an additional piece of the Menander text in another antiquity store in Cairo and purchased it at a low price. In the same way he had done with Dattari, he advised the merchant of its true value. Having originally bought it for a modest price, the merchant did not regret the sale; instead, he readily divulged his practice of obtaining good prices with his 'Arab colleagues':

> I start by knowing how much they charge for the whole. Then I casually put aside what I want to acquire, setting aside what seems uninteresting to me, while reviewing [it] with the greatest care. I ask the value of this last lot. Assuming I want to buy this one, my interlocutors, duped by this merry-go-round, indicate a very high figure. I deduct it from the total sum. I leave with the stock apparently disdained and obtained for next to nothing.

Upon seeing Nicole's look of disapproval, he declared; 'They are thieves, they deserve to be deceived.' Yet, while Nicole disapproved of deception, he did not scruple to offer his own disparaging descriptions of the Arab dealers. When he published the Menander text in 1898, he noted that one could not trust the Abydos provenance given by a native to Dattari as the Arabs 'almost always lie about the origin of their goods'.[23]

In early January, while Schechter was emptying genizot, Jules and Albert Nicole travelled to the Fayum where 'Grenfell and Hunt had made sensational discoveries'.

Albert, who recorded the events of their trip many decades later, described a visit to a village notable who killed a sheep in their honour and organized a tour to see people who might be able to sell them papyri. Due to the misery of bedbugs, part of the tour was cancelled, and it seems from Albert's silence on the matter, that they did not get to see Grenfell and Hunt at Oxyrhynchus. It's also possible that the actual excavation work had only begun some days after the Nicoles had already returned to Cairo. As Grenfell recalled:

> On January 11th we sallied forth at sunrise with some seventy workmen and boys, and set them to dig trenches through a mound near a large space covered with piles of limestone chips. . . . The choice proved a very fortunate one, for papyrus scraps at once began to come to light in considerable quantities. . . . Since this rubbish mound had proved so fruitful, I proceeded to increase the number of workmen gradually up to 110 . . . the flow of papyri soon became a torrent which it was difficult to cope with. . . . We engaged two men to make tin boxes for storing the papyri, but for the next ten weeks they could hardly keep pace with us.[24]

What the two excavators had discovered was a wealth of early Christian writings, one century older than any previously found. Over the course of several multi-year excavations, they would eventually amass the world's largest collection of papyri. However, in a somewhat analogous way to the discovery of genizah fragments, pieces from known find spots soon became mixed up with other pieces purchased from dealers. Most of the fragments in the Oxyrhynchus Papyri Collection were in Greek, but there were also texts in Demotic, Coptic, Latin and Arabic. A small percentage of fragments were in Hebrew, Aramaic and Syriac.[25]

When the Nicoles returned from their papyrus hunting trip, they went back to see Dattari in Cairo to find out if, in the meantime, he had acquired any more precious papyri fragments. According to Albert, Dattari showed them 'a large tin box, filled with parchments from the geniza of the synagogue in Cairo'. Albert did not say whether the provenance had been directly supplied by Dattari. It may have been so; alternatively, this provenance may have been applied to the fragments by Albert after he spent time in Oxford two years later, working with Adolf Neubauer to identify some of the pieces. In fact, the most likely scenario is that Dattari purchased the tin box on the assumption that the fragments inside held the sort of treasures that would appeal to Nicole, little knowing that they were mostly medieval Hebrew and Arabic scraps. The universally recognized tin box, so suggestive of the precious papyrus within, may have been a factor in causing the confusion. Albert was allowed to purchase the tin of fragments on the same condition as the scroll of Esther. If it proved to be valuable, he would have to give it to the library; if it proved to be monetarily worthless, he could keep it for himself.

When Albert continued his theological training in Edinburgh and Oxford the following year, he heard an Anglican pastor, Frederick William Puller, speak of 'the sensational discovery' of the Hebrew Ecclesiasticus that had been made by Neubauer and Cowley among fragments from the Cairo Genizah. His imagination sparked, Albert wondered if his tin from Dattari could hold fragments from the same work, and he approached Neubauer to help him find out. Among the pieces that caught

Neubauer's eye was a palimpsest: rubbed out Greek uncials overwritten with Hebrew script. With Neubauer's help, Albert produced a five-page summary of the contents of the tin, but most of the fragments were left unidentified. The tin, together with some of Nicole's other metal tins of uncatalogued papyri, was placed in the library where it lay forgotten until it was finally rediscovered in 2002. The lid of the tin was curiously inscribed thus:

> Hebrew texts (from the 13th century?) Parchments and papers from the Old Cairo Synagogue, purchased in 1896-1897 in Cairo at Philippe's by J[ules] Nicole. Read and identified (in part) by Al[bert] Nicole in Oxford in 1898 (work supervised by Prof. Neubauer).[26]

The inscription was clearly made after Albert returned from Oxford and probably after he turned over his tin box to a librarian. The discovery of a valuable palimpsest among the fragments meant that he had to keep his side of the bargain with his father and turn the tin over to the Geneva University Library. Since Albert maintained that the box had come from Dattari, it's possible that the attribution to *chez Phillipe* may have been added by a librarian who marked it in accordance with the provenance of the other tins. Phillipe was most likely the Cairo-based French dealer, Paul L. Philip who sold a cache of carbonized papyri to the Earl of Crawford in 1899, and he may have been the additional anonymous supplier of Nicole's Menander fragments.[27]

WRITING TO FRANCIS JENKINSON ON 12 JANUARY 1897, Schechter revealed that conditions inside the genizah chamber were so challenging that he simply grabbed whatever he could rather than spending time examining the contents. However, the main purpose of his letter was to ask for a special favour. Given his worries about fragments being stolen, he decided to get them sent on ahead of him. But he was equally worried that someone in Cambridge would get to them first and somehow make a great discovery before him. He therefore asked Jenkinson if the manuscripts could be stored in the library while, at the same time, marked as his private property. He assured him that the sacks contained many important things and that they were ultimately destined to become the library's property.[28]

Two days later, Schechter reported to Mathilde that he now had about seventeen sacks of fragments. He still complained that the synagogue beadle and his helpers were treating the *bakshish* as a steady source of income, slowing down the process, and making it difficult for him to finish the work. Worse still, they continued to supplement this 'income' by surreptitiously removing pieces from the sack overnight and selling them on to the dealers. The warden (presumably one of the Cattaouis) promised to send additional help along to seal up the sacks. Despite his anxiety at leaving unguarded manuscripts at the site, Schechter revealed to his wife that the only way to get a 'free permit' to ship them was to send them directly to the library; otherwise, they could get held up in customs. He reiterated his concern that they would remain sealed in Cambridge and marked as his private property until he returned. If Jenkinson did not agree to this request, he told her, then he would try to send the boxes to their home, to which alternative solution he hoped she had no objection. He was weary; it was not pleasant to spend time 'in the terrible bad smelling dusty places'. But he urged her not to worry about him; instead, he tasked her with finding 200 used stamps to send to the chief rabbi for his collection.

With nothing fresh to say, he didn't write for another four days. He was tired of the 'beastly, unhealthy' genizah. He dined with Rabbi again and with the Cattaouis. He also visited and prayed with the Karaites, who made a fuss of him. Everything, he complained, involved *bakshish*, suggesting that he had also given *bakshish* to the Karaites for some reason. Words of praise were reserved for the chief rabbi alone, who Schechter said acted only out of kindness. But now there was some new excitement on the horizon: someone had given him news about the ancient synagogue of al-Mahallah al-Kubra and he was keen to go there and see if it had a genizah.

On 20 January, he felt that the end was in sight. He had amassed thirty bags of fragments and had spent a fortune in *bakshish* and carriages which 'will have to be paid by the Library'. He also contended that he had given 'such a lot' of money to the dealers. Yet, he conceded, 'by buying from them, I get what is most valuable'. The beadle, a man named Bechor (or Behor) confounded him the most: he was, proclaimed Schechter, 'the greatest thief that ever lived'. Having spent a great deal of his own money on the venture so far, Schechter had come to feel that every single fragment was his 'by rights'. Bechor, on the other hand, may well have been involved with the fragments for years: moving the pieces discovered in the 1889–92 rebuild to other locations; sourcing and uncovering buried pieces for ardent collectors; and just finding a way to make a better standard of living from scraps of old paper. Indeed, the regular income generated by selling fragments piecemeal was now coming to an abrupt end, which may have been an alarming prospect for Bechor, leading him to sell whatever he could while ever he could. To this end, he confided to Schechter that he had once buried ten bags of manuscripts in a graveyard, which he was willing to retrieve and sell to him. The graveyard was far from town, and Bechor claimed that he would need travel expenses to go there. Schechter expressed curiosity about what he would bring, but the results of that expedition, if any, were either never disclosed in writing or, if they were written down in a letter, they are now lost. Still, the few details Schechter divulged here are intriguing. What might have caused Bechor to bury fragments far from town? Was the graveyard the Bassatine or some other Jewish cemetery? Did he transport them there, or was he once involved in operations to bury fragments from the genizah of another local synagogue?

Meanwhile, Schechter divulged that the chief rabbi's son had agreed to travel with him around the villages near Cairo to check on other genizot. By son, he probably meant son-in-law: the same Mas'ud Hay Ben-Simeon who was also the Rabbi's brother. Mas'ud's wife (Raphael's daughter) was pregnant, and so the expedition would likely be postponed until after Schechter's planned visit to his own brother in Palestine. The Cattaouis continued to show him hospitality, and he dined with them three or four times a week. Nevertheless, he confided to Mathilde that he felt most beholden to the Rabbi and his son: the latter having worked with him 'for days in the Genizahs'. To thank him, Schechter planned to give him a gift of 'three or four pounds' (roughly equivalent to £500 today).[29] Eager to get the materials sent to England, he was planning to send off the boxes by the end of the week. But he warned Mathilde against storing them in the house, should they have to take them in. Instead, he advised her to transfer them to a warehouse and to insure them for £300 (around £34,000 today). In addition to writing to Mathilde, Schechter sent letters to Charles Taylor, Donald MacAlister and David Kaufmann.

Agnes Lewis and Margaret Gibson arrived in town two days later and checked into the Hotel d'Angleterre, near to Dean Butcher's All Saints Church and not far from the Métropole. They called on their friends, Dr Watson and Dr Burney, at the American Mission, who told the twins how they had been helping advise Schechter on the practicalities of living in Cairo. After leaving the mission, they went to find their friend, taking with them a respirator (Mathilde's inspirational idea), some quinine, a magnifying glass and some novels. Back in the hotel, Agnes immediately wrote to Mathilde to report on Schechter and allay any fears she may have about him. Overall, they found him to be in good spirits but 'tired with the work'. Among the heaps of 'unimportant stuff' he had found 'a few good things': an outcome the sisters described as being 'the way in all Eastern libraries'.[30]

In Oxford, Neubauer and Cowley had separated out a heap of 'unimportant stuff' from the boxes of fragments sent over by d'Hulst in 1896. As sanctioned by the library curators, the unwanted fragments were earmarked for sale. Pressure to discard the fragments may have also come from Nicholson who, since his election to the position of Bodley's Librarian in 1882, had waged a constant battle against the problems of storage. The library's sorely needed expansion had only recently got under way; although space was still wanting, and Nicholson's reportedly 'omnivorous appetite for every form of publication' and less-than-sound financial decisions undermined his own efforts.

The Bodleian's Annual Report publicly recorded that 'a private collector of well-known position' had made an offer for the unwanted fragments. In one of the library's internal sales ledgers, on a page marked 'sale of waste', the buyer was named as E. N. Adler.[31] Since no formal sale was publicly announced, it can only be assumed that Neubauer, wanting to keep the fragments in the safe hands of trusted Jewish collector, reached out to Adler over the matter. Yet, the unwanted fragments remained largely unexamined and under-appreciated in Adler's home. When he came to describe his 3,800-piece manuscript collection to the Jewish Historical Society of England in 1915, he revealed, 'Besides my bound volumes, I have great numbers of Geniza pieces in boxes.'[32]

When the boxes finally reached America through the sale of his private library in the 1920s, many of them re-entered another genizah-like state in the vaults of New York's Jewish Theological Seminary Library. Only recently, thanks to key funding and increased interest, have they been removed and fully examined. The fact that so many of them were originally derived from the Count d'Hulst's 1895 discoveries in a subterranean place near the Ben Ezra Synagogue remained unknown until recently.[33]

In Cairo, Schechter took the twin sisters on a tour to see the Ben Ezra Synagogue. Uncharacteristically, Agnes had not brought along her camera, and she later expressed great regret at not being able to share an image of the place. Still, she later used her pen to recreate a memorable scene that turned out to have significance beyond mere description:

It is a very plain synagogue in one of the most densely populated quarters of old Cairo. A very broad gallery runs round three sides of it, and above one of these there is a door high up in the white-washed wall, to which the roughest of rude ladders gave access. As its rungs were very wide apart, I dared not attempt to mount it; but the servant of the synagogue did so, and as he jumped down on the other side we could hear the crinkling of vellum leaves under his feet.[34]

This genizah 'loft', she explained, based on her memory of Schechter's explanation, was like 'a tomb of books'. Seemingly unaware that the building had been newly restored, she described how the manuscripts had ended up inside: 'When a manuscript had become useless, the synagogue authorities would neither take on themselves the responsibility of destroying nor of selling a holy thing, so they just tossed it in there.' Similarly, not realizing that the contents of the space had been transferred from location to location, she couldn't understand why they were so different in their state of preservation from the Sinai manuscripts, and she reasoned their present condition thus:

> The whitewash of the walls tumbled on it in the course of centuries, dust from the streets, not too pure, and sand from the desert blew in, a tap of water was turned on, whence it were perhaps better not to enquire, and the fragments all stuck together and got mixed in a way that is simply indescribable. The MSS. at Sinai may have been exposed to rough usage, but they were at least protected by being packed up in boxes and baskets, and the most neglected of them never got torn up, nor was it ever exposed to being embedded in a heterogeneous mass of confusion such as filled the loft of the Genizah.

Schechter confided in them his great frustration that the beadle and his helpers had been lifting fragments from the unguarded sacks and selling them on to the dealers. The sisters, with Schechter's 'full approbation', embarked on a mission to scour the local antiquity shops to track down the fragments that had been grabbed by these 'light-fingered gentry'. As a result of their efforts, Agnes explained 'a considerable quantity came into the possession of Mrs. Gibson and myself'.

Schechter told Mathilde privately that he had felt unable to prevent the sisters from pursuing the pieces on the market, but he felt reassured by their promise that no one would be allowed to examine the manuscripts until he had done so. In his estimation, the two women were not discerning enough to buy truly important pieces and therefore must have swooped up only what he had declined to buy. Agnes, on the other hand, viewed the purchase of all and any fragment on the market as a necessary step since any piece might contain a portion of Ecclesiasticus. Nevertheless, the scraps were in so parlous a state, they were compelled to apply some sort of rudimentary conservation treatment to them in their hotel room before packing them in their luggage:

> I found each little bundle of heterogeneous leaves glued together, some loosely, through having been dried after immersion in water; some tightly, by a treacle-like sticky substance formed out of their own decay . . . and amongst the dust that covered them I discovered not a few very tiny insects.

What Agnes was describing were pieces of parchment that had reached an advanced stage of destruction. When parchment is exposed to moisture, it goes through a process of gelatinization. The collagen fibres of the former animal skin relax and change shape leading to deformation of the page and visible spots. When parchment is exposed to prolonged damp conditions, it grows microorganisms that attack it from within, causing it to change wholly or in part to 'a gelatinous, stinking mass', that then sticks to other materials surrounding it.[35]

Medieval buildings in Cairo were constructed from natural limestone-clad walls that enabled the buildings to breathe and prevented drastic fluctuations in temperature. Had parchment manuscripts been left in an unstable environment for 700 years or so, they would have entirely perished. The manuscripts that Agnes held in her hand, unbeknown to her at the time, were testifying to the strange journeys they had undergone after being removed from their medieval tombs, buried, disinterred, reburied or sent out into the antiquity shops.[36]

SCHECHTER HAD FINALLY CLEARED THE LARGE GENIZAH by 28 January 1897. As he relayed in a letter to his wife: 'I have emptied all, the whole rubbish down to the bottom.' The work was hard, not only physically, but also in trying to persuade the workers to remove everything. The beadle clearly still hoped to retain fragments for future sales. No mention was made of his ten bags of buried materials. From the other genizahs, Schechter claimed that he had retrieved 'barely a sack and a half'.

While tens of thousands of fragments awaited shipping, Schechter's nervousness about them increased. He would stay another ten days, he informed Mathilde, to have a look around Cairo and Memphis, but also 'to watch the dealers'. The locals, he told her, were starting to grumble and complain that he had taken away so much. As far as he could tell, he had got everything 'except their area'. This odd reference may have been to the area where the custodians' local housing once stood and was being rebuilt: the area down by the eastern boundary wall where Schechter took his one and only photograph.

When the time came to ship the sacks, however, Schechter realized he faced an additional problem. Under Egyptian law, antiquities could not be excavated without a permit; without a permit, the official licence for their export would not be issued, and the materials would be confiscated at the Customs House. It was no doubt thanks to his new friendship with Henriques (a seasoned exporter of goods from Egypt) and his good friend, Harry Boyle (Cromer's right-hand man) that Schechter was able to obtain a last-minute written petition. Boyle delivered his petition to the director of the Customs House on Friday, 29 January, and the proper permit was issued the very next day. Boyle also told Schechter that Lord Cromer, having heard a good deal about him by now, had requested an introduction.[37] Writing of these things to Mathilde, on this last day of January, Schechter informed her that he planned to stay in Cairo until the 8th or 9th of February. While he was making preparations to travel to Palestine, he planned to see other parts of Cairo, and he wanted to see the ruins of Memphis. It is perhaps, no coincidence, that the places he'd identified to visit were on the Jewish pilgrims' tourist map.

12

In the footsteps of Jewish pilgrims (1897)

THE RUINS OF THE ANCIENT ROYAL CAPITAL OF MEMPHIS are situated in a region south of al-Fustat, near Giza, where the site of an ancient Jewish colony, and the ruins of the former Kanīsat Mūsā (Synagogue of Moses) at Dammuh also lie. The name of the synagogue comes from traditions that associated it with the biblical figure of Moses; and the synagogue was a major site on the map of Jewish pilgrims.[1] What, if anything, Schechter found during his trip to these sites, he didn't divulge, nor did he share in writing his impression of these places. But as genizah documents in his collection later proved, the area was visited often in the Middle Ages as part of a seasonal pilgrimage. The event was so popular that, according to al-Maqrizi, who also provided an account of the synagogue, even non-Jews took part in some of the activities associated with it. Indeed, at one time, the festivities even became too rowdy, and according to evidence provided by a Cambridge genizah fragment (T-S 20.117), an ordinance was created to set standards of behaviour and decorum there. From the list of banned activities (such as playing chess) it's possible to reconstruct what might have taken place at these events before order was restored.[2] Had anything actually been written down at Dammuh during these annual festivities, the pieces may have eventually found their way into a genizah, and certainly any inter-communal documents, like the twelfth-century lease of land agreement found in the genizah fragment T-S 10J4.11, may have been placed later in the genizah nearest the final recipient.

The physical structure of the Kanīsat Mūsā in Dammuh appears on a rare Middle Eastern scroll from the fourteenth century that provides colourful images of the sites of Jewish pilgrimage from Egypt to the mountains of Lebanon. Another illustration of the synagogue also appears on a sixteenth-century manuscript held in the British Library.[3] The latter lists and describes the main sites of pilgrimage for Jews, including the Mount of Olives and the Cave of Machpelah. The drawing shows that the Kanīsat Mūsā had numerous niches for Torah scrolls, including one dedicated location where the scrolls were unrolled for the women to see. The scrolls kept in such major sites of pilgrimage were highly venerated and in times of danger they would be transported to other locations. When the synagogue was largely destroyed by order of a Mamluk Sultan in 1498, any manuscripts kept at the site may also have been transferred elsewhere, or else they may have become entombed in situ, waiting for the dealers of Giza to unearth them as they scouted around the ruins in the area looking for Coptic manuscripts, papyri and more.

Schechter also sent a short note to Mathilde that month from another major site of medieval Jewish pilgrimage, the Delta town of al-Mahallah al-Kubra. The town and its synagogue were well documented in Jewish literature. In the medieval period, it had been a busy urban centre: it was the country's largest producer of silk weaving and dyeing and, at one point, the third-largest city in the country. Like the synagogue at Dammuh, the al-Amshati Synagogue of al-Mahallah al-Kubra, and its purportedly ancient scroll, had long been a focus of an annual visit for Egyptian Jewry, probably based on the Muslim festival of *Mawlid*.[4] The Egyptian Jewish chronicler Joseph Sambari mentioned the synagogue and its scroll in the seventeenth century. It was also described by Jacob Saphir, who visited in 1864.

In the wake of the cotton boom, the town, situated in the heart of the Nile Delta, expanded massively, bringing in foreigners, particularly large numbers of Greek merchants and investors, as well as locals to work and manage the cotton gins and financial institutions that underpinned the industry.[5] By the time of Schechter's visit, around 200 Jews lived there. In line with other restorations taking place in the 1880s, the community had decided to rebuild the al-Amshati and, like the Ben Ezra Synagogue, it was replaced with an exact replica. Schechter was unimpressed, or maybe disappointed, with the place. His brief note to Mathilde reveals that he had examined the synagogue and found nothing there apart from a rather 'old-new' building. On the whereabouts of its genizah and any possibility of its recovery, Schechter had either not asked or, if he did, he had not received a satisfactory answer. Most likely the contents had been removed during the rebuild and either buried in the cemetery (which was very close by) or sold off. If fragments from the al-Amshati Synagogue began circulating in the Egyptian antiquities market in the 1880s, they may even have reached the Jerusalem stores and dealers.

Aside from his excursions out of the city to key sites, Schechter remained obsessed with keeping an eye on the local Cairene dealers, or 'thieves' as he called them. One of them, he said, had promised to look around another genizah for him. But Schechter was distrustful, and he suspected that any additional fragments coming to light would probably be those fragments already 'stolen' from him. On 4 February, Schechter wrote to his good friend Mayer Sulzberger who had apparently asked him to look for some manuscripts for him while in Egypt. He hadn't been able to get him any, he explained, as he'd promised to make all his acquisitions for Cambridge and, anyway, until now 'there are none to be had'. But, he continued, rather enigmatically, 'you shall get a few things *lemazkeret* [as a souvenir] for which you *must not* pay'.[6]

SCHECHTER LEFT EGYPT FOR PALESTINE the day after his trip to al-Mahallah. Upon seeing the Holy Land, he expressed sadness that his parents, who had longed to see it, did not get to do so. Yet, despite staying in Palestine for several weeks, and despite his Zionist beliefs, he recorded hardly any information about his visit there. In Zikhron Yaakov, he visited his brother who had been a resident of the colony since 1882.[7] The town struck him as beautiful and spiritual, and Jerusalem 'surpassed his expectations'. In a report on the Anglo-Jewish Association's activities in the city, Schechter was said to have paid 'frequent visits to the Jewish Public Library', and he was later listed as one of its supporters.[8] He most likely connected with members of the library's committee, including key figures such as Ephraim Cohen-Reiss, who endeavoured to enlist his support. Such a connection could explain how Cambridge University Library came to purchase a Karaite ketubah that was written in Jerusalem in the eleventh century from an Ephraim Cohen of Jerusalem in 1897.

It can only be supposed that like most Jewish first-time visitors to Palestine, Schechter would have gone to see the Holy Sites on the Jewish pilgrim's map, including the tombs of the prophets and the pool of Siloam in Jerusalem. Yet, again, he did not disclose his itinerary, but it seems that he was somewhere that afforded him an interaction with the Yemenites. Indeed, of all Jerusalem's inhabitants, Schechter praised the Yemenites for being 'the most interesting and the most honest people in the place'. This brief mention of the Yemenite community suggests that he may have visited the town of Silwan, near the pool of Siloam, where they were situated and that he must have had a commercial interaction with them. Aside from this, the only other written evidence that he obtained manuscripts in Palestine is found in a short notice by the 'Jerusalem correspondent' for *The Jewish Chronicle*:

> Mr. Schechter has been rather successful in his search for Hebrew manuscripts not only in Egypt, but also in Palestine. His keen eye has not only discovered but also obtained in Hebron a few of these MSS., to acquire which, many other scholars before him have tried in vain. There were in the Jeshibah [Yeshivah] in Hebron, many years ago, about a thousand different copies which the Wardens and Rabbis would not consent to sell, but allowed to be stolen or eaten by mice. To hide the theft, and also to make as much profit as possible, these ill-gotten manuscripts were sold in fragments which, thus separated from the book of which they were part, were of but little critical value. Thus, of this entire treasure, Mr. Schechter found only a small number of manuscripts, which he saved from destruction by persuading the community to sell them in the interest of scholarship, and employ the proceeds for the good of the community.[9]

The trip to Hebron, another pilgrimage site, may have been facilitated by his old school friend, Mordechai Adelmann, who had obtained manuscripts from Hebron at an earlier period. When, in the next year, Israel Abrahams, travelling on behalf of the Anglo-Jewish Association, followed in Schechter's footsteps, he met Adelmann, Yosef Mejohas and David Yellin on the journey and travelled with them to Hebron. Abrahams noted that Adelmann was 'a school fellow of Schechter's and resembles him in many ways'. In Hebron, Adelmann's good friend Dr Jermans offered them a place to stay as there was no hotel. Unlike Schechter, however, Abrahams did not encounter any manuscripts in Hebron and only reported on the poverty, dirt and danger of the place.

Of Schechter's own dealings with Adelmann barely a trace remains. Only one letter that hints at a long relationship exists in Schechter's archive. The letter was sent by Adelmann from Jerusalem in 1914. It begins full of warm greetings for his 'dear friend' and then proceeds to relate matters relating to fundraising and the public controversy caused by the 'War of the Languages'. The war was between Jewish educators in Palestine at loggerheads over the proposed language of instruction for the newly formed Technion. The *Hilsverein der deutschen Juden*, a German relief agency similar to the French Alliance Israélite, which had established schools in Palestine beginning in the early twentieth century, had insisted that the first institute of higher learning should teach in German whereas the Zionists had pushed for Hebrew. Adelmann added a postscript to his letter asking Schechter whatever became of the manuscripts belonging to their good friend David Kaufmann, who had died unexpectedly at the age of forty-seven in 1899.

If nothing else, Adelmann may have introduced Schechter to the antiquities and coin dealer Samuel Raffalovich either during his visit or afterwards by letter. In one of his missives to Mathilde sent later in March, Schechter enclosed some rare stamps he had purchased which bore 'the stamp of Jerusalem in Hebrew'. In a later exchange with Elkan Adler, he disclosed having been introduced to Raffalovich by a Jerusalem friend. Alternatively, his introduction to Raffalovich may have come about thanks to Rabbi Solomon Aaron Wertheimer, since both Wertheimer and Raffalovich were known to each other (as attested in a later letter sent from Raffalovich to David Simonsen, chief rabbi of Denmark).[10] It also makes sense that Schechter would visit someone he knew had supplied him with manuscripts from 'the genizahs of Old Egypt'.

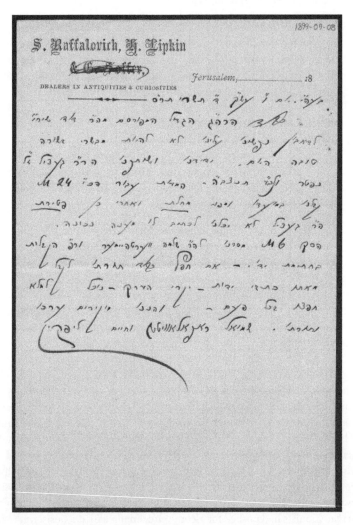

Figure 12.1 David Simonsen Archives, a letter from Samuel Raffalovich to Rabbi David Simonsen in Copenhagen, 8 September 1899.

Indeed, Wertheimer had continued to supply manuscripts to Cambridge through 1896 and to Oxford through 1897. From the latter he received payments amounting to just over eight pounds that year. Most of the items he sent were manuscripts rather than fragments, and they included a copy of Hunain b. Ishaq's introduction to Galen, a copy of Ibn al-Jazzar's *Viaticum*, some Spanish medical recipes, and a history of the Turks from 1391 CE. However, one manuscript, a 64-folio copy of the 'Singalese' (Sinhalese or Ceylonese) Jewish liturgical rite, something that could have easily been floating around the Jerusalem markets thanks to Jacob Saphir's travels to India, was later designated by the Bodleian as 'from the Geniza'.[11]

WERTHEIMER ALSO CLAIMED A MORE SIGNIFICANT CONNECTION to Schechter's trip to Egypt and Palestine and the discovery of the Genizah. The story was retold by his son, Rabbi Moses Wertheimer, in a letter to the Hebrew-language newspaper *Ha-Zofeh*. It was as follows:

> Rabbi Solomon Aaron Wertheimer sold the first leaf of Ben Sira to Moses Gaster who passed it on to Solomon Schechter. Alerted to the idea of the Genizah, Schechter travelled to see Wertheimer in Jerusalem in 1896. He invited him to go with him to Cairo to find the Genizah, but Wertheimer was too busy working on his book and couldn't go. Schechter went alone, retrieved many manuscripts from the Genizah, and thereafter went down in history as its discoverer. In 1927, Wertheimer bitterly wrote that no-one remembered the 'miserable miscreant who first discovered the city and brought all this treasure into the light of day'.[12]

The obvious errors in Wertheimer's version of the events – namely, that it wasn't Moses Gaster who first alerted Schechter to Ben Sira but rather Lewis and Gibson; Schechter hadn't discovered '*the* Genizah' after travelling to Jerusalem, it was the other way around; and he didn't travel to Jerusalem in 1896, he went there in 1897 – have meant that this abiding family story has had to be disregarded. Yet, by assuming a simple mix-up of the dates on Wertheimer's part, the story can start to make sense when also reconsidered in light of a later discovery of additional leaves of Ben Sira and in light of Schechter's actual itinerary.

The leaves that were later discovered were in fact the *first pages* of the Book of Ben Sira (MS A); and they came to light in a rather mysterious fashion after Schechter returned to Cambridge. Schechter did visit Jerusalem and afterwards he did indeed return to Cairo where he then paid a visit to at least one other unnamed synagogue. This visit may have arisen thanks to intelligence supplied by Wertheimer. In his recollections of the events, Wertheimer may have mistaken or conflated the two things and assumed that Schechter had found and despoiled *the* Genizah after his trip to Jerusalem.

SCHECHTER SENT A LETTER TO FRANCIS JENKINSON on 18 February 1897 to let him know that eight large boxes of fragments were on their way. The shipment was being handled by the firm 'Large & Co.', and the boxes would arrive within the next few weeks. In his previous letter, he had disclosed that he had been given 'the full permission of the authorities' to take as much as he liked. Going forward, thanks largely to Schechter repeating this fact, the impression that the community had given away the manuscripts became part of the official genizah narrative. Yet, the fact that Mathilde had insured the shipment for £300 suggests that this was the amount that had been expended to acquire them. D'hulst later disclosed to Nicholson that Schechter's layout of 'hundreds of pounds' had hampered his own abilities to negotiate for fragments. Sayce also separately confirmed to Nicholson that he had heard from some unknown source (probably d'Hulst) that the amount expended by Schechter had been £300.[13]

Nevertheless, questions remain as to Schechter's outlay. He not only expended an amount on acquiring material from the 'large genizah' but also on purchasing fragments from other locations. Mathilde had privately revealed to Mayer Sulzberger that Charles Taylor had initially earmarked a £200 fund for the expedition, and Schechter likewise told him that the university had defrayed his expenses and that all purchases were for the library. But in addition to buying manuscripts, money was needed for Schechter's travel costs and for shipping and carriage fees. Schechter had also spent a great deal in terms of *bakshish* and on the cost of buying manuscripts in antiquities shops and elsewhere in Egypt and Palestine.

In October 1897, Jenkinson recorded in his diary the receipt of a cheque from Taylor for £100. He was to use it to repay himself £37.96, which he broke down as follows: £19.5.3 the cost of carriage for eight large boxes; £8.4.3 for Hebrew manuscripts, and £10 paid to a 'Mrs. Smith' (presumably a reimbursement to Agnes Smith Lewis). The remaining £60 was sent to Schechter.[14] Schechter's own outlay (whether eventually fully reimbursed or not) may have been the reason why upon his return to Cambridge he told Mathilde that he had made no decision with regard to the manuscripts and that 'for the time being everything belongs to me'.

SCHECHTER RETURNED FROM JERUSALEM TO EGYPT in March 1897. In his letter to Jenkinson, he stated that one of his aims once back in Cairo was to 'have a look at a certain synagogue which I have not seen yet'. Having already seen the Karaite Synagogue and the Maimonides Synagogue, that may have left the Haim Capoussi Synagogue in the Harat al-Yahud. The synagogue had been built in the seventeenth century in memory of Haim Capoussi, a Kabbalist of the same period who studied in Safed and lived for a part of his life in Cairo, and whose family had been among the first Jews expelled from Spain in 1391 CE. The synagogue and Capoussi's tomb, like the al-Amshati Synagogue in al-Mahallah al-Kubra, was also a site of annual pilgrimage. The building itself was unusual, having been partly hewn out of the wall, and the arrangement of the interior rooms was unlike any other synagogue.[15] If he did indeed visit, Schechter would have found the building in a poor state of preservation (it wasn't renovated until 1900). Nevertheless, he would have had every great expectation of finding materials there from at least as early as the seventeenth century.

In addition to seeking out synagogues in Cairo and the surrounding area, he also took a tour of the region south of the Fayum near where Flinders Petrie was engaged in excavations at Deshasheh. Petrie had begun the archaeological season at Oxyrhynchus with Grenfell and Hunt but on seeing that the area only promised papyri and not 'Egyptian remains' he left to explore the area further south.[16] Schechter's trip to see archaeological sites may have come about thanks to the rumours about the papyri discoveries. Coincidently, apparently unbeknown to him, Schechter had shipped off to England an eighth- or ninth-century papyrus codex with his genizah hoard. The codex, bound with string, containing Hebrew liturgical poems by the sixth-century Palestinian poet Joseph b. Nissan was the only example of papyrus found in the 'Cairo Genizah'. It was also the only surviving example of a papyrus codex to have been written in Hebrew characters.[17]

By mid-March, having scouted around for additional manuscripts, Schechter was ready to leave Egypt. In addition to the fragments, he found, or was given, some discarded wood panels carved with medieval inscriptions. These were some of the panels that had so captivated Adler's interest during his visit in 1888, and they may also have included the boards Jacob Saphir noted had been removed to a 'special room' upstairs in the synagogue. The boards were shipped off together with the rest of his haul. Schechter himself never publicly mentioned them, even though they represented a genuinely fascinating artefact from the medieval period. He later donated them to the Jewish Theological Seminary in New York where they became part of a uniquely constructed ark that was sanctified at Schechter's inauguration as the Seminary's president.[18]

But for now, as he confided in his wife, he had greater things to ponder. He had just received an offer from America to lead the new Seminary, and it threw into sharp contrast his status at Cambridge. They had clearly exchanged letters discussing how the donation of the manuscripts would impact that status, but Schechter advised her that they should discuss it when they met up again in Paris. Nevertheless, he added, he felt that his scholarship stood on its own merits and, having just recovered the world's largest cache of medieval Hebrew manuscripts, he believed that it was worth more than just an honorary doctorate.

On board the ship, which departed Alexandria on March 20, he met again with Flinders Petrie. The journey was certainly burned in Petrie's memory as the ship ran aground near Marseille. He recalled it vividly in his memoir, including the detail that he was so convinced the boat would sink he rescued in his pocket a black figurine he had purchased from Ali el-Arabi. He also remembered sharing the journey with 'Dr. Schechter, the Rumanian' who had been 'active over his clearance of Jewish MSS in Cairo'. Unbeknown to Petrie, even though Schechter had, as Adler later observed, 'made the best use of his opportunities', Cairo was by no means cleared of its Jewish MSS.

No leaf left unturned (1897–8)

THE PIECES OF THE PUZZLE FELL INTO PLACE for David Kaufmann at some point during the year 1896. The fragment from the Archduke Rainer papyrus collection he had published together with D. H. Müller in 1892, plus the fragments that had reached his home in 1894 and after, together with the fragments that had been acquired by the Bodleian and Elkan Nathan Adler could only add up to one thing: a shared source. While his own negotiations to acquire the source were underway, Kaufmann set to work on an article to explain the history of the ancient synagogue in Old Cairo and its equally ancient genizah and how its manuscripts had reached Europe.

In relating the first complete written history of this particular genizah, Kaufmann started with Simon Von Geldern, the ancestor of his much studied and greatly admired subject Heinrich Heine, and he posited him as the first European to have visited it. Next, he advanced Jacob Saphir as the first person to realize its potential when he uncovered it from the roof of the Ezra Synagogue. The fragments that reached his house, he now believed, had come his way from this genizah through Jerusalem thanks to Saphir and other later visitors to the synagogue. The article, which was published in the Hebrew journal *Ha-Shiloah* between April and September of 1897, was written in two parts and before it was completed, Kaufmann had heard about Schechter's success in Cairo. Despite having been piped to the post, he was able to complete the puzzle by linking the many recent manuscript discoveries published over the years, including his own, to the chain provided by Lewis and Gibson's Ben Sira fragment through to the Genizah's final denouement by Schechter. Thus, by Kaufmann's pen, the story of '*the* Genizah' – an ancient and undisturbed single shared source and find spot – was born.[1]

They may have discussed these ideas, or perhaps Adler had seen a draft of Kaufmann's work, either by letter or on his way home from Persia, for when Adler came to publish his Barzillai fragment in *The Jewish Quarterly Review* in July 1897, he laid out an almost identical history of 'the Genizah'. Like Kaufmann, Adler relayed the story of the Genizah's discovery from Von Geldern to Saphir. He likewise linked the fragments brought by Sayce and Neubauer in Oxford to the fragments that had reached Berlin, Cambridge and the Archduke Rainer in Vienna, and he also connected the Lewis and Gibson fragment, and *especially* the fragments of Kaufmann, 'the future historian of the Jews of Egypt' to the Genizah. And, according to Adler's best information, some fragments had recently been sold at public auction in Cologne, and Wertheimer of Jerusalem was a seller. After relaying his own encounters with the old-new synagogue, which helped him to defend why he had assumed in 1888 that no manuscripts of importance to be found in Cairo, he brought the story to an end with Schechter's exhaustive ransacking of 'the Genizah' and his return home 'laden with the spoils of the Egyptians'.[2]

SCHECHTER PUBLICLY SHARED THE STORY OF HIS DISCOVERY in August 1897 in articles for *The Times* of London and *The Sunday-School Times* of Philadelphia. The idea for the piece, it seems, had come from Sulzberger, who suggested that he write something about his Cairo adventure for Henry Clay Trumbull, editor of the Philadelphia based periodical.[3] Entitled 'A Hoard of Hebrew MSS.' in London and 'A Hunt in the Genizah' in Philadelphia, the article shared the details of his visit to Cairo and his encounter with 'the real old Genizah'. That he may have seen other genizot was only hinted at when explaining away the idea that old books were usually buried in the grave of a scholar: 'More often, however, as I have had occasion to observe, they dug for the dead books a grave by themselves in the cemetery, or hid them in some sort of shed adjoining the synagogue.' He also acknowledged how his discovery of the original Ecclesiasticus fragment in the Lewis-Gibson collection had led to further discoveries of fragments at Oxford, and he assured the reader that all these fragments were undoubtedly from '*a* Genizah'.

Schechter explained for his broad audience that whereas a genizah was traditionally a 'hiding place' for sacred, semi-sacred and disgraced books, over time 'the Genizah' had 'extended its protection' to anything else for which the sacred language was used, such as letters, leases and contracts. Thus, 'the Genizah of the old Jewish community', he explained, was part 'sacred lumber-room' and part 'secular record office'. Rather than disseminating knowledge about the many different types of genizot he'd encountered in Egypt and Palestine, where they were located and what they held, Schechter used his pen to promote the idea of '*the* Genizah', which afterwards became synonymous with the act or practice of 'genizah'.

Schechter's article for *The Times* then proceeded to make several inaccurately worded statements of gratitude to the chief rabbi, 'Rev. Aaron Bensimon' (Raphael Aaron Ben-Simeon), and to a 'Mr. Youssef M. Cattaui' (Moïse Cattaoui) the president of the Jewish community, as well as a deliberately inaccurate acknowledgement to England's own chief rabbi Dr Hermann Adler for his letter of introduction.

He related the journey with Rabbi Ben-Simeon to see the synagogue of Ezra the Scribe in the Fortress of Babylon, and he gave a brief overview of its more than 1,000-year history. As to the scene that awaited him in the Genizah, he stated that 'one can hardly realize the confusion in such a real old Genizah until one has seen it'. He went on to describe the 'battlefield of books', the '*disjecta membra*', the 'general crush' and the 'big unshapely lumps', and how he had spent most of his time in the Genizah fighting to separate the comparatively modern printed matter from the fragments. The amount of printed matter, he revealed, was 'very large' having been placed in the Genizah during the last 400 years.[4]

The same notion about the age of the Genizah was amplified in an article written the following month by an unknown writer for *The Churchman* of New York. Here the author set about explaining Schechter's adventures and discoveries for a Christian audience. In addition to describing the Genizah as a 'sort of old church garret', he explained that all manner of documents were placed in the Genizah and that in 'the synagogue of Ezra the Scribe, in Cairo, there is a Genizah having an authentic record extending over more than a thousand years'.[5]

In his own original piece, Schechter shared his frustrations with the beadles publicly, and the need to constantly offer them *bakshish* for their help. Worse still was 'a certain dealer in antiquities' (named as a Greek dealer in *The Sunday-School Times*) who he explained had 'some mysterious relations with the Genizah, which enabled him to offer me a fair number of fragments for sale . . . but which were mine by right and on which he put exorbitant prices'. Finally, before going on to describe the important content of some of the spoils – medieval Bible MSS, liturgies, rabbinic materials, autograph fragments and a wealth of documents and miscellaneous matter – he announced that the hoard amounted to 'about 40,000' fragments.

SOMEONE WAS TROUBLED BY SCHECHTER'S ACCOUNT of the discovery. The day after the article appeared in *The Times*, the editor received an anonymous letter:

> Sir, – In the interesting description of the ancient 'Geniza' in Cairo, Mr. Schechter omits to mention that the honour of the discovery of this treasure belongs truly to the learned librarian of the Bodleian, Dr. A. Neubauer, who was the first to light upon it and to obtain a large number of important fragments for that library. He has published, already some years ago, a few of these documents and has placed others at the disposal of scholars, such as Dr. M. Friedlander, the principal of Jews' College, London. This latter has studied the hitherto unknown system of punctuation in a paper read before the Society of Biblical Archaeology, in whose 'Proceedings' it has appeared already in March, 1896. The other who went to that 'hiding-place' of the ancient synagogue in Cairo was Mr. Elkan N. Adler, who not only brought last year very valuable MSS. from there, but practically gave the key to it to Mr. Schechter. In appointing the honours of the discovery we must be just and fair. Suum Cuique.[6]

The identity of the anonymous letter writer remains unknown, but all evidence points towards Arthur Ernest Cowley who, being aware of Neubauer's long involvement with the search and discovery of genizah fragments, was upset by Schechter's failure to mention his 'revered teacher and friend'. Cowley was also the person who had originally donated the documents with the 'hitherto unknown system of punctuation' that were published by Friedländer. As a fellow of Magdalene College, Oxford, he would have regularly repeated his institution's Latin toast *ius suum cuique* (to each one his due).[7] Schechter was enraged and immediately suspected Adler, but by the time he came to crafting a response to Suum Cuique, it seems his suspicions were raised towards Oxford. His short letter, published three days later, downplayed Adler's role in helping him while hinting at other contentious discoveries:

> Sir, – The honour of discovering the Genizah belongs to the 'nameless' dealers in antiquities of Cairo, who for many years have continually offered its contents to the various libraries of Europe. Manuscripts were acquired by these libraries

without any reference to purchases previously made for the Bodleian Library. The first acquisitions that reached Cambridge from this source were presented by the late Mr. Greville Chester in 1890. Mr. E. N. Adler spent half a day in the Genizah. I learnt from him that he had been presented with some MSS. by the authorities. This is 'the key he gave me.' As to being fair and just 'in apportioning the honours of the discovery of MSS.,' I could tell, unfortunately, a long tale about it, as 'Suum Cuique' is perhaps aware. Priority questions, however, are tedious, and I do not intend to become a burden to your readers.[8]

After he received a letter from Adler confirming that he wasn't the anonymous writer, Schechter sent him an explanation of his failure to give him credit in *The Times* article. It had been done on purpose for a good reason; namely, to underscore and legitimize the whole process of removing the Genizah by giving it the stamp of a higher rabbinical authority:

For putting in the name of your brother in such a stiff formal way I [purposed] to show the gentiles that the letter of our Chief Rabbi has with the Eastern [Jewries] as much authority as that of the Archbishop with the Coptic Churches (I know of such a case). Your name would have undone the effected and intended. Will you understand me now. You shall soon P. G. [Please God] be compensated by me. I have to lecture on the subject.[9]

In the version of the discovery printed for *The Sunday-School Times* in Philadelphia, however, no mention was made of either the Chief Rabbi Hermann Adler, or his brother, Elkan. In addition to the new reference to the Greek dealer who tried to thwart Schechter's aims, Schechter also divulged that 'Some few original specimens will, I have good reason to believe, soon be seen in the library of Judge Sulzberger in Philadelphia'. Indeed, he had written to Sulzberger earlier in April promising that he would soon have 'a few nice things'.

Neubauer was anxious to know how much Schechter had hauled away with him. Before Schechter broke the news in *The Times*, Sayce sent a letter to d'Hulst to ask if he could 'keep an eye on the Hebrew MSS.', and to let him know when anything could be done in regard to them. In June 1897, d'Hulst was staying in England at Bolehall Manor in Tamworth with his friend and antiquities client, William MacGregor. Sayce wrote to him there and asked him to meet Neubauer at Oxford. The main driving factor for the Oxford scholars continued to be Ben Sira (Ecclesiasticus):

Neubauer has told the Press to send you a copy of Ecclesiasticus addressed to Bolehall. He also wants to see you very much & to have a talk about the MSS. & the advisability or not of his coming to Cairo next winter. If you would like to come to Oxford, he would put you up at his house, or he could go & see you if you preferred. I am returning to London in a day or two to be here during the month of August, & if you wished to come to Oxford then I could put you up in College. Neubauer thinks that if you went back to Cairo early, you might be able to get the MSS. or at all events to prepare the way for him but that if you do not go back till November it would be best for him to start for Egypt at the same time.[10]

Neubauer followed up with d'Hulst, and the two men arranged to meet for lunch at Exeter College. Meanwhile, Schechter was busy in Cambridge searching through his hoard for additional pieces of Ben Sira (Ecclesiasticus). Surprisingly, given the logistics of checking 40,000 fragments, he was quickly rewarded. In July, Francis Jenkinson recorded in his diary: 'Schechter found a double leaf of Hebrew Ecclesiasticus, & nearly went off his head.' The double leaf, it turned out, was part of the book's colophon.

During the long and painstaking process of sorting his fragments, Schechter uncovered a great many other important documents, including autograph letters of Maimonides, copies of parts of the Jerusalem Talmud, and palimpsests of Hebrew liturgy with Syriac underwriting. He also uncovered fragments in Coptic and old French. In reporting these finds to Sulzberger, he exclaimed: 'the contents of the Genizah turn out to be of much greater importance than I ever dared to hope for.' An iconic photograph was taken of him sitting in the Old Library room (later dubbed 'the Cairo Room') surrounded by the boxes and piles of fragments strewn across multiple tables. As he told Sulzberger, the room had become 'one of the sights of Cambridge'.

Twenty-five days later, he penned another letter to Sulzberger and, among other matters, informed him that a 'nice little box or "Schachtel" full of fragments' was being brought to him by their mutual friend in London, Mrs Fannie Muhr, sister of Simon Muhr, a prominent Philadelphia merchant and philanthropist. He hoped that the fragments would bring him happiness, and he asked him to consider them as a *minhat azkerah* (memorial offering) of his travels in the East. Given Schechter's prior statement to Sulzberger that he had been duty bound to buy everything in Cairo for the library, it doesn't seem likely that he siphoned off some of the fragments paid for by Charles Taylor to send to Sulzberger. The fragments may have been pieces he purchased from his own funds in Egypt or Palestine. Another scenario also presents itself. This scenario posits that the fragments had already been in Schechter's possession for some time having been passed along to him years before by Moses Gaster. Such a strange set of circumstances can only be understood by considering the later, and much maligned, testimony of Solomon Aaron Wertheimer with regard to the discovery of '*ha-daf ha-rishon*' (the first 'leaf' or 'page') of Ben Sira.

SCHECHTER DISCOVERED FOUR LEAVES OF BEN SIRA on two separate days in September 1897, according to Charles Taylor. The four leaves (two consecutive pairs) were from a different manuscript version of the text. The version could have been easily missed by anyone unfamiliar with the rabbinical quotations of Ben Sira: the leaves were small and the lines of handwriting closer together than the version first brought to light by Lewis and Gibson. This version was also closer to the Syriac translation of Ben Sira than the better-known Greek translation. Together, these leaves supplied some of the missing first sections of the work, starting at Chapter 3. Indeed, as Taylor pointed out, these manuscripts 'could only have been singled out from a collection of so many thousands by a careful though necessarily rapid scrutiny. They altogether lack the striking Biblical and Masoretic appearance which distinguished the Ben Sira fragments previously found.'

Most remarkably, given the importance of discovering an alternate medieval manuscript version of Ben Sira (particularly given its differing relationship to later translations), Schechter did not broadcast the news of this significant find until much later. Jenkinson, who noted many of Schechter's great discoveries in his diary, did not make any mention of an MS A, and no mention of it was made to close friends such as Sulzberger. In the October pages of *The Jewish Chronicle*, Israel Abrahams shared the news of Schechter's 'latest discovery of fresh fragments', without specifying what they contained, but he promised that a specimen page would be provided in the next issue of *The Jewish Quarterly Review*. In that issue (January 1898), Schechter announced his discovery of parts of the colophon, that is, additional leaves of the known version (MS B). The discovery of the MS A version only came to public attention via the publication of his book *The Wisdom of Ben Sira* early in 1900, and any fanfare surrounding it was given over to the volume as a whole. Even stranger, no facsimile of this incredible new discovery was provided in the publication even though a plate from MS B – the Lewis and Gibson fragment – was included.

It is entirely reasonable to accept at face value Taylor's statement that Schechter discovered the two pairs of leaves of MS A within the genizah collection on two

Figure 13.1 MS. T-S 12.863: a copy of Ben Sira 3:6, 3: 8-4:10, labelled by Solomon Schechter and Charles Taylor as 'MS A.'

separate days in September 1897. The subsequent high level of secrecy surrounding the find would have been deemed a necessary course of action to prevent others from rushing to find similar leaves in their collections, bringing about a nightmarish repeat of the events surrounding Schechter's first discovery of Ben Sira in the spring of 1896. Yet, an alternative state of affairs surrounding the discovery of parts of MS A, based on Wertheimer's claim that he sold the first leaf of Ben Sira to Moses Gaster who passed it on to Solomon Schechter, is worth considering here.

Moses Gaster had been building up his collection from the mid-1880s. He encouraged individuals with private collections to donate them to the safe environment of his library and he instructed his book dealers to buy in bulk. In his memoir 'The Story of My Library', he related how his strategic and valuable purchases of Romanian literature had alerted other Romanians to the value of what he was collecting and the competition for them grew exponentially. When he was forced to leave Romania, he had to abandon his collecting mission, and when he finally returned to that field of collecting, there was very little left. This anecdote was followed by an even more enigmatic observation:

> And this is how it always was with me. First I made people aware of the value of these things, then I had to pay for it. The same was also true for Hebrew literature. In any case, I am happy that in this way many books and manuscripts were saved. They are in safe [private] hands, or in larger libraries.[11]

In the case of genizah fragments, it would appear at first glance as though his 'awareness' of their value had worked in the opposite direction. Gaster is known to have purchased fragments from Raffalovich in the wake of Schechter's grand genizah discoveries, and his publications of genizah fragments are all post-1899. At present, barely any written evidence that Gaster made earlier genizah purchases has come to light. Nevertheless, since his correspondence proves that Wertheimer was one of his suppliers, it is highly likely that some genizah fragments had come to him from that source in or before early 1896. This may have been the type of purchase he described in his memoir as being 'a mixed bag' of fifty-plus items 'old and new, valuable and worthless, all together'.

The proposition of this date is also based on the story recently uncovered surrounding the near loss of some of his precious manuscripts in a fire in 1898.[12] Gaster had left the manuscripts (including genizah fragments) with the lithographic firm of Vincent Brooks, Day & Son in London, and after their building caught fire in April 1898, he rushed over to check on them. Gaster divulged that these almost 1,000-year-old manuscripts had been in the firm's possession for 'upwards of two years', and he was deeply relieved to find that they had survived the fire intact. If they had been with the Vincent Brooks, Day & Son company upwards of two years, then they would have belonged to Gaster at least prior to April 1896.

Thus, based on Wertheimer's testimony, the story of MS A could be reconstructed as follows: Gaster purchased a mixed bag of fragments from Wertheimer at some point before April 1896. He selected those that interested him, including those he subsequently took to Vincent Brooks, Day & Son. At the same time, he passed along fragments he didn't want into the safe hands of his good friend Solomon Schechter. Depending on the number of fragments he received from Gaster and the timing of their arrival, Schechter may not have looked at them immediately. Prior to the discovery of Ben Sira, he was even dismissive of some of Wertheimer's fragmentary offerings to the library. However, in the wake of finding Ben Sira in the Lewis-Gibson fragment, and the upset caused soon after by Neubauer's own Ben Sira discoveries, Schechter may have decided to look more carefully through the Gaster fragments.

After he spotted on the one small leaf of close writing an early section of the Book of Ben Sira (MS A), his obsession to find the source of these fragments now representing two distinct codices doubly intensified. This particular leaf of Ben Sira, however, he kept absolutely secret until he could discover the rest of the book. After encountering multiple genizot in Cairo, he decided to consult with Wertheimer in Jerusalem as to the find spot of the leaf of Ben Sira he had supplied to Gaster.

At the time of his original sale to Gaster, Wertheimer may have recognized the content of Ben Sira but not its great import, that is, that it represented a medieval copy of the original Hebrew text from ancient times. Gaster, likewise, may have recognized parts of the text but not connected the dots. To Schechter's great credit, it was his incredible, encyclopaedic knowledge of Ben Sira in the rabbinic sources that enabled him to arrive at such a realization, and even then, there were those who questioned his conclusions. The only other person equipped with similar knowledge, who could arrive at the same speedy conclusion about Ben Sira, was Neubauer.

When Schechter visited Wertheimer in Jerusalem, he took the leaf of Ben Sira he'd got from Gaster with him, and he queried its provenience. Wertheimer sent him either back in the direction of Old Cairo or towards some other synagogue genizah. Schechter's invitation to Wertheimer to accompany him to Cairo may have been issued half-heartedly, or perhaps he hoped that Wertheimer could lead him to other as yet untapped sources. At any rate, Wertheimer clearly did not realize that Schechter had ransacked the synagogue at Old Cairo before visiting Jerusalem. When he came to recall the whole incident many years later, Wertheimer's only other mistake was to misremember the date of their encounter.

If this leaf from the first pages of Ben Sira had been sold by Wertheimer to Gaster and then passed on to Schechter, the other leaves of MS A could have come to light during Schechter's subsequent searches in his hoard from Cairo on exactly the days posited by Charles Taylor. Upon finding the first matching leaf, Schechter may have placed the Wertheimer-Gaster leaf into the Cambridge collection to join it. Jenkinson's diary records that in late August and September, he had worked with Schechter to sort 'select' and 'choice' fragments into drawers. Perhaps the mix-up was done inadvertently: he had been working long hours and battling with poor lighting for many months now as he poured over bundles of manuscripts strewn about the room. Schechter even admitted to Sulzberger that he once forgot that he was carrying around an eleventh-century letter in his pocket, and Jenkinson criticized him for trampling over fragments as he hurriedly turned over the piles. On the other hand, if he had purposely obscured the fragment's provenance, Schechter may have justified his actions by explaining to himself that it didn't matter exactly where it came from and how he got it; the Gaster fragments had been properly paid for and transferred to his keeping after all. The most important thing was his ability to identify the content and enrich the world through his knowledge, particularly in contradistinction to the tendentious claims of the Higher Critics.

Three days before the official discovery of the first pair of MS A leaves on 2 September 1897, Schechter had dispatched the 'schachtel' of promised fragments off to Sulzberger. Sulzberger's genizah collection, which he later donated to Dropsie College in Philadelphia, comprised a mixed bag of fifty-seven items, it included the range of materials found in other genizah collections: medieval scraps of biblical, rabbinic and liturgical texts; documents written in al-Fustat and other places, like Alexandria, Damyat, Aleppo, Salonica, Sicily and Tunis; and scraps of pen trials. It also included a seventeen-page grocer's account book from 1703 CE bound with string and written in Yemenite script.[13] The pieces may have been purchased by Schechter after his work in the Ben Ezra Synagogue genizah was finished and during his subsequent travels between Palestine and Egypt, or perhaps they were the unwanted fragments from the Wertheimer-Gaster bundle. This reconstruction, while complex and based entirely on circumstantial evidence, could finally help explain the Wertheimer family story, as well as the great secrecy surrounding MS A. Yet, without any further corroborating evidence it must, like so many other genizah stories, remain in the realm of pure speculation.

ADDITIONAL TUSSLES OVER PURCHASES AND OWNERSHIP took place in the autumn of 1897. Samuel Raffalovich and his partner M. Goldstein had recently arrived in England to set up a business dedicated to the sale of 'Ancient Phoenician Glass and Palestine Antiquities'. Their arrival was noted by the journal *Jewish World* who interviewed them for news about the state of their Jewish brethren in Palestine. Goldstein, it noted, was 'English by birth and American by citizenship' and had 'for five years past been a resident in Jerusalem' and Raffalovich was 'an American citizen and of Russian-Polish birth' who had been resident in Jerusalem for the past seven years. He was, the journal said, 'A learned Hebraist, formerly editor of an American Hebrew journal'. Among the objects the antiquarians had brought with them were 'a collection of manuscripts, a Yemen Scroll of the Law, a half-shekel of the second year of Simon Maccabaeus, and incense shovels probably used in the Temple itself'.[14] Among the prospective clients they visited were Elkan Nathan Adler, Solomon Schechter, and Moses Gaster.

On 13 October 1897, they travelled to Cambridge and met with Schechter. Jenkinson did not trust them and noted the visit in his diary: 'I found Schechter & "Raffalovitch & Co." – from whom we eventually bought some MSS. for £21. They professed to <u>know</u> more about glass & antiquities, & shekels. They had appeared to me <u>false</u>.'[15] In early December 1897, Raffalovich sent news to Adler that he had 'received some fragments from the *genizah* of *Mizrayim* (Egypt)'. Having promised to let him see them first, he requested an appointment to call on him. During their meeting, Adler selected twelve fragments that interested him and offered £5 for them. Raffalovich was due to visit Schechter in Cambridge and, according to Adler, he preferred to wait and see what value Schechter assigned to the rest before agreeing on the £5. However, five days after he arrived back in London, Raffalovich told Adler that he had sold all of the fragments to Schechter: 'Mr. Schechter said that for you even £5 will be to [*sic*] much to pay for the fragments, but he was kind enough & tried his best for me & I sold them to the University of Cambridge for £20.'[16] Since a payment of £20 was a high sum for a bundle of fragments, it's likely that Schechter had spotted among them items of great interest.

Adler was outraged and wrote back immediately: 'I am sure you have treated me most dishonestly to sell the fragments over my head after your solemn promise to let me buy them – or at least the portion I selected – at the price to be fixed by Mr. Schechter.' Raffalovich responded quickly that he was shocked by Adler's tone. He insisted he was telling the truth and that Schechter had advised him that the pre-selected fragments would be too costly for Adler and since he had also advised him that the other fragments on offer were 'valueless', Raffalovich had seized at the opportunity to accept the lump sum of £20 rather than lose £15 on the deal. He hoped that Adler would understand, and he asked him to let him know if, when he received his next instalment of manuscripts, he would like to be informed of it first.

Adler also sent a disgruntled letter to Schechter calling him a *masig gvul* (usurper). Schechter responded that he had known Raffalovich from the month that Adler was away in Bokhara and that he had 'introduced himself to me by a letter from a friend in Jerusalem' and it was 'at that time (when he sold me the Yemen MSS) that he promised me that he would write for Genizah MSS. He came here to fulfill his promise.' Schechter further claimed:

> It is a lie when he says that I told him that you will pay £5 for 12 select fragments. I gave him no answer to this, but simply bought what you declined to take. To say the truth, I did not find the fragments you selected particularly exciting. Perhaps it will do you good to know that there was neither Sirach [Ben Sira] or Aquila nor any signature or letter of any importance in the whole collection.

In attempting to lighten the tone, he ended: 'That you would suspect me of being *masig gvul* is too bad and we shall have a fight when I meet you next.' Adler, however, was not easily deterred from the argument:

> I accept your explanation, but it does not alter the fact that I knew the man first, ordered the MSS first, sorted these particular fragments first & promised to buy them at the price you fixed for me – not your library. I beg you to keep the parcel intact till the Librarian returns & then ask him to decide the point. Probably the fairest thing will be for each party to pay £10 & to choose fragment by fragment in succession. I know there is nothing particularly exciting in the lot but still there are several I should like to have. You see I am perfectly frank & not *noges ve-noter* (biting and spiteful). With all Maccabean greetings.

Schechter, likewise, would not concede the fight:

> My explanation does alter the facts. I did know the man before you returned from Persia. He did then promise the Genizah MSS before you had with him any transaction. I did not in the least take note of your sorting the fragments. The MSS which interested me most were not among the 12 fragments you selected; as I will

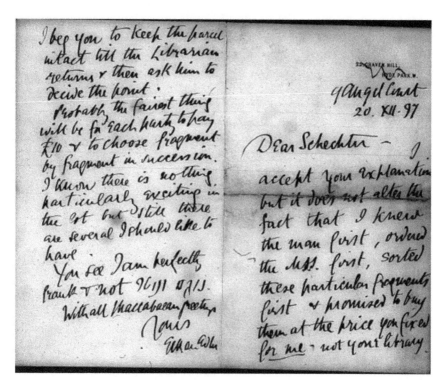

Figure 13.2 Solomon Schechter Collection. Box 1/15, a letter from Elkan Nathan Adler in London to Solomon Schechter, 20 December 1897.

show you when you are here. Neither you nor he did tell me with a single word that I have to fix prices <u>for you</u>. Would you refuse to buy MSS which you knew were in my hands? I cannot possibly understand you. However, I am not *noges ve-noter* as you say. (I do not see why you should be).

The final word, it seems, was offered by Adler, who pointed out the flaw in Schechter's argument; namely, that he admitted he was not interested in the twelve fragments selected by Adler:

It is evident that Raffalovich did not explain to you the true position, but it is also evident that you knew that an offer from me of £5 was given for fragments & that 'the MSS which interested you most were not among them.' Why then didn't you buy the batch for £15 and leave me my little vineyard for £5?

Signing off his letter as 'Yours all the same', it seems that, after almost twenty days of wrangling, the matter was at an end.

But not quite: Raffalovich and Goldstein did indeed have fragments of 'Sirach' among their wares. On their way back to Jerusalem, either at the end 1897 or at the beginning of 1898, they stopped off in Paris where they visited Israel Lévi, Talmudic scholar, editor of the journal *Revue des Études Juives* and future chief rabbi of France. Lévi had been following closely the Ben Sira discoveries, and he was working on his own edition of the fragments discovered to date based on his interpretation and understanding of their contents. His perspective on the fragments differed from Schechter's, particularly with regard to the phase of Hebrew represented in them, and he had criticisms of the transcriptions produced by Neubauer and Cowley.[17]

When Lévi finally came to publish his own discovery of fragments of Ben Sira held in the Bibliothèque du Consistoire Israélite de Paris, he provided the following explanation of how they had been acquired:

> Some dealers who had been in England selling many bundles of leaves, found in the *gueniza* (and perhaps in the cemetery) of Cairo, came to Paris to offer the remainder of their lot, which no one wanted. At my request, Baron Edmond de Rothschild, whose generous zeal for Jewish studies cannot be praised too much, was kind enough to purchase these scrap pieces and donated them to the Bibliothèque du Consistoire Israélite de Paris.[18]

The fragments were afterwards transferred to the Alliance Israélite Universelle (AIU) Library in Paris. Some years later, Elkan Adler recalled visiting Lévi and being shown a page of the Ben Sira fragments 'which he had bought from Goldstein and Raffalovich'.[19]

The leaves that Rothschild had purchased for the Bibliothèque du Consistoire included two additional Hebrew versions of Ben Sira: afterwards dubbed MS C and MS D. One month after Lévi's article on them appeared in print, Schechter published fragments of MS C in *The Jewish Quarterly Review*. Three months after that, another Raffalovich and Goldstein client, Moses Gaster, published his own fragment of MS C in the same journal. Lévi's statement that the dealers had brought over to Paris 'the remainder of their lot, which no one wanted' suggests that none of the English buyers had spotted the fragments of MS C among the bundles they purchased, unless the two businessmen had carefully divided up their fragments to maximize sales and at each turn, based on the prices offered by others, they got their next set of clients to put in a higher bid.

After his run-in with Schechter, Adler was determined not to be further outdone, and he went on to snap up fragments at every opportunity. In 1898, he collected additional fragments from Egypt and 'important MSS from Palestine and a Geniza in Alexandria' and in 1901, as reported in *The Jewish Chronicle*, he returned to England with 'the spoils of Genizoth at Corfu, Damascus, Tiberias, Nablous, Jerusalem, Hebron and Cairo'. By the time he came to sell his library to the Jewish Theological Seminary in New York, his little vineyard of fragments had grown to around 35,000 items. Among them he discovered fragments from Ben Sira MS A in 1900, and in 1931 scraps of a fifth version, MS E, emerged.[20]

Neubauer and Cowley were still looking for the rest of MS B unaware that other versions of Ben Sira could be found. In October 1897, Neubauer heard from d'Hulst that he had been active again on behalf of the library and he wrote to thank him 'for all the trouble you have taken about the Genizah'. He was glad to receive the information that 'the fragments are still there', and he informed d'Hulst that Schechter had found ten or twelve leaves of Ecclesiasticus and that if he found the rest his name would 'be mentioned as the finder'. Neubauer was no doubt aware that d'Hulst had been upset to discover in his presentation copy of Neubauer and Cowley's Ecclesiasticus, that only Sayce had been acknowledged in the Preface. Sayce had mollified him at the time by telling him that it was done to keep their future plans secret and 'in order not to impede' his pending work. Nonetheless, Sayce himself would never publicly acknowledge d'Hulst's early role in recovering parts of Ecclesiasticus for Oxford.

Neubauer informed d'Hulst in December that Oxford had agreed to provide funds for an excavation. Oxford's vice chancellor had written to Sir William E. Garstin as d'Hulst had suggested to Sayce.[21] A civil engineer by profession, Garstin served as the Inspector-General of Irrigation in Egypt and Under-Secretary of State for Public Works in the Public Works Ministry under Sir Colin Scott Montcrieff. D'Hulst understood that his plan to excavate the area near the synagogue compound would need the support of the ministry, particularly if the Jewish community opposed the idea.

In January 1898, d'Hulst sent Neubauer a packet of fragments that were 'taken from the heap, <u>without choosing</u>' so that he could judge the quality of the material. He reported that the expected price of a packet had risen to eight shillings in the wake of Schechter's visit and that there was talk of 'another secreted heap of similar papers'. He would not begin his excavation work until Neubauer gave the go-ahead and also because of the heavy rains.[22] Neubauer responded that he wished the excavation to proceed; despite not containing any startling discovery, the fragments were worth the eight shillings. Neubauer was certain that Schechter had not found the remainder of Ecclesiasticus and he therefore hoped that d'Hulst would be 'the fortunate discoverer of some part of it' in his excavations.[23]

By February, d'Hulst had obtained permission for the excavation from Garstin and from Mr A. H. Perry, the Director General of Towns and Buildings (*Tanzim*) and Harvey Pasha, the chief of the police. After a slight delay caused by the paperwork and the need for another visit to the ministry, d'Hulst's work got underway and he forwarded eight bags of fragments to Oxford. The pile, he afterwards discovered, had been created at some point when the synagogue caretakers had thrown out 'the last of their rubbish' in December 1889.[24] D'Hulst also located the large heap that had been created several months prior to that, in the months before he had started the pottery excavation for the Egypt Exploration Fund. He reported that this pile contained 'papers of the same nature . . . as those I sent you & in the same proportion', and he warned that there could be refuse hidden underneath of another provenience.

If Neubauer were to give the go-ahead, he calculated that it would take about 'six weeks to turn'. The work would be impeded by the open water conduit and road that lay before the heap and the piles of rubbish would need to be carried a short distance to get the necessary space for turning and examining the contents. But a speedy decision was needed because the synagogue had purchased the plot of land upon which the rubbish lay and building operations could be imminent. A new permit for digging there would also be necessary.

D'Hulst then checked on the status of the manuscripts still inside the hiding place in the synagogue. For these manuscripts, he reported, the caretakers would not accept any less than £35. He estimated that there were around ten sacks worth of material there, but that around nine-tenths were printed. The rest was paper with barely any parchment. The locals, he suspected, 'have carried & carry all sorts of rubbish paper together, to mix them up with what was left with a view to selling them'. He also informed Neubauer that they were expecting Schechter to return in August. The latter information may have been a ruse to deter d'Hulst or others from buying what was left.

After d'Hulst's first bags of fragments arrived in Oxford, Neubauer and Cowley went through them and found pieces interesting enough to warrant a continued search. This was conveyed to Nicholson who asked d'Hulst to incur a further expenditure on behalf of the library up to the amount of ten pounds. In early March, Nicholson requested an estimate of the amount of work remaining so that he could get the Bodleian Curators to agree on the project continuing.[25]

Schechter continued to sort through piles of fragments in the 'Cairo Room'. He lamented to Sulzberger how little time he had left over to study manuscripts more pertinent to his own scholarship. His eyes were sore from closely examining thousands of fragments, and any spare time left over was devoted to preparing his monumental edition of *The Wisdom of Ben Sira* for publication. Going back in time from the early rabbinic era, his usual period of study, he found himself having to read everything of pertinence to the pre-Maccabean age, 'about which tradition and history know nothing and our critics know too much'. His reading, however, was causing him to feel a certain amount of rebelliousness towards the 'omniscience' of the German Higher Critic, Wellhausen, so much so that he eventually came to feel that his Ben Sira would be 'a declaration of war to certain results of higher criticism concerning the Writings'.

While Schechter endeavoured to get to grips with late biblical history, he sympathized with Sulzberger's struggles to identify pieces among the genizah fragments he'd sent him. He promised that he would be rewarded for his labour by the gift of a few more pieces when he could find someone to transport them to America. The fragments sent to Sulzberger were not the only manuscripts that Schechter gave to others as gifts. The Old Library at Trinity College, Dublin, holds three manuscripts whose provenance is stated as 'the Cairo Genizah'. The first, a twelfth-century copy of a Hebrew treatise on medicine by Avicenna, comprising 163 folios, was given to the library in 1943 by R. A. S. Macalister. The library's records state that it was a gift from 'Dr. Solomon Schechter'. Macalister, a biblical archaeologist, had consulted with Schechter over the first chapter of his book *Ecclesiastical Vestments: Their Development and History* (London, 1896), and he acknowledged his help in the preface. Still, it's unlikely that Schechter presented him with a gift whose subject matter was remote from his research interests, and doubly strange for Schechter to give away a substantial manuscript, a rarity among genizah fragments, to someone with whom he did not have a particularly close relationship.

A more likely scenario is that Schechter gave this manuscript to his great ally, and a supporter of his trip to Cairo, Sir Donald MacAlister, Fellow of St John's College, Cambridge, and a Physician to Addenbrooke's Hospital. Donald MacAlister's interests in medicine, languages and philosophy and his closer relationship with Schechter make him a better candidate for the recipient of the gift. Donald MacAlister's wife, Edith

Florence Boyle MacAlister, also happened to be R. A. S. Macalister's sister, and it's possible that it came to him after her death as she did not have any children. The other two manuscripts, a book of Leviticus with Arabic translation in Hebrew characters (eight leaves) and fragments of regulations for prayer (two leaves), both twelfth to thirteenth-century pieces, may well have been given directly to R. A. S. Macalister given his interest in how church vestments related to the vestments of the Levitical priesthood.[26]

In the midst of negotiations to donate Schechter's hoard of Hebrew manuscripts to Cambridge University Library, Charles Taylor wrote to Jenkinson on 5 March 1898 to help clear up some misunderstandings concerning the long-term care of the collection. Taylor asked for clarification on what would be considered a reasonable sum to conserve, bind and classify such a large collection, given that some members of the Library Syndicate 'advocates of expenditure on modern books of science etc. – would object to <u>much</u> expenditure on the Cairo MSS'. Schechter, he reported, felt that the library should take as long as it needed to work on the collection as the work could not and should not be hurried. But one Syndicate member, Arthur Thomas Chapman, a professor of mathematics, Greek and Hebrew at Emmanuel College, was concerned that the rest of the Syndicate would object to a lengthy, drawn-out undertaking. He suggested that the amount of expenditure should be decided from the outset.

In addition, Taylor clarified Schechter's statement about their obligation to the Cairo community. Schechter, he told him, had promised the community that the manuscripts would be organized and made accessible to scholars. He made pains to correct Jenkinson who had described the manuscripts as a collection that had been 'shamefully neglected' at Cairo. It was not a 'collection', Taylor informed him, but rather 'a heap of MSS. put away as done with'.[27]

ISRAEL ABRAHAMS WAS ABOUT TO ENCOUNTER A HEAP OF MSS 'put away as done with' inside the Ben Ezra Synagogue. Having recently published his major work, *Jewish Life in the Middle Ages*, Abrahams decided that a trip to Palestine was necessary for his new study of the history of the Maccabeans. As a member of the Anglo-Jewish Association, he could also inspect the schools on the Association's behalf. Moreover, since he would be in the region, a new tourist attraction beckoned – the Ben Ezra Synagogue, which was now synonymous with the famous Cairo Genizah. On board the ship, Abrahams met Raffalovich, who introduced himself and told Abrahams that he'd been in England selling manuscripts to Schechter, Adler and Gaster. Gaster's genizah purchases from that quarter were later described as the 'gleaning which remained after the rich harvest', among them were a number of Yemenite fragments from the nineteenth century, a contract which, despite looking like a medieval fragment, was dated to 1880, and a bill of divorce dated to 1865.[28] According to Abrahams, it was Gaster who had told Raffalovich to seek him out on the journey. Abrahams, for his part, felt glad to have gained a contact in Jerusalem.

After a long and sickening sea journey, Abrahams reached Cairo on 15 March 1898, and checked in at the Shepheard's Hotel. Two days later, he met with the chief rabbi and they shared coffee, cigarettes and a 'capital' conversation in Hebrew with a smattering of French. After their conversation, Abrahams quickly realized that Schechter had 'by no means exhausted the Geniza', and he swore his wife, Freda, to secrecy while he tried to 'worm out more from them'.[29]

At the same time that Abrahams was trying to find out more about the Genizah, d'Hulst was running around the various government offices submitting plans of the proposed excavation work. Responding to a letter from Nicholson, he confessed to feeling relieved that they did not want him to purchase the materials still inside the synagogue building. He did not trust the locals when it came to making agreements 'when they see an advantage'. And in this case, d'Hulst stated, 'they had an advantage, have had hundreds of pounds from Prof. Schechter.' The official permission to turn the rubbish heaps, he believed would be issued the next day. He also took the opportunity to explain to Nicholson his long-standing connection to the fragments, beginning with his work for the Fund in 1889, and he included the information that 'all the papers could have been had at that time for £20'.[30]

The following day, as d'Hulst was getting his permit, Abrahams was taken on a visit to Old Cairo by a young *shamash* (caretaker). In recounting the days' events to Freda, he excitedly told her: 'I saw the Geniza – there is a great deal left. I should not wonder that there is as much again as Schechter took. Possibly I might get permission to look through some of the residue on Sunday.' He told her not to 'let this leak out yet', but he proposed writing an article about his visit and his discoveries there for his good friend, Asher Myers, the editor of *The Jewish Chronicle*.

Abrahams stayed in Old Cairo all afternoon. He took many photographs during the visit, including photos of the beadle and the chief rabbi, but he later discovered that they were all over-exposed. Still, he hoped to visit the Genizah again on the Sunday or Monday before leaving for Port Said on the Tuesday. Over the course of the next day, however, he began to doubt that he would manage to see it again, for he could not tell whether he would get the necessary authorization, and he confided to his wife that he might 'cry' if it were not possible. He also shared with her the secret that 'it is a real sell Schechter pretending that he had brought away everything. I daresay they deceived him into believing that he had.' The chief rabbi summoned him to his office on Monday, insisting that Abrahams retake his photographs. But when Abrahams arrived the next day, Ben-Simeon was busy with weddings, divorces and other matters, and he had to wait. Whether or not he shed tears over the matter, Abrahams's premonition was correct: he did not return to the Genizah.

His subsequent experiences in Palestine may have overtaken those of Egypt. He certainly dedicated a whole chapter of a book on his visit to the Maccabean site of Hebron, although that city did not yield up any treasures either: Schechter had been there before him and 'there was nothing left but modern Cabbalistic literature'.[31] In Jerusalem, Abrahams was invited by the Library Committee to give a lecture in Hebrew on 'Jewish travelling in the Middle Ages' and the standing-room-only event brought together leaders and representatives from a wide range of Jewish organizations and institutions. The audience members were impressed with his Hebrew, and two members of the Library Committee, Adelmann and Yellin, proposed a vote of thanks. Abrahams' popular lecture was followed by several weeks of touring the country and visiting the agricultural colonies. After he returned to England, his proposed article on the genizah was never written, and he never publicly shared the details of his genizah experience. A collection of twenty-one manuscript fragments, including some medieval fragments that were 'probably from the Cairo Genizah', were taken with him to Cambridge after he succeeded Schechter as Reader in Rabbinics in 1902. They were kept with his papers in the Library of Oriental Studies and transferred to the University Library in 1961.[32]

RAFFALOVICH HAD ALSO BEEN BUSY IN CAIRO that month. After taking leave of Abrahams when their ship embarked in Egypt, he had visited the city and engaged in undocumented activities surrounding the purchase of manuscripts. After he arrived back at his store near the Jaffa Gate in Jerusalem, he wrote to Schechter in March of 1898 to let him know that he was sending him two packets of fragments from the genizah. After experiencing 'great trouble' there, he was only able to take back to Jerusalem a portion of the manuscripts he'd purchased in Cairo. The remainder, about 1,000 fragments, were due to be mailed to him soon, but for the meantime he was sending on 512 leaves. They had cost him £18 and he hoped that Schechter would reimburse him for their true value. He promised to send on the rest and whatever else came to his hand while he was in Jerusalem. At the same time, he swore Schechter to secrecy, saying: 'I hope you will oblige me with that, & as to Mr Adler & other people in London are very interesting [*sic*] in that, please don't let them know that I sent to you any thing.' Raffalovich also requested that Schechter not let his former partner Mr Goldstein know about what he had sent and still planned to send.[33]

COUNT D'HULST REPORTED ON THE PROGRESS OF HIS EXCAVATIONS at the end of March 1898. He let Nicholson know that the fragments retrieved so far filled a box over one metre tall (or deep), and some of the pieces had up to twenty leaves still together. In order to avoid news of the dig leaking out to the French newspapers, the ministry had given him 'une permission officieuse' (unofficial authorization). With this in mind, he recommended that the work should go ahead without delay and anticipated that it would take another £15–£20 to complete.[34]

Sayce was back in Cairo having heard the news that Coptic manuscripts were for sale in the markets. He told Nicholson that d'Hulst had taken a sample along to the Scottish Coptologist Walter Ewing Crum to get his opinion of them.[35] On the progress of the excavations, he wrote: 'D'Hulst tells me that the Hebrew MSS you have already received from him are unfortunately not "earth-shaking" . . . Am I right in telling him to go on?' And he shared the news that the Ministry of Public Works had received a letter protesting the excavation work from Max Herz, the chief architect of the Comité de Conservation des Monuments de l'Art Arabe.

Herz, a Hungarian Jew, had lived in Egypt since 1880. His architectural background had gained him the appointment as chief architect for the Comité in 1890; a position he held until 1914. Having learnt of the excavation work, Herz, according to Sayce, wanted to acquire the manuscripts for Berlin. Sayce recommended moving ahead with the excavations without further pause. If they could continue digging for another week or two then the protest could be successfully ignored. Strictly speaking, he divulged, the ministry had no legal right to grant the permission without first consulting the Comité.[36]

REGINALD HENRIQUES WAS KEEPING A CLOSE EYE on what he called Schechter's 'Geniza'. On 5 April, he wrote to Schechter from the Turf Club: 'I have been having most exciting times lately in your Geniza & but for my timely intervention everything that is left would [as] now have been carried off to the Bodleian Library Oxford.' In a visit to the Ben Ezra Synagogue on the previous Saturday he had come across the 'Comte de Hulst'. The Count was digging 'outside the enclosed space of the synagogue' and being helped by twenty local workers to move 'considerable quantities of sand and rubbish'. Henriques challenged his authority to dig on private property and d'Hulst showed him his licence from the Ministry. Unaware that he was talking to Schechter's 'spy', he told him that the work was for 'Mr. Neubauer & the Bodleian Library'.

After their meeting, d'Hulst went to see Joseph Cattaoui at the Ministry for a full permit to dig and remove anything he could find 'within & without the precincts of the synagogue'. Henriques foresaw the danger and got to Cattaoui's office in time to get him to change the permit, authorizing him to work only outside the synagogue compound where there was 'probably nothing of value'. With a little further expenditure, Henriques felt certain that a considerable quantity of manuscripts would be found inside the courtyard 'on the site of the former synagogue'. Very soon, he told Schechter, he would be able to send him 'a fairly good lot', and the Comte d'Hulst would succeed in taking away only 'very very little'. Besides, his work of three weeks had only resulted in half a sack, and Henriques promised to continue to try to prevent him taking anything further. He signed off his letter to Schechter with greetings from Boyle, and a postscript to say that he was due to celebrate Passover with the Cattaouis.

Three days later, a letter from d'Hulst to Neubauer painted a different picture of the affair. The work, he reported, was going successfully and he felt confident that he would soon 'double the quantity of Egyptian fragments at the Bodleian'. He had already recovered 'more than two big grain sacks full' which, in addition to paper fragments, contained parchment manuscripts as well. Some of the pieces were damp and so he laid them out in the sun to dry before packing them away. But the work was difficult: the area outside the synagogue precinct offered no shade from the piping hot sun; the smell of dead animals thrown into the area exacerbated their discomfort, and black dust severely dried their eyes and caused additional respiratory difficulties. Many workers quit and had to be replaced. D'Hulst related how the previous Saturday they had been 'attacked by a number of Jews armed with sticks' claiming that he and his men were working illegally on synagogue property.

With Sir William Garstin's help, d'Hulst gained an introduction to the chief of the synagogue (Moïse Cattaoui), who promised to get him permission from the 'Israelitish Consistory' the following day. Feeling emboldened by Cattaoui's obliging ways, d'Hulst asked him for permission to dig within the synagogue compound, particularly as he had only just recently discovered that 'a large part of the courtyard has been covered about one meter high with the same papers – containing rubbish'. These may have been the fragments that Schechter had tossed out in his attempts to separate the 'wheat' of medieval manuscripts from the 'chaff' of printed matter.

On Tuesday, the official permit to excavate outside the synagogue compound came through, but permission to work inside the compound was denied. Nevertheless, d'Hulst comforted Neubauer, the materials he'd recovered for him from outside would most likely keep him occupied until the next winter season. In the meantime, no one was likely to tackle the rubbish pile in the synagogue courtyard in the hot summer months ahead. They could revisit the situation after Neubauer had a chance to assess the quality of the manuscripts being recovered, and no doubt some letters of support from influential English Jews would help resolve the problem of gaining further permissions going forward.[37]

Several weeks later, d'Hulst sent another update to Nicholson. He apologized for falling behind on the correspondence: he was living in Zeitoun and had to go into Cairo to collect his mail. Not having heard any further instructions from Oxford, he'd decided to forge ahead anyway. He was working every day now, including weekends and holidays. He didn't dare stop as the synagogue caretakers, no doubt resentful of having another stranger usurp their ability to earn an income again, were proving 'troublesome' and 'ill-willed'. But with relentless hard work, he had now recovered 'nine big grain sacks full of fragments'.[38]

Sayce sent his own letter to Nicholson: he had resolved the Count's difficulties and the project was progressing thanks to the protection of the police and Ministry of Public Works. He had even received an approval from the community leaders. Cattaoui promised them, Sayce averred, that d'Hulst could excavate in the synagogue garden the following summer 'where, it seems, no end of MSS are buried'. One box of manuscript fragments had been packed up for Oxford, he noted, and there were more 'under the ground' than anticipated.[39]

Sayce also mentioned that the Coptic manuscripts had been purchased by Bouriant (probably the French Egyptologist and coptologist, Urbain Bouriant), and he enclosed a letter from Max Herz's colleague, Bernhard Moritz, the head of the Khedivial Library. Moritz was relatively new to the position having previously been an Arabic paleographer and librarian at the Friedrich-Wilhelms University in Berlin. Sayce noted enigmatically that he had told Moritz that Nicholson would do everything he could to accommodate the Khedivial Library. The issue may have related to Arabic papyri and perhaps to some sort of agreement concerning any Arabic manuscripts found in the excavations. The Egyptian National Library's collection of over 2,000 pieces of Arabic papyri was first put together by Moritz in 1897. He also amassed his own personal collection, which was eventually donated to the University of Pennsylvania, and he was involved in passing along a collection of papyri to Wilhelm Max Müller in 1910, a consignment that included genizah fragments.[40]

Nicholson confirmed to d'Hulst that he was willing to 'run the risk' of the additional outlay, and he asked him to kindly cover the cost of another twenty pounds to complete the work. He hoped they could avoid bringing attention to d'Hulst's excavation as he was concerned not to irritate the Egyptian officials.[41] But d'Hulst had decided to proceed before getting the firm go-ahead. With other buyers on the scene, it probably occurred to him that his outlay would somehow get reimbursed regardless of whether Oxford wanted the fragments or not. Eight days later, he informed Nicholson that the work was complete: the excavation project was brought to a close. After fifty-five working days spent on the project, he reported that he had accumulated 'sixteen big grain sacs full of fragments'. The sacks had been packed into four big wooden packing cases and shipped with the forwarding agency Large & Co.[42]

D'Hulst was about to depart for England to stay with MacGregor at Bolehall Manor, and he requested that all mail be redirected to him there. Nicholson sent a response to Bolehall on 20 May 1898 that he would 'take an early opportunity of asking the Curators to express their sense of your most unusual services to the Bodleian, and am only sorry that I can't let the University know of them without the risk of hindering our future designs on the synagogue garden'. Entries in the Bodleian ledgers show that d'Hulst was reimbursed for the full amount, and a handwritten draft of a letter of acknowledgement, dated June 15, was retained in the library's archives. In the draft letter, d'Hulst was thanked on behalf of the Bodleian Curators for his great trouble: 'Your exceeding kindness would under any circumstances have claimed their thanks, but the exceptional difficulties which you had to surmount make their indebtedness to you still greater.' When d'Hulst received the official letter, dated 17 June, it was signed by John R. Magrath, the university vice chancellor.

Finding every last fragment (1898–9)

IN THE SUMMER OF 1898, NEUBAUER AND COWLEY UNPACKED D'HULST'S LATEST BOXES of excavated genizah materials with great anticipation. As for Schechter, even though he'd sent off his transcriptions of *The Wisdom of Ben Sira* for publication and was working on the introduction, the idea that he might have overlooked fragments of Ben Sira constantly nagged at him. He was also aware, thanks to communications from Henriques, that Neubauer had an agent in Cairo. Only another scan through the collection could ease his mind, and he sent a letter to Jenkinson requesting his help to get the Cairo room rearranged to give him the best means of examining the fragments quickly and efficiently. His anxiety about the matter was so great that he barged into one of Jenkinson's meetings to press him on the matter.[1]

Jenkinson was informed that sacks of fragments were still available for purchase in Cairo through another source – his friends, Walter Ewing Crum and his wife, and Mr and Mrs George Darwin. The visitors announced their arrival at the library by throwing a pebble at his window. After he showed them the Coptic and Ethiopic manuscripts in the library's collection, he took them to see the genizah fragments. They demonstrated great interest in these as they'd been offered five sacks of fragments while visiting Cairo. The seller may have been d'Hulst who had been tasked by Sayce with taking a Coptic manuscript to show Crum. The sale fell through after someone warned them that Schechter had taken away with him all the manuscripts of value. Though it appears that his reaction to that statement was shared only with his diary, Jenkinson noted his surprise at this rather 'hasty assumption.'[2]

RAFFALOVICH CONTINUED TO OFFER GENIZAH FRAGMENTS to various institutions. By now he had two additional partners in Jerusalem, Haim Lipkin and Getzil Cohen Sofer, and the partners had sent some pieces over to Cambridge for review, as well as reminders for payment.[3] On 1 July 1898 the records of the British Museum noted that the dealer, W. S. Raffalovich of Jerusalem, was offering 'eight manuscripts and five collections of manuscript fragments' for sale. The price for the lot was £111.16. Raffalovich did not claim the 'Cairo Genizah' provenance for the pieces in this offering; he simply highlighted their antique appearance and interesting orthography. Some months later, having sensed great interest in his fragments, Raffalovich offered the British Museum a collection from 'a Genizah in Cairo' for the sum of £1,000. He also sent two packages of fragments to Cambridge for

Schechter to review. On 4 December 1898, Jenkinson recorded in his diary that he spent two hours with Schechter going over one of the packages, and he concluded that it was 'very poor stuff'. They returned to examine the fragments on the 8th and, once again, Jenkinson pronounced them to be 'a very poor lot indeed'. That same day, the British Museum recommended the purchase of the Raffalovich fragments, which he had now reduced to the price of £250. Having spent some time examining the pieces and deciding he wanted them, the curator, George Margoliouth, wrote a glowing report recommending their purchase on the grounds that 'the importance of the collection from the religious, literary and social point of view can scarcely be overestimated'.[4] He wasn't wrong: in addition to autograph pieces by Maimonides, the collection included some much-coveted missing sections of the MS B version of Ben Sira.

While Jenkinson had regarded Raffalovich's latest offerings as 'rubbishy', Anthony Ashley Bevan, Lord Almoner's professor of Arabic at Cambridge, had found some things there that interested him, including some Arabic fragments. Jenkinson showed him some of the other pieces that had been sent from Egypt on approval: a seventeenth-century Koran; an old grammatical manuscript; and two medical manuscripts, one of which was declared 'no good at all'. This latter may have been sent back or it could have been the one that Schechter gifted to MacAlister. The British Museum, in the meantime, had officially accepted Raffalovich's offer of fragments.

The tremendous scholarly value of the Taylor-Schechter Genizah Collection was formerly recognized in September when the 'Doctor of Literature' was finally conferred on Schechter. The degree, reported *The Jewish Chronicle*, was given 'in recognition of his remarkable service to Hebrew literature generally, and to Cambridge University in particular, by his epoch-making discoveries in the Cairo Genizah'.[5] The gift was formally accepted 'by Grace of the Senate' on 10 November 1898, and a further Grace placed the sum of £500 at the disposal of the Library Syndicate for 'obtaining expert assistance in classifying and making a catalogue of the collection of manuscripts'.[6] The agreement was made with the understanding that Schechter had returned from Cairo with approximately 40,000 fragments, yet additional fragments were still arriving. These included the pieces purchased from Raffalovich, as well as a donation from Lewis and Gibson of all the fragments they had purchased in the markets, apart from pieces of the Old Testament they set aside for themselves.[7] Even more fragments would soon be on their way; yet no funds existed for their decipherment and care, and many would languish in boxes for decades to come.[8]

HENRIQUES KEPT SCHECHTER ABREAST OF DEVELOPMENTS IN CAIRO, and in December 1898 he wrote to let him know that 'the matter of the Ghenisa is by no means finished'. Forgetting about his earlier interaction with the 'Compte de Hulst', he divulged that while he'd been away in England, a German or Austrian man had succeeded in digging up 'at least 20 to 25 bags of manuscripts'. Now someone else, a Dr Muller, had arrived on the scene and was offering the synagogue beadle £2 per bag. After he heard about this, Henriques intercepted the sale and 'collared what was already dug up', which amounted to five sacks. The sacks were being kept in

Henriques's own warehouse in Cairo while he waited for Schechter's response. If no agreement could be made on the price, he would have to relinquish them again. He asked Schechter if he was willing to pay the £2 for each bag in addition to packing and shipping. If Schechter agreed, he could secure everything that had been dug up and ship over between ten and fifteen bags. In describing the type of material, Henriques stressed that it was 'all manuscript' and 'mostly of same type as sent you before' although these were much dustier and dirtier pieces having been buried in the sand. He reiterated the need for speed as he feared that 'too much already has been lost to you during my absence'.[9]

Henriques' letter is revealing and inscrutable all at the same time. Clearly fragments were still being unearthed, but the find spot is not divulged, and it may or may not have been in the area of the Ben Ezra Synagogue. His statement that the material being sent was the same as 'sent you before' is also intriguing since no record of anything sent from Henriques to Schechter prior to this letter has been found. One possible scenario is that he enclosed a sample in the letter he sent on 5 April 1898 when he first encountered d'Hulst digging. If there had been an accompanying explanatory note, it may have been discarded after Schechter added the sample pieces to the existing Cambridge genizah collection.

The rival for the bags, who willingly gave his card, may have been the Austrian Orientalist David Heinrich Müller, David Kaufmann's good friend. Müller was connected to at least one Hebrew fragment: the piece he published with Kaufmann from the Rainer collection, and he was no doubt aware of his friend's abiding interest in them. The timing was right: he had left Europe in November to embark on a scientific mission to Yemen with the Count Carlo de Landberg. Their expedition, under the auspices of the Vienna Academy of Sciences, also took them through Egypt.[10] Another candidate could be Wilhelm Max Müller, the American orientalist and son of the German philologist and orientalist Friedrich Max Müller. Wilhelm eventually acquired some genizah fragments through Bernard Moritz in 1910, but it seems that he only spent time in Egypt beginning in 1900.[11]

At the end of the month, when 1898 was at a close, Henriques was still trying hard to get additional bags of manuscripts and keep hold of those already appropriated. Their price had increased to £2.10.0 for a bag, reflecting the growing interest from other buyers, and it was applied retroactively to the bags in his warehouse. As other buyers before him, with little regard for the economic consequences of such purchases on the sellers, he described the synagogue caretakers as 'the most annoying & unprincipled crowd one can possibly imagine'. He apologized for the wait and the additional cost, but he had hopes that three or four more sacks would be available in the next week.

In the top corner of Henriques's letter, Jenkinson made a note early in the new year that he'd been answered with the instruction to 'buy'. Direct correspondence between Schechter and Henriques came to an end at this time. Schechter had been appointed a professor at University College London, and for a while found himself too busy to write, even to close friends like Sulzberger. Henriques's follow-up letters negotiating the purchase and shipping of the sacks of fragments were addressed to Jenkinson.

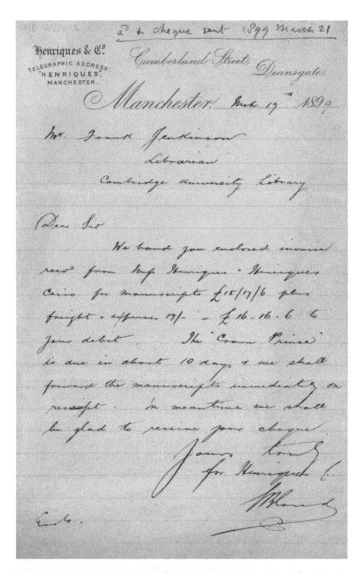

Figure 14.1 MS ULIB 6/6/1/2, a letter from Henriques & Co. confirming shipment of manuscripts to Cambridge, 19 March 1899.

ELKAN ADLER EMBARKED ON HIS THIRD TOUR OF THE NEAR EAST towards the end of 1898 with a 'head full of apocrypha'. In search of untapped genizot, in addition to Palestine and Egypt, he decided to visit Aleppo. In the Great Synagogue of Aleppo, he was allowed to view the famous Aleppo Codex, as well as several other medieval Bible codices. He was permitted to enter the (or 'a') genizah which was located in the eaves of the roof of a side chapel. Yet, he did not find anything of interest, only printed matter. He attributed the lack of manuscripts to the fact that the genizah at Aleppo was periodically emptied and taken for ceremonial burial, a process that the locals believed helped bring on the rain. A few good manuscripts were recovered from other quarters, however, including a *divan* (anthology) of poems citing unknown contemporaries of Maimonides and a fourteenth-century Masoretic Bible with a reference to China in its colophon.[12]

In Egypt, he obtained additional 'Geniza fragments' in Cairo (although he did not say exactly how he got them) and 'important MSS' from 'a Geniza in Alexandria'. An unknown number of fragments also came into his possession thanks to an excavation conducted in the middle of the night, as he explained in 1904 to members of the Jews' College Literary Society:

> One learns at Cairo that the last of the Jews of Rosetta had carried away with him the Genizah from that city and brought it to Alexandria for re-burial. One goes to the Chief Rabbi, an intelligent man and one who, since Schechter's discovery of the Hebrew Ecclesiasticus, knows why people are so interested in Egyptian relics. One tells him about the Rosetta Genizah, but he has not heard of it. He asks his myrmidons, and at last one says, 'Oh yes, I know where it was buried.' In my courtly French I beg him to allow me to dig for it. 'Certainly,' says he, 'we will arrange for it; come next week.' 'Oh but my boat leaves to-morrow for Marseilles.' 'Then I am afraid it will be impossible.' 'But if one pays the diggers?' 'It is too late now.' 'Oh, but let them over night.' 'Well, how much will you give?' And so the Genizah is uncovered and one rescues from the grave some quite important fragments of early MSS. as well as documents so late as a Cretan Ketubah of a poor divorcée of fifty years ago.[13]

Adler was also about to acquire fragments from another source closer to home. On 11 January 1899, an Acta of the Bodleian Library declared that Nicholson 'was authorised to sell for £20 a quantity of MS. fragments from Egypt put aside by Dr. Neubauer and Mr. Cowley as not worth retention'. The price was exactly the same as the amount expended on d'Hulst's excavation, suggesting that very little of his hoard was retained. Fourteen days later, the Bodleian Library Receipts Ledger noted that Mr E. N. Adler was the happy recipient of their 'sale of useless Hebrew MS fragments'.[14]

Although the number of fragments Adler purchased was not recorded, it can only be conjectured that of the sixteen big grain sacks of fragments sent over by d'Hulst, most were sold off after Neubauer and Cowley had made their selection of a mere 73 items (199 folios).[15] That his strenuous efforts on behalf of the Bodleian had come to this sorry pass remained unknown to the Count d'Hulst.

D'Hulst likewise had no knowledge that some of the manuscripts brought to light through his excavations were on their way to Cambridge. On 7 March 1899, Henriques informed Jenkinson that the sacks of fragments were on board the Crown Prince ship and headed to Manchester. He was sure that more manuscripts would be unearthed soon but more money was being demanded for them in light of the cost of 'digging & removing soil'. Future bags would likely cost between three to four pounds each and so he wanted to know if Jenkinson wished to give him 'faculty to secure them'. Thirteen days later, Jenkinson noted at the head of the letter that he had instructed Henriques to 'go on', and that going forward he would receive a coded telegram with instructions to either stop or to purchase the bags at the price of five pounds each.

THE LURE OF ACQUIRING IMPORTANT PIECES OF 'THE CAIRO GENIZAH' remained in the air. Dealers were aware of the new interest in items of this provenance, and scholarly travellers in the know were now alert to such items being offered for sale in the markets. Such was the case of the German Orientalist and Semiticist Eugene Mittwoch who, in the spring of 1899, travelled with fellow Orientalist Moritz Sobernheim to visit archaeological sites in Syria, Palestine and Egypt on behalf of the Institut-Français D'Archéologie Orientale. While visiting Egypt, Mittwoch purchased around forty Hebrew fragments from 'the Cairo Genizah'. When he published one of the fragments that same year, he noted that most of the pieces in his small collection were liturgical in content; although there were also pieces of medical, exegetical and philosophical works, poems, letters, bills and the like. The piece that he was keen to share with the world, however, was a letter by Rabbi Hanan'el ben Samuel al-Amshati the Judge (*c.* 1170–1250), who became related to Moses Maimonides by marriage. The letter concerns questions surrounding the study of Greek philosophy and Maimonides' views on the issue. Since the location of the addressee and the details of the recipient were missing from al-Amshati's letter, Mittwoch assumed that it may have well migrated from 'somewhere else to Cairo and so into the Geniza'. The al-Amshati family dynasty of rabbis and merchants was connected to the synagogue in al-Mahallah al-Kubra.[16]

Five years after Germany came under Nazi rule, Mittwoch escaped to England. After his death in 1942, 20 or so fragments were acquired by the Central Library of the Selly Oaks Colleges in Birmingham and incorporated into a collection of over 3,000 Middle Eastern manuscripts gathered by the Iraqi-born theologian and Syriacist Alphonse Mingana. There they met up with nineteen other similar Hebrew fragments of unknown provenance, including one set of 'twenty small, darkened leaves containing tales in colloquial Arabic' from around the eighteenth century.[17] The twelfth-century al-Amshati fragment, however, had further journeys to undertake. Mittwoch's dire circumstances probably induced him to sell the piece, and it was eventually picked up by London collector David Sofer, from a dealer in Jerusalem. It was later identified as Mittwoch's fragment by the Semiticist Paul Fenton. The much-travelled fragment was sold off once again in 2017, and privately purchased by the Green Collection in Oklahoma City for the National Christian Foundation. It now resides under the curatorial care of the Museum of the Bible in Washington, DC.[18]

SIX SACKS OF FRAGMENTS SEQUESTERED BY HENRIQUES had meanwhile arrived at the firm of Henriques & Co. in Manchester, and they were awaiting a payment of £16.16.6, including freight and expenses, before they could travel to Cambridge. The cheque was sent out while Schechter was finishing up his prefatory remarks for *The Wisdom of Ben Sira*. On 5 April 1899, following his letter-writing hiatus, Schechter confirmed to Mayer Sulzberger that he would soon receive a copy of his 'Sirach' which was due out next May. For all he knew, additional portions of Ben Sira could still be on their way to Cambridge, but it was too late for this volume. At least they would be at Cambridge and not elsewhere. On 21 April 1899, Jenkinson recorded in his diary that he had written a letter to Henriques 'Thanking him, reporting progress, & saying we would pay what was necessary to secure further sacks'. In May, Henriques told Jenkinson that he was continuing to act on the library's behalf to procure the manuscripts which they seemed 'anxious to secure'. One difficulty he proclaimed was that several people were still 'scheming to obtain whatever is brought to light especially an Austrian whose name I communicated to Professor Schechter some time ago'. Yet, despite the continued digging, only one sack had been prepared and Henriques feared that the supply was at an end.

Together with his letter, he enclosed a manuscript book that the 'Austrian Count' had found 'in the same place'. The Count, presumably d'Hulst, had offered £2 for the book, but Henriques had managed to wrest it away from him and now enclosed it on approval pending their decision. Whether it ever found its way back to d'Hulst isn't known, but on 29 May, Jenkinson noted in his diary that the manuscript 'being pronounced no good by Schechter, was at once sent back with thanks for the trouble taken'.

From this time, communications between Henriques and Cambridge University Library ceased. The lack of interest in his latest offering may have been off-putting, or perhaps more important personal matters intervened. The death of his father, Edward Micholls Henriques, in 1901, may well have delayed his final consignment of bags, which did not arrive in Cambridge until 1902. The Henriques collection of six sacks (1899) and three bags (1902) were subsumed into the larger Taylor-Schechter Collection. Schechter's first estimation of his hoard in 1897 was 40,000 fragments, but by 1908 he estimated that the collection was around 100,000 fragments. Even allowing for an initial underestimation and a final overestimation, this is still a divergent number, and it may never be known how much Henriques, Raffalovich and others contributed to that total. In 1906, after the library had finished cleaning, pressing and sorting 34,335 fragments, a handwritten report for sharing with the members of the Library Syndicate listed the residue stored in twenty-four wooden boxes. The list included some materials that had been examined and cast aside as 'unimportant'; four boxes of small fragments 'put aside in course of sorting'; one box of unexamined materials that were mostly in bad condition and 'two boxes of rubbish'. A note at the end of the list stated:

> It may be well to remind the Syndicate that a considerable quantity of fragments from the same source as the Taylor-Schechter Collection has been purchased by the Library within the last few years. Only a small amount of work has been done on them and it is very desirable that steps should be taken for their further examination.[19]

When a new phase of sorting through the collection was undertaken in the 1950s, materials from the boxes of residue were classified into a 'New Series' or set aside and redistributed into new boxes. The leftover materials were finally examined and conserved beginning in the 1970s, and they were classified into an 'Additional Series'. By 2009, an inventory project determined that the Taylor-Schechter Genizah Collection amounted to 193,654 fragments. Of the entire collection, only one folder of materials in the New Series, 189 miscellaneous items, was attributed to Henriques.[20]

Given that he had a high regard for Schechter's mission and supported it by acting as the library's agent, Henriques would not have expected his sacksful of unearthed fragments to be distinguished in any way. In his preface to *The Wisdom of Ben Sira*, Schechter provided an intriguing hint at the size and extent of Henriques's involvement by expressing thanks 'to my friend Mr Reginald Q. Henriques of Cairo (originally of Manchester), to whose kindness, beginning during my stay and still continuing, I am indebted for many a precious document and important MS'.

AT THE CENTURY'S CLOSE, NEUBAUER WAS FORCED TO LEAVE THE LIBRARY: with diminishing cognitive abilities and increasingly poor eyesight, the 68-year-old could no longer carry out his duties. In recognition of his great services to the Bodleian, he was awarded an annual pension of £250 (£50 higher than the regular pension). The work of finishing the *Catalogue of Hebrew Manuscripts in the Bodleian Library* was left in Cowley's hands. Neubauer had compiled all of the catalogue entries up to column 226 of the catalogue (a little less than half of the final printed book), and Cowley continued to catalogue the 'later acquisitions' mostly from the post-1895 period. When the work was finally published in 1906, it failed to acknowledge the help of the Count d'Hulst. D'Hulst came across a copy in 1909, and he wrote to Nicholson to complain about the omission; after much wrangling back and forth, the work was re-issued with an addendum dated 7 May 1910.

In the newly printed addendum, Nicholson acknowledged 'the great services of Count R. d'Hulst during the early part of 1898 in procuring *Geniza* fragments for the Bodleian'. That they had failed to record his activities in the Bodleian Annual Report, he claimed, was because 'absolute secrecy as to the Cairo fragments was, for the time being, necessary to the interests of the Library'. That they also overlooked his help in the *Catalogue* was because he and the author always had 'far more work waiting for us than we can do, and probably we both wrote our preliminary statements under severe pressure of time'. What Nicholson failed to mention, however, is that the library now barely contained any fragments from d'Hulst's massive 1898 consignment and only a small portion of the fragments recovered in 1895-6. With regard to d'Hulst's earlier consignments, which included the Bodleian fragments of Ecclesiasticus, Nicholson wrote:

> I am told by Count d'Hulst that another part of the Bodleian collection of *Geniza* fragments appear to be derived from excavations carried out by him in 1889 for the Egypt Exploration Fund, and that others again were obtained by him in 1893 and 1895. Of these things I believe both Dr. Cowley and myself were unaware, and Dr. Neubauer, who might just possibly have been able to inform us, was totally incapacitated by ill health in 1899, and died on Apr. 6, 1907, at the age of 76.[21]

Thus, the full story of d'Hulst's involvement in discovering genizah fragments was obscured, and it's only thanks to subsequent letters sent by him and his wife during and after the First World War that it can be partially reconstructed and the provenance of the fragments better understood. Having been reduced to poverty after losing money on several investments, d'Hulst soon became an object of suspicion. In 1916, he was interned as an enemy alien in the Ras-el-Tin camp in Alexandria. Meanwhile, his possessions were sold off at public auction, including a vast set of photographs taken in Egypt and various Egyptian artefacts he had amassed over the years. He died not long after of tuberculosis. At some point after 1932, after making a third attempt to seek restitution from Oxford, his wife, Laura, died in penury. The scores of historical letters in her possession from members of the Egypt Exploration Fund, MacGregor, Nicholson, Sayce, Neubauer and others from which she had quoted in her attempts to retell her husband's story were forever lost.[22]

Genizah fragments acquired in Germany late in 1899 would eventually become a casualty of the Second World War. Under the leadership of Dr Markus Horovitz, an Orthodox rabbi in Frankfurt, a local community consortium agreed to purchase 4,314 genizah fragments from an undertermined source for the Stadt-und Universitätsbibliothek in Frankfurt Am Main. The purchase had been guided by Aron Freimann, the great Hebrew bibliographer and librarian of the Hebraica and Judaica division of the Stadt-und Universitätsbibliothek, who was also Horovitz's nephew and future son-in-law. Freimann was himself a close friend of Elkan Adler and, purportedly, the first person to whom Adler showed all his treasures. The two travelled together in Italy and parts of North Africa, where Freimann made purchases for the library.

Freimann was also a member of the Berlin-based *Mekitze Nirdamim* Literary Society for the publication of medieval Hebrew literature, which since its founding boasted many illustrious members with connections to genizah fragments, such as Abraham Firkovich, Abraham Harkavy and David Kaufmann, as well as others connected on the periphery like David Simonsen in Copenhagen and David Yellin in Jerusalem. With personal contact between the scholarly members positively encouraged by the society, Aron Freimann was well situated to find a supplier. When he took up the position of librarian in 1898, the Hebraica and Judaica division comprised 11,000 Hebrew books; by the time he was dismissed by the Nazi regime in 1935, it held 40,000 Hebrew books, in addition to genizah fragments. During the allied bombing of Frankfurt, the library building was mostly decimated. Large parts of its holdings were lost or destroyed, including the Hebrew books and nearly all of the genizah fragments. Today, only photocopies of the medieval poetry fragments in the collection survive.

An inexhaustible supply (1900s)

BRINGING SCHECHTER TO AMERICA was one of the major goals of Cyrus Adler and other leading American Jewish intellectuals at the turn of the twentieth century. Schechter was seen as the ideal figurehead to lead the newly built Jewish Theological Seminary in New York. The *Jewish Exponent* of Philadelphia had already made the case that by the time he arrived there he would have 'made the most out of the Geniza find'. The work in America, it proposed, was more important: 'Here, too, he has original materials to work upon, not musty and illegible manuscripts, but a great, living, throbbing community. . . . Dr. Schechter will come where the need for him is greatest, and that greatest need is here.'[1] Nevertheless, 'musty and illegible manuscripts' were beginning to make their way to America to join those already collected by Cyrus Adler, and Adler's dream of building a great American Jewish library was starting to be realized.

Among the scholars who eventually sold or donated large numbers of genizah fragments to American libraries was the Philadelphia lawyer, David Werner Amram. Amram was deeply interested in the history of Jewish jurisprudence, and in 1896 he had authored a book on *The Jewish Law of Divorce According to the Bible and Talmud*. The idea that thousands of documents enabling the reconstruction of Jewish legal practice in the Middle Ages had been discovered in the Cairo Genizah, and that more were still to be had, led him to reach out to Solomon Schechter in 1899 or 1900 for advice on how to find them. Following a communication from Schechter, Amram corresponded with 'dealers in the city of Jerusalem, who were in possession of a portion of these Genizah manuscripts.'[2]

The dealers were most likely Samuel Raffalovich and Haim Lipkin. Their other partner Getzil Sofer had passed away in the autumn of 1899. On their new letterhead, they described themselves as 'Dealers in Antiquities & Curiosities', and they sent Hebrew books and manuscripts on approval to collectors, as well as fragments upon request. One of their clients was Elkan Nathan Adler who purchased several substantial sixteenth-century volumes from the three partners in June and around 79 manuscripts from Jerusalem and Hebron in 1901.[3] Amram was soon rewarded by his query to Jerusalem with a collection of around 363 genizah fragments. Among the copies of medieval biblical and rabbinic writings, literary pieces and legal documents from al-Fustat, Cairo, and Alexandria, however, were some pieces less likely to have surfaced from the Ben Ezra Synagogue genizah: a letter from a Jerusalemite living in Bethlehem written in 1835, and a marriage contract from Yemen conducted in 1892.[4]

Figure 15.1 CAJS MS Halper 374, a Yemenite marriage contract from 1892 purchased by Amram attributed to the Cairo Genizah.

RICHARD JAMES HORATIO GOTTHEIL TOURED THE MIDDLE EAST IN 1904 on a leave of absence from his academic post. In a series of popular articles for *The New Era Illustrated Magazine*,[5] the American orientalist captured his impressions of the Jewish communities of Florence, Rome, Alexandria and Cairo, and he gave accounts of their synagogues both in terms of history and architectural interest. He compared the newer synagogues in Rome unfavourably to the older ones which were unused and in a process of dilapidation. Noting what he felt was a Jewish 'disregard for the old when it is not institutional', he pointed to the case of the old ark in the synagogue in al-Fustat, which had survived purely because its Hebrew inscriptions rendered it worthy of placing in a genizah and not because of its age or artistic merits.

In his piece about Cairo, he offered scathing views of the state of Jewish community life in the city, particularly the community's leadership, which he regarded as autocratic. Power was wielded by the 'presidential firm' and 'nothing can be done in the "communité," as such, unless "the firm" approves of it and are technically "in it". The schools, he viewed as miserable, pitiable and profitless, and he pointed out a disparity between the amount of communal funds set aside for welfare as opposed to the amount of money that had recently been spent to build the magnificent new synagogue in the Ismailiyyah quarter. Aside from the time he spent subjecting the community to the scrutiny of his critical outsider lens, he was given access to the stores of manuscript codices still held in various parts of the city. In this work too, he expressed complaints, including the difficulty in studying such works closely when no books of reference were available to consult, as well as the state in which they were stored. The Ben Asher Codex in the Karaite synagogue, he reported with great consternation, was stuffed inside a wooden box:

> *stuffed*: the word is no exaggeration; the box is not large enough, and the pages must be fitted to its size! The others are tied up in bandana handkerchiefs, or rags of equal cleanliness, and stuffed into the cupboards. Their resting-place touches a wall, through which water seems to percolate, in such a manner that damp and mould are gradually eating their way into the parchments. Pages that fifteen or twenty years ago must have been quite legible are becoming a mass of pulp.[6]

Nevertheless, when the pages of these old Bible codices were placed open on the table before him, he confessed to being overcome with feelings of awe at the sight and wonder at the labour of love that went into constructing 'these venerable monuments'. In drawing up this first systematic review of the Hebrew manuscripts still existing in Cairo, in addition to noting their dimensions, content and colophons, he gave a description of their present whereabouts. In all, he located and described thirty-three ancient books and thirty-four major manuscripts, which had been mostly ignored.[7]

Gottheil's call to the community to institute educational reforms and to take better care of their heritage, which included helping to establish a local Hebrew Literary Association, caught the attention of at least one member of Cairo's leading families. This individual, Jacques Mosseri, had recently returned to Cairo from his undergraduate studies in England, and it's likely that he had his first encounter with Gottheil at the time of the latter's stay in Cairo. Some years later, he recalled discussing with him the possibility that there were additional sites of buried genizot in and around Cairo that could be unearthed: an idea that Gottheil apparently dismissed.[8]

A COLLECTION OF FRAGMENTS ARRIVED AT THE BODLEIAN IN 1906. The sender was Joseph Offord, a London-based businessman who ran his father's illustrious coach company, supplying coaches for European nobility. In his spare time, Offord indulged a passion for Egyptian archaeology and collecting antiquities. He contributed numerous notes and articles to various journals such as *Biblia*; and he was an active member of several professional societies in the field of archaeology. His personal collection was geared towards tablets, seals and ostraca rather than manuscripts. However, an encounter with an Arab dealer in the winter of 1903–4 led him to buy some fragments which he afterwards donated to McGill University in Montreal.

The dealer was most likely Ali el-Arabi, who supplied biblical manuscripts to Charles Lang Freer between 1906 and 1909, as well as manuscripts subsequently given Cairo Genizah provenance in 1908. Offord took his fragments to show a Mr Margoliouth (probably George Margoliouth of the British Museum) who helped him to identify them. Margoliouth's notes were included in the donation.[9] These fragments may have been part of the larger collection of fragments that he subsequently sent along to the Bodleian in 1906, or he may have been induced to return to the same dealer, or someone else, to find more at Arthur Cowley's behest.

In the letter accompanying the 'box with Hebrew and Aramaic manuscripts', he informed Cowley that 'I do not think many more MSS from the Geniza will turn up, I saw Count d'Hulst who thinks that the store is quite exhausted'.[10] The true size of Offord's collection will never be known: the Bodleian kept 713 items (most of which were poorly preserved fragments of paper) and, in a repeat of the familiar story, got rid of others in a 'sale of waste' the following year. The happy recipient was once again Elkan Nathan Adler.[11] When he came to catalogue Offord's fragments, Cowley discovered that one of the pieces came from a philosophical legal treatise in Judeo-Arabic, and that it matched fragments in the library given 'by exchange' from Christian David Ginsburg, as well as a fragment that he himself had donated in 1910. But for each individual catalogue entry, whereas he noted that Offord's piece was 'ultimately from the Geniza', and Ginsburg's piece was 'originally from the Geniza', of his own piece he said nothing.

Other small collections of fragments were acquired over the course of the early part of the twentieth century and accorded Cairo Genizah provenance. Cowley himself added 245 items to the library. Most of them were described as 'from the Geniza', but some were given the new label 'originally from the Geniza'. In some cases, he was less certain: in cataloguing a 63-folio copy of Maimonides's *Mishneh Torah* in Yemenite script from 1636 CE, he noted that it was 'Probably from the Geniza'. But with regard to all these pieces, he was mostly silent on the matter of how he acquired them, apart from in a few cases where he indicated that they came through an Egyptian dealer.[12]

Another set of fragments that were acquired through an Egyptian dealer were those that came into the possession of the art collector, Charles Lang Freer, in 1908. In the catalogue of Freer's fragments, published in 1927, William H. Worrell noted in his introduction that the dealer had probably got them directly from the synagogue or from others who had picked them up 'at the time when the synagogue was being repaired'. Yet, here for the first time, other scenarios were added: 'It is, of course, also possible that they were dug up by natives after being regularly buried by the authorities of the Synagogue. It is even possible that they never were in the Synagogue, but that they were obtained from some ancient cemetery, where they had been originally buried with the dead.'[13]

JACQUES MOSSERI SET ABOUT EXPLORING CAIRO THE FOLLOWING YEAR at the request of the French scholar Israel Lévi. In the first decade of the twentieth century, in addition to serving as the secretary of the Société des Études Juives and editing its scholarly journal *Revue des Études Juives*, Lévi included the study of genizah fragments held in the Bibliothèque du Consistoire Israélite de Paris among his many scholarly endeavours. His work on Ben Sira had gained him the 'Prix Delalande-Guérineau' from the Académie des Inscriptions et Belles-Lettres, and he continued to publish articles on other important texts discovered among the genizah fragments, such as the Damascus Document. The contents of other genizah collections were also being revealed thanks to the publication of a catalogue of the British Museum's Hebrew manuscripts in 1905, and a catalogue of David Kaufmann's Hebrew manuscripts in 1906. Lévi's colleague, the scholar and librarian Moïse Schwab, was likewise busy preparing catalogues of the Hebrew manuscripts held in France, including the genizah fragments at the Bibliothèque du Consistoire.

Gottheil published his description of the additional Hebrew manuscripts still to be found in Cairo in 1905, and by the following year, an international scholarly collaboration to produce the twelve volumes of *The Jewish Encyclopedia* was completed, and it included Elkan Nathan Adler's article on the subject 'Genizah'. Thanks to his personal enquiries to Archibald Henry Sayce, Adler was able to reveal for the first time that fragments from 'the Cairo Genizah' had been 'thrown out and buried in the ground' and regarding genizah practices in the Orient he declared that 'not the least important part of the Taylor-Schechter collection has come from the graveyard'.

In 1907, Lévi was working closely with Bernard Eliezer Dov Chapira, scholar and librarian at the Alliance Israélite Universelle, on the decipherment of fragments from the *diwan* (anthology) of a Spanish Hebrew poet, Todros ben Judah Halevi Abulafia, that had surfaced among the genizah fragments in the Bibliothèque; these were found to match to fragments held in Adler's private collection and other pieces held by Moses Gaster. Yet, portions of the *diwan* were still missing and the idea of conducting further searches in Cairo seemed ever more appealing.[14]

After Gottheil's departure from Egypt, Mosseri developed a strong interest in local heritage, and he set about researching and writing an article on the history of the synagogues. He also began to dream about establishing a Jewish museum and library in Cairo. In 1910, most likely in connection to such initiatives, Moïse Cattaoui, sent a letter to Solomon Schechter in New York on behalf of the Communauté Israélite. He was pleased to inform him that the Jewish community intended to create a museum dedicated to Jewish history in general and to the history of the Jews of Egypt in particular. He kindly asked him if he would donate a copy of his publication of documents found in the 'Guenizah of Old Cairo'.[15] Other leading scholars were approached for copies of their published works too. According to an interview conducted with Mosseri for *The Jewish Chronicle*, the response was decidedly underwhelming:

The Jews are bitterly regretting the transference of the Geniza . . . for they now regard the documents as precious property stolen from its rightful owners. They desire to possess, at least, photographs of the chief manuscripts and to form a collection of all the articles that have appeared on this subject. They have written to all authors begging for 'Sonderabdrucke,' (reprints) but so far the response has been practically nil. As Mr. Mosseri pathetically observed 'Not only have they taken the originals, but when we write and humbly beg for a copy of what they have written, our appeal goes straight into the waste paper basket.' Perhaps they may yet make amends?[16]

Whether the lack of interest from those who had depleted Cairo's treasures had added extra incentive to his mission is not clear, but Mosseri doubled down on the hunt. His local contacts must have informed him that fragments had been buried in the Bassatine Cemetery, and that there were fragments still buried in and around the synagogue precinct. Between 1910 and 1912, under the auspices of the Société des études juives, Mosseri and a French archaeologist, Captain Raymond Weill, together with help from Gottheil and Bernard Chapira, unearthed over 7,000 items. Chapira compiled a catalogue of the items with the intention that they would be integrated into a new Jewish educational institution; however, due to unknown circumstances, the pieces remained in Mosseri's possession. The collection included fragments of biblical, rabbinical and liturgical writings, belle-lettres, medicine and documents. Among the treasures were portions of the *Sefer Ha-Galuy* by Saadia Gaon, the personal seal of the Babylonian Gaon Nehemiah and an autograph letter by Moses Maimonides. It also incorporated a great many papers from the eighteenth and nineteenth centuries produced by the Jewish communities of Egypt. Chapira's catalogue of the Mosseri fragments was never published, and it disappeared when the collection itself went out of sight for many decades following Jacques Mosseri's premature death in 1934.

Today, thanks to an agreement with his family, the collection resides on long-term loan at Cambridge, where it is undergoing conservation, cataloguing and digitization.[17] In Egypt, ideas that Mosseri advocated in the early 1900s are being revived. Under the leadership of Magda Haroun and Samy Ibrahim, a group of Egyptian Jews, Jews of Egyptian descent, and international supporters, working collectively as the non-profit 'Drop of Milk Association', won an ARCE-funded grant in 2017 to survey and document Cairo's synagogues. Their work has also inspired funding support for the restoration of the Bassatine Cemetery, a project championed by former community leader, Carmen Weinstein. In close collaboration with international scholars, such as Yoram Meital, the manuscripts in the Karaite synagogue and the books in the community library are being studied, preserved and catalogued. Recently, during the course of this work, Meital rediscovered an eleventh-century Hebrew Bible Codex hidden in white paper wrapping on a bookshelf in the Karaite synagogue. The Codex is one of the oldest and best-preserved copies of the 'Writings' section of the Hebrew Bible. The Drop of Milk Association hopes that this treasure will one day form one of the crowning glories of a Jewish heritage library or museum in Cairo.[18]

BY THE SECOND DECADE OF THE TWENTIETH CENTURY, THE GENIZAH STORES WERE STILL NOT EXHAUSTED, and fragments continued to be offered for sale through the antiquities trade well into the second decade of the twentieth century. In 1915, responding to a decision by the Bodleian Curators to award him twenty-five pounds for his excavation work on their behalf, the disgruntled and impoverished d'Hulst told them that he knew that there was 'still a number of them – possibly and probably as large a quantity as I have excavated – buried'.[19] However, he averred, this was a secret that he would now take to the grave. Additional buried material may have been located somewhere in the Bassatine, or perhaps on the former wasteland that later became Jewish community housing, or to the east of the Roman wall adjacent to the Greek Catholic cemetery. This may be the same location where another cache of fragments was discovered through excavations conducted in the 1980s. Most of the fragments found on this occasion were printed materials from the late nineteenth century and early twentieth century. And some pieces may have come from private homes and institutions through the hands of individuals wishing to take advantage of the demand for fragments.[20] At the time of writing his unhappy letter of 1915, d'Hulst claimed that native dealers were buying leaves at ten to sixteen shillings each and selling them off to tourists at between one and three pounds for each leaf. In addition to discreet sales of Hebrew fragments, leaves were also sold mixed up in bundles to collectors seeking papyri.

Among the European and American institutions that acquired additional fragment collections around the time of Mosseri's excavations were the University of Pennsylvania Museum (from Wilhelm Max Müller who procured them in 1910 through Bernard Moritz, director of the Khedieval Library in Cairo); the Bodleian Library (from A. E. Cowley in 1910 and 1915 through an Egyptian dealer); and CAJS in the University of Pennsylvania (originally purchased by Dropsie College from the Reverend Camden McCormick Cobern in Cairo who bought them from an Arab dealer in 1913–14). In the 1920s and 1930s, genizah fragments were bundled up in purchases of papyri made on behalf of institutions such as Michigan University Library (through Bernard Pyne Grenfell and Francis W. Kelsey) and the Oriental Institute Museum Collection in Chicago (through Erik von Scherling). Most of these collections were originally purchased from Maurice Nahman in Cairo. Other small collections that were obtained during the course of the twentieth century were gained either through the absorption of one collection into another (e.g. the Pevzner Library into the University of Haifa), or as part of a large-scale purchase (e.g. Salo Baron for Columbia University), or through donations from later family members (e.g. the British Library from Aron Wertheimer). The provenance of some small collections is still undetermined (e.g. the RAR MSS at CAJS). Around eighteen small collections are held in private hands. They were either inherited, acquired through booksellers or purchased on auction. With little to no information pertaining to their history being available at present, they have not been included in this investigation of the Cairo Genizah story.

Epilogue

In the end, it was not possible to cover the history of every genizah collection, and what is presented here is only part of the story. Today, fifty institutions and around eighteen private individuals are believed to own collections of fragments deemed to be part of the Cairo Genizah. Yet, as this book has proved, the history of these collections is more convoluted than once assumed. Had the entire contents of the Ben Ezra Synagogue been removed and restored intact during the building reconstruction in 1889–92, the label 'from the Cairo Genizah' would have been entirely accurate. But whereas large numbers of the medieval fragments did indeed originate from the Ben Ezra Synagogue and its environs, many others did not. As we have seen, manuscripts and fragments were acquired in additional towns and cities like Rosetta and Alexandria; some were from places in Palestine, like Hebron and Jerusalem; some were derived from other parts of the Middle East, in countries such as Iraq and Yemen. Some of the manuscripts were held in personal collections and became fragmented during book sales; some had been stashed away in various hiding places inside Karaite and Rabbanite synagogues; others were buried whole or in parts in tombs, caves and other plots of land, and some may have even originated from non-Jewish genizah-type hiding places. As they were transposed into new settings, many losses occurred. Manuscripts were destroyed or damaged during disinterment, various stages of dismemberment, poor handling and care, natural and man-made disasters, unsuitable rehousing solutions and even institutional policies.

Beyond charting the fragments' many fascinating journeys, these stories have wider implications and touch upon important ethical issues. While the situation of the genizah fragments is different to the dramatic Arabic 'book drain to Europe' that Ahmed El Shamsy describes in *Rediscovering the Islamic Classics*, the mode of acquiring the fragments, using whatever means necessary, presents another example of the ways in which European and American Orientalism impacted the cultural heritage of the Middle East.[1] In this respect, efforts to reveal the full history of the Cairo Genizah can contribute towards understanding the deeply entangled and problematic history of the West's coetaneous appreciation and despoilation of the East.

The dispersal of genizah fragments likewise raises questions of ownership and custodianship with regard to materials consigned to genizot. These questions concern not only the different ways one may treat an object that has been discarded versus one that has been hidden away but also the degree to which Western Jewish scholars felt themselves entitled to acquire the writings of their compatriots in the East by any means and at any cost. As this book has shown, some communities attached special significance to genizot and any attempt to open them was believed to invite a disaster or calamity. In violation of their customs and practices, such concerns were often dismissed by manuscript hunters as mere superstition or ignorance. While most genizah acquisitions came about through sales, the stories uncovered here raise questions about the extent to which local sellers were exploited by collectors who subsequently realized greater returns on the resale of items or by institutions enriched by previously unrecognized treasures. And while the scholars who were involved in acquiring genizah fragments lambasted local dealers for dismantling books, the evidence presented calls into question the extent to which their insatiable desires for copies of ancient works made them complicit in such acts.

Finally, with regard to institutions, the investigation at hand raises many questions surrounding late-nineteenth- and early-twentieth-century collecting practices that have implications for the collections as they stand today. Some of these practices included the variable treatment of materials based on what was considered historically or monetarily valuable, which sometimes involved casting aside or discarding medieval writings considered as mere 'waste'. In efforts to build world-class collections, some nineteenth-century curators accepted collections with dubious provenance. As Donna Yates and Emiline Smith outline in 'Antiquities Trafficking and the Provenance Problem', this often involved creating false narratives to justify the acquisition.[2] Such justifications included the idea that wealthy institutions as a matter of course provided better protection for materials than local environments, or that purchases of antiquities helped sustain poor people in low-income countries. Yet, as we have seen, some institutions in this period practised poor or inaccurate record keeping, neglected their holdings (either by forgetting about them, failing to catalogue them or keeping them in poor environmental conditions), or they jumbled materials during the various stages of conserving, rehousing and cataloguing them.

Even today, many institutions supply only limited ownership history and acquisition information with their collections, possibly in the belief that tracking down this information is barely worth the effort, especially since the label 'from the Genizah' is regarded as sufficient to explain the fragment's origins. The process is often regarded as too complex and time consuming as it can involve a painstaking and not necessarily straightforward investigation of institutional archives and records. In other situations, the exercise may be deemed hopeless since it is believed that relevant documentation no longer exists.

Nevertheless, as the stories in this book prove, key information can be found, and lost histories recovered. Thanks to advances in the digital realm and the sharing of resources, additional information about the exceptional 'archive' known as the Cairo Genizah continues to surface. And, as we persistently question the evidence before us, many more wonderful things will emerge.

Appendix

Genizah collections

The list of collections is mostly derived from the Friedberg Jewish Manuscript Society database: (https://fjms.genizah.org) and Oded Zinger's 'Finding A Fragment in a Pile of Genizah'; it also incorporates some institutional information gathered from Benjamin Richler's *Catalogue of Hebrew Manuscripts*, institutional websites and catalogues and the sources listed in the Bibliography. Within each section, collections are listed in alphabetical order according to current location. Sub-collections are listed according to the known acquisition date. Undetermined provenance (find spot or chain of ownership) simply means that the author has not been able to find or determine the provenance of a collection.

Institutions with collections of 500+ fragments

(1) Budapest, Hungary: David Kaufmann Collection, Library of the Hungarian Academy of Sciences

Shelfmarks: MTA 1-465 and additional MSS labelled MTA AS, M (at one time all classified as MSS Kaufmann A592–594).

Provenance: David Kaufmann purchased a box of fragments from 'der Genisa einer egyptischen Synagoge' in 1894; he may also have made subsequent, unrecorded purchases. The source is undetermined, although the most likely candidate appears to be his long-time Jerusalem supplier, Mordechai Adelmann. According to M. S. Löwinger, the original collection comprised 710 pieces; some were loaned to other scholars and either given to other institutions or, as with the fragments labelled with 'M' numbers, they were lost. Some rediscovered fragments are labelled 'AS.' See Chapter 9.

(2) Cambridge, UK: Taylor-Schechter Genizah Collection, Cambridge University Library (CUL)

- Shelfmarks: MSS T-S A-K, T-S 6F-18K, T-S Ar., T-S Misc, T-S 8-32.
- Provenance: Discovered by Solomon Schechter in 1896–7 in the Ben Ezra Synagogue, in the Bassatine Cemetery and other genizot; some were purchased by Schechter from dealers in Cairo; some were purchased from dealers by Agnes Smith Lewis and Margaret Dunlop Gibson. See Chapter 11.

- Shelfmarks: MSS T-S NS, T-S NS J, T-S AS.
- Provenance: Discovered by Solomon Schechter in 1896–7 in the Ben Ezra Synagogue, in the Bassatine Cemetery and other genizot; some were purchased by Schechter from dealers in Cairo; some were purchased from dealers by Agnes Smith Lewis and Margaret Dunlop Gibson. Six sacks and three bags of fragments within this series were purchased by Reginald Q. Henriques from unnamed locals who acquired them from excavations conducted in Cairo in 1898–9. Henriques sold the fragments to the Cambridge University Library in 1899 and 1902. See Chapters 9–14.
- Shelfmarks: MSS Or. 1080-1081.
- Provenance: Catalogued as part of the T-S Series. Partly purchased from Solomon Aaron Wertheimer of Jerusalem between 1892 and 1896; partly purchased from Samuel Raffalovich of Jerusalem in December 1898. See Chapters 7–14.

(3) Cambridge, UK: Library Genizah Collections, CUL

- Shelfmarks: MSS Add. 863.2, Add. 2586, Add. 3339 (a-c), Add. 3356, Add. 4320a-d.
- Provenance: Add. 863.2, 3339 (a-c) and 3356 of undetermined provenance; Add. 2586 was acquired in 1880; Add. 4320 was acquired in 1899: no other information concerning these two manuscripts was recorded.
- Shelfmarks: MSS Add. 1034.
- Provenance: Offered for sale by a George Ellis of St. John's Wood, London, on 14 September 1892 (see also Chetham's Library genizah collection).
- Shelfmarks: MSS Add. 3158, 3159.1-15, 3160.1-16, 3161, 3162.
- Provenance: Purchased from Greville John Chester in 1891, who acquired them from an anonymous dealer in or near Cairo. See Chapter 7.
- Shelfmarks: MSS Add. 3430.
- Provenance: Purchased from an Ephraim Cohen in Jerusalem in 1897. A likely candidate is Ephraim Cohen-Reiss, who was the president of the Abarbanel Library committee and its director in 1899, and a pioneer of the Hebrew education system in Palestine. See Chapter 12.
- Shelfmarks: MSS Add. 3317, 3335, 3336-8, 3340-3, 3345, 3347-50, 3353-4, 3357-8, 3361-2, 2266, 3368-72, 3380-8, 3412-16, 3419-23, Or. 1035.1.
- Provenance: Purchased from Solomon Aaron Wertheimer in 1896, apart from Add. 3358 which was purchased from Wertheimer before 1895. See Chapters 10 and 11.
- Shelfmarks: MSS Or. 1102.
- Provenance: Fragment of Ben Sira (MS B) purchased by Agnes Smith Lewis and Margaret Dunlop Gibson during their trip to Palestine and Egypt in the spring of 1896. It was given to Cambridge University Library in 1926 through their bequest. See Chapter 10.
- Shelfmarks: MSS Or. 2116.4, Or. 2116.10, Or. 2116.12a.2-4, Or. 2116.14, Or. 2116.16, Or. 2116.17.2-4, Or. 2116.18, Or. 2116.19.1-2, 8-14.

- Provenance: Part of the Israel Abrahams Collection which was transferred from the Library of the Faculty of Oriental Studies in 1961. Abrahams probably acquired them during his trip to Palestine and Egypt in 1898. See Chapter 13.
- Shelfmarks: MSS Or. 2243, 2245-46
- Provenance: Given to Cambridge University Library from a collection of 25 manuscripts acquired by the British Government from the David Solomon Sassoon estate in lieu of taxes. They include two Karaite liturgical texts. Other pieces are dispersed to private collectors; two fragments are held at the NLI (5569/8, 5700/8). Sassoon purchased his fragments while on a journey to Damascus via Egypt in 1902.
- Shelfmarks: MSS Or. 1743.23.
- Provenance: Seven folio copy of a text of the Mishnah tied together with string and placed inside an envelope. A note on the envelope indicates that the owner was Elkan Nathan Adler. A second note written by Francis Jenkinson in 1904 states, 'I do not remember about this.'
- Shelfmarks: MSS Or. 1700.1-19.
- Provenance: Part of a collection of manuscripts donated by the Coptic scholar Sir Herbert Thompson in 1939. The genizah fragments were discovered by Ben Outhwaite in 2005 in a box together with some of Thompson's Coptic manuscripts. He probably acquired the Coptic manuscripts during his visit to Saqqara in 1907-8; they were ultimately from the White Monastery in Upper Egypt. The genizah fragments may have been part of a bundle purchased from an antiquities dealer, or they were mixed up with Thompson's collection at CUL in error.

(4) Cambridge, UK: Jacques Mosseri Genizah Collection, CUL

- Shelfmarks: Moss. I-X.
- Provenance: Discovered by Jacques Mosseri with Raymond Weil, Bernard Chapira and Richard Gottheil in the Bassatine Cemetery, and in the Ben Ezra Synagogue grounds and precinct during excavations funded by the AIU, as well as additional pieces from the Ben Ezra Synagogue and other synagogues in Cairo. The collection was privately held by the Mosseri family until they gave it on long-term loan to CUL in 2006. See Chapter 15.

(5) Cambridge, UK: Lewis-Gibson Genizah Collection, CUL

- Shelfmarks: Glass, Misc, Lit I-III, Talmudica I-II, Arabica I-II, Bib. I-VII, Add.
- Provenance: Partly purchased by Agnes Smith Lewis and Margaret Dunlop Gibson in 1896 during their trip to Palestine and Egypt, and partly from dealers in Cairo in 1897. Donated to Westminster College, Cambridge; jointly purchased by CUL and the Bodleian Libraries, Oxford, in 2013 and housed in CUL. See Chapters 10 and 11.

(6) **London, UK: British Library (formerly British Museum) Genizah Collections**

- Shelfmarks: Or. 2597-98.
- Provenance: Fragments purchased from Moses Wilhelm Shapira in 1882. Shapira claimed he acquired his manuscripts from Karaites in Hīt and in Cairo; some may have been derived from other genizot in Palestine and Egypt. See Chapter 4.
- Shelfmarks: MSS Or. 5517-66, Or. 6197.
- Provenance: Purchased from Samuel Raffalovich of Jerusalem in July and December 1898. See Chapter 13.
- Shelfmarks: MSS Or. 6666, Or. 7943.
- Provenance: Provenance unstated; probably Samuel Raffalovich in 1898.
- Shelfmarks: MSS Or. 6581.
- Provenance: Tiny fragments of a palimpsest with unrecorded provenance. The pieces were investigated by Robert Blake in 1921 who discovered matching fragments in CUL and the Bodleian Library Oxford. A. E. Cowley told Blake that the Bodleian pieces had been purchased from Solomon Wertheimer in 1894. See Chapter 9.
- Shelfmarks: MS Or. 7943.
- Provenance: Purchased in 1913 from a Mrs Dora Finn of Portsmouth: possibly originally from James Finn, the British Consul in Jerusalem from 1845 to 1863. Finn also donated Samaritan manuscripts to the BM in 1852–4, and a Torah scroll (presented to him by the Jews of Morocco) and a Samaritan manuscript to the Cambridge University Library in 1867.
- Shelfmarks: MSS Or. 8660-3.
- Provenance: Acquired in 1920; no other information is provided with these fragments.
- Shelfmarks: Or.9965, Or.10112A-C, + 100+ other shelfmarks within the Or.10100 to Or. 12300 range.
- Provenance: Purchased in 1924 from Moses Gaster.
- See Chapter 8.
- Shelfmarks: MSS Gaster 7-1789 (not consecutive).
- Provenance: Recorded as a purchase in 1927, together with the larger Moses Gaster Manuscript Collection. The purchase was formally agreed in 1924 but only fully made public in 1927. See Chapter 8.
- Shelfmarks: MS Or. 12186.
- Provenance: Purchased in 1958 from Joseph Halpern of Golders Green, London: formerly belonged to Marcus Nathan Adler (perhaps through Elkan Nathan Adler); all stated to be originally from 'the Genizah in Cairo'.
- Shelfmarks: MS Or. 13153, fol.1-29.
- Provenance: Purchased in 1986 from Aron Wertheimer, son of Solomon Aaron Wertheimer, from his father's collection.
- Shelfmarks: MS Or. 13956A-E.
- Provenance: Purchased from a Philips in Amsterdam; contained a note with the date 1896.

- Shelfmarks: MS Or. 9772.
- Provenance: Undetermined.

(7) Manchester, UK: The Rylands Cairo Genizah Collection, John Rylands Library (JRL), University of Manchester

- Shelfmarks: MSS A-C, G, L, P, Glass, Gaster Arabic, Gaster Hebrew, Gaster Hebrew MS., Gaster Printed, Genizah additional series, Bible Gaster series, Rylands Genizah fragments series.
- Provenance: Moses Gaster purchased fragments from the Jerusalemite dealers, Solomon Aaron Wertheimer in 1895 and Samuel Raffalovich in 1898, as well as from other undetermined sources. In 1969, John Rylands purchased 15,000 of these fragments through his eldest son, Vivian Gaster. See Chapter 8.

(8) New York, United States: Genizah Collections, Jewish Theological Seminary of America Library (JTSA)

- Shelfmarks: JTSA ENA 1-4200 (not consecutive), ENA unspecified volume, ENA II, ENA NS.
- Provenance: The Elkan Nathan Adler Genizah Collection forms the main bulk of the JTSA genizah collections. Parts of Elkan Nathan Adler's genizah collections were discovered in the Ben Ezra Synagogue in 1896; parts were purchased during subsequent visits to genizot in Cairo and Alexandria in 1898 and 1901; partly purchased from the Bodleian Library's Sale of Waste in 1897 and 1899 (originally from Count Riamo d'Hulst's 1898 excavations), and 1907 (originally from Joseph Offord's 1906 sale); partly purchased from Samuel Raffalovich in 1898; parts may have been acquired from other locations and genizot during travels to the Near East, including Morocco, Algeria, Tunis, Aleppo and Persia, in 1892, 1894, 1896 and 1900. See Chapters 5–14.
- Shelfmarks: MS, MS Rabbinica, MS Lutzki, MS Schechter, MS Krengel, KE, Scroll
- Provenance: Apart from the 'MS Schechter' fragments, which were probably among those he took with him when he moved to America. A suitcase of genizah fragments belonging to Rabbi Johann Krengel was discovered in the library in the 1970s. Krengel acquired them through Heinrich Frauberger in Frankfurt am Main. The provenance of the other fragments at JTS is undetermined.

(9) Oxford, UK: The Cairo Genizah Collection of the Bodleian Libraries

- Shelfmarks: MSS. Heb. b. 1-2, Heb. c. 8-14 (R), Heb. d. 19-29, Heb. d. 32, Heb. e. 22-30, Heb. f. 18-23, Heb. g. 2.
- Provenance: Purchased from Greville John Chester in 1890, who discovered them in the half-demolished medieval Ben Ezra Synagogue in December 1889. See Chapter 6.

- Shelfmarks: MS. Heb. b. 3, Heb. c. 16, Heb. d. 31, Heb. d. 39, Heb. f. 24-26, Heb. g. 3.
- Provenance: Donated by the Egypt Exploration Fund, who acquired them from Count Riamo d'Hulst in 1889; d'Hulst discovered them during excavations for pottery in the environs of the Ben Ezra Synagogue. See Chapter 6.
- Shelfmarks: MSS Heb. a. 1-2, Heb. b. 4, Heb. c. 1, Heb. c. 17-21, Heb. d. 33-38, Heb. d. 41-48, Heb. e. 31-41, Heb. e. 43-45, Heb. f. 27-33, Heb. f. 35 (P)-38.
- Provenance: Purchased from Greville John Chester, who purchased them from an anonymous dealer in or near Cairo in 1890, 1891 and 1892. See Chapter 7.
- Shelfmarks: MSS. Heb. b. 5, MS. Heb. c. 23, Heb. d. 49-51, Heb. d. 56-58, Heb. e. 46-56, Heb. e. 58, Heb. f. 39-40, Heb. f. 42-45, Heb. f. 47-48, Heb. f. 54, Heb. g. 5 (and possibly MSS Heb. a. 3, Heb. e. 82).
- Provenance: Purchased from Solomon Aaron Wertheimer in Jerusalem in 1892, 1893, 1895, 1896. See Chapters 7–11.
- Shelfmarks: MS Heb. f. 51-52.
- Provenance: Donated by Arthur Ernest Cowley in 1895 who acquired them during a trip to Egypt in 1894. See Chapter 9.
- Shelfmarks: MSS. Heb. b. 7-12, Heb. c. 26-28, Heb. d. 59-67, Heb. e. 62, Heb. e. 69-78, Heb. f. 34, Heb. f. 56-59, Heb. g. 8.
- Provenance: Discovered by Count Riamo d'Hulst in an underground chamber near the Ben Ezra Synagogue in 1895 and purchased by the Bodleian through Archibald Henry Sayce. See Chapter 10.
- Shelfmarks: MS. Heb. f. 61 (and possibly MSS. Heb. b. 13, Heb. d. 68).
- Provenance: Discovered by Count Riamo d'Hulst during excavations near the Ben Ezra Synagogue in 1898: funded by the Bodleian Library, sub-collection attributed to Archibald Henry Sayce. See Chapter 13.
- Shelfmarks: MSS. Heb. c. 50, Heb. d. 74-77, Heb. e. 93-101, Heb. f. 99-103 (and possibly Heb. g. 12).
- Provenance: Purchased from Joseph Offord, who purchased them from an Arab dealer in Egypt in 1906. See Chapter 15.
- Shelfmarks: MSS. Heb. a. 4, Heb. b. 18, Heb. c. 52-54, Heb. d. 73, Heb. d. 78, Heb. e. 102-105, Heb. f. 104-105.
- Provenance: Acquired by exchange with Christian David Ginsburg at some point after 1906 and before 1910.
- Shelfmarks: MSS. Heb. c. 55-56, Heb. d. 79-81, Heb. e. 106-108, Heb. f. 106-108, Heb. f. 110-111.
- Provenance: Donated by Arthur Ernest Cowley in 1910 and 1915, who seems to have acquired them from an anonymous dealer in Egypt. See Chapter 15.
- Shelfmarks: MSS. Heb. b. 17, Heb. c. 51, Heb. e. 105, Heb. e. 110.
- Provenance: Undetermined, apart from the 8 folios of MS Heb. e. 110 which F. Ll. Griffith passed on to the Bodleian from G. W. Murray, who had obtained them in the Fayum.

(10) Paris, France: Fragments de la Guéniza du Caire, Alliance Israélite Universelle (AIU)

- Shelfmarks: MSS IA-ID, IIA-B, IIIA-D, IVA-C, VA-C, VIA-C, VIIA-F, VIIIA-E, IXA-B, X-XII, H147A, BOITE 201 (unclassified).
- Provenance: Baron Edmond de Rothschild purchased these fragments in 1898 for the Bibliothèque du Consistoire Israélite de Paris from Samuel Raffalovich and his partner, M. Goldstein, at Israel Lévi's request. They were later transferred to the AIU. See Chapter 13.

(11) Philadelphia, PA, United States: Cairo Genizah Collections at Penn, Library at the Herbert D. Katz Center for Advanced Judaic Studies (CAJS), University of Pennsylvania

- Shelfmarks: MSS Halper Nos. 18, 29-30, 43, 45, 49-50, 59, 62, 68, 85, 98, 102, 104-6, 115-16, 119, 121, 127, 130, 136-37, 155, 157-58, 183, 212-13, 224, 227, 240-41, 247, 252-53, 259, 262, 273, 309, 312, 339, 436, 439-41, 443.
- Provenance: Cyrus Adler purchased these MSS in a market in Cairo in 1891. He donated them to Dropsie College after becoming its president in 1908. Dropsie became part of the University of Pennsylvania in 1993, and the former institution and its library evolved into Penn's Center for Advanced Judaic Studies in 1998. See Chapter 7.
- Shelfmarks: MSS Halper Nos. 4-8, 10, 12-14, 20, 22, 28, 33-34, 42, 44, 64-65, 76, 78, 83, 88, 159, 177, 209-10, 214, 216, 264, 332-34, 336, 344, 349, 357, 379, 381-82, 389-90, 392-93, 408, 413, 414, 449, 471, 474, 478-82, 485-87.
- Provenance: Donated to Dropsie College by Judge Mayer Sulzberger. Solomon Schechter sent him MSS as a gift after he returned from Egypt and Palestine in 1897. Another source for some of these fragments may have been his long-time supplier, Ephraim Deinard. See Chapters 11 and 12.
- Shelfmarks: MSS Halper Nos. 2-3, 9, 15-16, 19, 23-27, 31-32, 35, 37-38, 46-48, 51-53, 56, 58, 61, 63, 66, 69-71, 74, 79, 81-82, 84, 87, 89-91, 93-95, 97, 99-101, 108-114, 118, 123-26, 129, 132-35, 138, 143-52, 154, 156, 160-70, 172, 174-76, 178-81, 184-198, 200, 200-2, 204-5, 208, 211, 215, 217-18, 220-23, 225, 228-29, 231-38, 243-45, 248-51, 256-58, 260-61, 265-72, 274, 276-79, 281-83, 285, 287-96, 298-307, 310-11, 313-31, 335, 340-43, 345-46, 348, 350-56, 358-78, 380, 383-88, 391, 394-412, 415-28, 432-34, 442, 445-48, 450-55, 457-70, 472-73, 475-77, 483-84.
- Provenance: Purchased from David Amram Werner in 1920-1. Werner originally acquired his fragments from a dealer in Jerusalem in c.1900. The dealer was probably Samuel Raffalovich. See Chapter 15.
- Shelfmarks: MSS Halper Nos. 21, 40-41, 75, 80, 86, 103, 117, 120, 182, 263, 435, 437-38.
- Provenance: Donated by Harry Friedenwald to Dropsie College. Friedenwald may have acquired the fragments during his visit to Jerusalem in 1911.
- Shelfmarks: MSS Halper Nos. 55, 73, 203.

- Provenance: Purchased from Rev. Camden McCormick Cobern in 1920–1 who, according to Romain Butin, obtained them in Cairo in 1913 or 1914 from 'a trusty town Arab who had been with him previously on several exploring missions'. See Chapter 15.
- Shelfmarks: MSS Halper Nos. 36, 92, 96, 239, 255, 284, 286.
- Provenance: Given by David Amram Werner to Ephraim Lederer in 1901. Lederer donated them to Dropsie College in 1920 and 1922.
- Shelfmarks: MSS Halper Nos. 1, 11, 17, 39, 173, 199.
- Provenance: Given by David Amram Werner to the Young Men's Hebrew Association in 1901.
- Shelfmarks: MSS Halper Nos. 338, 347.
- Provenance: Given by David Amram Werner to the University of Pennsylvania Law School in 1901.
- Shelfmarks: MSS Halper Nos. 54, 57, 60, 67, 72, 77, 122, 128, 131, 139-42, 153, 171, 206-7, 219, 226, 230, 242, 246, 254, 280, 297, 308, 429-31, 444, 456.
- Provenance: Given by David Amram Werner to the University of Pennsylvania in 1901.
- Shelfmarks: RAR MS 82.313.1-53, 85.126.1-43 (not consecutive).
- Provenance: Undetermined, either omitted from original Halper catalogue or acquired by Penn separately.

(12) Strasbourg, France: Manuscrits de la Bibliothèque nationale et universitaire de Strasbourg

- Shelfmarks: MSS 4.017-5.138 (non-consecutive) + papyrus.
- Provenance: The fragments were most likely purchased by Wilhelm Spiegelberg, head of Institute of Egyptology in Strasburg, who in 1899 was commissioned to purchase papyri in the antiquities markets of Egypt for the Strasbourg collection. Included are several fragments of liturgy of St. Jean Chrysostom. Some fragments are marked 'Aus der Genīza von Cairo'.

(13) St. Petersburg, Russia: Archimandrite Antonin (Kapustin) Collection, National Library of Russian (NLR)

- Shelfmarks: MSS Yevr. III A, Yevr. III B1-1200.
- Provenance: Probably acquired by Antonin Kapustin from dealers in Cairo during the period when the Ben Ezra Synagogue was being restored: 1889–92. The fragments were given to the NLR in 1899 in accordance with his bequest. See Chapter 6.

(14) St. Petersburg, Russia: Second Firkovich Collection, NLR

- Shelfmarks: Yevr. II A-C, Yevr. II K, Yevr-Arab. I-II, Arab-Yevr, Yevr. IV.
- Provenance: Acquired by Abraham Firkovich largely from the Karaite Synagogue in Cairo in 1863–4, but fragments were also derived from other places he visited in the Near East, including Istanbul, Beirut, Jaffa, Jerusalem, Nablus and Aleppo, as well as through mailings. See Chapter 2.

Institutions with collections comprising less than 500 fragments

(1) **Berlin, Germany: Bibliothek der Jüdischen Gemeinde zu Berlin (photocopies in the Schocken Institute, Jerusalem).**

- Shelfmarks: MSS 27.1-10, 152.1-36, A1 I-III, A1.1-4, A2-A4, A4.27, A5.30.
- Provenance: Collected by either the first librarian, Jakob Fromer, during his four-year tenure from 1898 to 1902, or by the subsequent librarian, Rabbi Dr Moritz Stern who, between 1902 and 1919, built up the bibliothek to comprise over 70,000 books. Original size of the genizah collection unknown. Some fragments are now held at HUC.

(2) **Birmingham, UK: The Mingana Collection, Cadbury Research Library, University of Birmingham**

- Shelfmarks: Mingana 1-18.
- Provenance: Acquired by Dr Alphonse Mingana, who may have collected them during his travels to Sinai and Upper Egypt in 1929 to collect Syriac manuscripts from monasteries in the region. See Chapter 15.
- Shelfmarks: Mittwoch 1-22.
- Provenance: The fragments were added to the Mingana Collection together with the books of Professor Eugen Mittwoch. Mittwoch made his first visit to the East with Moritz Sobernheim in 1899 and probably acquired these fragments during that trip. One of Mittwoch's fragment (Genizah 29), a letter written by a member of the al-Amshati family, is now in the Museum of the Bible in Washington, DC. See Chapter 14.

(3) **Cincinnati, United States: Hebrew Union College (HUC) Library**

- Shelfmarks: MSS 403, 1001-1311, 2065 (not consecutive); Acc.944-985 (not consecutive); Roseman A-F
- Provenance: The HUC genizah collection is derived from multiple sources: some of the fragments were part of a collection formerly owned by the Hungarian scholar Ludwig Blau; some fragments were purchased by the genizah scholar Jacob Mann in 1924. The liturgical fragments came from the Berlin Judische Geimeinde. A number of fragments are from undetermined sources.

(4) **Frankfurt am Main: Stadt-und Universitätsbibliothek (photocopies in the Schocken Institute, Jerusalem)**

- Shelfmarks: MSS 1-220.
- Provenance: Probably originally collected in 1899 by Aron Freimann, the librarian of the Hebraica and Judaica division of the Stadt-und Universitätsbibliothek Frankfurt am Main. Freimann travelled with Elkan Nathan Adler in the Near East, collecting materials for the library, which he developed into a leading world collection of Judaica and Hebraica. The original genizah collection, now mostly lost, was 4,314 fragments. See Chapter 14.

(5) **Geneva, Switzerland: The Cairo Genizah Collection in Geneva, Bibliothèque publique et universitaire**

- Shelfmarks: MSS 1-150.
- Provenance: Purchased by the Greek scholar and papyrologist Jules Nicole for his son Albert, while they were both in Cairo in 1897. The fragments were requested by Albert from among items offered for sale by the dealer Giovanni Dattari. Adolf Neubauer helped with their partial identification and thanks to an agreement between father and son; they were donated to the Geneva University Bibliothèque. They were rediscovered in the library in a tin box in 2006. See Chapter 11.

(6) **Heidelberg, Germany: Bibliothek des Instituts für Papyrologie**

- Shelfmarks: p. Heid. Aram. 1-2; Hebr.1-33.
- Provenance: These fragments may have been part of a bundle of papyri purchased by Karl Reinhardt in Cairo in 1897 from an antiquities dealer in Akhmim, or through the German *Papyruskartell* (1902–14), or possibly later through Carl Schmidt, who purchased papyri from Maurice Nahman in 1930.

(7) **Jerusalem, Israel: Rare Collection, National Library of Israel**

- Shelfmarks: MSS 577.1-10, 1087, 1149, 2242, 5156, 5699, 5700, 6964, 7036, 7396, 8199.1-38.
- Provenance: According to an article written by Avinoam Yellin in 1923, genizah fragments were sold to the Jewish National Library by Solomon Aaron Wertheimer. Yellin states that the fragments arrived at the library thirty years prior to his article (thus around 1893). It is not clear whether all the genizah fragments in the NLI are from Wertheimer; some may be later additions. One fragment (MS 1149) appears to be from a binding; MSS 5699-7000 previously had 'Sassoon' numbers (presumably the collector, David Sassoon). The tiny fragments in MS 8199.1-38 may be connected to Samuel Raffalovich, the Jerusalem supplier of many very fragmented collections. See Chapter 8.

(8) **New York, United States: Norman E. Alexander Jewish Studies Library, Columbia University Libraries**

- Shelfmarks: MSS Fr.4, Fr.627a, General 163.1-8, X893 (various within call no. range).
- Provenance: The precise provenance of the genizah manuscripts is undetermined. They arrived at Columbia University with a collection of 700 manuscripts purchased by Professor Salo Baron from the bookdealer David Fraenkel in Vienna in 1933–4. Some fragments were also removed from book bindings.

(9) **Moscow, Russia: Baron Günzburg Collection of Hebrew Manuscripts, Russian State Library**

- Shelfmarks: Guenzburg MS 773, 920.1-59, MSS 1181, 1340-44.

- Provenance: Collected by Baron David Günzburg as part of his family's library building endeavour; supplier unknown; possibly through Günzburg's connections to either Adolf Neubauer or Elkan Nathan Adler.
- Shelfmarks: Or. F.173.II., 118.1-11.
- Provenance: Undetermined: formerly in the library of the Imperial Theological Academy in Moscow.

(10) Paris, France: Institut de France

- Shelfmarks: MSS 3381.1-49.
- Provenance: Probably acquired by Joseph Derenbourg, who partly identified them. They are most likely the fragments he reportedly 'procured from Jerusalem' together with a larger Yemenite manuscript of Saadiah Gaon's translation of the Pentateuch at some point between 1892 and 1895. See Chapter 8.

(11) Vienna, Austria: Papyrussammlung Erzherzog Rainer, Österreichische National Bibliothek, Papyrussammlung und Papyrusmuseum

- Shelfmarks: Papyrussammlung Erzherzog Rainer Per H1-H210.
- Provenance: Otto Theodor Graf acquired the fragments while amassing a large papyri collection from the Fayum and other sites in Lower Egypt. The collection was purchased by the Archduke Rainer Ferdinand in Austria. See Chapters 5-7.

(12) Warsaw, Poland: Jewish Studies Library, Tlomackie Synagogue (photocopies in the Schocken Institute, Jerusalem)

- Shelfmarks: MSS 54.1-43.
- Provenance: Possibly acquired by Ignace Bernstein, who collected Jewish folklore and was a founder and patron of the great synagogue library. Bernstein purchased manuscripts in 1898 from the Frankfurt bookseller and publisher, J. Kaufmann.

(13) Washington, DC, United States: Smithsonian National Museum of Asian Art: combining Freer and Sackler Galleries
- Shelfmarks: MSS F1-F50 (alt. F1908. 44A-44Z and previously labelled with Roman numerals).
- Provenance: Acquired by the American industrialist and art collector Charles Lang Freer, who claimed that he had purchased them from a 'dealer in Gizeh' in 1908. The dealer was most likely Ali el-Arabi through his agent Haggi Mahomedo. See Chapters 5, 6 and 15.

Institutions holding thirty or less fragments

(1) Ann Arbor, MI, United States: University of Michigan Papyrology Collection, University of Michigan Library

- Shelfmarks: P. Mich. Inv. 531-533.

- Provenance: Purchased in Egypt by B. P. Grenfell and F. W. Kelsey in March–April 1920, most probably from Maurice Nahman in Cairo who was a regular supplier to Kelsey. See Chapter 15.

(2) **Basel, Switzerland: Handschriften-Signaturen, Universitätsbibliothek Basel, University of Basel**

- Shelfmarks: MS UBH RII 5.
- Provenance: Reached the University of Basel as part of a larger collection of papyri in 1900.

(3) **Berlin, Germany, Orientabteilung (Oriental Department: Hebrew Manuscript Collection), Staatsbibliothek zu Berlin**

- Shelfmarks: MSS Or. Oct. 1637-1650.
- Provenance: Unclear: Moritz Steinschneider added MSS to the collection in the 1890s; Arthur Spanier purchased MSS for the collection in the 1920s.

(4) **Cambridge, MA, United States: Hebrew manuscript collection, Houghton Library of the Harvard College Library, Harvard University**

- Shelfmarks: MSS Heb.29, fols. 1-2
- Provenance: undetermined; fol. 2 Hilkhot Alfasi may match with JRL MS B4811.

(5) **Chicago, IL, United States: Oriental Institute Museum Collection: Manuscripts, University of Chicago**

- Shelfmarks: OIM A11241-7.
- Provenance: A Dutch dealer, Erik von Scherling, sold the fragments to the Oriental Institute in December 1932. Von Scherling acquired them during a visit to Cairo, where he purchased Egyptian, Coptic and Greek papyri from Maurice Nahman and other Cairo dealers. He distributed the papyri bundles to institutions in the United States. See Chapter 15.

(6) **Copenhagen, Denmark: The David Simonsen Manuscript Collection, Det Kgl. Bibliotek (Royal Danish Library)**

- Shelfmarks: Sim. Jud.-Arab 6.
- Provenance: Included in the digital scan of this fragmentary letter (Egypt, *c.* twelfth century) is a folder containing the following words in Danish: Til Overrabbiner Simonsen fra גניזה I den samle synagogue I Fostat Egypten fra Deres hengiven E. N. Adler 10. 3. 1896 (To Chief Rabbi Simonsen from גניזה [genizah] in the old synagogue in Fostat, Egypt, from your devotee, E. N. Adler, 10. 3. 1896). Simonsen added in pencil: 'via Gottf. Ruben' which may be a reference to the Jewish Danish merchant and Consul General, Gottfried Moses Ruben. See Chapter 10.

(7) **Dublin, Ireland: Asian, Middle Eastern and Ethiopic Manuscripts, Trinity College Library Dublin**

- Shelfmarks: IE TCD MS 2243
- Provenance: A twelfth to thirteenth century, 163ff., Hebrew rabbinical treatise on medicine. The catalogue (MARLOC) states: 'Found in the Cairo Genizah. Presented by R.A.S. Macalister, (who received it from Dr. Solomon Schechter), 8 September 1943.' The MS may have come to him from Sir Donald MacAlister (1854–1934). Donald MacAlister's closer relationship with Schechter made him a more likely recipient of this gift. MacAlister's wife, Edith Florence Boyle, was also R. A. S. Macalister's sister, and she may have given it to her brother after Donald's death in 1934. See Chapter 15.
- Shelfmarks: IE TCD MS 2715/1-2.
- Provenance: The catalogue describes these two manuscripts as 'Book of Leviticus with Arabic translation in Hebrew characters (8 folios)' and 'Regulations for prayer (2 folios)' and states that both are 'Possibly of the 12th or 13th cent., probably from the Cairo Genizah'. It records that they are part of a collection of Asian and Middle Eastern manuscripts (IE TCD MSS 2684-2747) which were classified and alphabetically arranged on 13 June 1962. The donor for these manuscripts and their date of acquisition is generally unknown. This manuscript seems a more likely candidate for a donation from Schechter to R. A. S. Macalister, given Macalister's interests in biblical history and his publication dealing with church vestments and their origins in the vestments of the Levitical priesthood.

(8) **Durham, NC, United States: Ashkar-Gilson Manuscripts, David M. Rubenstein Rare Book and Manuscript Library, Duke University**

- Shelfmarks: MSS 1-23.
- Provenance: Fragments of an early medieval Torah scroll purchased in 1970 by Dr Fuad Ashkar, a specialist in nuclear medicine and biology, and his wife, Theresa, from a dealer in Beirut, Lebanon, named Mohamed Taha Nassar. Additional fragments were purchased on behalf of Ashkar and his colleague, Dr Albert Gilson, at the University of Miami, through Ashkar's sister, Nayla, who was living in Beirut. The remaining pieces were sold to unnamed German investors in 1972. The provenance story was revealed in 1991 in a court case *Fuad S. and Theresa N. Ashkar v. Commissioner* (61 T.C.M. 1657 (1991)) relating to Ashkar's tax claims for these manuscripts.

(9) **Erfurt, Germany: Erfurt Jewish Community**

- Shelfmarks: MS. frag. 1
- Provenance: Present location and provenance undetermined

(10) Haifa, Israel: Younes & Soraya Nazarian Library, University of Haifa

- Shelfmarks: MSS GEN B, C, LT, M.
- Provenance: The University of Haifa Library acquired the fragments from the Pevzner public library of Haifa. They were originally donated to the Pevzner library by a Mr Benjamin Ben-Israel Berstein, who immigrated to Palestine from Italy during the 1920s. Pencil notes on the fragments indicate a former Russian owner.

(11) Heidelberg, Germany: Universitätsbibliothek Heidelberg

- Shelfmarks: MSS Cod. Heid. Or. 78-80.
- Provenance: These were acquired by Adalbert Merx, who purchased them from a Yemenite dealer in Cairo prior to 1894. Merx believed that they had been stored in a private home. Merx was a professor of Theology at the University of Heidelberg until his death in 1909. See Chapter 8.

(12) Jerusalem, Israel: Ben Zvi Institute

- Shelfmarks: MS. 64
- Provenance: Fragments from the prayer book of Solomon ben Nathan of Sijilmasa; provenance undetermined.

(13) Jerusalem, Israel: The Central Archives for the History of the Jewish People

- Shelfmarks: MS 2588
- Provenance: Document written in medieval Fustat; additional provenance details undetermined.

(14) Kiev: Academy of Sciences, Abraham Harkavy Collection, The Vernadsky National Library of Ukraine

- Shelfmarks: MSS Harkavy E8, E32, K5, M13, P11, R14, R45.3, R 45.5 R64.2-5, R 66.3, R67.
- Provenance: The Vernadsky Library inherited its collection from the Institut Evreiskoi Proletarskoi Kul'tury (Library of the Institute for Jewish Proletarian Culture). The institute was from the former archives and library of the Society for the Promotion of Culture among the Jews of Russia (1863–1929). A large part of the manuscript collection was originally donated to the OPE by Abraham Harkavy, including these genizah fragments. See Chapter 5.

(15) Leeds, UK: Cecil Roth Collection, Leeds University Special Collections, Leeds University Library

- Shelfmarks: MSS Roth 723.1-29.
- Provenance: Roth noted that these fragments were 'from Genizah', but it is not clear how he acquired them. Additional uncatalogued fragments in his collection (in Box D) were described as 'Fragments from a North African Genizah'; they were acquired in Jerusalem in 1959.

(16) Mainz, Germany: Mainz Jewish community

- Shelfmarks: MS 2.
- Provenance: Identified as a match to MS Freer 19, which comprises secular poetry and a Fatimid Chancery document. The original manuscript and the photograph of it that used to exist in Mainz and which appears in the Friedberg database are both missing.

(17) Manchester, UK: Chetham's Library, Manchester

- Shelfmarks: Mun. D.5-8/A-F.
- Provenance: Offered for sale by George Ellis of London on 15 September 1892 (see also Cambridge Library Genizah Collections).

(18) Montreal, Canada: Rare Books and Special Collections, McGill University Library and Archives

- Shelfmarks: MSS Hebrew 1-3
- Provenance: Sold to the collection by Joseph Offord, who purchased the fragments from an unnamed Arab dealer in Egypt in the winter of 1903–4. See Chapter 15.

(19) Munich: Bayerische Staatsbibliothek

- Shelfmarks: Cod. Hebr. 419.I-V, XIV.
- Provenance: Possibly James Loeb, an American philanthropist and Hellenist, who donated materials to the Bayerische Staatsbibliothek in 1927. In the same year, the German scholar, Wilhelm Spiegelberg, donated a Demotic papyrus found at Elephantine to the Staatliche Sammlung Ägyptischer Kunst, Munich. It was named for Loeb who was funding the excavations. Two fragments are matched with other fragments in genizah collections in Cambridge, Oxford, JTSA, London and Geneva.

(20) New York, United States: Yeshiva University Library

- Shelfmarks: MSS 296.1-2.
- Provenance: A fragment of liturgical poetry on paper, and a fragment of biblical commentary on parchment; provenance undetermined.

(21) Paris, France: Département des Manuscrits, Bibliothèque Nationale de France (BNF)

- Shelfmarks: MSS Heb 1463, 1489.1-14.
- Provenance: MSS 1489, 1-14 were either acquired by William Charles Auguste Mayor during his visit to Egypt in 1872, or they were acquired in Jerusalem from the Swiss scholar and pastor Paul Laufer, who toured Egypt and the Holy Land in 1893. The evidence for both is included in a small archive of papers that were wrapped around the fragments; however, the timing and interest in such fragments points more towards Laufer.See Chapter 8.

(22) Philadelphia, PA, United States: University of Pennsylvania Museum Collection

- Shelfmarks: MSS E16250, E16275, E16504-E16527.
- Provenance: Purchased together with a large collection of manuscripts and papyri by Wilhelm Max Müller in 1910 through Bernard Moritz, the director of the Khedieval Library in Cairo, as well as through some other dealers in Cairo. See Chapter 15.

(23) Ramat Gan, Israel: Bar Ilan University Library

- Shelfmarks: MS 182, MS 626.
- Provenance: Possibly part of the collection acquired by Bar Ilan from Mordecai Margaliot, a Polish-born scholar of Midrashic and geonic literature. Another possibility is the Moussaieff Collection, which includes rare books and manuscripts gathered by the Kabbalist Rabbi Shlomo Moussaieff, who emigrated to Palestine in 1890. Nevertheless, these 2 pieces are not included in the Moussaieff digital collection of 221 manuscripts.

(24) St. Petersburg, Russia: Institute of Oriental Manuscripts (IOM)

- Shelfmarks: MSS D 55.1-30.
- Provenance: The institute possesses over 1,100 Hebrew manuscripts, 600 of which are Karaite. Parts of the collection were derived from the Moses Aryeh Leib Friedland, who had amassed a collection of printed Hebrew works and manuscripts and donated them to the IOM in 1892. Parts of the IOM collection came from the private collections of Daniel Chwolson and David Maggid. No other provenance information has been found to date relating to these fragments.

(25) Tel Aviv, Israel: Herbert Cohen Collection, Sourasky Central Library, Tel Aviv University

- Shelfmarks: MSS 1-16.
- Provenance: MS 7 previously belonged to the Berlin community (MS152.2). Otherwise, it is still undetermined how Herbert Cohen acquired his fragments.

(26) Toronto, Canada: Friedberg collection, Thomas Fisher Rare Book Library, University of Toronto

- Shelfmarks: Friedberg MSS 9-002, 9-003, 9-004.1-32.
- Provenance: Around 35 fragments privately collected by Albert Dov Friedberg and donated to the Thomas Fisher Rare Book Library in the late 1990s together with his collection of 40 medieval manuscripts and 240 printed books.

(27) Turin, Italy: Biblioteca Nazionale Universitaria di Torino

- Shelfmarks: MSS Ebr. 1-6, Sam. 1.
- Provenance: Possibly collected by the German biblical scholar, Paul E. Kahle

(28) Vatican City, Italy: Biblioteca Apostolica Vaticana

- Shelfmarks: MSS Ebr. 530.
- Provenance: One of the fragments under this shelfmark, a fourteenth-century fragment of the Babylonian Talmud, Avodah Zarah, joins with fragments in the Taylor-Schechter Genizah Collection and the Mosseri Genizah Collection. Nevertheless, the supplier of the fragments in the Vatican is still undetermined.

Notes

Prologue

1   The bibliography includes as comprehensive a list of works dealing with the Cairo Genizah discovery as possible.
2   Marina Rustow, *The Lost Archive: Traces of a Caliphate in a Cairo Synagogue* (Princeton and Oxford: Princeton University Press, 2020), 47–8.
3   See Brent Nongbri, *God's Library: The Archaeology of the Earliest Christian Manuscripts* (New Haven and London: Yale University Press, 2018), 222.
4   Chris Gosden and Yvonne Marshall, 'The Cultural Biography of Objects', *World Archaeology* 31, no. 2 (October 1999): 169–78.
5   J. C. Milosch and N. Pearce (eds.), *Collecting and Provenance: A Multidisciplinary Approach* (New York and London: Rowman & Littlefield, 2012), xv.

Chapter 1

1   Jacob Saphir, *Even Sapir*, Volume I (Lyck, 1866), 21b.
2   E. R. J. Owen, *Cotton and the Egyptian Economy 1820–1914* (Oxford: Oxford at the Clarendon Press, 1969), 89–121.
3   Najat Abdulhaq, *Jewish and Greek Communities in Egypt, Jewish and Greek Communities in Egypt: Entrepreneurship and Business before Nasser*, Library of Middle East History; 58 (UK: I.B. Tauris, 2016), 72–7.
4   Andre Raymond, *Cairo*, trans. Willard Wood (Harvard, MA: Harvard University Press, 2000), 309–15.
5   For the scant mention of the presence of Jews in early Greek and Arabic papyri, see Petra Sijpesteijn, 'Visible Identities: In Search of Egypt's Jews in Early Islamic Egypt', in *Israel in Egypt: The Land of Egypt as Concept and Reality for Jews in Antiquity and the Early Medieval Period*, ed. Alison Salvesen, Sarah Pearce and Miriam Frenkel (Leiden: Brill, 2020), 424–40. See also, Tal Ilan, 'Between the Hellenistic World and the Cairo Genizah: The Jewish Community in Late Antique Egypt', in *The Jews in Medieval Egypt*, ed. Miriam Frenkel (Boston: Academic Studies Press, 2021), 1–21. Ilan mentions a papyrus from Oxyrhynchus as providing the most substantial evidence for the existence of an organized Jewish community in the area at the end of the third century CE.
6   For a history of the area, see Wladyslaw B. Kubiak, *Al-Fustat: Its Foundation and Early Urban Development* (Cairo and New York: The American University in Cairo Press, 1987), Peter Sheehan, *Babylon of Egypt: The Archaeology of Old Cairo and the Origins of the City* (Cairo and New York: The American University in Cairo Press, 2010), and Jill Kamil, *Coptic Egypt: History and Guide* (Cairo and New York: The American University in Cairo Press, 1987).

7   Paula Sanders, *Creating Medieval Cairo: Empire, Religion, and Architectural Preservation in Nineteenth Century Egypt* (Cairo and New York: The American University in Cairo Press, 2008), 24–5.

8   Details about the rebuilding of the churches can be found in Sheehan, *Babylon of Egypt*, 121–7. For more details about Cairo's synagogues, see the online exhibition, 'The Synagogues of Cairo and Alexandria, Egypt, selected sites', *Diarna*, accessed 25 April 2019. http://diarna.org/exhibits/the-synagogues-of-cairo-and-alexandria-egypt -selected-sites/.

9   Mercedes Volait, *Antique Dealing and Creative Reuse in Cairo and Damascus, 1850–1890* (Leiden: Brill, 2021), 54–89.

10   In some historical accounts, the synagogue was referred to by the name of the prophet Elijah or Jeremiah; it was also known locally as the *al-Shamiyin* (a reference to it having once been the synagogue of the medieval Jerusalemite community). In the twentieth century, after the discovery of its genizah, it became popularly known as the Ben Ezra Synagogue. See Jacques Mosseri, 'The Synagogues of Egypt: Past and Present', *The Jewish Review* 5, no. 1 (1914): 31–44.

11   The translation is taken from Jacob Saphir, *My Footsteps Echo: The Yemen Journal of Rabbi Yaakov Sapir*, ed. and trans. Yaakov Lavon (Jerusalem: Feldheim, 1997), 281.

12   For more on Saphir, see Noah S. Gerber, *Ourselves or Our Holy Books: The Cultural Discovery of Yemenite Jewry* (Jerusalem: Ben Zvi Institute, 2013) [Hebrew], and Raymond Apple, 'Rabbi Jacob Levi Saphir & his voyage to Australia', *Australian Jewish Historical Society* 6, no. 4 (1968).

13   For the history of the Bible and Masorah, see David Stern, *The Jewish Bible: A Material History* (Seattle and London: University of Washington Press, 2017).

14   For the vocalization systems and their history, see Paul E. Kahle, *The Cairo Geniza* [The Schweich Lectures of the British Academy 1941] (London: Oxford University Press, 1947).

15   'Miscellanies', *The Journal of Sacred Literature and Biblical Record* 10 (1867): 502–3.

16   For the history of this scroll and its discovery, see the essays in Mauro Perani (ed.), *The Ancient Sefer Torah of Bologna: Features and History, European Genizah Texts and Studies*, Volume 4 (Leiden: Brill, 2019).

17   For the history of the Aleppo Codex, see Hayim Tawil and Bernard Schneider, *Crown of Aleppo: The Mystery of the Oldest Hebrew Bible Codex* (Philadelphia: The Jewish Publication Society, 2010) and Matti Friedman, *The Aleppo Codex: In Pursuit of One of the World's Most Coveted, Sacred, and Mysterious Books* (New York: Algonquin Books, 2012).

18   See the section on 'The Annotation Enterprise of the Egyptian Torah Scholars', *Kedem Auction Catalogue* no. 66 (Jerusalem, 15 May 2019): 214–18.

19   Gerber, *Ourselves or Our Holy Books*, 28–9. Saphir was also well known as a poet, composing songs in praise of Zion for festive events in the city of Jerusalem, and for other special occasions. His skills in speaking Arabic were developed through his work in the Etrog (citrus) Trade. See Apple, 'Rabbi Jacob Levi Saphir',198.

20   Norman Golb, 'The Typography of the Jews of Medieval Egypt: VI. Places of Settlement of the Jews of Medieval Egypt', *Journal of Near Eastern Studies* 33, no. 1 (1974): 116–49.

21   S. D. Goitein, *A Mediterranean Society: The Jewish Communities of the Arab World as Portrayed in the Documents of the Cairo Geniza, Vol. V: The Individual* (Berkeley, Los Angeles, London: University of California Press, 1988), 19–25.

22   See the extracts from Saphir's travelogue '1858. General Situation of the Jews in Egypt', in *Jews in Nineteenth-Century Egypt*, ed. Jacob M. Landau (New York: New

York University Press; London: University of London Press Ltd, 1969), 171–5. The translation 'chattering of words' is taken from Richard G. Marks, 'Hinduism, Torah, and Travel: Jacob Sapir in India', *Shofar: An Interdisciplinary Journal of Jewish Studies* 30, no. 2 (2012): 30.

23 Marina Rustow, *Heresy and the Politics of Community: The Jews of the Fatimid Caliphate* (New York: Cornell University Press, 2008), 46.

24 Elinoar Bareket, 'Karaite Communities in the Middle East during the Tenth to Fifteenth Centuries', in *Karaite Judaism: A Guide to its History and Literary Sources*, ed. Meira Polliack (Leiden and Boston: Brill, 2003), 237–8.

25 See Adolf Neubauer, *Medieval Jewish Chronicles and Chronological Notes, ed. from Printed Books and Manuscripts*, Volume I (Oxford: Clarendon Press, 1887–95), 118.

26 Saphir, *Even Sapir*, 14b–15b.

27 See M. Beit-Arie, C. Sirat, M. Glatzer (eds.), *Codices Hebraicis Litteris Exarati Quo Tempore Scripti Fuerint Exhibentes, I, Jusqu'à 1020, Monumenta Palaeographica Medii Aevi*, Series Hebraica, 1 (Turnhout: Brepols; Paris: Institut de Recherche et d'Histoire des Textes, C. N. R. S.; and Jerusalem: Académie Nationale des Sciences et des Lettres d'Israël, 1997), 28.

28 Richard J. H. Gottheil, 'Some Hebrew Manuscripts in Cairo', *The Jewish Quarterly Review* 17, no. 4 (July 1905): 609–55.

29 T. W. Aveling, *Voices of Many Waters, or Travels in the Lands of the Tiber, the Jordan, and the Nile* (London: John Snow, Paternoster Row, 1855), 269.

30 The attribution to Ezra the scribe in numerous Jewish Bibles from the Middle Ages suggests that this was an archetype that perhaps referred back to an original exemplar or model scroll. See Saverio Campanini, 'The "Ezra Scroll" of Bologna: Vicissitudes of an Archetype between Memory and Oblivion', in *The Ancient Sefer Torah of Bologna*, 29–52.

31 For Jacob Saphir's activities in the Yemen, see Gerber, *Ourselves or Our Holy Books*, 30–5 and the translation of Saphir's journal in *My Footsteps Echo*, edited by Lavon.

32 Dan Shapira, 'On Firkowicz, Forgeries and Forging Jewish Identities', in *Manufacturing a Past for the Present: Forgery and Authenticity in Medievalist Texts and Objects in Nineteenth-Century Europe*, ed. János M. Bak, Patrick J. Geary and Gábor Klaniczay (Leiden and Boston: Brill, 2014), 159–60.

33 Dan Shapira, *Abraham Firkowicz in Istanbul (1830–1832): Paving the Way for Turkic Nationalism* (Ankara: Karam, 2003), 7–18.

34 Avihai Shivtiel, 'The Genizah and its Roots', in *The Written Word Remains: The Archive and the Achievement: Articles in Honour of Professor Stefan C. Reif*, ed. Shulamit Reif (Cambridge: Cambridge University Library, 2004), 4–8.

35 Emanuel Tov, 'A Qumran Origin for the Masada Non-Biblical Texts?' *Dead Sea Discoveries* 7, no. 1 (2000): 62–3.

36 For the references to the 'practice of genizah' in rabbinic literature, see *Babylonian Talmud*, Tractate Megillah, 26b, Tractate Shabbat, 13b, 30b, 115a, and the *Mishneh Torah, Yesodei Ha-Torah*, 6:8.

37 J. J. Benjamin II, *Eight Years in Asia and Africa: from 1846 to 1855* (Hanover: Published by the Author, 1863), 160.

38 Philip Abraham, *Curiosities of Judaism: Facts, Opinions, Anecdotes, and Remarks Relative to the Hebrew Nation* (London: Philip Abraham, 1879), 226–7.

39 Mark Cohen and Yedida Stillman, 'The Cairo Geniza and the Custom of Geniza among Oriental Jewry: An Historical and Ethnographic Survey', *Pe'amim* 24 (1985): 3–35. [Hebrew].

40 'The Revised Version of the Old Testament', *Church Quarterly Review* 20 (1885): 455.

41 George Edmands Merrill, *The Parchments of the Faith* (Philadelphia: American Baptist Publication Society, 1894), 46.

42 David Kaufmann, *Aus Heinrich Heine's Ahnensaal* (Breslau: S. Schottlaender, 1896), 283–96. Kaufmann reproduces select pages from Von Geldern's diary, excluding folios 22–3. A photocopy of folio 23, which includes the mention of two visits to the *Kahal Eliyahu ha-Navi* as well as the mention of a visit to a genizah, is provided by A. M. Habermann in *The Cairo Genizah and Other Genizoth: Their Character, Contents and Development* (Jerusalem: Rubin Mass, 1971), 90 [Hebrew], from the original held in the Schocken Institute.

43 Kaufmann writes that Von Geldern recalled seeing the room set aside for salvaging unused books and writings (*Aus Heinrich Heine's Ahnensaal*, 123). Based on Kaufman's account, subsequent historians would write that Von Geldern was impressed by the 'wealth of possibility that lay hidden amid the rubbish of the genizot' (e.g. Adler, 'Genizah' *Jewish Encyclopedia*, 1906). Yet Kaufmann only references the abovementioned phrase '*Hipasti be-genizah*' (I searched the (or a) genizah) on folio 23 of the diary (*Aus Heinrich Heine's Ahnensaal*, 123, fn. 2), which suggests that any attempt to record Von Geldern's impressions is mere speculation.

44 Claudius Buchanan, *Christian Researches in Asia: With Notices of the Translation of the Scriptures into the Oriental Languages*, 2nd edition (London: T. Cadell and W. Davies; Cambridge: J. Deighton, 1811), 208–9.

Chapter 2

1 Tapani Harviainen, 'Abraham Firkovich', in *Karaite Judaism: A Guide to Its History and Literary Sources*, ed. Meira Polliack (Leiden and Boston: Brill, 2003), 880–2.

2 Harviainen, 'Abraham Firkovich', 885.

3 Avraham Firkovich, *Sefer Avne Zikaron* (Vilna: Samuel Joseph Finn and Abraham Zevi Rozenkranz Press, 1872), 16–18. [Hebrew]. The translated quote is from Harviainen, 'Abraham Firkovich', 887. For a description of the Odessa Collection, see also Olga Vasilyeva, 'The Firkovich Odessa Collection: The History of Its Acquisition and Research, Present Condition and Historical Value', *Studia Orientalia* 95 (2003): 45–53.

4 See Golda Akhiezer, 'Rabbanite Manuscripts in Karaite Hands: Findings from the Crimean Genizot and Libraries', *Journal of Jewish Studies* LXX, no. 2 (2019): 332–56. Akhiezer is the first person to explore Firkovich's experiences with the Crimean genizot in depth. This account is a blend of her discoveries and Firkovich's own testimony.

5 Firkovich, *Sefer Avne Zikaron*, 22–3.

6 August Freiherr Von Haxthausen, *The Russian Empire: Its People, Institutions, and Resources*, trans. Robert Farie, Volume II (London: Chapman and Hall, 1856), 104–5.

7 See Akhiezer, 'Rabbanite Manuscripts in Karaite Hands', 342–3. Akhiezer discovered this evidence in the archives of the Jewish Theological Seminary in New York.

8 'Our Weekly Gossip', *The Athenaeum: Journal of English and Foreign Literature, Science, and the Fine Arts* 1845 (7 March 1863): 135.

9 Akhiezer, 'Rabbanite Manuscripts in Karaite Hands', 343.

10 See Ben Outhwaite, 'The First Owners of the Leningrad Codex: T-S 10J30.7', *Fragment of the Month*, November 2017, https://doi.org/10.17863/CAM.28071, and the provenance possibilities outlined by Vasilyeva, 'The Firkovich Odessa Collection', 48–9.

11 Tapani Harviainen, 'Abraham Firkovich as Collector of Dispersed Minorities and their Manuscripts in the Light of his Personal Archive in St. Petersburg', *Jewish Studies* 39 (1999): 101.

12 Tapani Harviainen, 'Abraham Firkovich and the Karaite Community in Jerusalem in 1864', *Manuscripta Orientalia* 4, no. 2 (1998): 66–70.

13 Tapani Harviainen, 'Abraham Firkovich, the Aleppo Codex, and Its Dedication', in *Jewish Studies at the Turn of the Twentieth Century: Proceedings of the 6th EAJS Congress, Toledo, July 1998. Volume 1: Biblical, Rabbinical, and Medieval Studies*, ed. Judit Targarona Borrás and Angel Sáenz-Badillos (Leiden and Boston: Brill, 1999), 133.

14 See Tawil and Schneider, *Crown of Aleppo* and Friedman, *The Aleppo Codex* for fascinating accounts of the manuscript's disappearance and re-emergence.

15 The complex story of the dedication page and the questions of forgery surrounding it are investigated in detail by Yosef Ofer in 'Abraham Firkovich and the Dedication Inscription of the Aleppo Codex', *Hebrew Union College Annual* 76 (2005): 259–72.

16 Henry A. Stern, *Dawnings of Light in the East* (London: Charles H. Purday, 1854), 32, 226.

17 Tapani Harviainen, 'Abraham Firkovitsh, Karaites in Hīt and the Provenance of Karaite Transcriptions of Biblical Hebrew Texts into Arabic Script', *Folio Orientalia* XXVIII (1991): 181.

18 Harviainen, 'Abraham Firkovitsh, Karaites in Hīt', 182.

19 Harviainen, 'Abraham Firkovitsh, Karaites in Hīt', 182–4.

20 The testimony is found in Zev Wolf Schur's travelogue, *Mahazot Ha-Hayim*, Vien: G. Breg, 1884, 66. [Hebrew]. Schur's informant told him that the community's stay in Jerusalem was short.

21 Reinhart Hoerning, *British Museum Karaite MSS. Descriptions and Collation of Six Karaite Manuscripts of Portions of the Hebrew Bible . . .* (London: Williams and Norgate, 1889), v.

22 Stefan C. Reif, 'A Fresh Look at Adolf Neubauer as Scholar, Librarian and Jewish Personality', [unpublished paper read before the Jewish Historical Society of England, 2005].

23 Shapira, 'Remarks on Avraham Firkowicz', 138–9.

24 Adolf Neubauer, 'Die Firkowitzsche Sammlung', *Melanges Asiatiques* 4, no. 16 (Marz 1864): 121–7.

25 Adolf Neubauer, *Aus der Petersburger Bibliothek: Beiträge und Documente zur Geschichte des Karäerthums und der Karäischen Literatur* (Leipzig: Oskar Leiner, 1866), 42–3.

26 Tapani Harviainen, 'Abraham Firkovich and the Karaite Community', 68.

27 The complex historical relationship between the two groups is examined in Gary Knoppers, *Jews and Samaritans: The Origins and History of their Early Relations* (Oxford: Oxford University Press, 2013).

28 Akhiezer, 'Between Samaritans and Karaites', 239–41.

29 Firkovich's report of his acquisition of genizah manuscripts from the Samaritan synagogue is translated in Tapani Harviainen and Haseeb Shehadeh, 'The Acquisition of the Samaritan Collection', *Studia Orientalia* 97 (2003): 52–5.

30 Tapani Harviainen and Haseeb Shehadeh, 'How Did Abraham Firkovich Acquire the Great Collection of Samaritan Manuscripts in Nablus in 1864?' *Studia Orientalia* 73 (1994): 178.

31 The excerpts quoted in this chapter are translated from Saphir's travelogue, *Even Sapir*, 21b.

32 Lily Kahn, *A Grammar of the Eastern European Hasidic Hebrew Tale* (Leiden and Boston: Brill, 2014), 46.

33 Firkovich's exploits in Cairo were examined in detail by Zeev Elkin and Menahem Ben-Sasson, 'Abraham Firkovich and the Cairo Genizas in the Light of his Personal Archive', *Pe'amim* 90 (2002): 51–95 [Hebrew], showing that he travelled from Jerusalem to Egypt in the middle of May 1864 and left back to Jerusalem on 6 June 1864, leaving his grandson to continue emptying the genizah. Elkin and Ben-Sasson identified the synagogue on the basis of the stone commemorating the date of its renovation (68–9).

34 The Codex was seen and photographed in the Karaite synagogue as late as 1979 by Boruch Helman (a visiting scholar) and J. Zel Lurie (Hadassah Magazine editor), see Helman, Boruch, 'The Karaite Jews of Cairo', *Hadassah Magazine* (March 1979), 5, and it was microfilmed in the 1980s. After that period, it disappeared and Zel Lurie, who tried to track it down several decades later, believes it was taken to the National Library of Israel (see J. Zel Lurie, 'Mysteries of the Cairo Codex: Part II', *Florida Jewish Journal* (13 June 2012)).

35 For example, Simon Hopkins in 'The Discovery of the Cairo Genizah', *Bibliophilia Africana* IV (1981): 150, even translated Saphir's words in capital letters: 'BUT WHO KNOWS WHAT IS STILL BENEATH?' David Cassuto's reconstruction of the synagogue in 'The Synagogues in Cairo', in *The Jews in Ottoman Egypt (1517–1914)*, ed. Jacob M. Landau (Jerusalem: Misgav Yerushalaim, 1988), 204–19 argues that the rooftop was entirely open as in other courtyard synagogues like the one in Aleppo, and that the genizah was a deep chute-like structure. I also attempted to explain the unusual-seeming size of the genizah and align both discoveries in previous articles.

36 Translation of the text provided in Elkin and Ben-Sasson, 'Abraham Firkovich and the Cairo Genizas', 75. [Hebrew].

37 Elkin and Ben-Sasson, 'Abraham Firkovich and the Cairo Genizas', 90–1.

Chapter 3

1 Greville John Chester, 'Donkey Rides Around Cairo', in *Aunt Judy's Christmas Volume For 1879*, ed. H. K. F. Gatty (London: George Bell & Sons, 1879), 157–63, 224–9, 270–5, 356–62, 416–21, 485–94.

2 Gertrud Seidmann, 'Forgotten Pioneers of Archaeology in Victorian Oxford: The Rev. Greville John Chester (1830–1892)', *Oxoniensia* LXXI (2006): 147.

3 W. J. Loftie, *A Ride in Egypt: From Sioot to Luxor in 1879* (London: Macmillan and Co., 1879), ix.

4 'Obituary', *The Academy and Literature* 41, no. 1048 (June 1892): 550.

5 'Notes and News', *Palestine Exploration Fund: Quarterly Statement*, London (July 1892): 179.

6 Stephen Emmel, 'Reconstructing a Dismembered Coptic Library', in *Gnosticism and the Early Christian World: In Honor of James M. Robinson*, ed. James E. Goehring,

Charles W. Hedrick, Jack T. Sanders, and Hans Dieter Betz (Sonoma: Polebridge Press, 1990), 145–61.

7 Greville John Chester, 'Notes on the Coptic Dayrs of the Wady Natrûn and on Dayr Antonios in the Eastern Desert', *The Archaeological Journal* 30 (June 1873): 116.

8 William Wright (ed.), *Catalogue of Syriac Manuscripts in the British Museum Acquired Since the Year 1838* (London: Longmans & Co., 1872).

9 See Ahmed El Shamsy, *Rediscovering the Islamic Classics: How Editors and Print Culture Transformed an Intellectual Tradition* (New Jersey: Princeton University Press, 2020), 10–19.

10 Wright, *Catalogue of the Syriac Manuscripts,* viii–ix.

11 Robert Curzon, *Visits to Monasteries in the Levant*, 5th edition (London: John Murray, 1865), 76.

12 *Journal [by Miss Platt] of a Tour through Egypt, the Peninsula of Sinai, and the Holy Land in 1838, 1839 in two volumes*, Volume 1 (London: printed solely for private circulation by Richard Watts, 1841), 133.

13 Lucas Van Rompay, 'Coptic Christianity, Syriac Contacts With', in *Gorgias Encyclopedic Dictionary of the Syriac Heritage: Electronic Edition*, ed. Sebastian P. Brock, Aaron M. Butts, George A. Kiraz and Lucas Van Rompay: https://gedsh .bethmardutho.org/Coptic-Christianity-Syriac-contacts-with.

14 Wright, *Catalogue of the Syriac Manuscripts*, xii–xiii.

15 *Journal [by Miss Platt]*, 279.

16 Wright, *Catalogue of the Syriac Manuscripts*, xii–xiii.

17 *Association for the Furtherance of Christianity: Letters and Papers Concerning the Coptic Church in Relation to the Church of England: Under the Primacy of Archbishop Howley, 1836–1848* (London: Printed for the Use of the Committee, 1883), 83–7.

18 Wright, *Catalogue of the Syriac Manuscripts*, xiii–xiv.

19 Wright, *Catalogue of the Syriac Manuscripts*, xv.

20 Sebastian Brock, 'Abbot Mushe and the Poll Tax', *Newsletter of the Levantine Foundation* no. 2 (September 2007): 2.

21 Wright, *Catalogue of the Syriac Manuscripts*, xvi.

22 Emmel, 'Reconstructing a Dismembered Coptic Library', 150.

23 Chester, 'Notes on the Coptic Dayrs', 110.

24 Greville John Chester, 'Notes on the Ancient Christian Churches of Musr El Ateekah, or Old Cairo, and its Neighbourhood', *The Archaeological Journal* 29 (1872): 126–7.

25 Chester, 'Notes on the Coptic Dayrs', 116.

26 Translation in Richard J. H. Gottheil, 'An Eleventh-Century Document Concerning a Cairo Synagogue', *Jewish Quarterly Review* 19, no. 3 (April 1907): 506–7.

27 David Salomons (ed.), *Miscellany of Hebrew Literature*, Volume I (London: N. Trübner and Co., 1872), 133.

28 In the Kedem Auction Catalogue, no. 66, 218: 'Joseph Sambari in his book *Divrei Yosef* (Ahavat Shalom edition, 53) related that he found a gloss handwritten by R. Menach (to the book Tikun Yissachar, Venice 1579), in which R. Menachem de Lonzano recounted that while in Cairo, he went to the Ben Ezra Synagogue, and personally inspected the Torah scroll attributed to Ezra.'

29 Richard Pococke, *Description of the East, and Some Other Countries*, Volume 5: Observations on Egypt (London: W. Bowyer, 1743), 28.

30 See 'Obituary', *British Medical Journal* (15 August 1896): 427–8.

31 H. E. James A. S. Grant, 'An Introduction to Ancient Egyptian History', *Transactions of the Aberdeen Philosophical Society* III (1900): 1–30: 'For nearly a quarter of a

century (the period of my residence in Egypt) I have devoted a considerable portion of my spare time to the study of the History of Ancient Egypt and in collecting antiquities illustrative of that history, so that I have now a large museum of my own in Cairo, where every Wednesday evening during the winter season I read papers on Egyptological subjects, and illustrate my lectures by means of the specimens of antiquities I have collected.' J. M. Buckley, *Travels in Three Continents: Europe & Africa & Asia* (New York: Hunt & Eaton; Cincinnati: Cranston & Curts, 1895), 334: 'So numerous and valuable are Dr. Grant's possessions that they would give fame to any city in this country, if collected and classified in a museum of antiquities.'

32 *The Athenaeum*, No. 2344 (28 September 1872): 403.
33 See also Eleazar Hurvitz, *Catalogue of the Cairo Geniza Fragments in the Westminster College Library, Cambridge*, Volume I (New York: Yeshiva University, 2006), [Hebrew] for an in-depth discussion of the synagogue's hiding places.
34 The friendship between the Grants and Chester is mentioned in Margaret S. Drower, *Flinders Petrie: A Life in Archaeology* (Madison, WI: The University of Wisconsin Press, 1995), 40.
35 F. Robert Hunter, 'Tourism and Empire: The Thomas Cook & Son Enterprise on the Nile, 1868–1914', *Middle Eastern Studies* 40, no. 5 (September 2004): 34–5.
36 See Waleed Hazbun, 'The East as an Exhibit: Thomas Cook & Son and the Origins of the International Tourism Industry in Egypt', in *The Business of Tourism: Place, Faith, and History*, ed. Philip Scranton and Janet F. Davidson (Philadelphia: University of Pennsylvania Press, 2007), 19 and Margarita Díaz-Andreu, *A World History of Nineteenth Century Archaeology: Nationalism, Colonialism, and the Past* (Oxford: Oxford University Press, 2007), 123.
37 Brian Fagan, *The Rape of the Nile: Tomb Robbers, Tourists, and Archaeologists in Egypt*, 3rd edition. (USA: Westview Press, 2004), 192.
38 See Edwards's lament on the 'work of destruction', in Amelia B. Edwards, *A Thousand Miles Up the Nile* (London: Longmans, Green & Co., 1877), 519–20.
39 Edwards, *A Thousand Miles*, 658.
40 Fredrik Hagen and Kim Ryholt, *The Antiquities Trade in Egypt 1880–1930: The H. O. Lange Papers*, Scientia Danica. Series H., Humanistica 4, Volume 8 (Copenhagen, Denmark: Det Kongelige Danske Videnskabernes Selskab, 2016), 32–3.
41 See El Shamsy, *Rediscovering the Islamic Classics*, 13–14.
42 Stanley H. Skreslet II, 'The American Presbyterian Mission in Egypt: Significant Factors in its Establishment', *American Presbyterians* 64, no. 2 (Summer, 1986): 83–95.
43 See Agnes Lewis, 'Zu H. Duensing, Christlich-palästinisch-aramäische Texte und Fragmente', *Zeitschrift der deutschen morgenländischen Gessellschaft* 61 (1907): 630–2.
44 See also Heather J. Sharkey, *American Evangelicals in Egypt: Missionary Encounters in an Age of Empire* (Princeton and Oxford: Princeton University Press, 2008), 20–6.
45 Gulian Lansing, *Egypt's Princes: A Narrative of Missionary Labor in the Valley of the Nile* (New York: Robert Carter and Brothers, 1865), 370.
46 John C. Van Dyke, 'Notes on the Sage Library of the Theological Seminary at New Brunswick', Reprinted from the 'Christian Intelligencer' of 4, 11 and 18 July 1888 (New Brunswick, NJ, 1888), 8–9. See also the entry for 'Rev Dr Gulian Lansing' in the collections database of the British Museum: https://www.britishmuseum.org/collection/term/BIOG54299.
47 See Nongbri, *God's Library*, for the full story behind these papyri finds.
48 Adolph Bauer, 'Neue Funde griechischer Papyrusrollen in Aegypten', *Zeitschrift für Ägyptische Sprache und Altertumskunde* 16 (1878): 108–10.

49 *The Athenaeum* no. 2623 (2 February 1878): 160.
50 Edmund Craster, *History of the Bodleian Library* (Oxford: Clarendon Press, 1952), 200.
51 Adolf Grohmann, *Arabische Chronologie I, Arabische Papyruskunde II* (Leiden; Koln: E. J. Brill, 1966), 54–6.
52 Adolf Neubauer, 'Report to Convocation of Hebrew-Arabic Manuscripts at St. Petersburg', *Oxford University Gazette* (21 November 1876): 99–101.
53 'The Massorah', *The Times* (2 March 1877), 4.

Chapter 4

1 A detailed account of Shapira's life is provided in Chanan Tigay, *The Lost Book of Moses: The Hunt for the World's Oldest Bible* (USA: HarperCollins, 2016).
2 John Blackburn, *A Hand-Book Round Jerusalem* (London: F. and J. Rivington, 1846), 11.
3 Albert M. Hyamson (ed.), *The British Consulate in Jerusalem in Relation to the Jews of Palestine, 1838–1914. Part 1: 1838–1861* (London: Edward Goldston Ltd, 1939), 76–8.
4 'Letter No. III. From Dr. Tobler', *Palestine Exploration Fund Quarterly Statement* (April 1876): 103–4.
5 William Cowper Prime, *Tent Life in the Holy Land* (New York: Harper & Brothers, 1857), 156–61.
6 *Quarterly Statement: Palestine Exploration Fund* (1869–1871): 54. Capt. Wilson and Capt. Warren, *The Recovery of Jerusalem: A Narrative of Exploration and Discovery in the City and the Holy Land* (London: Richard Bentley: 1871), 228.
7 T. G. E., 'A Few Days in Jerusalem', *The Monthly Packet of Evening Readings for Members of the English Church* (January 1870): 378, 382.
8 A similar scroll was taken from the Cochin Jews of India by the Rev. Charles Buchanan, see S. M. Schiller-Szinessy, *Catalogue of the Hebrew Manuscripts Preserved in the University Library Cambridge*, Volume 1 (Cambridge: Printed for the University Library, 1876), 1–4.
9 S. Baer, *Zwei alte Thora-Rollen aus Arabien und Palästina, beschreiben von S. Baer . . .* (Frankfurt A. M.: Verlag von Johannes Alt, 1870).
10 Amy Fullerton-Fullerton, *A Lady's Ride Through Palestine & Syria: With Notices of Egypt and the Canal of Suez* (UK: S.W. Partridge, 1872), 226.
11 George A. Smith et al., *Correspondence of Palestine Tourists; Comprising a Series of Letters by George A. Smith, Lorenzo Snow, Paul A. Schettler, and Eliza R. Snow of Utah . . .* (Salt Lake City, Utah Territory: Descret News Steam Printing Establishment, 1875), 225.
12 See Gerber, *Ourselves or Our Holy Books*, 71–5, for the scholarly reception of the Yemenite *Midrash Ha-Gadol*.
13 Yosef Tobi, 'An Unknown Study by Joseph Halévy on his Journey to Yemen', *Proceedings of the Seminar for Arabian Studies* 35 (2005): 287–92.
14 *Bulletin de l'Alliance Israélite Universelle* (2 January 1860): 22–5.
15 *Bulletin de l'Alliance Israélite Universelle* (1 January 1865): 8.
16 See Gerber, *Ourselves or Our Holy Books*, 22–5, 30–4, for a full account of the Yemenite encounter with the emissaries and collectors from Jerusalem and Europe from the Yemenite perspective.
17 For the details of Halévy's mission and the contents of Habshush's journal, see Alan Verskin, *A Vision of Yemen: The Travels of a European Orientalist and His Native Guide* (Stanford, CA: Stanford University Press, 2018).

18 Verskin, *A Vision of Yemen*, 157.
19 Verskin, *A Vision of Yemen*, 144.
20 M. W. Shapira, *Eigenhändiges Verzeichnis der von Shapira gesammelten hebr. Handschriften,* Staatsbibliothek zu Berlin (MS or. Fol. 1342): https://digital .staatsbibliothek-berlin.de/werkansicht/?PPN=PPN777461838, 160.
21 Paul B. Fenton, 'Moses Shapira's Journey to the Yemen', in *Mittuv Yosef: Yosef Tobi Jubilee Volume,* ed. Ayelet Oettinger and Danny Bar-Maoz, Volume 2 (Haifa: University of Haifa Press, 2011), LXVIII–LXXXI.
22 *The Athenaeum* 2733 (13 March 1880): 346–7.
23 Gottheil, 'Some Hebrew Manuscripts in Cairo', 610–11.
24 Translation from Saphir, *My Footsteps Echo,* ed. Lavon, 168.
25 Merav Mack and Benjamin Balint, *Jerusalem: City of the Book* (New Haven and London: Yale University Press, 2019), 127–8.
26 A. H. Sayce, 'Oxford Letter', *The Academy,* 11 June 1881, no. 475, 434.
27 C. D. Ginsburg, 'Hebrew MSS. at the British Museum', *The Academy* XIX, no. 476 (18 June 1881): 455–6. See also Archibald Henry Sayce's announcement about Shapira's hoard in *The Athenaeum,* No. 2783 (26 February 1881): 301.
28 Shapira, *Eigenhändiges Verzeichnis der von Shapira,* 60.
29 Ari Ariel, *Jewish-Muslim Relations and Migration from Yemen to Palestine in the Late Nineteenth and Twentieth Centuries* (Leiden, Boston: Brill, 2014), 48–50.
30 Rabbi Benjamin, 'Mi-Tipuse Yerushalayim', *Ha-Aretz,* 27 February 1925, 4.
31 For a short biography of Adelmann, see George Mandel, *Who Was Ben-Yehuda with in Boulevard Montmartre?* (Oxford Centre Papers; 2) (Oxford: Oxford Center for Postgraduate Hebrew Studies, 1984), 13–15 and 'Mordechai Edelman' in Joseph Galron-Goldschläger, *Modern Hebrew Literature- a Bio-Bibliographical Lexicon* (Ohio State University), https://library.osu.edu/projects/hebrew-lexicon/index.htm. [Hebrew]. Adelmann's activities are recorded in the pages of various German and Hebrew journals of the 1880s and 1890s, such as *Ha-Tzvi, Ha-Tzvira, Die Judishe Presse* and the *Beilage zur 'Judischen Presse': Spenden-Verzeichnisse für alle Zweige jüdischer Wohlthätigkeit.*
32 See also Gerber, *Ourselves or Our Holy Books,* 64–71 on the activities of Adelmann and others in purchasing manuscripts from the Yemenite immigrants newly arrived in Jerusalem.
33 *A Summary Catalogue of Western Manuscripts in the Bodleian Library at Oxford which have hitherto been catalogued in the Quarto Series with references to the Oriental and other manuscripts,* ed. Falconer Madan, Volume V (Oxford: Clarendon Press, 1905), 589 and George Margoliouth, *Catalogue of the Hebrew and Samaritan manuscripts in the British Museum,* Volume I (1899): Introduction.
34 Shapira, *Eigenhändiges Verzeichnis der von Shapira,* 98–100.
35 Shapira, *Eigenhändiges Verzeichnis der von Shapira,* 426.
36 Andrew Watson, *The American Mission in Egypt: 1854–1896* (Pittsburgh: United Presbyterian Board of Publication, 1904), 400.
37 Skreslet II, 'The American Presbyterian Mission', 89.
38 Henry Clay Trumbull in *Old Time Student Volunteers; My Memories of Missionaries* (New York, Chicago, Toronto: Fleming H. Revell Company, 1902), recalled the way that Lansing received greetings from everyone he passed as he walked through the streets of Cairo.
39 James M. Ludlow, 'Ancient Hebrew Manuscript at Cairo', *Friends' Review. A Religious, Literary and Miscellaneous Journal* 34, no. 44 (1881): 693–4. Ludlow was an American Presbyterian clergyman and author.

40 For example, Gabriel Charmes, *Five Months at Cairo and in Lower Egypt*, trans. William Conn (London, 1883), 137, described the Ben Ezra Synagogue as 'a place so dark and dirty' it would cause Jeremiah 'to weep'.

41 *Universalist Quarterly and General Review* NS 20 (July 1883), 364–5.

42 E. L. Butcher, *The Story of the Church of Egypt*, Volume I (London: Smith, Elder, & Co., 1897).

43 Their 'warm' friendship is mentioned in Trumbull's *Old Time Student Volunteers*, 204.

44 Mourad el-Kodsi, *The Karaite Jews of Egypt 1882–1986* (Lyons, NY: Wilprint Inc., 1987), 267–8. For information about bookselling, see also Yaron Ben-Naeh and Noah Gerber, 'Libraries and Book Collections of Ottoman Jews: The Case of Late Ottoman Jerusalem', *Sefunot* 26 (2019): 360–1. [Hebrew].

45 Shapira, *Eigenhändiges Verzeichnis der von Shapira*, No. 2 refers to catalogue entry Kd. No. 2, which was later classified as BL MS. Or. 2524, a thirteenth-century copy of abstracts of Al-Qirqisani's Kitab al-Anwar. The nineteenth century copy of this work, Shapira's Kd. No. 7a, by Moshe Ha-Levi, is now classified as BL MS. Or. 2526.

46 British Museum Records, British Museum Department of MSS Report Respecting Offers for Purchase, 4 July 1882.

47 See Shapira, *Eigenhändiges Verzeichnis der von Shapira*, 568, section 'KC' where he describes Karaite prayer books in his possession that comprised hundreds of leaves. An example in the British Library collection is BL. Or. 2533 (KC. No. 5), a 350-page codex comprising a collection of piyyutim (hymns) from the seventeenth century.

48 *The Times* (10 July 1882): 4.

49 See Kaufmann MSS A407 and A410 in Max Weisz, *Katalog der Hebräischen Handschriften und Bücher in der Bibliothek des Professors Dr. David Kaufman S. A.* (Frankfurt A. M.: J. Kaufmann, 1906).

50 David Kaufmann, 'Die Grabschrift des R. Isak Bar Scheschet', *Monatschrift für Geschicte und Wissenschaft des Judenthums* 32, no. 4 (1883): 190–2.

51 The movement of these collections is discussed in Ben-Naeh and Gerber, 'Libraries and book collections of Ottoman Jews', 341–404. [Hebrew].

52 Weisz, *Katalog der Hebräischen Handschriften*, 183.

53 See a transcription of the letters in Samuel Krauss, *David Kaufmann. Eine Biographie* (Berlin: S. Calvary & Co., 1901), 56–7.

Chapter 5

1 Harkavy's encounters with manuscripts are recorded in Abraham Harkavy, *Hadashim ve-Yeshanim, Meqorot ve-Mehkarim be-toledot Yisrael u-be-Sifruto* (Hebrew; facsimile edition; Jerusalem, 1970).

2 For example, see the Harkavy MSS listed in Judith Olszowy-Schlanger, *Karaite Marriage Documents from the Cairo Genizah . . .* (Leiden, New York, Köln, 1998).

3 Harkavy, *Hadashim ve-Yeshanim*, 106–8. Also Gottheil, 'An Eleventh-Century Document', 518–22. Harkavy's reference may have been to the *Kehilat Kodesh Mizrayim* (Synagogue of the Egyptian Jews).

4 Harkavy, *Hadashim ve-Yeshanim*, 101.

5 Zachary M. Baker, 'History of the Jewish Collections at the Vernadsky Library in Kiev', *Shofar* 10, no. 4 (1992): 31–48.

6 *The Acts and Proceedings of the . . . Regular Session of the General Synod of the Reformed Church in America* 81 (1886): 4–5, 446.

7 One such journal, penned by a visitor to the Egyptian Museum's sales room in 1894, noted that a mummy and case could be had for £20 and scarabs for pennies. Hagen and Ryholt, *Antiquities Dealers*, 47–8.

8 *The Independent*, 24 November 1887, 9.

9 Twenty-two manuscripts were viewed and described by Richard Gottheil after his visit to the Karaite Synagogue in 1905. This particular codex mentioned by Lansing in listed as 'no. 18' in Gottheil's article, 'Some Hebrew Manuscripts in Cairo.'

10 Van Dyke, *Notes on the Sage Library*, 9.

11 Adolf Neubauer, 'The Introduction of the Square Characters in Biblical MSS, and an Account of the Earliest MSS. of the Old Testament', in *Studia Biblica Et Ecclesiastica: Essays Chiefly in Biblical and Patristic Criticism*, vol. 3, edited by S. R. Driver, T. K. Cheyne and W. Sanday (Oxford: Clarendon Press, 1891), 22, 25.

12 When the biblical scholar Paul Kahle examined the codex in the 1950s, he concluded that Neubauer had relied too heavily on Seligman's method of dating and that the date supplied in the colophon could be trusted (see Paul E. Kahle, 'The Hebrew Ben Asher Bible Manuscripts', *Vetus Testamentum* 1, no. 3 (1951): 161–7, 161–3). In 1997, the codicologist Malachi Beit-Arie vindicated Neubauer's theory and provided evidence to show that the colophon had been copied from an earlier codex (see Beit-Arie, Sirat, Glatzer (eds.), *Codices Hebraicis*, 28).

13 Harris's trips to the East are described in Alessandro Falcetta, *The Daily Discoveries of a Bible Scholar and Manuscript Hunter: A Biography of James Rendel Harris, 1852–1941* (Great Britain: T&T Clarke, Bloomsbury Publishing, 2018). Harris's explanation about not providing provenance is added as a note to Robert W. Rogers, 'A Catalogue of Manuscripts (chiefly Oriental) in the Library of Haverford College', *Haverford College Studies*, no. 4, 28–50.

14 Falcetta, *The Daily Discoveries*, 75, 98.

15 See the preface of E. N. Adler, *Jews in Many Lands* (Philadelphia: Jewish Publication Society of America, 1905) where Adler provides details of his journeys, 11–14.

16 See E. N. Adler, 'The Hebrew Treasures of England', presidential address delivered on 9 February 1914, *The Jewish Historical Society of England: Transactions* 8–9 (1915–1917): 16.

17 Donald Malcom Reid, *Whose Pharaohs? Archaeology, Museums, and Egyptian National Identity from Napoleon to World War I* (Berkeley, Los Angeles, London: University of California Press, 2003), 54–8.

18 Hagen and Ryholt, *Antiquities Dealers*, 138.

19 Andrew Humphreys, *Grand Hotels of Egypt in the Golden Age of Travel* (Cairo and New York: The American University in Cairo Press, 2015), 79.

20 Chester, 'Donkey Rides Around Cairo', 272.

21 For example, see the entry for 'Mohammed *Effendi*' in Hagen and Ryholt, *Antiquities Dealers*, 244.

22 Humphreys, *Grand Hotels of Egypt*, 59.

23 See the biographies of the dealers in Hagen and Ryholt, *Antiquities Dealers*, 183–274.

24 Hagen and Ryholt, *The Antiquities Trade*, 217.

25 Hagen and Ryholt, *The Antiquities Trade*, 217.

26 Abdulhaq, *Jewish and Greek Communities in Egypt*, 76–80.

27 Alessia Di Santi, 'From Egypt to Copenhagen. The Provenance of the Portraits of Augustus, Livia, and Tiberius at the Ny Carlsberg Glyptotek', *Analecta Romana*

Instituti Danici XLII (2017): 33–46. Bakhoum Soheir & Marie-Christine Hellmann, 'Wilhelm Froehner, le commerce et les collections d'antiquités égyptiennes', *Journal des Savants* 1 (1992): 164.

28 See, for example, the dealers who worked with Charles Lang Freer in Kent D. Clarke, 'Paleography and Philanthropy: Charles Lang Freer and His Acquisition of the "Freer Biblical Manuscripts"', in *The Freer Biblical Manuscripts: Fresh Studies of an American Treasure Trove*, ed. Larry W. Hurtado (Leiden and Boston: Brill, 2006), 29, fn. 30. See Solomon Schechter's account of his genizah discoveries in *The Friend: A Religious and Literary Journal* LXXI (28 August 1897), 46.

29 Hagen and Ryholt, *Antiquities Dealers*, 250.

30 See Hagen and Ryholt, *Antiquities Dealers*, 189–90, and Renee Levy's testimony about the family in Alisa Douer, *Egypt – The Lost Homeland. Exodus from Egypt, 1947–1967* (Berlin, Logos Verlag Berlin GmbH, 2015), 217.

31 Robert S. Hichens, 'Street Scenes in Cairo', *The Pall Mall Magazine IV* (September–December 1894): 605, 608.

32 Douglas Sladen, *Oriental Cairo: The City of the 'Arabian Nights'* (Philadelphia: J. B. Lippincott Company, 1911), 97–8.

33 Hagen and Ryholt, *Antiquities Dealers*, 79, fig. 59.

34 See C. E. Baxter, *Talofa: Letters from Foreign Parts* (London: Sampson Low, Marston, Searle & Rivington, 1884), 171, and Russell James Colman, *Trifles from a Tourist in Letters from Abroad* (Norwich: Fletcher and Son, 1886), 240.

35 Samir Raafat, 'Death, The Great Homogenizer . . .', *Historical Society of Jews from Egypt* 3 (11–24 November 1999): http://www.hsje.org/Whoswho/Robert_Nahman/Robert _Nahman.htm

36 See the genealogical tree compiled by Samir W. Raafat in *Bassatine News*: http://bassatine.net/nahman.php.

37 Ann C. Gunter, *A Collector's Journey: Charles Lang Freer and Egypt* (Washington, DC: Smithsonian Freer Gallery of Art, 2002), 105.

38 Samir W. Raafat, *Maadi 1904–1962: Society and History in a Cairo Suburb* (Zamalek, Cairo, Egypt: Palm Press, 1994), 15.

39 Robert Vitalis, *When Capitalists Collide: Business Conflict and the End of the Empire in Egypt* (Berkeley, Los Angeles, London: University of California Press, 1995), 32–9.

40 Adler, *Jews in Many Lands*, 29.

41 E. N. Adler, 'An Eleventh Century Introduction to the Hebrew Bible: Being a Fragment from the Sepher Ha-Ittim of Rabbi Judah ben Barzilai of Barcelona', *The Jewish Quarterly Review* 9, no. 4 (1897): 672, and *Jews in Many Lands*, 23–30.

Chapter 6

1 'The Cairo Genizah: How It was Found', *The Jewish Chronicle*, 5 May 1933, 4.

2 Alfred Butler, *The Ancient Coptic Churches of Egypt*, Volume 1 (Oxford: Clarendon Press, 1884), 235.

3 Sheehan, *Babylon of Egypt*, 84, 121.

4 Nelly Shafik Ramzy, 'The Impact of Local Environment Aspects on Coptic Architecture in Egypt', *Alexandria Engineering Journal* 51 (2012): 326–7.

5 On the trade in used interior furniture, see Sanders, *Creating Medieval Cairo*, 37–8; Sheehan, *Babylon of Egypt*, 122, discusses the relocation of the Hanging Church doors,

and *The Jewish Theological Seminary of America Biennial Report, 1902–1904* (New York, 1906), 126–9 provides information about the Synagogue Ark.

6 Loftie, *A Ride in Egypt*, 176.

7 G. J. Chester, *Catalogue of the Egyptian Antiquities in the Ashmolean Museum, Oxford* (Oxford: Parker & Col, 1881), 87–8.

8 Details about Henry Wallis's excavations and collecting habits can be found in Timothy Wilson, 'A Victorian Artist as Ceramic-Collector', *Journal of the History of Collections* 14, no. 2 (2002): 231–2.

9 'Discovery of an early Christian cemetery near Alexandria', *The Times* (4 May 1887), 15.

10 Rebecca J. W. Jefferson, 'A Genizah Secret: The Count d'Hulst and Letters Revealing the Race to Recover the Lost Leaves of the Original Ecclesiasticus', *Journal of the History of Collections* 21, no. 1 (2009): 126.

11 The Count d'Hulst's activities at Bubastis are described in A. Edwards, 'Bubastis: An Historical Sketch', *The Century Magazine* 39, no. 3 (1890): 334. In a discussion regarding Arabic pronunciation, Sayce wrote: 'I especially want the Count to be clear on the subject, as he is one of those on whom we depend for a knowledge of the actual pronunciation of the Egyptian *fellahin*', *The Academy* 42, no. 1066 (1892): 315.

12 See d'Hulst's letters to Naville in Bibliothèque de Genève, Ms. fr. 2542, ff. 226–39 and his letters to Amelia Edwards and Reginald Stuart Poole in the Egypt Exploration Society Lucy Gura Archives, Box III, k69–123.

13 Jefferson, 'A Genizah Secret', 127. Details of the pottery finds were published in Henry Wallis, *The Godman Collection: Persian Ceramic Art in the Collection of Mr. F. DuCane Godman, F. R. S. The Thirteenth Century Lustred Vases* (London; printed for private circulation, 1891).

14 Peter Sheehan, 'Archaeological Survey of the Ben Ezra Synagogue Site', in *Fortifications and the Synagogue: The Fortress of Babylon and the Ben Ezra Synagogue, Cairo*, ed. Phyllis Lambert (Montreal: Canadian Center for Architecture, 1994), 65–77.

15 Mosseri, 'The Synagogues of Egypt', 31–44, and Charles Le Quesne, 'The Synagogue', in *Fortifications and the Synagogue: The Fortress of Babylon and the Ben Ezra Synagogue, Cairo*, ed. Phyllis Lambert (Montreal: Canadian Center for Architecture, 1994), 79–87.

16 The *mezuzot* pieces are classified as MS Heb.g.8 in Adolf Neubauer and Arthur Ernest Cowley (eds.), *Catalogue of the Hebrew Manuscripts in the Bodleian Library*, Volume II (Oxford: Clarendon Press, 1906), 22. Their provenance is unknown.

17 For an in-depth account of Chester's involvement with genizah fragments, see also Rebecca J. W. Jefferson, 'What Cannot Often Be Obtainable': The Revd Greville John Chester and the Bodleian Genizah Collection', *Journal of the History of Collections* 31, no. 2 (July 2019): 271–89. The letters from Chester to E. W. B. Nicholson, quoted in this chapter, are all preserved in the Bodleian Library Records: MS Bodl.e.479.

18 The pieces were described in the Annual Report of the Bodleian Curators, 5 May 1891, 443. For an analysis of the collection, see Rebecca J. W. Jefferson, 'Data Analysis of the Genizah Fragments at the Bodleian Libraries', University of Florida Institutional Repository: https://ufdc.ufl.edu/IR00011094/00001.

19 Elliott Horowitz, '"A Jew of the Old Type": Neubauer as Cataloguer, Critic, and Necrologist', *The Jewish Quarterly Review* 100, no. 4 (Fall 2010): 649.

20 David Kaufmann, *Die letzte Vertreibung der Juden aus Wien und Niederösterreich: ihre Vorgeschichte (1625 1670) und ihre Opfer* (Budapest: Buchdrukerei Der Act. G. Athenaeum, 1889).

21 Nongbri, *God's Library*, 216.

22 See a description of the British Museum's Hebrew manuscript collection in Ilana Tahan, 'The Hebrew Collection of the British Library: Past and Present', *European Judaism: A Journal for the New Europe* 41, no. 2 (Autumn, 2008): 43–55.

23 Richard Gottheil and William H. Worrel (eds.), *Fragments from the Cairo Genizah in the Freer Collection* (New York: The Macmillan Company, 1927), xiii, fn. 10.

24 Elena Astafieva, 'How to Transfer "Holy Russia" into the Holy Land? Russian Policy in Palestine in the Late Imperial Period', *Jerusalem Quarterly* 71 (Autumn 2017): 8–11.

25 Abraham I. Katsch, *The Antonin Genizah in the Saltykov-Schedrin Public Library in Leningrad* (New York, 1963), 1 and Jefferson, 'What Cannot Often Be Obtainable', 276.

26 Jeffrey Mark Puall and Janet Billstein Akaha, 'Using Autosomal DNA Analysis to Connect Rabbinical Lineages: A Case Study of the Wertheimer and Wertheim Dynasties', *Avotaynu* XXVIII, no. 4 (2012): 62.

27 See Sara Jo Ben Zvi, 'Whose Geniza?' *Segula* 5 (June 2011): 60–70. A helpful list of the works published by Wertheimer together with the present location of the manuscripts he used and then sold on has been compiled by Dr Ezra Chwat, bibliographer at the National Library of Israel: https://www.academia.edu/9970575/Notes_on_R_Shlomoh_Aharon_Wertheimers_Genizah.

28 Jefferson 'What Cannot Often Be Obtainable', 277.

Chapter 7

1 See Neubauer and Cowley (eds.), *Catalogue of the Hebrew Manuscripts*, xiv, 58–59, MS Heb.e.21 (no. 2662).

2 Greville John Chester to Henry Bradshaw, Bloomsbury Court, London WC, 1886, Cambridge University Library, MS Add. 2592.959. Chester had also consulted with Lanzone on aspects of his Phoenician gem collection in 1885, see Greville John Chester, 'Notes on Some Phoenician Gems', *Palestine Exploration Fund: Quarterly Statement* (January 1885): 129–32.

3 Jefferson, 'What Cannot Often Be Obtainable', 278.

4 See Charles R. Watson, 'Sarah B. Dales Lansing – "The Personal Element in Missionary Service"', in *In the King's Service*, ed. Charles R. Watson (Philadelphia, PA: Board of Foreign Missions Presbyterian Church of N. A., 1905), 83–114 and *The Missionary Review of the World III* (NS) (December 1890), 960.

5 See Jefferson, 'A Genizah Secret', 137–8, fn. 48.

6 Brent Nongbri, *God's Library*, 87–90. See also the list of Coptic magical fragments associated with Nahman at http://www.coptic-magic.phil.uni-wuerzburg.de/index.php/2020/03/20/looking-at-the-coptic-magical-papyri-xiv-modern-collections/.

7 Jefferson, 'What Cannot Often be Obtainable', 280. For a description of Ali el-Arabi's life and work, see Hagen and Ryholt, 192–5. For his connection to Genizah manuscripts and to Freer, see Ann C. Gunter, *A Collector's Journey: Charles Lang Freer and Egypt* (Washington, DC, 2002), 102.

8 Clarke, 'Paleography and Philanthropy', 50–3.

9 Jefferson, 'What Cannot Often Be Obtainable', 280.

10 Roth-Lochner, Barbara, 'Un voyage en Egypte (1896–1897), extrait des Souvenirs d'Albert Nicole', in *Voyages en Égypte de l'Antiquité au début du 20e s*, ed. J. L. Chappaz et C. Ritschard (Genève: Genève Musée d'art et d'histoire, 2003), 250.

11 Bernard P. Grenfell, 'Oxyrhynchus and its Papyri', in *Egypt Exploration Fund. Archaeological Report, 1896–1897*, ed. F. Ll. Griffith (London: Egypt Exploration Fund, 1897), 7–10.

12 Hagen and Ryholt, *The Antiquities Trade*, 253–4, fig. 23.

13 Jean Capart, 'Nécrologie: Maurice Nahman', *Chronique d'Égypte* 44 (1947): 300–1. Capart wrote this premature obituary as a result of a miscommunication: Nahman was not deceased at this point.

14 Jefferson, 'What Cannot Often Be Obtainable', 280, fn. 85.

15 Elizabeth Dospel Williams, '"Into the Hands of a Well-Known Antiquary of Cairo": The Assiut Treasure and the Making of an Archaeological Hoard', *West 86th: A Journal of Decorative Arts, Design History, and Material Culture* 21, no. 2 (Fall–Winter, 2014): 267.

16 Andrew Watson, 'Reforms Among the Copts', *Evangelical Christendom* (1 October 1891): 318.

17 The letters from Chester to E. W. B. Nicholson, quoted in this chapter, are all preserved in the Bodleian Library Records: MS Bodl.e.479.

18 Jefferson, 'What Cannot Often Be Obtainable', 281.

19 Neubauer and Cowley (eds.), *Catalogue of the Hebrew Manuscripts*, xvi. Chester's contribution was also overlooked in the second publication of these fragments.

20 When he later came to examine a box of manuscripts that Jules Nicole had acquired from Cairo in 1898, Neubauer's attention was mostly fixed on a Greek palimpsest. See Jefferson, 'What Cannot Often Be Obtainable', fn, 93.

21 Jefferson, 'What Cannot Often Be Obtainable', 282.

22 Jefferson, 'What Cannot Often Be Obtainable', 283.

23 E. A. Wallis Budge, *By Nile and Tigris. A Narrative of Journeys in Egypt and Mesopotamia on Behalf of the British Museum Between the Years 1886 and 1913, by Sir E. A. Wallis Budge* (London, 1920), 85.

24 Stefan C. Reif, *Hebrew Manuscripts at Cambridge University Library* (Cambridge: Cambridge University Press: 1997), 30.

25 Cyrus Adler, *I Have Considered the Days* (Philadelphia: Jewish Publication Society of America, 1941), 116–17. For details of Adler's trip to the East, see also Cyrus Adler, *Selected Letters*, ed. Ira Robinson, Volume 1 (Philadelphia and New York: The Jewish Publication Society of America & The Jewish Theological Seminary of America, 1985), 27–55.

26 Jefferson, 'What Cannot Often Be Obtainable', 284. This may be Bodl. ms Heb.35.f (p) which is described as a tiny papyrus fragment from the Fayoum.

27 See Agnes's description of her stay in the mission in Agnes Smith, *Through Cyprus* (London: Hurst and Blackett, 1887), 49–71.

28 Margaret Dunlop Gibson, *How the Codex Was Found: A Narrative of Two Visits to Sinai from Mrs. Lewis's Journals, 1892–1893* (Cambridge: Macmillan and Bowes, 1893). For a complete account of their life and discoveries, see Janet Soskice, *The Sisters of Sinai: How Two Lady Adventurers Discovered the Hidden Gospels* (New York: Alfred A. Knopf, 2009).

29 Jefferson, 'What Cannot Often Be Obtainable', 284–85 and fn. 23. A later survey of the site concluded that the original marble pillars had been replaced with cast-iron pillars painted to imitate marble.

30 *The Academy* (4 February 1893), 113.

31 Jefferson, 'What Cannot Often Be Obtainable', 285.

32 His life and experiences are captured in his memoir: Abbas Hilmi II, *The Last Khedive of Egypt: Memoirs of Abbas Hilmi II,* trans. and ed. Amira Sonbol (Reading: Ithaca Press, 1998).

Chapter 8

1 A. H. Sayce, *Reminiscences* (London: Macmillan & Co., Limited, 1923), 119.
2 The letters from d'Hulst to E. W. B. Nicholson, Adolf Neubauer and Falconer Madan, quoted in this chapter, are all preserved in Bodleian Library Records: MS Bodl.d.1084. In the later letters to Madan, d'Hulst quoted from letters sent to him by Neubauer, Sayce and others.
3 Bodleian Library Records (BLR) C.59 'Payments for MSS'.
4 J. T. S. Solomon Schechter Papers, Solomon Schechter to Mathilde Schecter, Cairo, 20 January 1897.
5 Riamo d'Hulst to Édouard Naville, 22 June 1888, Bibliothèque de Genève, Ms. fr. 2542, ff.231.
6 James E. Keenan, 'The History of the Discipline', in *Oxford Handbook of Papyrology,* ed. Roger S. Bagnall (Oxford and New York: Oxford University Press, 2009), 60.
7 D. H. Müller and David Kaufmann, 'Der Brief Eines Ägyptischen Rabbi an Den Gaon [Salomo] Ben Jehuda', *Mittheilungen Aus Der Sammlung Der Papyrus Erzherzog Rainer* V, nos. 3–4 (Wien, 1892): 127.
8 Abraham Epstein, 'Review of H. D. Muller et David Kaufmann. Der Brief eines aegyptischen Rabbi an den Gaon [Salomon] ben Jehuda. Tirage à part du Ve volume des *Mittheilungen aus Der Sammlung der Papyrus Erzherzog Rainer, 1892 . . .*', *Revue des Etudes Juives* 25 (1892): 272–3.
9 Wertheimer's letters to Cambridge have been partly transcribed and translated in an appendix in Eleazar Gutwirth, '*Coplas de Yocef* from the Genizah', *Revue des Études Juives* 155, nos. 3–4 (1996): 397–400.
10 César Merchán-Hamann, 'Introduction to the Bodleian Library & College Collections', in *Jewish Treasures from Oxford Libraries,* ed. Rebecca Abrams and César Merchán-Hamann (Oxford: Bodleian Library, University of Oxford, 2020), 31–2.
11 R. Loewe, 'Solomon Marcus Schiller-Szinessy, 1820–1890: First Reader in Talmudic and Rabbinic Literature at Cambridge', *Transactions (Jewish Historical Society of England)* 21 (1962–1967): 160–1. A complete catalogue of the Cambridge Hebrew manuscript collection was finally undertaken and completed by Stefan C. Reif in 1997.
12 Stefan C. Reif, 'Jenkinson and Schechter at Cambridge: An Expanded and Updated Assessment', *Jewish Historical Studies* 32 (1990–1992): 285–8.
13 Mirjam Thulin, '*Wissenschaft* and Correspondence: Solomon Schechter between Europe and America', *Jewish Historical Studies* 48, no. 1 (2017): 117–18.
14 Mel Scult, 'The Baale Boste Reconsidered: The Life of Mathilde Roth Schechter (M. R. S.)', *Modern Judaism* 7, no. 1 (February 1987): 4.
15 See Theodor Gaster, 'Moses Gaster 1856–1939', in *Studies and Texts in Folklore, Magic, Mediaeval Romance, Hebrew Apocrypha, and Samaritan Archaeology,* ed. Moses Gaster (New York: Ktav, 1971), xv–xxxix, and Maria (Cioată) Haralambakis, 'Representations of Moses Gaster (1856–1939) in Anglophone and Romanian Scholarship', *New Europe College Yearbook 2012–2013,* Vol. 13 (2015): 89–128.

16 Adolf Neubauer, 'Review: Two Monographs by Dr. M. Gaster', *The Jewish Quarterly Review* 6, no. 3 (April 1894): 577.

17 Moses Gaster, 'The Story of My Library', trans. Brad Sabin Hill, *The British Library Journal* 21, no 1 (Spring 1995): 19.

18 Adolf Neubauer, 'Post-Biblical Bibliography, 1888–9', *The Jewish Quarterly Review* 2, no. 2 (January 1890): 194.

19 Solomon Schechter, 'The Riddles of Solomon in Rabbinic Literature', *Folklore* 1, no. 3 (September 1890): 358.

20 Solomon Schechter, 'Jewish Literature in 1890', *The Jewish Quarterly Review* 3, no. 2 (January 1891): 314–42.

21 Insights into Schechter's life and work in Cambridge, particularly his relationships with Cambridge scholars and the University Librarian can be found in Stefan C. Reif, *A Jewish Archive from Old Cairo: The History of Cambridge University's Genizah Collection* (Richmond, Surrey: Curzon, 2000).

22 'Obituary: Dr. Adolf Neubauer', *The Jewish Chronicle*, 12 April 1907, 9 and Jefferson, 'A Genizah Secret', 138–9, fn. 75.

23 Solomon Schechter, 'The Quotations from Ecclesiasticus in Rabbinic Literature', *The Jewish Quarterly Review* 3, no. 4 (July 1891): 689, and Jefferson, 'A Genizah Secret', 129.

24 David Starr, 'Loving Is Believing: Solomon Schechter and the Bible', *The Initiative on Bridging Scholarship and Pedagogy in Jewish Studies, Working Paper 7* (Brandeis University, 2010), 15.

25 A. H. Sayce, *The 'Higher Criticism' and the Verdict of the Monuments* (Published Under the Direction of the Tract Committee) London: Society for Promoting Christian Knowledge, 1894.

26 Neubauer, 'Post-Biblical Bibliography', 194.

27 Adolf Neubauer, 'Review of "Notes on a Hitherto Unknown Exegetical, Theological, and Philosophical Commentary to the Pentateuch by Alexander Kohut: The Columbia College MS. of Megilla (Babylonian Talmud) by Max Leopold Margolis"', *The Jewish Quarterly Review* 5, no. 2 (January 1893): 338–42.

28 The articles were entitled 'Notes on Hebrew MSS. in the University Library at Cambridge', and they ran from I–VI in *The Jewish Quarterly Review* 4, no. 1 (October 1891) to 6, no. 1 (October 1893).

29 Cambridge University Reporter, 8 June 1892, 907.

30 Adalbert Merx, *Documents de paléographie hébraïque et arabe, publiés avec sept planches photo-lithographiques* (Leyde: Brill, 1894), 10.

31 E. J. Pilcher, 'An Arabic Version of the Book of Job', *Biblia* XIV (1901): 37–42.

32 Wertheimers letters, postcards and lists are kept together with folders of genizah manuscripts in Cambridge University Library, MS Or.1080.13 and Or.1080.2, see Rebecca J. W. Jefferson, 'The Historical Significance of the Cambridge Genizah Inventory Project', in *Language, Culture, Computation. Computing of the Humanities, Law, and Narratives. Lecture Notes in Computer Science*, ed. N. Dershowitz and E. Nissan E., Volume 8002 (Berlin, Heidelberg: Springer, 2014), 26.

33 The fragments were first identified and analysed in Judith Olszowy-Schlanger and Roni Shweka, 'Newly Discovered Early Palimpsest Fragments of the Talmud Yerushalmi from the Cairo Genizah', *Revue des études Juives* 172, no. 1–2 (January–June, 2013): 49–81.

34 See Eustace Alfred Reynolds-Ball, *Jerusalem. A Practical Guide to Jerusalem and Its Environs, with Excursions to Bethlehem, Hebron, Jericho* (London: Adam and Charles

Black, 1901) where Singer is listed on pp. 6, 8, 193. His name and profession also appear in the membership list of *Mittheilungen und Nachbrichten des Deutschen Palestina-Vereins* (the German Society for the Exploration of Palestine) 6 (1896): 48, 63.

35 Ben Zvi, 'Whose Geniza?', 60–70.

36 Moses Gaster, 'The Story of My Library', 19.

37 See Renate Smithuis, 'Short Introduction to the Genizah Collection in the John Rylands Library', in *From Cairo to Manchester: Studies in the Rylands Genizah Fragments*, ed. Renate Smithuis and Philip S. Alexander (Journal of Semitic Studies; Supplement 31), (Oxford: Oxford University Press, 2013), 3.

38 For the story of their discovery, see Ronny Vollandt, 'A Muslim Genizah in Damascus', *Fragment of the Month*, June 2018. https://doi.org/10.17863/CAM.34051.

39 This highly plausible scenario is suggested by Rustow in *The Lost Archive*, 47–8.

Chapter 9

1 *The Educational Times* XLVII, 1 January 1894, 34.

2 Adolf Neubauer, 'Literary Gleanings. XII. The Hebrew Bible in Shorthand Writing', *Jewish Quarterly Review* 7, no. 2 (January 1895): 361–4.

3 Robert P. Blake, 'Khanmeti Palimpsest Fragments of the Old Georgian Version of Jeremiah', *The Harvard Theological Review* 25, no. 3 (1932): 225–72. In Craster, *History of the Bodleian Library*, 310, the palimpsest Georg. c. I (P) is ascribed in error to the Sir Oliver Wardrop collection of Georgian MSS.

4 See Reif, *Hebrew Manuscripts*, SCR nos 955–6, 963, for example.

5 Abigail Green, 'Old Networks, New Connections: The Emergence of the Jewish International', in *Religious Internationals in the Modern World: Globalization and Faith Communities since 1750*, ed. Abigail Green and Vincent Viaene (UK: Palgrave Macmillan, 2012), 61.

6 Oded Shay, 'Collectors and Collections in Palestine at the Conclusion of the Ottoman Era', *Le Muséon* 122, nos. 3–4 (2009): 19–23.

7 Cyrus Adler and I. M. Casanowicz, *Biblical Antiquities: A Description of the Exhibit at the Cotton States International Exposition* (Atlanta, Washington: Government Printing Office, 1895).

8 Adler, *Selected Letters*, Volume 1, 69.

9 Adler, *Selected Letters*, Volume 1, 55. See also William M. Brinner, *Sutro Library Hebraica: A Handlist* (California State Library, 1966).

10 Jewish Theological Seminary, Solomon Schechter Collection Jewish Theological Seminary, Solomon Schechter Collection, Box 1/11 – Correspondence: Adler, Cyrus, letter from Sutro, 11 November 1890.

11 BLR.d.1084: Rev. William MacGregor to Count Riamo d'Hulst (dated 23 November 1894) quoted in a letter sent by Count Riamo d'Hulst, 24 December 1914.

12 Drower, *Flinders Petrie*, 85.

13 See Jefferson, 'A Genizah Secret', 128. Details of d'Hulst's last days at the Fund can be found in the Egypt Exploration Society, Lucy Gura Archives, EES Box III, K and in the letters between d'Hulst and Naville in the Bibliothèque de Genève, Ms. fr. 2542.

14 See the online study: David Kaufmann and his Collection: http://kaufmann.mtak .hu/en/study01.htm, and David Kaufmann, 'Or ha-Ganuz, Ginzei ha-Genizah asher hayitah be-Mitzrayim ha-Atiqah', *Hashiloah* II (1897): 389.

15 *Jewish Chronicle*, 14 July 1899, 17.

16 Thulin, '*Wissenschaft* and Correspondence', 122–3.

17 *The Menorah*, XIII, no. 4 (October 1892), 305–6.

18 *The Menorah*, XV, no. 2 (August 1893), 65–73. [68, 70]

19 Asher Weill, *B'nai B'rith and Israel: The Unbroken Covenant* (Jerusalem: B'nai Brith World Center, 1998), 9–10.

20 Avinoam Yellin, 'Genizah Fragments in the Jewish National Library', *The Journal of the Palestine Oriental Society* III (1923): 200–2.

21 Hermann Adler, 'The Chief Rabbis of England', *Papers Read at the Anglo-Jewish Historical Exhibition, Royal Albert Hall, London, 1887* (London: Office of the Jewish Chronicle, 1888), 276.

22 David Kaufmann, 'The Prayer-Book According to the Ritual of England before 1290', *The Jewish Quarterly Review* 4, no. 1 (October 1891): 20–63.

23 David Kaufmann, 'The Etz Chayimm of Jacob B. Jehudah of London, and the History of His Manuscript', *The Jewish Quarterly Review* 5, no. 3 (April 1893): 353–74.

24 Adolf Neubauer, 'Miscellanea Liturgica: The Etz Chayim', *The Jewish Quarterly Review* 6, no. 2 (January 1894): 348–54. Neubauer was the first person to produce a scholarly edition of a genizah fragment in that journal: see Eve Krakowski, '"Elhanan, Son of Shemariah": The Old Series and the Cairo Geniza', *Jewish Quarterly Review* 110, no. 4 (2020): 593–8.

Chapter 10

1 Jefferson, 'Cairo Genizah Unearthed', 179.

2 Sheehan, 'Archaeological Survey', 71.

3 H. Legrand, Dr Burlazzi and A. J. Gauthier, 'Origin of Cholera in Egypt in 1895', *Public Health Reports (1896–1970)* 11, no. 3 (17 January 1896): 55.

4 The photograph is published in Peter Sheehan, 'The Roman Fortifications', in *Fortifications and the Synagogue: The Fortress of Babylon and the Ben Ezra Synagogue, Cairo*, ed. Phyllis Lambert (Montreal: Canadian Center for Architecture, 1994), 63.

5 Sayce, *Reminiscences*, 213, 285–6.

6 The letters between Sayce, d'Hulst, Nicholson and Neubauer are all preserved in one volume in the Bodleian Library Records: BLR d.1084. Some of the original correspondence is only preserved in excerpts quoted by d'Hulst and his wife in letters sent to the Bodleian in the twentieth century. Those later letters are also part of this archive.

7 *Report on the Epidemic of Cholera in Egypt during the Years 1895 & 1896*, Ministry of Interior. Sanitary Department (Cairo: National Printing Office, 1897).

8 Shehab Ismail, *Engineering Metropolis: Contagion, Capital, and the Making of British Colonial Cairo, 1882–1922*. Thesis (Columbia University, 2017), 66.

9 See Jefferson, 'Cairo Genizah Unearthed', 179–80. The author mistakenly assumed that all four boxes were shipped based on later testimony by the Count d'Hulst that in 1895 he had procured 'a number of very large boxes'. But there is no evidence that four arrived at the Bodleian. Only one payment to Sayce is recorded that year. A second box may have arrived in June 1896 since a payment to Sayce is recorded on the 19th of that month.

10 See the list of restrictions in the appendices to *Report on the epidemic of cholera in Egypt*.

11 Elkan Nathan Adler, *About Hebrew Manuscripts* (Oxford: Henry Frowde, 1905), 109.

12 *The Jewish Chronicle*, 11 October 1895, 8.

13 Tawil and Schneider, *Crown of Aleppo*, 120.

14 For more on Behar, see Joseph M. Papo, 'The Sephardim in North America in the Twentieth Century', *American Jewish Archives* 44, no. 1 (1992): 267–308, and for his sisters, see Amalia Skarlatou Levi, *Evanescent Happiness: Ottoman Jews Encounter Modernity: The Case of Lea Mitrani and Joseph Niego (1863–1923)* (Istanbul: Libra Kitapçılık ve Yayıncılık, 2015).

15 For the history of the National Library, see Dov Bernhard Schidorsky, *The Origins of the Jewish National and University Library Against the Background of the Modern Jewish National* Movement (University of California, Berkeley, 1977) (PhD Thesis) and Zvi Baras, *A Century of Books: The Jewish National and University Library 1892– 1992 Centennial Anniversary Exhibition* (Jerusalem: Jewish National and University Library, 1992) [Hebrew].

16 Adler, *Jews in Many Lands*, 31.

17 *The Jewish Chronicle*, 7 February 1896, 16.

18 David Kaufmann, 'Dedicatory Poem to Jehudah ha-Nagid', *Jewish Quarterly Review* 9, no. 2 (January 1897): 360–1.

19 Adolf Neubauer, 'Egyptian Fragments. מגלות', Scrolls Analagous to that of Purim, with an Appendix on the First 'נגידים, *The Jewish Quarterly Review* 8, no. 4 (July 1896): 541–61.

20 A. E. Cowley, 'Some Remarks on Samaritan Literature and Religion', *The Jewish Quarterly Review* 8, no. 4 (July 1896): 575.

21 *The Jewish Chronicle*, 6 March 1896, 18.

22 Moses Gaster, 'The Story of My Library', 16–22.

23 E. N. Adler, 'MS. of Haftaras of the Triennial Cycle', *The Jewish Quarterly Review* 8, no. 3 (April 1896): 528–9.

24 Det KGL. Bibliotek, Denmark: Judaica Collection: The David Simonsen Manuscript, Cod. Sim. Jud.-Arab 6.

25 Sayce's reaction was discovered by Stefan Reif and described in 'A Fresh Look at Adolf Neubauer'. (unpublished).

26 Agnes Smith Lewis, *In the Shadow of Sinai: A Story of Travel and Research from 1895 to 1897* (Cambridge: Macmillan & Bowes, 1898), 143–6.

27 Jewish Theological Seminary, New York, Solomon Schechter Collection, Mathilde Schechter Papers – Writings: Mrs Schechter's Memoirs: Discovery of Jesus Ben Sira.

28 The quote is from Schechter's note to the sisters (preserved with CUL MS Or.1102). The comment to his wife is quoted in JTS MSP – Writings, Discovery of Jesus Ben Sira.

29 Anders Gerdmar, *Roots of Theological Anti-Semitism: German Biblical Interpretation and the Jews, from Herder and Semler to Kittel and Bultmann*. Studies in Jewish History and Culture 20 (Leiden: Brill, 2009), 77–95.

30 Solomon Schechter, 'The Quotations from Ecclesiaticus in Rabbinic Literature', *The Jewish Quarterly Review* 3, no. 4 (July 1891): 682–706.

31 D. S. Margoliouth, *An Essay on the Place of Ecclesiasticus in Semitic Literature* (Oxford: Clarendon Press, 1890), 21–2.

32 *The Athenaeum*, 3577, 16 May 1896, 652.

33 *The Athenaeum*, 3583, 27 June 1896, 846.
34 A. E. Cowley and A. Neubauer (eds.), *The Original Hebrew of a Portion of Ecclesiasticus (XXXIX. 15 to XLIX. 11) Together with the Early Versions and an English Translation* (Oxford: Clarendon Press, 1897), xii.
35 Lewis, *In the Shadow of Sinai*, 176.
36 Bodleian Library Records, d. 14, 9 May 1896, Minutes compiled by the Reverend Dr Macgrath, V. C.
37 BLR.d.1084: Dr Adolf Neubauer to Count Riamo d'Hulst (dated 29 December 1897), quoted in a letter sent by Laura M. A. d'Hulst, 22 August 1932.
38 Solomon Schechter, 'The Lewis-Gibson Hebrew Collection', *The Jewish Quarterly Review* 9, no. 1 (October 1896): 115.
39 Mathilde Schechter Papers – Writings: Mrs Schechter's Memoirs: Discovery of Jesus Ben Sira.
40 For more on Charles Taylor, his life, work and relationship with Schechter, see Stefan Reif (ed.), *Charles Taylor and the Genizah Collection: A Centenary Seminar and Exhibition, St. John's College, Cambridge 2 November 2008: Papers Delivered and Items Exhibited* (Cambridge: St. John's College, 2009).
41 BLR d.1084: Archibald Henry Sayce to Count Riamo d'Hulst (dated 26 October 1896), quoted in a letter sent by d'Hulst to the Bodleian on 20 May 1915.
42 E. N. Adler, 'An Eleventh Century Introduction', 673.
43 Jewish Theological Seminary, Solomon Schechter Collection, Box 1/15 – correspondence: Adler, Elkan N. The date is smudged and it is not clear whether Schechter has written the Roman numeral X or XI for the month.
44 'Ecclesiasticus', *The Jewish Chronicle* (11 March 1904): 29.
45 BLR d.1084: Archibald Henry Sayce to Count Riamo d'Hulst (dated 28 November 1896), quoted in a letter sent by d'Hulst to the Bodleian on 20 May 1915.
46 Jewish Theological Seminary, Solomon Schechter Collection, Box 1/15 – correspondence: Adler, Elkan N., dated 14 December 1896.
47 'Ecclesiasticus', 29.

Chapter 11

1 All of the letters between Solomon and Mathilde Schechter quoted in this chapter can be found in the Jewish Theological Seminary Solomon Schechter Collection: Mathilde Schechter Correspondence: Solomon Schechter's Letters to Marthilde, Boxes 26/2–3 (1894–1906). For additional insights into Schechter's discovery of Ben Sira and his trip to Cairo, see A. Hoffman and Peter Cole, *Sacred Trash: The Lost and Found World of the Cairo Geniza* (New York: Nextbook, Schocken, 2011). Hoffman and Cole also provide a wealth of material on the reception of the manuscripts during Schechter's day and by the next generation of genizah scholars. See the publications of Stefan C. Reif for in-depth analyses of Schechter's relationships with his Cambridge colleagues and other scholars.
2 Jewish Theological Seminary, Solomon Schechter Collection, Box 2/7 – Correspondence: Ben Simon, Raphael Aaron, letter dated 20 November 1896.
3 Maurice Fargeon, *Les Juifs en Egypte* (Le Caire: Paul Barbey, 1938), 201 and Zvi Zohar, 'Ben-Shim'on, Raphael Aaron', in *Encyclopedia of Jews in the Islamic World*, Executive Editor Norman A. Stillman. [Consulted online].

4 Yigal Nizri, "'The Missing Corpus" A Rabbinical Perspective on the Question of
   the Case of Rabbi Raphael Aharon Ben-Shim'on', *Jewish Thought in Arab Societies,
   1880–1960. An International Workshop, 26–28 May 2014.* [PDF online].

5 Zvi Zohar, 'Ben-Shim'on, Mas'ūd Ḥayy', in *Encyclopedia of Jews in the Islamic World*,
   Executive Editor Norman A. Stillman. [Consulted online].

6 'The Guardian of Egypt: Ribbi Refael Aharon ben Shimon זצ"ל', *The Sephardic Halacha
   Center.* https://theshc.org/the-guardian-of-egypt-ribbi-refael-aharon-ben-shimon-זצל/.

7 The Cattauis were large in number, but their names followed clear patterns: the
   children all taking their father's name as a middle name; thus, Hector, a son of Moïse
   de Cattaui, was known as Hector Moïse Cattaui; whereas Joseph, son of Aslan Bey
   Ya'qub Cattaui, was known as Joseph Aslan Cattaui. See the genealogical tree on: ,
   compiled by Egyptian historian Samir Raafat.

8 See the section on 'Joseph Aslan Cattaui Pacha', in Moshe Behar and Zvi Ben-Dor
   Benite (eds), *Modern Middle Eastern Jewish Thought: Writings on Identity, Politics, and
   Culture, 1893–1958* (Brandeis University Press, 2013): 80–5.

9 Andrew Humphreys, *Grand Hotels of Egypt in the Golden Age of Travel*, 161.

10 Schechter mixed languages in his writing; therefore extensive quotes given here are
   rendered into plain English. http://bassatine.net/cattaui.php

11 Meir Ben-Horin, 'Solomon Schechter to Judge Mayer Sulzberger: Part I. Letters from
   the Pre-Seminary Period (1895–1901)', *Jewish Social Studies* 25, no. 4 (October 1963):
   259–60.

12 See 'Solomon Schechter: A Postcard from Cairo', *Yeshiva University Library Blog*,
   30 September 2013: https://blogs.yu.edu/library/2013/09/30/solomon-schechter-a
   -postcard-from-cairo/. Guttmann was probably Jacob Guttmann (1845–1919), the
   historian of Jewish philosophy.

13 Lajos Blau, 'Fosztat városa, Maimonides müködésének színhelye', *Magyar Zsidó
   Szemle* (January–April, 1938): 57.

14 J. M. C. Toynbee, H. D. A. Major, revised by David Gill. 'Gardner, Ernest Arthur
   (1862–1939), classical scholar and archaeologist'. *Oxford Dictionary of National
   Biography* (Oxford: Oxford University Press, 2004) [online].

15 Ben-Horin, 'Solomon Schechter to Judge Mayer Sulzberger', 260.

16 Rebecca J. W. Jefferson, 'Dangerous Liaisons in Cairo: Reginald Q. Henriques and the
   Taylor-Schechter Genizah Manuscript Collection', *Judaica Librarianship* 20 (2017):
   25–6, 21–51.

17 Joel Beinin, 'The Karaites in Modern Egypt', in *Karaite Judaism: A Guide to Its History
   and Literary Sources*, ed. Meira Polliack (Leiden and Boston: Brill, 2003), 419.

18 See an edition of the letter in M. Schmierer-Lee, 'Add.6463(e)3416: Breathing the 'dust
   of centuries', *Fragment of the Month*, October 2014. https://doi.org/10.17863/CAM
   .7800. The letter to Jenkinson is dated 12 January 1897.

19 Solomon Schechter, 'A Hunt in the Genizah', *The Friend: A Religious and Literary
   Journal* 71, no. 6 (28 August, 1897): 45–7, 46. This is a reproduction of the article
   in *The Sunday-School Times*, and 'A Hoard of Hebrew Manuscripts', *The Times*
   (London), 3 August, 1897. 13.

20 Paul Whelan, 'The Marquis' Excavations: A Tale of Two Diaries', in *Talking Along the
   Nile: Ippolito Rosellini, Travellers and Scholars of the 19th Century in Egypt, Proceedings
   of the International Conference held on the occasion of the presentation of Progetto
   Rosellini. Pisa, June 14–16, 2012*, ed. Marilina Betrò and Gianluca Miniaci (Pisa
   University Press, 2013), 238.

21 Sayce, *Reminiscences*, 294, and Tom Hardwick, 'The Obsidian King's Origins. Further Light on the Purchasers and Prices at the MacGregor sale, 1922', *Discussions in Egyptology* 65 (2012): 9–10, and Di Santi, 'From Egypt to Copenhagen', 34.

22 The account of the Nicoles's stay in Egypt and the excerpts quoted (and translated) in this chapter are derived from Roth-Lochner, Barbara, 'Un voyage en Egypte (1896–1897), extrait des Souvenirs d'Albert Nicole', in *Voyages en Égypte de l'Antiquité au début du 20e s*, ed. J. L. Chappaz et C. Ritschard (Genève: Genève Musée d'art et d'histoire, 2003), 244–58.

23 Jules Nicole, *Le Laboureur de Ménandre: fragments inédits sur papyrus d'Égypte* (Bale et Genève: Georg & Co., Libraries-Éditeurs, 1898).

24 Bernard P. Grenfell, 'Oxyrhynchus and its Papyri', *Egypt Exploration Fund. Archaeological Report, 1896–1897*, ed. F. Ll. Griffith (London: Egypt Exploration Fund, 1897), 6–7.

25 Nongbri, *God's Library*, 222: 'despite their stated concern for context and provenance . . . interspersed with the pieces published in *The Oxyrhynchus Papyri* series are pieces Grenfell purchased from dealers, and not all of them are clearly identified as such'.

26 Barbara Roth-Lochner, 'Fragments of the Cairo Genizah at the Bibliothèque de Genève', in *The Cairo Geniza Collection in Geneva – Catalogue and Studies*, ed. David Rozenthal (Jerusalem: The Hebrew University Magnes Press, 2010), 42–5. [Hebrew].

27 Malcolm Choat, 'Lord Crawford's Search for Papyri: on the Origin of the Rylands Papyrus Collection', in *Actes du 26e Congres International de Papyrologies, Geneve 16–21 aout 2010*, ed. P. Schubert (Geneva: Droz, 2012), 143.

28 Schmierer-Lee, 'Add.6463(e)3416: Breathing the "dust of centuries"'.

29 The calculations are taken from the website, MeasuringWorth.com.

30 Jewish Theological Seminary, Solomon Schechter Collection, Box 27/33: Mathilde Schechter Correspondence – Lewis, Agnes, Cairo, 21 January 1897.

31 Jefferson, 'Cairo Genizah Unearthed', 190–2.

32 Adler, 'The Hebrew Treasures of England', 16.

33 See Jefferson, 'Cairo Genizah Unearthed' for the story of Adler's purchases from Oxford. For the cataloguing project on the JTS ENA collection and its problems, see Jay Rovner, 'The Computerized Genizah Cataloguing Project of the Jewish Theological Seminary of America: Its History, Current Status, and Future Prospects, with some General Considerations of Bibliographic Control of Genizah Fragments', *Shofar* 8, no. 4 (1990): 37–58.

34 The twins' encounter with the synagogue genizah and their experiences finding fragments with the dealers is recounted in chapter eight of Lewis, *In the Shadow of Sinai*. This excerpt and the two below it in this section are derived from pages 184–8.

35 See 'Leather and Leather Products', in *Handbook of Material Biodegradation, Biodeterioration, and Biostablization*, ed. Michalina Falkiewicz-Dulik, Katarzyna Janda and George Wypych, 2nd ed. (Toronto: ChemTec Publishing, 2015), 150.

36 Rebecca J. W. Jefferson, 'Deconstructing "the Cairo Genizah": A Fresh Look at Genizah Manuscript Discoveries in Cairo before 1897', *The Jewish Quarterly Review* 108, no. 4 (Fall 2018): 445–6.

37 Jefferson, 'Dangerous Liaisons in Cairo', 26–8.

Chapter 12

1 For the fascinating history of Dammuh and its connection to the Ezra Synagogue, see Hurvitz, *Catalogue of the Cairo Geniza Fragments*, 139–47.

2 For a translation of the ordinance, see Goitein, *A Mediterranean Society* V, 21–2.

3 The fourteenth-century scroll is MS. Magll. III 43, Biblioteca Nazionale Centrale, Florence and the sixteenth-century MS is MS Add. 27125, British Library, London. For a full description of these manuscripts, together with images, and an analysis of the architecture of Dammuh, see Rachel Sarfati, 'Between Heaven and Earth: Places of Worship in Egypt and Syria through the Mirror of Visual Evidence', *Arts 2020* 9, no. 3 (2020): 90–113. The Florence scroll is described in Rachel Sarfati, 'Real and Fictive Travels to the Holy Land as Painted in the Florence Scroll', in *Maps and Travel in the Middle Ages and the Early Modern Period: Knowledge, Imagination, and Visual Culture*, ed. Ingrid Baumgärtner et al. (Berlin and Boston: De Gruyter, 2019), 232–51.

4 Landau, *Jews in Nineteenth-Century Egypt*, 44–5.

5 Hanan Hassan Hammad, *Mechanizing People, Localizing Modernity. Industrialization and Social Tranformation in Modern Egypt: al-Mahalla al-Kubra, 1910–1958* (University of Texas at Austin, 2009), 17–28. [PhD Dissertation].

6 Ben-Horin, 'Solomon Schechter to Judge Mayer Sulzberger', 260–1.

7 Norman Bentwich, *Solomon Schechter: A Biography* (Cambridge: University Press, 1938), 131–3.

8 *The Jewish Chronicle*, 6 May 1898, 13, and *The Menorah: A Monthly Magazine for the Jewish Home* XXXII (January–June, 1902): 224–6.

9 *The Jewish Chronicle*, 9 April 1897, 22.

10 Det KGL Bibliotek, Denmark, David Simonsen Archives – Correspondents: Samuel Raffalovich, Jerusalem, 9 August 1899.

11 Neubauer and Cowley (eds.). *Catalogue of the Hebrew Manuscripts*, see MS Heb. f. 54.

12 *Ha-Zofeh*, 20 October 1961, 5, and Ben-Zvi, 'Whose Geniza?', 69.

13 Jefferson, 'Dangerous Liaisons in Cairo', 35.

14 Cambridge University Library MS. Add. 7420 (1897).

15 Yoram Meital, *Jewish Sites in Egypt* (Jerusalem: Ben Zvi Institute, 1995), 56–60. [Hebrew]. Gottheil in "An Eleventh Century Document", 518–22, listed synagogues still extant.

16 W. M. Flinders Petrie, *Deshasheh 1897*. Fifteenth Memoir of the Egypt Exploration Fund, London, 1898, 1–3.

17 Rebecca J. W. Jefferson, 'T-S 6H9 – 21, the papyrus codex rebound'. *Fragment of the Month*, July 2009. https://doi.org/10.17863/CAM.48228.

18 The history of these panels, and the ark that was recreated from them at JTS, was recently researched by David Selis for a paper entitled: '"The Oldest Piece of Ecclesiastical Furniture in this Country": On Solomon Schechter, His Torah Ark, and the Cairo Genizah' (forthcoming).

Chapter 13

1 David Kaufmann, 'Or ha-Ganuz, Ginzei ha-Genizah asher hayitah be-Mitzrayim ha-Atiqah', *Hashiloah* II (1897): 385–93, 481–90. [Hebrew].

2 Adler, 'An Eleventh Century Introduction', 671–3.

3 Ben-Horin, 'Solomon Schechter to Judge Mayer Sulzberger', 262.

4 Solomon Schechter, 'A Hoard of Hebrew MSS', *The Times*, 3 August 1897.
5 *The Churchman*, 18 September 1897, 323.
6 *The Times*, 4 August 1897, 6.
7 Hoffman and Cole, *Sacred Trash*, 88. Adina Hoffman was the first person to suggest Cowley after discovering the use of this phrase as a toast at Magdalene College.
8 *The Times*, 7 August 1897, 11.
9 Jewish Theological Seminary, Solomon Schechter Collection, Box 2/7 – Correspondence: Adler, Elkan N., letter dated 5 August 1897.
10 Letters sent from Sayce on 21 June 1897 and from Neubauer on 23 June 1897 were quoted in a letter sent by d'Hulst to the Bodleian on 20 May 1915 (BLR d.1084).
11 Gaster, 'The Story of My Library', 21.
12 The story of the fire was uncovered by Renate Smithuis as part of her investigations into the history of the Moses Gaster collections in the John Rylands Library, see Renate Smithuis, 'Short Introduction to the Genizah Collection in the John Rylands Library', in *From Cairo to Manchester: Studies in the Rylands Genizah Fragments*, ed. Renate Smithuis and Philip S. Alexander (Journal of Semitic Studies; Supplement 31) (Oxford: Oxford University Press, 2013), 1–32.
13 See Benzion Halper, *Descriptive Catalogue of Genizah Fragments in Philadelphia* (Philadelphia: The Dropsie College for Hebrew and Cognate Learning, 1924) where each fragment is described and noted with its supplier.
14 *The Jewish World*, 22 October 1897, 52.
15 See Jenkinson's diary in Cambridge University Library MS Add.7420 (1897).
16 All of the letters between Solomon Schechter, Elkan Nathan Adler and Samuel Raffalovich quoted in this chapter can be found in the Jewish Theological Seminary, Solomon Schechter Collection, Box 1/15 – correspondence: Adler, Elkan N.
17 Stefan C. Reif, 'Some First Editions of Genizah Manuscripts of Ben Sira', in *Discovering, Deciphering and Dissenting: Ben Sira Manuscripts after 120 Years*, edited by James K. Aitken, Renate Egger-Wenzel and Stefan C. Reif (Berlin: De Gruyter, 2019), 50–1.
18 Translated text from Israël Lévi, 'Fragments de deux nouveaux manuscrits hébreux de l'Ecclésiastique', *Revue des Études Juives* 40, no. 79 (Janvier–Mars, 1900): 1.
19 *The Jewish Chronicle*, 11 March 1904, 29.
20 See *The Jewish Chronicle*, 17 May 1901, 30, and Elkan N. Adler, *Catalogue of Hebrew Manuscripts in the Collection of Elkan Nathan Adler* (Cambridge: The University Press, 1921), v.
21 BLR.d.1084: Dr Adolf Neubauer to Count Riamo d'Hulst (dated 29 December 1897), quoted in a letter sent by d'Hulst to the Bodleian, 20 May 1915.
22 BLR.d.1084: Count Riamo d'Hulst to Dr Adolf Neubauer, Cairo, 6 January 1898. BLR d.1084.
23 BLR.d.1084: Dr Adolf Neubauer to Count Riamo d'Hulst (dated 18 January 1898), quoted in a letter sent by d'Hulst to the Bodleian, 20 May 1915.
24 BLR.d.1084: Count Riamo d'Hulst to Dr Adolf Neubauer, Cairo, 17 February 1898.
25 BLR.d.1084: E. W. B. Nicholson to Count Riamo d'Hulst (dated 4 March 1898), quoted in a letter sent by d'Hulst to the Bodleian, 20 May 1915.
26 Hilary Richardson, 'Macalister, Robert Alexander Stewart', in *Dictionary of Irish Biography*, ed. James McGuire and James Quinn (Cambridge: Cambridge University Press, 2009), https://www.dib.ie/biography/macalister-robert-alexander-stewart-a5093, accessed 15 Sept. 2021. For the relationship between Schechter and Donald MacAlister, see Reif, *A Jewish Archive*, 78.

27   Cambridge University Library MS. Add.6463.3811: Charles Taylor to Francis Jenkinson, Cambridge, 5 March 1898.

28   S. D. Goitein, 'Geniza Papers of a Documentary Character in the Gaster Collection of the British Museum', *The Jewish Quarterly Review* 51, no. 1 (1960): 35, 46.

29   Phyllis Abrahams, 'The Letters of Israel Abrahams from Egypt and Palestine in 1898', *Transactions & Miscellanies (Jewish Historical Society of England)* 24 (1970–3): 8–9.

30   BLR.d.1084: Count Riamo d'Hulst to E. W. B. Nicholson, Cairo, 17 March 1898.

31   Israel Abrahams, *The Book of Delight and Other Papers* (Philadelphia: The Jewish Publication Society of America, 1912), 82.

32   See Reif, *Hebrew Manuscripts at Cambridge University Library*, for a list of Abraham's manuscripts.

33   Cambridge University Library MS. Add.6463.3825: Samuel Raffalovitch to Solomon Schechter, 24 March 1898.

34   BLR.d.1084: Count Riamo d'Hulst to E. W. B. Nicholson, Cairo, 31 March 1898.

35   BLR.d.1084: Archibald Henry Sayce to E. W. B. Nicholson, Cairo, 31 March 1898.

36   Jefferson, 'Dangerous Liaisons', 35.

37   BLR.d.1084: Count Riamo d'Hulst to Adolf Neubauer, Cairo, 8 April 1898.

38   BLR.d.1084: Count Riamo d'Hulst to E. W. B. Nicholson, Cairo, 21 April 1898.

39   BLR.d.1084: Archibald Henry Sayce to E. W. B. Nicholson, Dahabia Istar, Cairo, 22 April 1898.

40   Mohammed Saied Moghawery, 'The Historical and Cultural Significance of the Arabic Papyri Kept in the National Library'. [Accessed online at: https://www.austriaca.at /0xc1aa5576%200x001499e9.pdf], 449–53.

41   BLR.d.1084: E. W. B. Nicholson to Count Riamo d'Hulst (dated 4 May 1898), quoted in a letter sent by d'Hulst to the Bodleian, 20 May 1915.

42   BLR.d.1084: Count Riamo d'Hulst to E. W. B. Nicholson, Cairo, 12 May 1898.

Chapter 14

1   Reif, 'Jenkinson and Schechter at Cambridge', 297–300. He sent Jenkinson a letter in 1901 in which he thanked him for his kind goodwill and patience during that time.

2   Cambridge University Library MS. CUL Add.7421 (1898): Jenkinson's diary, 24 July 1898).

3   See the letters in the Cambridge University Library MSS. CUL. Add. 6463 (e). series.

4   Diana Rowland Smith, 'Genizah Collections in the British Library', in Hebrew Studies: Papers presented at a colloquium on resources for Hebraica in Europe held at the School of Oriental and African Studies, University of London, 11–13 September 1989 (British Library Occasional Papers; 13), ed. Diana Rowland Smith and Peter Shmuel Salinger (UK: British Library, 1991), 21.

5   *The Jewish Chronicle*, 16 September 1898, 18.

6   Cambridge University Library: Annual Report of the Library Syndicate, 1897, 8.

7   Lewis, *In the Shadow of Sinai*, 188.

8   The storage and transfer of the leftover materials is examined in Jefferson, 'The Historical Significance'.

9   The letters are discussed in Jefferson, 'Dangerous Liaisons', 37–8.

10   Harold N. Fowler, 'Archaeological News', *American Journal of Archaeology* 3 (September–December 1899): 241–77.

11 John R. Abercrombie, *A History of the Acquisition of Papyri and Related Written Material in the University (of Pennsylvania (Museum))*. http://ccat.sas.upenn.edu/rak/ppenn/paphist.htm.

12 Adler, *Jews in Many Lands*, 163–4.

13 Adler, *About Hebrew Manuscripts*, 112.

14 Bodleian Library Records (BLR) c.37: Receipts Ledger, 1890–1916: Sale of Waste.

15 For a breakdown of the Oxford collections by seller/donor, see Jefferson, 'Data Analysis of the Genizah Fragments'.

16 Eugen Mittwoch, 'Ein Geniza-Fragment', *Zeitschrift der Deutschen Morgnelandischen Gesellschaft* 57 (1903): 61–6. On the al-Amshati family, see also Mordechai Friedman, 'The Ibn al-Amshati Family-Maimonides' In-Laws', *Zion* 69, no. 3 (2004): 271–97. [Hebrew].

17 M. H. Gottstein, 'Hebrew fragments in the Mingana Collection', *Journal of Jewish Studies* V (1956): 172–6.

18 Paul B. Fenton, 'A Re-Discovered Description of Maimonides by a Contemporary', in *Maimonidean Studies*, Volume 5, edited by Arthur Hyman, (New York: Yeshiva University Press, 2008), 267–91.

19 See the lists in Jefferson, 'The Historical Significance', 14.

20 Jefferson, 'Dangerous Liaisons', 43–4.

21 Neubauer and Cowley, *Catalogue of the Hebrew Manuscripts*, addendum.

22 Jefferson, 'A Genizah Secret', 134–5.

Chapter 15

1 *The Jewish Chronicle*, 10 November 1899, 26.

2 David Werner Amram, 'Two Legal Documents of the Eleventh Century', *The Green Bag: An Entertaining Magazine for Lawyers* XIII (1901): 115–20.

3 Jewish Theological Seminary, Elkan Nathan Adler Archive – Correspondents: Samuel Raffalovich, 6 June 1899 and Det KGL Bibliotek, Denmark, David Simonsen Archives – Correspondents: Samuel Raffalovich, Jerusalem, 9 August 1899. Raffalovich informed Simonsen of Getzil Sofer's demise.

4 See the Amram entries in Halper, *Descriptive Catalogue of Genizah Fragments in Philadelphia*.

5 Richard Gottheil, 'In Ancient Footsteps: Florence', *New Era Illustrated Magazine* VI, no. 3 (February 1905): 272–80; 'Rome', VI, no. 4 (March–April 1905): 364–74; 'Alexandria', VI, no. 6 (June 1905): 622–31; 'Cairo' VII, no. 1 (July 1905): 40–7.

6 Gottheil, 'Some Hebrew Manuscripts in Cairo', 610–11.

7 For the rediscovery of these treasures, see Helman, 'The Karaite Jews of Cairo', 4–9, and Yoram Meital, 'A Thousand-Year-Old Biblical Manuscript Rediscovered in Cairo: The Future of the Egyptian Jewish Past', *The Jewish Quarterly Review* 110, no. 1 (Winter 2020): 194–219.

8 *The Jewish Chronicle*, 5 May 1911, 18, 28.

9 Jason Kalman, 'A Cairo Genizah Fragment of Genesis Rabbah from the Collection of McGill University', in *To Fix Torah in their Hearts: Essays on Biblical Interpretation and Jewish Studies in Honor of B. Barry Levy*, ed. Jaqueline S. Du Toit, Jason Kalman, Hartley Lachter and Vanessa R. Sasson (Cincinnati: Hebrew Union College Press, 2018), 120–5.

10 BLR d.1083: Joseph Offord to Arthur Ernest Cowley, 8 January 1906.
11 BLR.c.37: Receipts Ledger, 1890–1916: Sale of Waste.
12 Arthur Ernest Cowley, *Catalogue of Additional Genizah Fragments*, Oxford ca. 1929 [unpublished typescript].
13 Gottheil and Worrell (eds.), *Fragments from the Cairo Genizah*, xiv.
14 Bernard Chapira, 'Contribution à l'étude du Divan de Todros ben Iehouda Halévi Aboulafia', *Revue des études Juives* 106 (1941): 2–3.
15 Jewish Theological Seminary, Solomon Schechter Collection, Box 2/52 – Correspondence: Consistoire du Caire, Cairo, 2 March, 1910.
16 *The Jewish Chronicle*, 18 April 1912, 28.
17 Rebecca J. W. Jefferson and Ngaio Vince-Dewerse, 'When Curator and Conservator Meet: Some Issues Arising from the Preservation and Conservation of the Jacques Mosseri Genizah Collection at Cambridge University Library', *Journal of the Society of Archivists* 29, no. 1 (2008): 41–56, and I. Adler, *Catalogue of the Mosseri Collection* (Jerusalem: The Jewish National and University Library, 1990).
18 See Meital, 'A Thousand-Year-Old Biblical Manuscript', 217–19, and https://www.arce.org/project/egypts-synagogues-past-present and https://eg.usembassy.gov/bassatine-cemetery/.
19 Jefferson, 'Cairo Genizah Unearthed', 196.
20 For the material uncovered in the 1980s, see Mark R. Cohen, 'Geniza for Islamicists, Islamic Geniza, and the "New Cairo Geniza"', *Harvard Middle Eastern and Islamic Review* 7 (2006): 129–45. An example of a fragment that may have entered directly into the nineteenth-century markets could be the one discussed by Nick Posegay, 'Following the Links in T-S NS 192.11: A Qur'anic Exercise from a Cairene Public School', Fragment of the Month, January 2020. https://doi.org/10.17863/CAM.65165.

Epilogue

1 El Shamsy, *Rediscovering the Islamic Classics*, 10–19.
2 Donna Yates and Emiline Smith, 'Antiquities Trafficking and the Provenance Problem', in *Collecting and Provenance: A Multidisciplinary Approach*, ed. J. C. Milosch and N. Pearce (New York and London: Rowman & Littlefield, 2012), 385–6.

Bibliography

Archival sources

Bibliothèque de Genève, Ms. fr. 2542.
Bodleian Library Records: MS Bodl.c.59.
Bodleian Library Records: MS Bodl.c.37.
Bodleian Library Records: MS Bodl.d.1084.
Bodleian Library Records: MS Bodl.e.479.
British Foreign Office Archives: NA FO 141/671.
British Library Records: Charles Rieu.
Cambridge University Library Archives: Add.2592.959, Add.6463.1489, 2984, 3523, 3561,
    4817, 5106, 5112, 5309, 6937, Add. 4251.530, Add. 5359, Add. 6463 (e) 3825, Add.
    6463 (e) 3903, Add. 6463 (e) 3908, Add. 6463 (e) 4040, Add. 6463 (e) 4104, Add. 6463
    (e) 4067, Add. 6463 (e) 4079, Add. 6463 (e) 4111, Add. 6463 (e) 4120, Add. 6463 (e)
    4136, Add. 7413 (1890), Add. 7419 (1896), Add. 7420 (1897), Add. 7421 (1898), Add.
    7422 (1899), Add.8781, 272–73.
Cambridge University Library, Taylor-Schechter Genizah Research Unit Archives.
Cyrus Adler Papers, 1886–1942, University of Pennsylvania.
Det KGL Bibliotek, Denmark, David Simonsen Archives [accessed online].
Egypt Exploration Society, Lucy Gura Archives: EES Box III, k.
Jewish Theological Seminary, New York, Solomon Schechter Collection.
Jewish Theological Seminary, New York, Elkan Nathan Adler Collection.

Articles

Abrahams, Phyllis. 'The Letters of Israel Abrahams from Egypt and Palestine in 1898'.
    Transactions & Miscellanies (Jewish Historical Society of England) 24 (1970–1973): 1–23.
Adler, E. N. 'MS. of Haftaras of the Triennial Cycle'. *The Jewish Quarterly Review* 8, no. 3
    (April 1896): 528–529.
Adler, E. N. 'An Eleventh Century Introduction to the Hebrew Bible: Being a Fragment
    from the Sepher Ha-Ittim of Rabbi Judah ben Barzilai of Barcelona'. *The Jewish
    Quarterly Review* 9, no. 4 (1897): 669–716.
Adler, E. N. 'The Hebrew Treasures of England'. Presidential address delivered on 9 February
    1914, *The Jewish Historical Society of England: Transactions* 8–9 (1915–1917): 1–18.
Adler, Hermann. 'The Chief Rabbis of England'. *Papers Read at the Anglo-Jewish Historical
    Exhibition, Royal Albert Hall, London, 1887.* London: Office of the Jewish Chronicle,
    1888. 253–288.
Akhiezer, Golda. 'Between Samaritans and Karaites: Abraham Firkovich and His
    Perception of Samaritanism'. In *The Samaritans in Historical, Cultural, and Linguistic
    Perspectives*, edited by Jan Dušek, 235–244. Berlin, Boston: Walter de Gruyter, 2018.

Akhiezer, Golda. 'Rabbanite Manuscripts in Karaite Hands: Findings from the Crimean Genizot and Libraries'. *Journal of Jewish Studies* LXX, no. 2 (2019): 332–356.

Allony, N. 'Genizah and Hebrew Manuscripts in Cambridge Libraries'. *Areshet* 3 (1961): 395–425. [Hebrew].

Allony, N. 'Genizah Practices among the Jews'. *Sinai* LXXIX (1976): 193–201. [Hebrew].

Amram, David Werner. 'Two Legal Documents of the Eleventh Century'. *The Green Bag: An Entertaining Magazine for Lawyers* XIII (1901): 115–120.

Apple, Raymond. 'Rabbi Jacob Levi Saphir & His Voyage to Australia'. *Australian Jewish Historical Society* 6, no.4 (1968): 195–295.

Astafieva, Elena. 'How to Transfer "Holy Russia" into the Holy Land? Russian Policy in Palestine in the Late Imperial Period'. *Jerusalem Quarterly* 71 (Autumn, 2017): 8–11.

Baker, Zachary M. 'History of the Jewish Collections at the Vernadsky Library in Kiev'. *Shofar* 10, no. 4 (1992): 31–48.

Bakhoum, Soheir, and Marie-Christine Hellmann. 'Wilhelm Froehner, le commerce et les collections d'antiquités égyptiennes'. *Journal des Savants* 1 (1992): 155–186.

Bareket, Elinoar. 'Karaite Communities in the Middle East During the Tenth to Fifteenth Centuries'. In *Karaite Judaism: A Guide to its History and Literary Sources*, edited by Meira Polliack, 237–252. Leiden and Boston: Brill, 2003.

Bartal, Israel. 'Eastern European Haskalah and the Karaites: Christian Hebraism and Imperial Politics'. In *Eastern European Karaites in the Last Generations*, edited by D. Shapira and D. Lasker. 47–57, Jerusalem: Ben Zvi Institute, 2011. [Hebrew and English].

Bar-Ilan, Meir. 'The Genizah: Antonin's and Wertheimer's Collections,' *Alei Sefer* 23 (2013) 121–37.

Bauer, Adolph. 'Neue Funde griechischer Papyrusrollen in Aegypten'. *Zeitschrift für Ägyptische Sprache und Altertumskunde* 16 (1878): 108–110.

Beinin, Joel. 'The Karaites in Modern Egypt'. In *Karaite Judaism: A Guide to its History and Literary Sources*, edited by Meira Polliack, 415–430. Leiden and Boston: Brill, 2003.

Ben-Horin, Meir. 'Solomon Schechter to Judge Mayer Sulzberger: Part I. Letters from the Pre-Seminary Period (1895–1901)'. *Jewish Social Studies* 25, no. 4 (October 1963): 249–287.

Ben-Sasson, Menahem. 'Firkovich's Second Collection: Remarks on Historical and Halakhic Material'. *Jewish Studies* 31 (1991): 47–67. [Hebrew].

Ben-Sasson, Menahem, and Ze'ev Elkin. 'Abraham Firkovich and the Cairo Genizas in the Light of his Personal Archive'. *Pe'amim* 90 (2002): 51–95. [Hebrew].

Ben-Shammai, Haggai. 'The Scholarly Study of Karaism in the Nineteenth and Twentieth Centuries'. In *Karaite Judaism: A Guide to its History and Literary Sources*, edited by Meira Polliack, 9–24. Leiden and Boston: Brill, 2003.

Ben-Shammai, H. 'Is "The Cairo Genizah" a Proper Name or a Generic Noun? On the Relationship between the Genizot of the Ben Ezra and the Dar Simha Synagogues'. In *From a Sacred Source: Genizah Studies in Honour of Professor Stefan C. Reif*, edited by B. M. Outhwaite and S. Bhayro, 43–52. Leiden and Boston: Brill, 2010.

Ben Zvi, Sara Jo. 'Whose Geniza?' *Segula* 5 (June, 2011): 60–70.

Blake, Robert P. 'Khanmeti Palimpsest Fragments of the Old Georgian Version of Jeremiah'. *The Harvard Theological Review* 25, no. 3 (1932): 225–272.

Blau, Lajos. 'Fosztat városa, Maimonides müködésének színhelye'. *Magyar Zsidó Szemle* (January–April, 1938): 45–63.

Brock, Sebastian. 'Abbot Mushe and the Poll Tax'. *Newsletter of the Levantine Foundation* 2 (September 2007): 2.

Büchler, Adolf. 'The Reading of the Law and Prophets in a Triennial Cycle'. *The Jewish Quarterly Review* 5, no. 3 (April 1893): 420–468.

Capart, Jean. 'Nécrologie: Maurice Nahman'. *Chronique d'Égypte* 44 (1947): 300–301.

Cassuto, David. 'The Synagogues in Cairo'. In *The Jews in Ottoman Egypt (1517–1914)*, edited by Jacob M. Landau, 204–219. Jerusalem: Misgav Yerushalaim, 1988.

Chapira, Bernard. 'Contribution à l'étude du Divan de Todros ben Iehouda Halévi Aboulafia'. *Revue des études Juives* 106 (1941): 1–33.

Chester, Greville John. 'Notes on the Ancient Christian Churches of Musr El Ateekah, or Old Cairo, and its Neighbourhood'. *The Archaeological Journal* 29 (1872): 120–34.

Chester, Greville John. 'Notes on the Coptic Dayrs of the Wady Natrûn and on Dayr Antonios in the Eastern Desert'. *The Archaeological Journal* 30 (June 1873): 105–116.

Chester, Greville John. 'Donkey Rides Around Cairo'. In *Aunt Judy's Christmas Volume For 1879*, edited by H. K. F. Gatty, 157–163, 224–229, 270–275, 356–362, 416–421, 485–494. London: George Bell & Sons, 1879.

Chester, Greville John. 'Notes on Some Phoenician Gems'. *Palestine Exploration Fund: Quarterly Statement* (January 1885): 129–32.

Choat, Malcolm. 'Lord Crawford's Search for Papyri: on the Origin of the Rylands Papyrus Collection'. In *Actes du 26e Congres International de Papyrologies, Geneve 16-21 aout 2010*, edited by P. Schubert, 141–47. Geneva: Droz, 2012.

Clarke, Kent D. 'Paleography and Philanthropy: Charles Lang Freer and His Acquisition of the "Freer Biblical Manuscripts"'. In *The Freer Biblical Manuscripts: Fresh Studies of an American Treasure Trove*, edited by Larry W. Hurtado, 17–74. Leiden and Boston: Brill, 2006.

Coenen, Marc. 'The Funerary Papyri of the Bodleian Library at Oxford'. *The Journal of Egyptian Archaeology* 86 (2000): 81–98.

Cohen, Mark and Yedida Stillman. 'The Cairo Geniza and the Custom of Geniza among Oriental Jewry: An Historical and Ethnographic Survey'. *Pe'amim* 24 (1985): 3–35. [Hebrew].

Cowley, A. E. 'Some Remarks on Samaritan Literature and Religion'. *The Jewish Quarterly Review* 8, no. 4 (July 1896): 562–575.

Di Santi, Alessia. 'From Egypt to Copenhagen: The Provenance of the Portraits of Augustus, Livia and Tiberius at the Ny Carlsberg Glyptotek'. *Analecta Romana Instituti Danici* XLII (2017): 33–46.

Dospel Williams, Elizabeth. '"Into the Hands of a Well-Known Antiquary of Cairo": The Assiut Treasure and the Making of an Archaeological Hoard'. *West 86th: A Journal of Decorative Arts, Design History, and Material Culture* 21, no. 2 (Fall–Winter, 2014): 251–272.

Drower, Margaret S. 'Gaston Maspero and the Birth of the Egypt Exploration Fund'. *The Journal of Egyptian Archaeology* 68 (1982): 299–317.

Edwards, A. 'Bubastis: An Historical Sketch'. *The Century Magazine* 39, no. 3 (1890): 323–348.

Elkin, Zeev and Menahem Ben-Sasson. 'Abraham Firkovich and the Cairo Genizas in the Light of his Personal Archive'. *Pe'amim* 90 (2002): 51–95. [Hebrew].

Emmel, Stephen. 'The Coptic Manuscript Collection of Alexander Lindsay, 25th Earl of Crawford'. In *Coptology—Past, Present and Future*, edited by Søren Giversen, Martin Krause, and Peter Nagel, 317–325. Louvain: Uitgeverij Peeters, 1994.

Emmel, Stephen. 'Reconstructing a Dismembered Coptic Library'. In *Gnosticism and the Early Christian World: In Honor of James M. Robinson*, edited by James E. Goehring,

Charles W. Hedrick, Jack T. Sanders, and Hans Dieter Betz, 145–161. Sonoma: Polebridge Press, 1990.

Epstein, Abraham. 'Review of H. D. Muller et David Kaufmann. Der Brief eines aegyptischen Rabbi an den Gaon [Salomon] ben Jehuda. Tirage à part du Ve volume des *Mittheilungen aus Der Sammlung der Papyrus Erzherzog Rainer, 1892 ...*'. *Revue des Etudes Juives* 25 (1892): 272–76.

Fenton, Paul B. 'A Re-Discovered Description of Maimonides by a Contemporary'. In *Maimonidean Studies*, Vol. 5, edited by Arthur Hyman, 267–291. New York: Yeshiva University Press, 2008.

Fenton, Paul B. 'Moses Shapira's Journey to the Yemen'. In *Ayelet Oettinger and Danny Bar-Maoz*, edited by Mittuv Yosef: *Yosef Tobi Jubilee Volume*, Vol. 2, lxviii–lxxxi. Haifa: University of Haifa Press, 2011.

Fowler, Harold N. 'Archaeological News'. *American Journal of Archaeology* 3 (September–December 1899): 241–277.

Frary, Lucien J. 'Russian Missions to the Orthodox East: Antonin Kapustin (1817–1894) and His World'. *Russian History* 40 (2013), 133–51.

Friedman, Mordechai. 'The Ibn al-Amshati Family-Maimonides' In-Laws'. *Zion* 69, no. 3 (2004): 271–297.

Frothingham, A. L. Jr. 'Archaeological News'. *The American Journal of Archaeology and of the History of the Fine Arts* 4, no. 3 (1888): 336.

Gaster, Moses. 'The Story of My Library'. (Translated by Brad Sabin Hill), *The British Library Journal* 21, no 1 (Spring 1995): 16–22.

Gaster, Theodor. 'Moses Gaster 1856–1939'. In *Studies and Texts in Folklore, Magic, Mediaeval Romance, Hebrew Apocrypha, and Samaritan Archaeology*, edited by Moses Gaster, xv–xxxix. New York: Ktav, 1971.

Goitein, S. D. 'The Geniza Collection of the University Museum of the University of Pennsylvania'. *Jewish Quarterly Review* 49, no. 1 (1958): 35–52.

Goitein, S. D. 'Geniza Papers of a Documentary Character in the Gaster Collection of the British Museum'. *The Jewish Quarterly Review* 51, no. 1 (1960): 34–46.

Golb, Norman. 'Sixty Years of Genizah Research'. *Judaism* 6 (1957): 3–16.

Golb, Norman. 'The Typography of the Jews of Medieval Egypt: VI. Places of Settlement of the Jews of Medieval Egypt'. *Journal of Near Eastern Studies* 33, no. 1 (1974): 116–149.

Gosden, Chris and Yvonne Marshall. 'The Cultural Biography of Objects'. *World Archaeology* 31, no. 2 (October 1999): 169–78.

Gottstein, M. H. 'Hebrew Fragments in the Mingana Collection'. *Journal of Jewish Studies* V (1956): 172–176.

Gottheil, Richard. 'In Ancient Footsteps: Florence'. *New Era Illustrated Magazine* VI, no. 3 (February 1905): 272–280; 'Rome' VI, no. 4 (March–April, 1905): 364–374; 'Alexandria'. VI, no. 6 (June 1905): 622–631; 'Cairo' VII, no. 1 (July 1905): 40–47.

Gottheil, Richard J. H. 'Some Hebrew Manuscripts in Cairo'. *The Jewish Quarterly Review* 17, no. 4 (July 1905): 609–655.

Gottheil, Richard J. H. 'An Eleventh-Century Document Concerning a Cairo Synagogue'. *The Jewish Quarterly Review* 19, no. 3 (April 1907): 506–7.

Grant, H. E. and James A. S. 'An Introduction to Ancient Egyptian History'. *Transactions of the Aberdeen Philosophical Society* III (1900): 1–30.

Green, Abigail. 'Old Networks, New Connections: The Emergence of the Jewish International'. In *Religious Internationals in the Modern World: Globalization and Faith Communities since 1750*, edited by Abigail Green and Vincent Viaene, 53–81. UK: Palgrave Macmillan, 2012.

Grenfell, Bernard P. 'Oxyrhynchus and its Papyri'. In *Egypt Exploration Fund. Archaeological Report, 1896–1897*, edited by F. Ll. Griffith, 1–12. London: Egypt Exploration Fund, 1897.

Gutwirth, Eleazar. 'Coplas de Yocef from the Genizah'. *Revue des Études Juives* 155, nos. 3–4 (1996): 387–400.

Haralambakis, Maria (Cioată). 'Representations of Moses Gaster (1856–1939) in Anglophone and Romanian Scholarship'. *New Europe College Yearbook 2012–2013*, 13 (2015): 89–128.

Hardwick, Tom. 'The Obsidian King's Origins. Further Light on the Purchasers and Prices at the MacGregor sale, 1922'. *Discussions in Egyptology* 65 (2012): 7–52.

Harviainen, Tapani. 'Abraham Firkovitsh, Karaites in Hīt and the Provenance of Karaite Transcriptions of Biblical Hebrew Texts into Arabic Script'. *Folio Orientalia* XXVIII (1991): 179–191.

Harviainen, Tapani. 'Abraham Firkovich and the Karaite Community in Jerusalem in 1864'. *Manuscripta Orientalia* 4, no. 2 (1998): 66–70.

Harviainen, Tapani. 'Abraham Firkovich, the Aleppo Codex, and its Dedication'. In *Jewish Studies at the Turn of the Twentieth Century: Proceedings of the 6th EAJS Congress, Toledo, July 1998. Volume 1: Biblical, Rabbinical, and Medieval Studies*, edited by Judit Targarona Borrás and Angel Sáenz-Badillos, 131–6. Leiden and Boston: Brill, 1999.

Harviainen, Tapani. 'Abraham Firkovich as Collector of Dispersed Minorities and their Manuscripts in the Light of his Personal Archive in St. Petersburg'. *Jewish Studies* 39 (1999): 97–106.

Harviainen, Tapani. 'Abraham Firkovich'. In *Karaite Judaism: A Guide to its History and Literary Sources*, edited by Meira Polliack, 875–92. Leiden and Boston: Brill, 2003.

Harviainen, Tapani, and Haseeb Shehadeh. 'How Did Abraham Firkovich Acquire the Great Collection of Samaritan Manuscripts in Nablus in 1864?'. *Studia Orientalia* 73 (1994): 167–192.

Harviainen, Tapani, and Haseeb Shehadeh. 'The Acquisition of the Samaritan Collection'. *Studia Orientalia* 97 (2003): 49–63.

Hazbun, Waleed. 'The East as an Exhibit: Thomas Cook & Son and the Origins of the International Tourism Industry in Egypt'. In *The Business of Tourism: Place, Faith, and History*, edited by Philip Scranton and Janet F. Davidson, 3–33. Philadelphia: University of Pennsylvania Press, 2007.

Helman, Boruch. 'The Karaite Jews of Cairo'. *Hadassah Magazine* (March 1979): 4–9.

Heuberger, Rachel. 'Aron Freimann–"Master of Jewish Bibliography"'. *Jewish Studies* 40 (2000): 97–107.

Hichens, Robert S. 'Street Scenes in Cairo'. *The Pall Mall Magazine* IV (September–December 1894): 601–615.

Hopkins, Simon. 'The Discovery of the Cairo Genizah'. *Bibliophilia Africana* IV (1981): 137–178.

Horowitz, Elliott. '"A Jew of the Old Type": Neubauer as Cataloguer, Critic, and Necrologist'. *The Jewish Quarterly Review* 100, no. 4 (Fall 2010): 649–65.

Hunter, F. Robert. 'Tourism and Empire: The Thomas Cook & Son Enterprise on the Nile, 1868–1914'. *Middle Eastern Studies* 40, no. 5 (September 2004): 28–54.

Ilan, Tal. 'Between the Hellenistic World and the Cairo Genizah: The Jewish Community in Late Antique Egypt'. In *The Jews in Medieval Egypt*, edited by Miriam Frenkel, 1–21. Boston: Academic Studies Press, 2021.

Jefferson, Rebecca J. W. 'T-S 6H9 –21, the Papyrus Codex Rebound'. *Fragment of the Month*, July 2009. https://doi.org/10.17863/CAM.48228.

Jefferson, Rebecca J. W. 'A Genizah Secret: The Count d'Hulst and Letters Revealing the Race to Recover the Lost Leaves of the Original Ecclesiasticus'. *Journal of the History of Collections* 21, no. 1 (2009): 125–142.

Jefferson, Rebecca J. W. 'Sisters of Semitics: A Fresh Appreciation of the Scholarship of Agnes Smith Lewis and Margaret Dunlop Gibson'. *Medieval Feminist Forum: A Journal of Gender and Sexuality* 45, no. 1 (2009): 23–49.

Jefferson, Rebecca J. W. 'The Cairo Genizah Unearthed: The Excavations Conducted by the Count d'Hulst on Behalf of the Bodleian Library and Their Significance for Genizah History'. In *From A Sacred Source: Genizah Studies in Honour of Stefan C. Reif*, edited by Ben Outhwaite and Siam Bhayro, 171–200. Leiden: Brill, 2010.

Jefferson, Rebecca J. W. 'The Historical Significance of the Cambridge Genizah Inventory Project'. In *Language, Culture, Computation. Computing of the Humanities, Law, and Narratives. Lecture Notes in Computer Science, vol 8002*, edited by N. Dershowitz and E. Nissan. Berlin, Heidelberg: Springer, 2014: 9–37.

Jefferson, Rebecca J. W. 'Dangerous Liaisons in Cairo: Reginald Q. Henriques and the Taylor-Schechter Genizah Manuscript Collection'. *Judaica Librarianship* 20 (2017): 25–26, 21–51.

Jefferson, Rebecca J. W. 'Deconstructing "the Cairo Genizah": A Fresh Look at Genizah Manuscript Discoveries in Cairo before 1897'. *The Jewish Quarterly Review* 108, no. 4 (Fall 2018): 422–448.

Jefferson, Rebecca J. W. '"What Cannot Often Be Obtainable": The Revd Greville John Chester and the Bodleian Genizah Collection'. *Journal of the History of Collections* 31, no. 2 (July 2019): 271–289.

Jefferson, Rebecca J. W. and Ngaio Vince-Dewerse. 'When Curator and Conservator Meet: Some Issues Arising from the Preservation and Conservation of the Jacques Mosseri Genizah Collection at Cambridge University Library'. *Journal of the Society of Archivists* 29, no. 1 (2008): 41–56.

Behar, Moshe and Zvi Ben-Dor Benite (eds), *Modern Middle Eastern Jewish Thought: Writings on Identity, Politics, and Culture, 1893–1958*, edited by Moshe Behar and Zvi Ben-Dor Benite, 80–85. Boston, MA: Brandeis University Press, 2013.

Kahle, Paul E. 'The Hebrew Ben Asher Bible Manuscripts'. *Vetus Testamentum* 1, no. 3 (1951): 161–167.

Kalman, Jason. 'A Cairo Genizah Fragment of Genesis Rabbah from the Collection of McGill University'. In *To Fix Torah in their Hearts: Essays on Biblical Interpretation and Jewish Studies in Honor of B. Barry Levy*, edited by Jaqueline S. Du Toit, Jason Kalman, Hartley Lachter, and Vanessa R. Sasson, 119–43. Cincinatti: Hebrew Union College Press, 2018.

Kaufmann, David. 'Die Grabschrift des R. Isak Bar Scheschet'. *Monatschrift für Geschicte und Wissenschaft des Judenthums* 32, no. 4 (1883): 190–192.

Kaufmann, David. 'The Prayer-Book According to the Ritual of England before 1290'. *The Jewish Quarterly Review* 4, no. 1 (October 1891): 20–63.

Kaufmann, David. 'The Etz Chayimm of Jacob B. Jehudah of London, and the History of His Manuscript'. *The Jewish Quarterly Review* 5, no. 3 (April 1893): 353–374.

Kaufmann, David. 'Dedicatory Poem to Jehudah ha-Nagid'. *Jewish Quarterly Review* 9, no. 2 (Jan 1897): 360–61.

Kaufmann, David. 'Or ha-Ganuz, Ginzei ha-Genizah asher hayitah be-Mitzrayim ha-Atiqah'. *Hashiloah* II (1897): 385–393, 481–490. [Hebrew].

Keenan, James E. 'The History of the Discipline'. In *Oxford Handbook of Papyrology*, edited by Roger S. Bagnall, 59–78. Oxford and New York: Oxford University Press, 2009.

Krakowski, Eve. "'Elhanan, Son of Shemariah": The Old Series and the Cairo Geniza'. *Jewish Quarterly Review* 110, no. 4 (Fall 2020): 593–598.

Le Quesne, Charles. 'The Synagogue'. In *Fortifications and the Synagogue: The Fortress of Babylon and the Ben Ezra Synagogue, Cairo*, edited by Phyllis Lambert, 79–87. Montreal: Canadian Center for Architecture, 1994.

Legrand, H., Dr. Burlazzi, and A. J. Gauthier. 'Origin of Cholera in Egypt in 1895'. *Public Health Reports (1896–1970)* 11, no. 3 (17 January 1896): 54–58.

Leturcq, Jean-Gabriel. 'The Museum of Arab Art in Cairo (1869–2014): A Disoriented Heritage?' In *After Orientalism: Critical Perspectives on Western Agency and Eastern Re-Appropriations*, edited by François Pouillon and Jean Claude Vatin, 145–161. Leiden and Boston: Brill, 2014.

Lévi, Israël. 'Fragments de deux nouveaux manuscrits hébreux de l'Ecclésiastique'. *Revue des Études Juives* 40, no. 79 (Janvier–Mars, 1900), 1–30.

Lewis, Agnes. 'Zu H. Duensing, Christlich-palästinisch-aramäische Texte und Fragmente'. *Zeitschrift der deutschen morgenländischen Gessellschaft* 61 (1907): 630–32.

Loewe, Herbert. 'Some Traditions of Old Cairo'. *The Jewish Chronicle* (20 July 1906): 40–41.

Loewe, R. 'Solomon Marcus Schiller-Szinessy, 1820–1890: First Reader in Talmudic and Rabbinic Literature at Cambridge'. *Transactions* (Jewish Historical Society of England) 21 (1962–1967): 148–189.

Löwinger, M. S. 'Report on the Hebrew Mss in Hungary with Special Regard to the Hungarian Fragments of the Cairo Genizah'. In *Actes du XXI e Congress International des Orientalistes, Paris 23–31 juillet 1948*, 117–123. Paris: Imprimerie Nationale, 1949.

Ludlow, James M. 'Ancient Hebrew Manuscript at Cairo'. *Friends' Review. A Religious, Literary and Miscellaneous Journal* 34, no. 44 (1881): 693–94.

Marx, Alexander. 'The Importance of the Geniza for Jewish History'. *Proceedings of the American Academy for Jewish Research* 16 (1946–1947): 183–204.

Marx, Alexander and Boaz Cohen. 'Necrology: Aron Freimann'. *Proceedings of the American Academy for Jewish Research* 17 (1947–1948): xxiii–xxviii.

Marks, Richard G. 'Hinduism, Torah, and Travel: Jacob Sapir in India'. *Shofar: An Interdisciplinary Journal of Jewish Studies* 30, no. 2 (2012): 26–51.

Meital, Yoram. 'A Thousand-Year-Old Biblical Manuscript Rediscovered in Cairo: The Future of the Egyptian Jewish Past'. *The Jewish Quarterly Review* 110, no. 1 (Winter 2020): 194–219.

Merchán-Hamann, César. 'Introduction to the Bodleian Library & College Collections'. In *Jewish Treasures from Oxford Libraries*, edited by Rebecca Abrams and César Merchán-Hamann, 13–35. Oxford: Bodleian Library, University of Oxford, 2020.

Mittwoch, Eugene. 'Ein Geniza-Fragment'. *Zeitschrift der Deutschen Morgnelandischen Gesellschaft* 57 (1903): 61–66.

Moghawery, Mohammed Saied. 'The Historical and Cultural Significance of the Arabic Papyri Kept in the National Library'. https://www.austriaca.at/0xc1aa5576 %200x001499e9.pdf.

Müller, D. H., and David Kaufmann. 'Der Brief Eines Ägyptischen Rabbi an Den Gaon [Salomo] Ben Jehuda'. *Mittheilungen Aus Der Sammlung Der Papyrus Erzherzog Rainer* V, nos. 3–4 (Wien, 1892): 127–132.

Mosseri, Jacques. 'A New Hoard of Jewish MSS in Cairo'. *The Jewish Review* 4 (1913): 208–216.

Mosseri, Jacques. 'The Synagogues of Egypt: Past and Present'. *Jewish Review* 5, no. 1 (1914): 31–44.

Neubauer, Adolf. 'Die Firkowitzsche Sammlung'. *Melanges Asiatiques* 4, no. 16 (Marz 1864): 121–127.

Neubauer, Adolf. 'Report to Convocation of Hebrew-Arabic Manuscripts at St. Petersburg'. *Oxford University Gazette* (21 November 1876): 99–101.

Neubauer, Adolf. 'Post-Biblical Bibliography, 1888–9'. *The Jewish Quarterly Review* 2, no. 2 (January 1890): 191–204.

Neubauer, Adolf. 'The Introduction of the Square Characters in Biblical MSS, and an Account of the Earliest MSS. of the Old Testament'. *Studia Biblica et ecclesiastica: essays chiefly in Bibliocal and patristic criticism*, vol. 3, edited by S. R. Driver, T. K. Cheyne and W. Sanday, 1–26. Oxford: Clarendon Press, 1891.

Neubauer, Adolf. 'Review of "Notes on a Hitherto Unknown Exegetical, Theological, and Philosophical Commentary to the Pentateuch by Alexander Kohut: The Columbia College MS. of Megilla (Babylonian Talmud) by Max Leopold Margolis"'. *The Jewish Quarterly Review* 5, no. 2 (January 1893): 338–342.

Neubauer, Adolf. 'Miscellanea Liturgica: The Etz Chayim'. *The Jewish Quarterly Review* 6, no. 2 (January 1894): 348–354.

Neubauer, Adolf. 'Review: Two Monographs by Dr. M. Gaster'. *The Jewish Quarterly Review* 6, no. 3 (April 1894): 570–77.

Neubauer, Adolf. 'Literary Gleanings. XII. The Hebrew Bible in Shorthand Writing'. *Jewish Quarterly Review*, 7, no. 2 (1895): 361–364.

Neubauer, Adolf. 'Egyptian Fragments. תולגמ, Scrolls Analagous to that of Purim, with an Appendix on the First מידיגנ'. *The Jewish Quarterly Review* 8, no. 4 (July 1896): 541–561.

Nizri, Yigal. '"The Missing Corpus" A Rabbinical Perspective on the Question of the Case of Rabbi Raphael Aharon Ben-Shim'on'. *Jewish Thought in Arab Societies, 1880–1960*. An International Workshop, May 26–28, 2014. [PDF online].

Ofer, Yosef. 'Abraham Firkovich and the Dedication Inscription of the Aleppo Codex'. *Hebrew Union College Annual* 76 (2005): 259–272.

Offord, Joseph. 'Egyptiaca. Egyptian Manuscripts at Oxford'. *The American Antiquarian and Oriental Journal* 31 (1909): 157–159.

Olszowy-Schlanger, Judith, and Roni Shweka. 'Newly Discovered Early Palimpsest Fragments of the Talmud Yerushalmi from the Cairo Genizah'. *Revue des études Juives* 172, no. 1–2 (January–June, 2013): 49–81.

Outhwaite, Ben. 'The First Owners of the Leningrad Codex: T-S 10J30.7'. *Fragment of the Month*, November 2017. https://doi.org/10.17863/CAM.28071.

Outhwaite, Ben. 'Library Yields Surprise Find'. *Genizah Fragments: the newsletter of Cambridge University Library's Taylor-Schechter Genizah Research Unit at Cambridge University Library* 49 (April 2005): 2.

Papo, Joseph M. 'The Sephardim in North America in the Twentieth Century'. *American Jewish Archives* 44, no. 1 (1992): 267–308.

Pilcher, E. J. 'An Arabic Version of the Book of Job'. *Biblia* XIV, no. 2 (May 1901): 37–42.

Posegay, Nick. 'Following the Links in T-S NS 192.11: A Qur'anic Exercise from a Cairene Public School'. *Fragment of the Month*, January 2020. https://doi.org/10.17863/CAM.65165.

Puall, Jeffrey Mark and Janet Billstein Akaha. 'Using Autosomal DNA Analysis to Connect Rabbinical Lineages: A Case Study of the Wertheimer and Wertheim Dynasties'. *Avotaynu* XXVIII, no. 4 (2012): 59–69.

Raafat, Samir W. 'Death, the Great Homogenizer …'. *Historical Society of Jews from Egypt* 3 (11–24 November 1999): http://www.hsje.org/Whoswho/Robert_Nahman/Robert_Nahman.htm

Regourd, Anne. 'Arabic Documents from the Cairo Genizah in the David Kaufmann Collection in the Library of the Hungarian Academy of Sciences-Budapest'. *Journal of Islamic Manuscripts* 3, no. 1 (2012): 1–19.

Reif, Stefan C. 'Jenkinson and Schechter at Cambridge: an expanded and updated assessment'. *Jewish Historical Studies* 32 (1990–1992): 279–316.

Reif, Stefan C. 'The Discovery of the Cambridge Genizah Fragments of Ben Sira: Scholars and Texts'. In *The Book of Ben Sira in Modern Research: Proceedings of the First International Ben Sira Conference, 28-31 July 1996, Soesterberg, Netherlands*, edited by P. C. Beentjes, 1–22. Berlin, 1997.

Reif, Stefan C. 'Giblews, Jews and Genizah Views'. *Journal of Jewish Studies* 55, no. 2 (2004): 332–46.

Reif, Stefan C. 'A Fresh Look at Adolf Neubauer as Scholar, Librarian and Jewish Personality'. [Unpublished paper read before the Jewish Historical Society of England, 2005].

Reif, Stefan C. 'Some First Editions of Genizah Manuscripts of Ben Sira'. In *Discovering, Deciphering and Dissenting: Ben Sira Manuscripts after 120 Years*, edited by James K. Aitken, Renate Egger-Wenzel and Stefan C. Reif, 39–65. Berlin: De Gruyter, 2019.

'The Revised Version of the Old Testament'. *Church Quarterly Review* 20 (1885): 455.

Richler, Benjamin. 'The Lost Manuscripts of the Library for Jewish Studies in Warsaw'. In *Omnia in Eo: Studies on Jewish Books and Libraries in Honour of Adri Offenberg. Celebrating the 125th Anniversary of the Bibliotheca Rosenthaliana in Amsterdam*, edited by Irene Zwiep et al., 360–87. Belgium: Peeters, 2006.

Rompay, Lucas Van. 'Coptic Christianity, Syriac Contacts With'. In *Gorgias Encyclopedic Dictionary of the Syriac Heritage: Electronic Edition*, edited by Sebastian P. Brock, Aaron M. Butts, George A. Kiraz and Lucas Van Rompay. https://gedsh.bethmardutho.org/Coptic-Christianity-Syriac-contacts-with.

Roth-Lochner, Barbara. 'Un voyage en Egypte (1896–1897), extrait des Souvenirs d'Albert Nicole'. In *Voyages en Égypte de l'Antiquité au début du 20e s*, edited by J. L. Chappaz et C. Ritschard, 244–258. Genève: Genève Musée d'art et d'histoire, 2003.

Roth-Lochner, Barbara. 'Fragments of the Cairo Genizah at the Bibliothèque de Genève'. In *The Cairo Geniza Collection in Geneva – Catalogue and Studies*, edited by David Rozenthal, 42–45. Jerusalem: The Hebrew University Magnes Press, 2010. [Hebrew].

Rovner, Jay. 'The Computerized Genizah Cataloguing Project of the Jewish Theological Seminary of America: Its History, Current Status, and Future Prospects, with some General Considerations of Bibliographic Control of Genizah Fragments'. *Shofar* 8, no. 4 (1990): 37–58.

Rowland Smith, Diana. 'Genizah Collections in the British Library'. In *Hebrew Studies: Papers presented at a colloquium on resources for Hebraica in Europe held at the School of Oriental and African Studies, University of London, 11–13 September 1989 (British Library Occasional Papers; 13)*, edited by Diana Rowland Smith and Peter Shmuel Salinger, 20–25. UK: British Library, 1991.

Sarfati, Rachel. 'Real and Fictive Travels to the Holy Land as Painted in the Florence Scroll'. In *Maps and Travel in the Middle Ages and the Early Modern Period: Knowledge, Imagination, and Visual Culture*, edited by Ingrid Baumgärtner et al., 232–251. Berlin and Boston: De Gruyter, 2019.

Sarfati, Rachel. 'Between Heaven and Earth: Places of Worship in Egypt and Syria through the Mirror of Visual Evidence'. *Arts 2020* 9, no. 3 (2020): 90–113.

Schechter, Solomon. 'The Riddles of Solomon in Rabbinic Literature'. *Folklore* 1, no. 3 (September 1890): 349–358.

Schechter, Solomon. 'Jewish Literature in 1890'. *The Jewish Quarterly Review* 3, no. 2 (January 1891): 314–342.

Schechter, Solomon. "The Quotations from Ecclesiasticus in Rabbinic Literature." *The Jewish Quarterly Review* 3, no. 4 (July 1891): 682–706.

Schechter, Solomon. 'The Quotations from Ecclesiasticus in Rabbinic Literature'. *The Jewish Quarterly Review* 3, no. 4 (July 1891): 682–706.

Schechter, Solomon. 'Notes on Hebrew MSS. in the University Library at Cambridge'. *The Jewish Quarterly Review* 4, no. 1 (October 1891): 90–101.

Schechter, Solomon. 'The Lewis-Gibson Hebrew Collection'. *The Jewish Quarterly Review* 9, no. 1 (October 1896): 115–121.

Schechter, Solomon. 'A Hoard of Hebrew Manuscripts'. *The Times (London)*, 3 August 1897. 13.

Schechter, Solomon. 'A Hunt in the Genizah'. *The Friend: A Religious and Literary Journal* 71, no. 6 (28 August, 1897): 45–47. This is a reproduction of the article in the *Sunday-School Times*.

Scheiber, Alexander. 'The Kaufmann-Genizah: Its Importance for the World of Scholarship'. In *Jubilee Volume of the Oriental Collection 1951–1976. Papers Presented on the Occasion of the 25th Anniversary of the Oriental Collection of the Library of the Hungarian Academy of Sciences*, edited by Eva Apor, 176–79. Budapest, 1978.

Schmelzer, Menahem. 'One Hundred Years of Genizah Discovery and Research: The American Share'. *National Foundation for Jewish Culture Lecture Series No. 2*. New York, 1998.

Schmierer-Lee, M. 'Add.6463(e)3416: Breathing the 'Dust of Centuries'. *Fragment of the Month*, October 2014. https://doi.org/10.17863/CAM.7800.

Scult, Mel. 'The Baale Boste Reconsidered: The Life of Mathilde Roth Schechter (M. R. S.)'. *Modern Judaism* 7, no. 1 (February 1987): 1–27.

Seidmann, Gertrud. 'The Rev. Greville John Chester and 'The Ashmolean Museum as a Home for Archaeology in Oxford'. *Bulletin of the History of Archaeology* 16, no. 1 (2006): 27–33.

Seidmann, Gertrud. 'Forgotten Pioneers of Archaeology in Victorian Oxford: The Rev. Greville John Chester (1830-1892)'. *Oxoniensia* LXXI (2006): 145–50.

Shafik Ramzy, Nelly. 'The Impact of Local Environment Aspects on Coptic Architecture in Egypt'. *Alexandria Engineering Journal* 51 (2012): 325–341.

Shapira, Dan. 'On Firkowicz, Forgeries and Forging Jewish Identities'. In *Manufacturing a Past for the Present: Forgery and Authenticity in Medievalist Texts and Objects in Nineteenth Century Europe*, edited by János M. Bak, Patrick J. Geary and Gábor Klaniczay, 156–172. Leiden and Boston: Brill, 2014.

Shay, Oded. 'Collectors and Collections in Palestine at the Conclusion of the Ottoman Era'. *Le Muséon* 122, nos. 3–4 (2009): 1–23.

Sheehan, Peter. 'The Roman Fortifications'. In *Fortifications and the Synagogue: The Fortress of Babylon and the Ben Ezra Synagogue, Cairo*, edited by Phyllis Lambert, 49–63. Montreal: Canadian Center for Architecture, 1994.

Sheehan, Peter. 'Archaeological Survey of the Ben Ezra Synagogue Site'. In *Fortifications and the Synagogue: The Fortress of Babylon and the Ben Ezra Synagogue, Cairo*, edited by Phyllis Lambert, 65–77. Montreal: Canadian Center for Architecture, 1994.

Shivtiel, Avihai. 'The Genizah and its Roots'. In *The Written Word Remains: The Archive and the Achievement: Articles in Honour of Professor Stefan C. Reif*, edited by Shulamit Reif, 4–8. Cambridge: Cambridge University Library, 2004.

Sijpesteijn, Petra. 'Visible Identities: In Search of Egypt's Jews in Early Islamic Egypt'. In *Israel in Egypt: The Land of Egypt as Concept and Reality for Jews in Antiquity and the Early Medieval Period*, edited by Alison Salvesen, Sarah Pearce and Miriam Frenkel, 424–40. Leiden: Brill, 2020.

Sklare, David. 'A Guide to Collections of Karaite Manuscripts'. In *Karaite Judaism: A Guide to its History and Literary Sources*, edited by Meira Polliack, 893–924. Leiden and Boston: Brill, 2003.

Skreslet II, Stanley H. 'The American Presbyterian Mission in Egypt: Significant Factors in its Establishment'. *American Presbyterians* 64, no. 2 (Summer 1986): 83–95.

Smithuis, Renate. 'Short Introduction to the Genizah Collection in the John Rylands Library'. In *From Cairo to Manchester: Studies in the Rylands Genizah Fragments*, edited by Renate Smithuis and Philip S. Alexander (Journal of Semitic Studies; Supplement 31), 1–32. Oxford: Oxford University Press, 2013.

Starr, David. 'Loving is Believing: Solomon Schechter and the Bible'. The Initiative on Bridging Scholarship and Pedagogy in Jewish Studies, Working Paper 7 (Brandeis University, 2010): 1–26.

Tahan, Ilana. 'The Hebrew Collection of the British Library: Past and Present'. *European Judaism: A Journal for the New Europe* 41, no. 2 (Autumn, 2008): 43–55.

T. G. E. 'A Few Days in Jerusalem'. *The Monthly Packet of Evening Readings for Members of the English Church* (January 1870): 373–391.

Thulin, Mirjam. '*Wissenschaft* and Correspondence: Solomon Schechter between Europe and America'. *Jewish Historical Studies* 48, no. 1 (2017): 109–137.

Tobi, Yosef. 'An Unknown Study by Joseph Halévy on his Journey to Yemen'. *Proceedings of the Seminar for Arabian Studies* 35 (2005): 287–92.

Tov, Emanuel. 'A Qumran Origin for the Masada Non-Biblical Texts?' *Dead Sea Discoveries* 7, no. 1 (2000): 57–73.

Toynbee, J. M. C. and H. D. A. Major, revised by David Gill. 'Gardner, Ernest Arthur (1862–1939), classical scholar and archaeologist'. *Oxford Dictionary of National Biography*. Oxford: Oxford University Press, 2004. [online].

Vasilyeva, Olga. 'The Firkovich Odessa Collection: The History of its Acquisition and Research, Present Condition and Historical Value'. *Studia Orientalia* 95 (2003): 45–53.

Vollandt, Ronny, 'A Muslim Genizah in Damascus'. *Fragment of the Month*, June, 2018. https://doi.org/10.17863/CAM.34051.

Walfish, Barry. 'A Major Collection of Jewish Books and Manuscripts in Kiev'. *Association of Jewish Studies Newsletter* 43 (1993): 4–5.

Watson, Charles R. 'Sarah B. Dales Lansing—"The Personal Element in Missionary Service"'. In The *King's Service*, edited by Charles R. Watson, 83–114. Philadelphia, PA: Board of Foreign Missions Presbyterian Church of N.A., 1905.

Watson, Andrew. 'Reforms among the Copts'. *Evangelical Christendom* (1 October 1891): 318–19.

Whelan, Paul. '"The Marquis" Excavations: A Tale of Two Diaries'. In *Talking Along the Nile: Ippolito Rosellini, Travellers and Scholars of the 19th Century in Egypt. Proceedings of the International Conference held on the occasion of the presentation of Progetto Rosellini. Pisa, June 14–16, 2012*, edited by Marilina Betrò and Gianluca, 229–256. Miniaci: Pisa University Press, 2013.

Wilson, Timothy. 'A Victorian Artist as Ceramic-Collector'. *Journal of the History of Collections* 14, no. 2 (2002): 231–269.

Yates, Donna and Emiline Smith. 'Antiquities Trafficking and the Provenance Problem'. In *Collecting and Provenance: A Multidisciplinary Approach*, edited by J. C. Milosch, and N. Pearce, 385–94. New York and London: Rowman & Littlefield, 2012.

Yellin, Avinoam. 'Genizah Fragments in the Jewish National Library'. *The Journal of the Palestinian Oriental Society* III (1923): 200–202.

Zel Lurie, J. 'Mysteries of the Cairo Codex: Part II'. *Florida Jewish Journal* (13 June 2012).

Zinger, Oded. 'Finding a Fragment in a Pile of Geniza: A Practical Guide to Collections, Editions, and Resources'. *Jewish History* 32, no. 2–4 (2019): 279–309.

Zohar, Zvi. 'Ben-Shimʿon, Masʿūd Ḥayy'. In *Encyclopedia of Jews in the Islamic World*, Executive Editor Norman A. Stillman [Consulted Online].

Zohar, Zvi. 'Ben-Shimʿon, Raphael Aaron'. In *Encyclopedia of Jews in the Islamic World*, Executive Editor Norman A. Stillman [Consulted Online].

Biographical accounts, collected letters and papers, memoirs, travelogues

Adler, Cyrus. *I Have Considered the Days*. Philadelphia: Jewish Publication Society of America, 1941.

Adler, Cyrus, *Selected Letters*. Vol. 1. Edited by Ira Robinson. Philadelphia and New York: The Jewish Publication Society of America & The Jewish Theological Seminary of America, 1985.

Adler, E. N. *Jews in Many Lands*. Philadelphia: Jewish Publication Society of America, 1905.

Association for the Furtherance of Christianity: Letters and papers concerning the Coptic Church in relation to the Church of England: under the primacy of Archbishop Howley, 1836–1848. London: Printed for the Use of the Committee, 1883.

Aveling, T. W. *Voices of Many Waters, or Travels in the Lands of the Tiber, the Jordan, and the Nile*. London: John Snow, Paternoster Row, 1855.

Baxter, C. E. *Talofa: Letters from Foreign Parts*, London: Sampson Low, Marston, Searle & Rivington, 1884.

Benjamin II, J. J. *Eight Years in Asia and Africa: from 1846 to 1855*. Hanover: Published by the Author, 1863.

Bentwich, Norman. *Solomon Schechter: A Biography*. Cambridge: University Press, 1938.

Blackburn, John. *A Hand-Book Round Jerusalem*. London: F. and J. Rivington, 1846.

Buchanan, Claudius. *Christian Researches in Asia: With Notices of the Translation of the Scriptures into the Oriental Languages*. 2nd edition. London: T. Cadell and W. Davies; Cambridge: J. Deighton, 1811.

Buckley, J. M. *Travels in Three Continents: Europe & Africa & Asia*. New York: Hunt & Eaton; Cincinnati: Cranston & Curts, 1895.

Capart, Jean (ed.). *Travels in Egypt: Letters of Charles Edwin Wilbour*, Brooklyn, NY: Brooklyn Museum, 1936.

Charmes, Gabriel. *Five Months at Cairo and in Lower Egypt*, trans. By William Conn. London, 1883.

Chester, Greville John. *Transatlantic Sketches in the West Indies, South America, Canada, and the United States*. London: Smith, Elder & Co., 1869.

Colman, Russell James. *Trifles from a Tourist: in Letters from Abroad*. Norwich: Fletcher and Son, 1886.

Curzon, Robert. *Visits to Monasteries in the Levant*, 5th edition. London: John Murray, 1865.

Edwards, Amelia B. *A Thousand Miles Up the Nile*. London: Longmans, Green & Co., 1877.

Firkovich, Abraham. *Sefer Avne Zikaron*. Vilna: Samuel Joseph Finn and Abraham Zevi Rozenkranz Press, 1872. [Hebrew].

Fullerton-Fullerton, Amy. *A Lady's Ride Through Palestine & Syria: With Notices of Egypt and the Canal of Suez*. United Kingdom: S.W. Partridge, 1872.

Gibson, Margaret Dunlop. *How the Codex Was Found: A Narrative of Two Visits to Sinai from Mrs. Lewis's Journals, 1892–1893*. Cambridge: Macmillan and Bowes, 1893.

Journal [by Miss Platt] of a Tour through Egypt, the Peninsula of Sinai, and the Holy Land in 1838, 1839 in two volumes. Vol. 1. London: printed solely for private circulation by Richard Watts, 1841).

Ghosh, Amitav. *In an Antique Land*. London: Granta, 1992.

Lansing, Gulian. *Egypt's Princes: A Narrative of Missionary Labor in the Valley of the Nile*. New York: Robert Carter and Brothers, 1865.

Lewis, Agnes Smith. *In the Shadow of Sinai: A Story of Travel and Research from 1895 to 1897*. Cambridge: Macmillan & Bowes, 1898.

Loftie, W. J. *A Ride in Egypt: From Sioot to Luxor in 1879*. London: Macmillan and Co., 1879.

Prime, William Cowper. *Tent Life in the Holy Land*. New York: Harper & Brothers, 1857.

Pococke, Richard. *Description of the East, and Some Other Countries*, Volume 5: Observations on Egypt. London: W. Bowyer, 1743.

Reynolds-Ball, Eustace Alfred. *Jerusalem. A Practical Guide to Jerusalem and Its Environs, with Excursions to Bethlehem, Hebron, Jericho*. London: Adam and Charles Black, 1901.

Richardson, Hilary. 'Macalister, Robert Alexander Stewart'. In *Dictionary of Irish Biography*, edited by James McGuire and James Quinn. Cambridge: Cambridge University Press, 2009. https://www.dib.ie/biography/macalister-robert-alexander -stewart-a5093, accessed 15 September 2021.

Saphir, Jacob. *Eben Sapir*. Vol. 1. Lyck, 1866. [Hebrew]

Saphir, Jacob. *Eben Sapir*. Vol. 2. 1872. [Hebrew]

Saphir, Jacob. *My Footsteps Echo: the Yemen Journal of Rabbi Yaakov Sapir*, Ed. and Trans. Yaakov Lavon. Jerusalem: Feldheim, 1997.

Sayce, A. H. *Reminiscences*. London: Macmillan & Co., Limited, 1923.

Schur, Zev Wolf. *Mahazot Ha-Hayim*. Vien: G. Breg, 1884. [Hebrew].

Smith, Agnes. *Through Cyprus*. London: Hurst and Blackett, 1887.

Smith, George A. et al. *Correspondence of Palestine Tourists; comprising A Series of Letters by George A. Smith, Lorenzo Snow, Paul A. Schettler, and Eliza R. Snow of Utah ...* Salt Lake City, Utah Territory: Descret News Steam Printing Establishment, 1875.

Spiegelberg, Richard. *Wilhelm Spiegelberg: A Life in Egyptology*. Chicago, IL: Oriental Institute of the University of Chicago, 2015.

Stern, Henry A. *Dawnings of Light in the East*. London: Charles H. Purday, 1854.

Trumbull, Henry Clay. *Old Time Student Volunteers; My Memories of Missionaries*. New York, Chicago, Toronto: Fleming H. Revell Company, 1902.

Von Haxthausen, August Freiherr. *The Russian Empire: its People, Institutions, and Resources*. Translated by Robert Farie. Vol. II. London: Chapman and Hall, 1856.

Wallis Budge, E. A. *By Nile and Tigris. A Narrative of Journeys in Egypt and Mesopotamia on behalf of the British Museum Between the Years 1886 and 1913, by Sir E. A. Wallis Budge*. London, 1920.

Books, theses

Abbas Hilmi II. *The Last Khedive of Egypt: Memoirs of Abbas Hilmi II*. Trans. and ed. Amira Sonbol, Reading: Ithaca Press, 1998.

Abdulhaq, Najat. *Jewish and Greek Communities in Egypt, Jewish and Greek Communities in Egypt: Entrepreneurship and Business before Nasser* (Library of Middle East History; 58). UK: I. B. Tauris, 2016.

Abrahams, Israel. *The Book of Delight and Other Papers*. Philadelphia: The Jewish Publication Society of America, 1912.

Abraham, Philip. *Curiosities of Judaism: Facts, Opinions, Anecdotes, and Remarks Relative to the Hebrew Nation*. London: Philip Abraham, 1879.

Adler, Elkan Nathan. *About Hebrew Manuscripts*. Oxford: Henry Frowde, 1905.

Ariel, Ari. *Jewish-Muslim Relations and Migration from Yemen to Palestine in the Late Nineteenth and Twentieth Centuries*. Leiden, Boston: Brill, 2014.

Beit-Arie, M., C. Sirat, and M. Glatzer (eds). *Codices Hebraicis Litteris Exarati Quo Tempore Scripti Fuerint Exhibentes, I, Jusqu'à 1020* (Monumenta Palaeographica Medii Aevi, Series Hebraica, 1). Turnhout: Brepols; Paris: Institut de Recherche et d'Histoire des Textes, C. N. R. S.; and Jerusalem: Académie Nationale des Sciences et des Lettres d'Israël, 1997.

Butcher, E. L. *The Story of the Church of Egypt*. Vol. I. London: Smith, Elder, & Co., 1897.

Butler, Alfred. *The Ancient Coptic Churches of Egypt*. 2 Vols. Oxford: Clarendon Press, 1884.

Cowley, A. E., and A. Neubauer (eds). *The Original Hebrew of a Portion of Ecclesiasticus (XXXIX. 15 to XLIX. 11) Together with the Early Versions and an English Translation*. Oxford: Clarendon Press, 1897.

Craster, Edmund. *History of the Bodleian Library*. Oxford: Clarendon Press, 1952.

Díaz-Andreu, Margarita. *A World History of Nineteenth Century Archaeology: Nationalism, Colonialism, and the Past*. Oxford: Oxford University Press, 2007.

Douer, Alisa. *Egypt- The Lost Homeland. Exodus from Egypt, 1947–1967*. Berlin, Logos Verlag Berlin GmbH, 2015.

Drower, Margaret S. *Flinders Petrie: A Life in Archaeology*. Madison, WI: The University of Wisconsin Press, 1995.

El-Kodsi, Mourad. *The Karaite Jews of Egypt 1882–1986*. Lyons, NY: Wilprint Inc., 1987.

El Shamsy, Ahmed. *Rediscovering the Islamic Classics: How Editors and Print Culture Transformed an Intellectual Tradition*. New Jersey: Princeton University Press, 2020.

Fagan, Brian. *The Rape of the Nile: Tomb Robbers, Tourists, and Archaeologists in Egypt*, 3rd edn. USA: Westview Press, 2004.

Falcetta, Alessandro. *The Daily Discoveries of a Bible Scholar and Manuscript Hunter: A Biography of James Rendel Harris, 1852–1941*. Great Britain: T&T Clarke, Bloomsbury Publishing, 2018.

Falkiewicz-Dulik, Michalina, Katarzyna Janda and George Wypych (eds). *Handbook of Material Biodegradation, Biodeterioration, and Biostablization*. 2nd ed. Toronto: ChemTec Publishing, 2015.

Fargeon, Maurice. *Les Juifs en Egypte*. Le Caire: Paul Barbey, 1938.

Friedman, Matti. *The Aleppo Codex: In Pursuit of One of the World's Most Coveted, Sacred, and Mysterious Books*. New York: Algonquin Books, 2012.

Gerber, Noah S. *Ourselves or Our Holy Books: The Cultural Discovery of Yemenite Jewry.* Jerusalem: Ben-Zvi Institute, 2013. [Hebrew].

Gerdmar, Anders. *Roots of Theological Anti-Semitism: German Biblical Interpretation and the Jews, from Herder and Semler to Kittel and Bultmann.* Studies in Jewish History and Culture 20. Leiden: Brill, 2009.

Glickman, Mark. *Sacred Treasure: the Cairo Genizah: the Amazing Discoveries of Forgotten Jewish History in an Egyptian Synagogue Attic.* Woodstock, Vermont: Jewish Lights Publishing, 2011.

Goitein, S. D. *A Mediterranean Society: The Jewish Communities of the Arab World as Portrayed in the Documents of the Cairo Geniza, Vols I–VI.* Berkeley, Los Angeles, London: University of California Press, 1967–1993.

Grohmann, Adolf, *Arabische Chronologie I, Arabische Papyruskunde II.* Leiden/Koln: E. J. Brill, 1966.

Gunter, Ann C., *A Collector's Journey: Charles Lang Freer and Egypt.* Washington, DC: Smithsonian Freer Gallery of Art, 2002.

Gwilliam, G. H., F. Crawford Burkitt, and John F. Stenning, *Biblical and Patristic Relics of the Palestinian Syriac Literature from MSS in the Bodleian Library and in the Library of Saint Catherine on Mount Sinai.* Oxford: The Clarendon Press, 1896.

Habermann, A. M. *The Cairo Genizah and Other Genizoth: Their Character, Contents and Development.* Jerusalem, 1971. [Hebrew].

Hagen, Fredrik and Kim Ryholt. *The Antiquities Trade in Egypt 1880–1930: The H. O. Lange Papers* (Scientia Danica. Series H., Humanistica 4, Vol. 8). Copenhagen, Denmark: Det Kongelige Danske Videnskabernes Selskab, 2016.

Hammad, Hanan Hassan. *Mechanizing People, Localizing Modernity. Industrialization and Social Transformation in Modern Egypt: al-Mahalla al-Kubra, 1910–1958.* PhD Dissertation, University of Texas at Austin, 2009.

Harkavy, Abraham. *Hadashim ve-Yeshanim, Meqorot ve-Mehkarim be-toledot Yisrael u-be-Sifruto.* Jerusalem, 1970. [Hebrew; facsimile edition].

Hoffman, A., and Peter Cole. *Sacred Trash: The Lost and Found World of the Cairo Geniza.* New York: Nextbook, Schocken, 2011.

Humphreys, Andrew. *Grand Hotels of Egypt in the Golden Age of Travel.* Cairo, New York: The American University in Cairo Press, 2015.

Hyamson, Albert M. (ed.). *The British Consulate in Jerusalem in Relation to the Jews of Palestine, 1838–1914. Part 1: 1838–1861.* London: Edward Goldston Ltd, 1939.

Ismail, Shehab. *Engineering Metropolis: Contagion, Capital, and the Making of British Colonial Cairo, 1882–1922.* Thesis, Columbia University, 2017, 66.

Kahle, Paul E. *The Cairo Geniza (The Schweich Lectures of the British Academy 1941).* London: Oxford University Press, 1947.

Kahn, Lily. *A Grammar of the Eastern European Hasidic Hebrew Tale.* Leiden; Boston: Brill, 2014.

Kamil, Jill. *Coptic Egypt: History and Guide.* Cairo and New York: The American University in Cairo Press, 1987.

Kaufmann, David. *Die letzte Vertreibung der Juden aus Wien und Niederösterreich: ihre Vorgeschichte (1625 1670) und ihre Opfer.* Budapest: Buchdrukerei Der Act. G. Athenaeum, 1889.

Kaufmann, David. *Aus Heinrich Heine's Ahnensaal.* Breslau: S. Schottlaender, 1896.

Knoppers, Gary. *Jews and Samaritans: The Origins and History of their Early Relations.* Oxford: Oxford University Press, 2013.

Krauss, Samuel. *David Kaufmann. Eine Biographie.* Berlin: S. Calvary & Co., 1901.

Kubiak, Wladyslaw B. *Al-Fustat: Its Foundation and Early Urban Development,* Cairo and New York: The American University in Cairo Press, 1987.

Landau, Jacob M. *Jews in Nineteenth Century Egypt.* New York: New York University Press & London: University of London Press Ltd, 1969.

Loewinger, S., and A. Scheiber. *Genizah Publications in Memory of Prof. Dr. David Kaufmann.* Budapest, 1949.

Mack, Merav, and Benjamin Balint. *Jerusalem: City of the Book.* New Haven and London: Yale University Press, 2019.

Mandel, George. *Who Was Ben-Yehuda with in Boulevard Montmartre?* (Oxford Centre Papers; 2). Oxford: Oxford Center for Postgraduate Hebrew Studies, 1984.

Mann, Jacob. *Texts and Studies in Jewish History and Literature.* Vol. II. Philadelphia: Jewish Publication Society of America, 1935.

Margoliouth, D. S. *An Essay on the Place of Ecclesiasticus in Semitic Literature.* Oxford: Clarendon Press, 1890.

Meital, Yoram. *Jewish Sites in Egypt.* Jerusalem: Ben Zvi Institute, 1995. [Hebrew].

Merrill, George Edmands Merrill. *The Parchments of the Faith.* Philadelphia: American Baptist Publication Society, 1894.

Merx, Adalbert. *Documents de paléographie hébraïque et arabe, publiés avec sept planches photo-lithographiques.* Leyde: Brill, 1894.

Milosch, J. C., and N. Pearce (eds). *Collecting and Provenance: A Multidisciplinary Approach.* New York and London: Rowman & Littlefield, 2012.

Neubauer, Adolf. *Aus der Petersburger Bibliothek: Beiträge und Documente zur Geschichte des Karäerthums und der Karäischen Literatur.* Leipzig: Oskar Leiner, 1866.

Neubauer, Adolf. *Medieval Jewish Chronicles and Chronological Notes, ed. from Printed Books and Manuscripts.* Vol. I. Oxford: Clarendon Press, 1887–95.

Nicole, Jules. *Le Laboureur de Ménandre: fragments inédits sur papyrus d'Égypte.* Bale et Genève: Georg & Co., Libraries-Éditeurs, 1898.

Nongbri, Brent. *God's Library: The Archaeology of the Earliest Christian Manuscripts.* New Haven and London: Yale University Press, 2018.

Odom, William. *Memorials of Sheffield: its Cathedral and Parish Churches.* Sheffield: J. W. Northend, 1922.

Olszowy-Schlanger, Judith. *Karaite Marriage Documents from the Cairo Geniza: Legal Tradition and Community Life in Mediaeval Egypt and Palestine.* Leiden, New York, Köln, 1998.

Owen, E. R. J. *Cotton and the Egyptian Economy 1820–1914.* Oxford: Oxford at the Clarendon Press, 1969.

Perani, Mauro (ed.). *The Ancient Sefer Torah of Bologna: Features and History, European Genizah Texts and Studies, Volume Four.* Leiden: Brill, 2019.

Petrie, W. M. Flinders. *Deshasheh 1897.* Fifteenth Memoir of The Egypt Exploration Fund. London, 1898.

Petrie, W. M. Flinders. *Seventy Years in Archaeology.* Cambridge: Cambridge University Press, 2013.

Raafat, Samir W. *Maadi 1904–1962: Society and History in a Cairo Suburb.* Zamalek, Cairo, Egypt: Palm Press, 1994.

Raymond, Andre. *Cairo,* translated by Willard Wood. Harvard, MA: Harvard University Press, 2000.

Rees, Joan. *Amelia Edwards: Traveller, Novelist & Egyptologist*. London: Rubicon Press, 1998.

Reid, Donald Malcom. *Whose Pharaohs? Archaeology, Museums, and Egyptian National Identity from Napoleon to World War I*. Berkeley, Los Angeles, London: University of California Press, 2003.

Reif, Stefan C. *A Jewish Archive from Old Cairo: The History of Cambridge University's Genizah Collection*. Richmond, Surrey: Curzon, 2000.

Reif, Stefan C. (ed). *Charles Taylor and the Genizah Collection: A Centenary Seminar and Exhibition, St. John's College, Cambridge 2 November 2008: Papers Delivered and Items Exhibited*. Cambridge: St. John's College, 2009.

Rustow, Marina. *Heresy and the Politics of Community: The Jews of the Fatimid Caliphate*. New York: Cornell University Press, 2008.

Rustow, Marina. *The Lost Archive: Traces of a Caliphate in a Cairo Synagogue*. Princeton and Oxford: Princeton University Press, 2020.

Salomons, David (ed.). *Miscellany of Hebrew Literature*. Vol. I. London: N. Trübner and Co., 1872.

Sanders, Paula. *Creating Medieval Cairo: Empire, Religion, and Architectural Preservation in Nineteenth Century Egypt*. Cairo and New York: The American University in Cairo Press, 2008.

Sayce, A. H. *The "Higher Criticism" and the Verdict of the Monuments* (Published Under the Direction of the Tract Committee). London: Society for Promoting Christian Knowledge, 1894.

Schechter, Solomon. *Studies in Judaism*. London: Macmillan & Co., Ltd, 1896.

Schidorsky, Dov Bernhard. *The Origins of the Jewish National and University Library Against the Background of the Modern Jewish National Movement*. PhD Thesis, University of California, Berkeley, 1977.

Sedra, Paul D. *From Mission to Modernity: Evangelicals, Reformers and Education in Nineteenth Century Egypt*. London: I. B. Tauris, 2001.

Shapira, Dan. *Abraham Firkowicz in Istanbul (1830–1832): Paving the Way for Turkic Nationalism*. Ankara: Karam, 2003.

Sharkey, Heather J. *American Evangelicals in Egypt: Missionary Encounters in an Age of Empire*. Princeton and Oxford: Princeton University Press, 2008.

Sheehan, Peter. *Babylon of Egypt: The Archaeology of Old Cairo and the Origins of the City*. Cairo and New York: The American University in Cairo Press, 2010.

Sladen, Douglas. *Oriental Cairo: The City of the 'Arabian Nights'*. Philadelphia: J. B. Lippincott Company, 1911.

Soskice, Janet. *The Sisters of Sinai: How Two Lady Adventurers Discovered the Hidden Gospels*. New York: Alfred A. Knopf, 2009.

Starr, David. *Catholic Israel: Solomon Schechter, A Study of Unity and Fragmentation in Modern Jewish History*. Thesis, Columbia University, 2003.

Stern, David. *The Jewish Bible: A Material History*. Seattle and London: University of Washington Press, 2017.

Stevenson, Alice (ed.). *The Petrie Museum of Egyptian Archaeology: Characters and Collections*. London: UCL Press, 2015.

Stevenson, Alice. *Scattered Finds: Archaeology, Egyptology, and Museums*. London: UCL Press, 2019.

Tawil, Hayim, and Bernard Schneider. *Crown of Aleppo: The Mystery of the Oldest Hebrew Bible Codex*. Philadelphia: The Jewish Publication Society, 2010.

Tigay, Chanan. *The Lost Book of Moses: The Hunt for the World's Oldest Bible*. USA: HarperCollins, 2016.

Tignor, Robert L. *Egypt: A Short History*. Princeton and Oxford: Princeton University Press, 2011.

Thompson, Jason. *Wonderful Things: A History of Egyptology, Volume 2: The Golden Age: 1881–1914*. Cairo and New York: The American University in Cairo Press, 2015.

Verskin, Alan. *A Vision of Yemen: The Travels of a European Orientalist and His Native Guide*. Stanford, California: Stanford University Press, 2018.

Vitalis, Robert Vitalis. *When Capitalists Collide: Business Conflict and the End of the Empire in Egypt*, Berkeley, Los Angeles, London: University of California Press, 1995.

Volait, Mercedes. *Antique Dealing and Creative Reuse in Cairo and Damascus, 1850–1890*. Leiden: Brill, 2021.

Watson, Andrew. *The American Mission in Egypt: 1854–1896*. Pittsburgh: United Presbyterian Board of Publication, 1904.

Weill, Asher. B'nai B'rith and Israel: The Unbroken Covenant. Jerusalem: B'nai Brith World Center, 1998, 1–26.

Wertheimer, Solomon Aaron. *Bate midrašot: yaḵilu midrašim qeṭanim mi-kitve yad yešanim*. Jerusalem: Moses Lilienthal, 1893–1897.

Wertheimer, Solomon Aaron. *Sefer ginze Yerušalayim*. Jerusalem: Y. N. Lewi, 1896.

Wilson, John A. *Signs & Wonders Upon Pharoah: A History of American Egyptology*. Chicago and London: The University of Chicago Press, 1964.

Catalogues, guides, handlists

Adler, C. and I. M. Casanowicz. *Biblical Antiquities: a Description of the Exhibit at the Cotton States International Exposition*. Atlanta, Washington: Government Printing Office, 1895.

Adler, I. (ed.), *Catalogue of the Mosseri Collection*. Jerusalem: The Jewish National and University Library, 1990. [Hebrew].

Baer, S. *Zwei alte Thora-Rollen aus Arabien und Palästina, beschreiben von S. Baer ...* Frankfurt A. M.: Verlag von Johannes Alt, 1870.

Baras, Zvi. *A Century of Books: the Jewish National and University Library 1892–1992 centennial anniversary exhibition*. Jerusalem: Jewish National and University Library, 1992. [Hebrew].

Bauer, Adolph. 'Neue Funde griechischer Papyrusrollen in Aegypten'. *Zeitschrift für Ägyptische Sprache und Altertumskunde* 16 (1878): 108–110.

Bierbrier, Morris L. (ed.). *Who Was Who in Egyptology*, 5th revised edition. London: The Egypt Exploration Society, 2019.

Brinner, William M. *Sutro Library Hebraica: A Handlist*. California State Library, 1966.

Chester, G. J. *Catalogue of the Egyptian Antiquities in the Ahsmolean Museum, Oxford*. Oxford: Parker & Co., 1881.

Cowley, Arthur Ernest. *Catalogue of Additional Genizah Fragments*. Oxford ca. 1929 [unpublished typescript].

Danzig, N. *A Catalogue of Fragments of Halakhah and Midrash from the Cairo Genizah in the Elkan Nathan Adler Collection of the Library of the Jewish Theological Seminary of America*. New York and Jerusalem: Bet-ha-Midrash, 1997. [Hebrew].

Halper, Benzion. *Descriptive Catalogue of Genizah Fragments in Philadelphia*. Philadelphia: The Dropsie College for Hebrew and Cognate Learning, 1924.

Harkavy, A. *Report of the Imperial Public Library for the Year 1899*. St Petersburg [Leningrad], 1903. [Russian].

Hoerning, Reinhart. *British Museum Karaite MSS. Descriptions and Collation of Six Karaite Manuscripts of Portions of the Hebrew Bible* ... London: Williams and Norgate, 1889.

Hurvitz, Eleazer. *Catalogue of the Cairo Geniza Fragments in the Westminster College Library, Cambridge.* Vol. I. New York: Yeshiva University, 2006. [Hebrew].

Gottheil, Richard and William H. Worrell (eds). *Fragments from the Cairo Genizah in the Freer Collection.* New York: The Macmillan Company, 1927.

Katsch, Abraham I. *The Antonin Genizah in the Saltykov-Schedrin Public Library in Leningrad.* New York, 1963.

Kedem Auction Catalogue, no. 66 (Jerusalem, 15 May 2019), 1–344.

Khan, Geoffrey. *Karaite Bible Manuscripts in the Cairo Genizah.* Cambridge: Cambridge University Press, 1990.

Ktav Yad veSefer Institute: Research Center for Scholarly Editions and Publications of Jewish Manuscripts in Memory of Rabbi Solomon Aaron Wertheimer. Jerusalem, 1990 [Hebrew].

Leveen, J. *Catalogues of Hebrew and Samaritan manuscripts in the British Museum. Part IV: Introduction, Indexes, brief description of accessions* .... London, 1935.

Lewis, Agnes Smith, and Margaret Dunlop Gibson. *Palestinian Syriac Texts: From Palimpsest Fragments in the Taylor-Schechter Collection.* London: C. J. Clay and Sons, 1900.

Madan, Falconer (ed.). *A Summary Catalogue of Western Manuscripts in the Bodleian Library at Oxford which have hitherto been catalogued in the Quarto Series with references to the Oriental and other manuscripts.* Vol. V. Oxford: Oxford at the Clarendon Press, 1905.

Margoliouth, George. *Catalogue of the Hebrew and Samaritan Manuscripts in the British Museum.* Vols I–IV. London: The British Museum, 1899–1915.

Neubauer, Adolf, and Arthur Ernest Cowley (eds). *Catalogue of the Hebrew Manuscripts in the Bodleian Library.* Vol. II. Oxford: Clarendon Press, 1906.

Quaritch, Bernard. *Catalogue of Works in the Oriental Languages together with Polynesian & African,* London, 1887. 3205.

Reif, Stefan C. *Hebrew Manuscripts at Cambridge University Library: A Description and Introduction.* Cambridge: Cambridge University Press, 1997.

Richler, Benjamin. *Guide to Hebrew Manuscript Collections.* Second revised edition. Jerusalem: The Israel Academy of Sciences and Humanities, 2014.

Rogers, Robert W. 'A Catalogue of Manuscripts (chiefly Oriental) in the Library of Haverford College'. *Haverford College Studies* 4 (1890): 28–50.

Schiller-Szinessy, S. M. *Catalogue of the Hebrew Manuscripts Preserved in the University Library Cambridge.* Vol. 1. Cambridge: Printed for the University Library, 1876.

Shapira, M. W. *Eigenhändiges Verzeichnis der von Shapira gesammelten hebr. Handschriften.* Staatsbibliothek zu Berlin (MS or. Fol. 1342): https://digital .staatsbibliothek-berlin.de/werkansicht/?PPN=PPN777461838

Van Dyke, John C. *Notes on the Sage Library of the Theological Seminary at New Brunswick.* New Brunswick, NJ, 1888.

Wallis, Henry. *The Godman Collection: Persian Ceramic Art in the Collection of Mr. F. DuCane Godman, F. R. S. The Thirteenth Century Lustred Vases.* London; printed for private circulation, 1891.

Weisz, Max. *Katalog der Hebräischen Handschriften und Bücher in der Bibliothek des Professors Dr. David Kaufman S. A.* Frankfurt A. M.: J. Kaufmann, 1906.

Wright, William (ed). *Catalogue of Syriac Manuscripts in the British Museum Acquired Since the Year 1838.* London: Longmans & Co., 1872.

Digital publications

Bassatine News: http://bassatine.net

David Kaufmann and His Collection of Medieval Hebrew Manuscripts in the Oriental Collection of the Library of the Hungarian Academy of Sciences, Section 3.5. Online publication edited by Dr. Tamás Sajóm, Budapest, Library of the Hungarian Academy of Sciences: http://kaufmann.mtak.hu/index-en.html

Egypt's Synagogues Past and Present: https://www.arce.org/project/egypts-synagogues -past-present

Galron-Goldschläger, Joseph. *Modern Hebrew Literature- a Bio-Bibliographical Lexicon,* Ohio State University: https://library.osu.edu/projects/hebrew-lexicon/index.htm. [Hebrew

Jefferson, Rebecca J. W. 'Data Analysis of the Genizah Fragments at the Bodleian Libraries'. University of Florida Institutional Repository: https://ufdc.ufl.edu/IR00011094/00001.

'Solomon Schechter: A Postcard from Cairo'. *Yeshiva University Library Blog,* 30 September 2013: https://blogs.yu.edu/library/2013/09/30/solomon-schechter-a-postcard-from -cairo/

Suciu, Alin. 'The Coptic Manuscripts of Monsieur Dujardin and the Crawford Collection in the John Rylands Library, Manchester': https://alinsuciu.com/2012/12/28/the-coptic -manuscripts-of-monsieur-dujardin-and-the-crawford-collection-in-the-john-rylands -library-manchester/

'The Guardian of Egypt: Ribbi Refael Aharon ben Shimon ל"צז'. *The Sephardic Halacha Center*: https://theshc.org/the-guardian-of-egypt-ribbi-refael-aharon-ben-shimon-זצ'ל/.

'The Synagogues of Cairo and Alexandria, Egypt, Selected Sites'. *Diarna,* accessed 25 April 2019: http://diarna.org/exhibits/the-synagogues-of-cairo-and-alexandria-egypt -selected-sites/.

Toolkit for Genizah Scholars: A Practical Guide for Neophytes, compiled by Gregor Schwarb: https://hcommons.org/deposits/download/hc:15904/CONTENT/toolkit_for _genizah_scholars.pdf/

Newspapers, periodicals, reports

The Academy.

The Acts and Proceedings of the … Regular Session of the General Synod of the Reformed Church in America.

The American.

The Archaeological Journal.

The Athenaeum: Journal of English and Foreign Literature, Science, and the Fine Arts.

Bodleian Library: Annual Report of the Curators of the Bodleian Library.

British Medical Journal.

Brooklyn Daily Eagle.

Cambridge University Library: Report of the Library Syndicate.

Church Quarterly Review.

The Friend: Religious and Literary Journal.

A Handbook for Travellers in Egypt.

Haòr (HaZvi) newspaper from Ottoman Palestine.

The Jewish Chronicle.
The Journal of Sacred Literature and Biblical Record.
The Menorah: A Monthly Magazine for the Jewish Home.
The Missionary Review of the World.
Mittheilungen und Nachbrichten des Deutschen Palestina-Vereins.
The Nation.
Oxford University Gazette.
The Pall Mall Magazine.
Palestine Exploration Fund: Quarterly Statement.
The Sunday-School Times.
The Jewish Theological Seminary of America Biennial Report.
The Times (London).
Universalist Quarterly and General Review.

Websites

Cairo Genizah Manuscripts at the University of Pennsylvania Libraries: https://openn
    .library.upenn.edu/html/genizah_contents.html
Cambridge University Library Cairo Genizah Collection: https://cudl.lib.cam.ac.uk/
    collections/genizah/1
Friedberg Jewish Manuscript Society: https://fjms.genizah.org
Genizah Fragments at the Bodleian Libraries: https://genizah.bodleian.ox.ac.uk
GenizaLab Princeton: https://genizalab.princeton.edu
John Rylands Genizah Collection: https://luna.manchester.ac.uk/luna/servlet/
    ManchesterDev~95~2
Judaica DH at the Penn Libraries: https://medium.com/@judaicadh

Index